The Black Student's
Guide to Colleges

The Black Student's Guide to Colleges

Fourth Edition

Barry Beckham

MADISON BOOKS
Lanham • New York • London

Copyright © 1997 by Barry Beckham

Published by Madison Books
4720 Boston Way
Lanham, Maryland 20706

3 Henrietta Street
London WC2E 8LU, England

ISBN 1–56833–080–4 (pbk : alk. paper)

Distributed by National Book Network

The paper used in this publication meets the minimum requirements of
American National Standard for Information Sciences—Permanence of
Paper for Printed Library Materials, ANSI Z39.48–1984.
Manufactured in the United States of America.

CONTENTS

INTRODUCTION

Now, fourteen years after the first edition of the guide was published, black students on predominantly white college campuses are still facing environments that foster isolation and hostility.

As students have said on countless occasions, the campus is a microcosm of the larger society. And just as there is no racial paradise in America, there is no racial paradise for students attending white colleges.

There are, of course, some collegiate environments that will offer a more comfortable experience than others. One premise of this guide is that you owe it to yourself to ask hard questions about these environments before you fill out the admission applications. Another premise is that if the colleges have not demonstrated a commitment to respecting and supporting your presence, you may do well to look elsewhere.

These profiles, therefore, focus on the what-have-you-done-for-me-lately aspects of academics, support services, black student organizations, social life and general climate. In some cases, the evidence will show that the colleges do not care about you at all. In other instances, you will find inspiring examples of campuses committed to doing their best to offer equality of opportunity.

Good luck, and remember that your primary purpose is to finish the requirements and walk.

Barry Beckham
August 1996
Silver Spring, Maryland

THE APPLICATION PROCESS

Applying to college is a very confusing ordeal. There are tests to take, fees to pay, recommendations to secure, forms to fill out, and deadlines to meet. The cardinal rule is to begin the process very early—an early start will give you a competitive edge.

Begin no later than your junior year. The first thing to do is to browse through the college catalog section of your high school or local library. Try to get an understanding of the different types of colleges available and of which type best suits your needs.

Remember, colleges differ in many very important ways. Some are very large, others quite small; some urban, some rural; some extremely expensive, others relatively inexpensive. There are traditionally black colleges and predominantly white colleges; residential colleges and commuting colleges. The many advantages and disadvantages involved in each relate closely to your own personal requirements.

One starting point is to find out which colleges offer the strongest programs in your major area of interest. Then, compare the other considerations of size, location, cost, academic rating and social factors that distinguish one school from the next. It is very important to have long discussions about those colleges with your guidance counselor, your teachers and your parents.

By junior year you should have already established a good record of academic achievement. Do not slack off now. Grades from junior year on are considered most important by admission officers. This should be a year of continued achievement and standardized test taking.

In September, you should register to take the Preliminary Scholastic Aptitude Test (PSAT) which will be given in October. The PSAT is a practice test for the Scholastic Aptitude Test (SAT) which will be given in May. Both tests are important, because it is primarily on the basis of your high school grades and these test scores that colleges decide whether or not to offer you admission.

Both exams test verbal and mathematical skills. The best way to prepare for them outside of a formal test-taking course is to read very widely, review your basic math skills and study carefully the practice test and information bulletin which come with your registration materials.

All of these tests require you to pay certain fees. If you do not have the money to pay for the tests, ask your guidance counselor about fee waivers.

During the summer before senior year you should continue to investigate your different college choices. This is a good time to write away for up-to-date college catalogs, handbooks, and application forms. Study these materials carefully so that you will understand what you will need to do in September to make the application process flow smoothly.

Most important, see what the average SAT score and high school grade-point averages are for students admitted to the schools you are interested in. If your SAT scores and grade-point average are not as high as they should be, don't despair. You will still have time to get better grades first semester senior year, and better SAT scores the following December.

The process of applying to college really gains momentum during the fall semester of your senior year. Write to colleges for any additional admission and financial aid materials. Spend more time talking with your guidance counselor about the different colleges, and ask if there are any additional tests you must take or scholarship programs you can apply to. Find out the earliest date that your parents can file a Free Application for Federal Student Aid (FAFSA). The FAFSA is a questionnaire which is used to determine your financial needs. If you file it early, you will have enough time to correct mistakes and discrepancies.

In September, you should approach teachers who know you well and ask them if they would be willing to write you a recommendation to college. Check back with them to see if they have mailed the forms.

Then begin to think about what you are going to say in the personal essay which many colleges require. Carefully construct a draft of your essay, including all of your achievements and extracurricular activities. After you have written the first draft, show it to some of your English teachers to get their critical response. Rewrite your essay on the basis of those responses, and then put it away until you finish the rest of your application.

Remember to register for the December SAT and the College Board Achievement Test which will be given in January. Make sure that all of the colleges that you are applying to are receiving copies of your high school transcripts, your SAT scores, your FAFSA reports and your teacher recommendations.

Be sure to apply to at least one school where your grade point average and SAT scores are above that of most students who were accepted the previous year. This school will be your "safety school" or school to which you are more than likely to gain admission. Then try to apply to at least one school where your grades and scores are slightly below those of previously admitted applicants. This school might be a long shot, but it is always possible that you can build a strong case for yourself.

Most of the schools that you apply to should be those in which your grades and SAT scores match those of the previously admitted applicants. At these schools, you are likely to gain admission, and the challenge of the curriculum is likely to he best suited to your abilities. You may consider that two safety schools, two long shots and six matches are enough to make your chances better than average.

Don't be put off by application fees. They can be waived at some schools if you can show financial hardship.

The last thing to do is to check back over your personal essay and your application forms. Does the essay have any typing or grammatical mistakes? If so, correct them. Does it say everything that needs to be said about you to build the strongest case possible? If not, try to think of what else can be added. Is your application form filled out as neatly as possible? If not, see if your guidance counselor has any extra forms that you can use to do it over again. Finally, are all of the questions answered and the spaces filled? If not, provide the necessary information in order to avoid delays in processing.

Make sure that your applications are complete and mailed well ahead of the deadline. During March and April, you will be notified about your college acceptances and financial aid decisions. Good luck!

ABOUT SCHOLARSHIPS

Getting in may be the biggest worry for students applying to college. But once you're in, how do you stay in, financially?

Students looking for ways to finance their education should remember that scholarships are an important, and often surprising, source of funds. Don't assume that you have to be a genius, an outstanding athlete or in dire need to qualify for one. Your minority status, leadership ability or your chosen major can be the basis for some grants: some are even based on such criteria as the ability to play the bagpipes or an employment history as a golf caddie. But to get a scholarship, you'll have to do your research, and you'll have to apply.

It's important to start early: your junior year of high school is a good time. And remember:

• Scholarships come from a variety of sources—individual colleges, independent special interest foundations, the federal government and corporations. The following reference books may help you find what's available. Be sure to check the most recent editions.

Athletic Scholarships for Women
Women's Sports Foundation
342 Madison Avenue
Suite 728
New York, NY 10173

Barron's Handbook of American College Financial Aid
Nicholas C. Proia & Vincent M. Gaspari
Barron's Educational Series
113 Crossways Pk. Dr.
Woodbury, NY 11797

The Black Student's Guide to Scholarships, 4th edition
Barry Beckham
Madison Books
4720 Boston Way
Lanham, MD 20706
Phone 800-462-6420

Chronicle Four-Year College Data Book
Catalog No. 502CM4
Chronicle Guidance Publications, Inc.
Moravia, NY 13118-1190

College Financial Aid Emergency Kit
Joyce Lain Kennedy, Dr. Herm Davis and Dr. Sharon Bob
Sun Features, Inc.
Box 368-MW
Cardiff, CA 92007

The Complete Grant Sourcebook for Higher Education
Public Management Institute
American Council on Education
1 Dupont Circle NW
Washington, DC 20036

Directory of Financial Aids for Minorities
Gail A. Schlachter with Sandra Goldstein
Reference Service Press
1100 Industrial Road, Suite 9
San Carlos, CA 94070

Don't Miss Out: The Ambitious Student's Guide to Financial Aid,
15th edition
Robert Leider and Anna Leider
Octameron Associates
P.O. Box 2748
Alexandria, VA 22301

Financial Aids for Higher Education
Oreon Keeslar
William C. Brown & Co. Publishers
2460 Kerper Rd.
Dubuque, IA 52001

Foundation Grants to Individuals
The Foundation Center
79 Fifth Avenue
New York, NY 10003

Need a Lift?
American Legion
P.O. Box 1050
Indianapolis, IN 46206

The Scholarship Book, 4th edition
Daniel J. Cassidy and Michael J. Arlen
Prentice Hall
Route 59 at Brookhill Drive
West Nyack, NY 10995-9900

•   You can find out about federal and state aid from your guidance counselor. Ask for information about financial aid opportunities and applications when you write to the admission office of each college to which you might apply.

•   Before you apply, assess yourself. Do you have special interests? Do you belong to any clubs or organizations? Take an inventory of your and your family's finances and compare them with the cost of the colleges you are considering. Can you make a case for need? Read scholarship requirements and apply for scholarships that fit you.

•   Apply for as many scholarships as you can, but give priority to those that offer the most or are renewable. (Don't forget, though, that every little bit helps!)

• Give yourself time. Keep a schedule of when applications and essays are due, and give yourself an earlier deadline so you can GET THEM IN.

• Be accurate. Read and follow all instructions for each application carefully. Before you send anything out, check for errors and omissions.

• AIM HIGH. If you want it, it's worth trying for.

COPING WITH STRESS

L iving on a college campus is a change in lifestyle which can add stress and tension to any problems you may already have. Here are some hints from the National Association for Mental Health which may make coping a little easier.

TALK IT OUT: When something worries you, don't bottle it up. Confide in some level-headed person you can trust. Talking things out helps to relieve your strain, assists you in seeing your worry in a clearer light and in finding a way you can deal with it.

ESCAPE FOR A WHILE: Making yourself "stand there and suffer" is a form of self-punishment, not a way to solve a problem. It is perfectly realistic and healthy to escape from your difficulty long enough to recover breath and balance, as long as you are prepared to come back and deal with it when you are more composed.

WORK OFF YOUR ANGER: Expend the pent-up energy in some physical activity or take a long walk. Anger often blocks you from being able to deal with a problem. Working the anger out of your system, and cooling it off for a day or two will leave you much better prepared.

GIVE IN OCCASIONALLY: Even if you're right and you know it, it's easier on your system to give in once in a while. If you yield, you'll usually find that others will too. And if you can work out a compromise, the result will be relief from tension and the achievement of a practical solution.

DO SOMETHING FOR OTHERS: This should take the steam out of your own worries, at least for a while, which may be all you need.

TAKE ONE THING AT A TIME: For people under tension, an ordinary workload can seem unbearable. The load looks so great that it seems impossible to tackle any part of it. Decide which are the things that most need to be done, do them, and the rest won't seem quite such a total mess.

SHUN THE "SUPERMAN" URGE: Some people expect too much from themselves and get into a constant state of worry and anxiety because they think they're not achieving as much as they should be. Don't try for perfection in everything; it's an open invitation to failure. Decide which things you do well. These are apt to be the things you like to do anyway, and giving them your major effort will probably provide you with the most satisfaction. Then, deal with the things you have more trouble with, and do them well. But don't take yourself to task if you can't achieve the impossible.

GO EASY WITH YOUR CRITICISM: You may be expecting too much of others; it's your own fault, then, if you feel frustrated or let down when they don't measure up to your preconceived pattern of achievement. Acknowledge that you may be trying to make others over to suit yourself. Learn to work with, and within the limits of, their good points.

GIVE THE OTHER PERSON A BREAK: Competition is contagious, but so is cooperation. When you give the other person a break, you often make things easier for yourself; if he no longer feels you are a threat to him, he stops being a threat to you. And if you constantly feel you must "get there first," take a minute to examine the goals you're after. Some of them may prove trivial, and you can well afford to relax.

MAKE YOURSELF "AVAILABLE": You may be feeling neglected or left out—and it may be all in your imagination. Often others are just waiting for you to make the first move. Don't be the one who always has to be asked; make some of the overtures yourself.

SCHEDULE YOUR RECREATION: Some people drive themselves so hard that they allow too little time for recreation. You may need a program of definite hours for "time out."

GET UP 15 MINUTES earlier in the morning; mishaps will be less stressful.

PREPARE FOR MORNING THE EVENING BEFORE; set the table, make lunch, put out clothes.

DON'T TURN PREFERENCES INTO NEEDS. Our basic physical needs translate into food and water, and keeping warm. Everything else is a preference. Don't get attached to preferences.

DO NOTHING WHICH, AFTER BEING DONE, LEADS YOU TO TELL A LIE.

MAKE DUPLICATES OF ALL KEYS. Bury a house key in a secret spot in the garden and carry a duplicate car key in your wallet, apart from your key ring.

PRACTICE PREVENTIVE MAINTENANCE. Your car, appliances, home and relationships will be unlikely to fall apart.

ELIMINATE OR RESTRICT CAFFEINE.

PROCRASTINATION IS STRESSFUL. Do today what you want to do tomorrow; whatever you want to do today, do it now.

SAY "NO!" Saying no to extra projects, social activities, and invitations you know you don't have the time or energy for takes practice, self-respect, and a belief that everyone, every day, needs quiet time to relax and to be alone.

BE PREPARED TO WAIT. A paperback can make a wait in a post office line almost pleasant.

TWENTY QUICK TIPS FOR ACADEMIC SUCCESS

1. Plan two hours of study time for every hour you spend in class.

2. Study difficult (or boring) subjects first. Get the difficult work done while you are fresh, and save the best for last.

3. Avoid long study sessions. Focus on short sessions, then give your brain a chance to absorb what you studied. One-hour breaks are reasonable.

4. Select your best time of day for study. Very early morning has proved to be a prime time for successful students. The mind is usually better able to focus without distractions in the early morning.

5. Use waiting time to study. Write equations, formulas, definitions, and other materials on index cards. Keep them with you and pull them out while waiting for friends, the bus, your doctor or between classes.

6. Select a special study area. For concentrated study, select the same place day after day. And don't sleep, eat, or watch television in the special study area.

7. Select an uncomfortable place to study. Study really is hard work. So avoid easy chairs, beds and comfortable sofas.

8. Use a library. Libraries are designed for learning. Go there for studying and for gathering information.

9. Check your attention span. Little children find it difficult to stick with a task or concentrate on one point. If you have difficulty sticking to the study task, you may be exhibiting childish behavior. Concentrate on sticking with the study task.

10. Make explicit agreements—written contracts, if necessary—about study time with your roommate. Guard your personal study time the same way you do your money. Don't let others steal study time from you.

11. Eliminate noise distraction. Television, stereos, and other noise makers can rob you of precious study time. Silence has been found to be the best form of music for academic success.

12. Beware of those who misuse your time. Sincere friends want you to be successful. If your so-called friends can't understand why you must study, you don't need them. Avoid those who insist on taking you from your studies.

13. Avoid the telephone during study time. If you are studying, simply refuse to answer or accept the call. Tell your close friends that you will not interrupt your study time for a telephone call.

14. Learn to say "No!" Academic success is your most important agenda. Success means saying NO to all activities that take time from study as well as those that will lead to illegal or antisocial behavior. Say NO and mean it!

15. Hang a DO NOT DISTURB sign on your door, chair or desk. Let your friends know that you have scheduled a time for study, time for fun, and a time for rest. The DO NOT DISTURB sign tells them that you are about the business of preparing for academic success.

16. Go to class prepared, on time, and avoid cuts. Teachers are sympathetic to those who exhibit mature behavior.

17. Check with your instructor at the first sign of difficulty. Don't wait until you have failed the course to seek help.

18. Prepare reports, term papers, and other assignments at least seven days before they are due. Early preparations will give you time to check typing and sources for accuracy.

19. Avoid cheating to help you pass the course. Honesty is the best policy in college as well as in life.

20. Budget your time wisely. Time management is critical to academic success. Remember that there are 24 hours in a day and 168 hours in a week. You have enough time to make good grades and enjoy college. Just remember to give your priority to study.

HOW TO SURVIVE AT A WHITE COLLEGE

Eugene Williams, Jr., a 1991 graduate of Emory University, knows what it's like to be the only black in a classroom—and survive the experience.

An English major at Emory, he had to adjust to the new academic demands as well as deal with cultural challenges.

Adjusting successfully requires a plan, he says. Now, based in Washington, D.C., he gives workshops for black college-bound students who may find themselves navigating what he calls a milky terrain. He lists these tips in his book, *The Raisin-In-Milk Syndrome: Ten Survival Tips for Black Students at Predominantly White Colleges and Universities:*

1. Get to know your teachers.

2. Get good grades/study hard.

3. Get involved in campus-wide organizations.

4. Get involved with black organizations.

5. Observe students of other minority groups.

6. Don't be too much of a revolutionary.

7. Get to know the administration.

8. Don't emulate negative behavior.

9. Never publicly denounce a black student.

10. Don't spread yourself too thin!

KEY TO TERMS

Admission Policy: The degree of selectiveness a college uses in its admission process is described by the following terms: most selective; highly selective; very selective; selective; less selective and not selective.

Alumn: Substitute for alumni/alumnae, alumnus, alumna.

Frosh: Freshmen and Freshwomen.

NA: Not available.

NSSFMS: National Scholarship Service and Fund for Minority Students.

Total Expenses: Includes tuition, room and board; for state institutions with resident and non-resident tuition amounts, the resident tuition cost is followed by the non-resident cost.

Tuition: Cost for instruction alone for one school year; for state institutions with resident and non-resident amounts, the resident cost is followed by the non-resident expenses.

METHODOLOGY

These profiles of 500 to 1,000 words are the result of collecting two kinds of information: interview and survey results from black students, and documentation supplied by the colleges themselves. In some instances, documentation from other sources like periodicals, reports and other publications were used.

Our focus is on five major areas: (1) academics; (2) support services; (3) black student organizations; (4) social life; and (5) the overall climate.

You may notice that some profiles are much more thorough than others. Some schools send us a great deal of material. Others send us very little.

We will write a profile of any college that returns the materials to us in time. So if your favorite college is not listed, it is probably because it did not reply. The absence of so many black colleges is especially disappointing. Of the 192 schools appearing in this edition, only 20 are predominantly black. Perhaps if enough students and parents ask them to participate, their numbers will increase for the fifth edition.

ADELPHI UNIVERSITY
Garden City, New York 11530

Undergrads: 3,272
Black Undergrads: 393
Faculty: 631
Black Faculty: NA
Tuition: $13,870
Total Expenses: $19,890

Conservative and career-oriented, Adelphi presents challenging options for African-American students. The education is solid, but the drawbacks...?

The college draws mainly New York metropolitan area students interested in business, health and public service-related fields. Admission is selective.

Founded in 1896 as a liberal arts college, Adelphi has expanded its curriculum to include Schools of Banking and Money Management, Business Administration, Nursing and Social Work. Other academic programs include a summer session for skill-building, part-time degree programs, extension courses throughout the New York City area and enrichment courses. The university grants CLEP credit and has a work-study program in social work. Adelphi also grants a BFA in dance and theater. A minor in African-American studies is possible, and a substantial number of courses in black history, art and the minority experience are offered.

Admission officers recruit at all high schools in the New York City area, including schools with a large percentage of minority students. Both freshmen and transfers apply under a rolling admission policy. Applicants are notified about six weeks after the application comes in. Adelphi has an innovative early admission policy: it is possible to enroll as a full-time student without a high school diploma, or to enroll as a freshman while completing the senior year of high school. Under this plan, the student goes to high school in the morning and to Adelphi in the afternoon and/or evening. All early admission applicants must have completed the eleventh grade.

Students arriving without a good preparation in English and math generally find themselves at quite a disadvantage, and many have trouble bridging the gap. Free tutoring is a viable solution for many. The Higher Education Opportunity Program, considered an excellent resource by past respondents, has been dismantled. No study skills workshops exist. Students are expected to work out study problems with their professors, most of whom are white and reportedly difficult to approach. The Psychology Department provides general counseling, but black students reportedly do not take much advantage of the counseling services.

Black students socialize together informally or in black fraternities or sororities. The African People's Organization is the umbrella group for the politically inclined. They sponsor Black Solidarity Day and a Kwanzaa celebration, among other activities. Look for weekend jaunts at Roosevelt Field, a major mall in nearby Hempstead, and at a West Indian club, Nagasaki. Relationships with white students are not close, but they are not tense either. Yet there is close communication between black faculty and students.

The residents of Garden City do not welcome Adelphi's black and Hispanic minorities. Despite the severity of the situation, black students do not consider the tension to be a major drawback to their experience at Adelphi.

Black pre-professionals are supported in the pre-med and pre-law societies which do a good job of helping students succeed in those rigorous programs. There are not many other black student groups, although black theater is produced in connection with the drama courses in African-American Studies and several black fraternities and sororities are active. Few blacks get involved in student government, according to respondents. The only regularly scheduled black entertainment is music—soul, rhythm and blues, and jazz—on the radio.

Activities bringing black students into contact with the local community are few and far between, and usually not just for blacks. Adelphi has worked with Garden City on a "Save the Children" campaign, in which undergrads and grad students tutor local high school students.

Four-fifths of Adelphi's students commute, but most blacks don't because they are from out of state. Students living on campus tend to have a social life centered around dorm parties, but for African Americans, the options don't seem satisfying.

AGNES SCOTT COLLEGE
Decatur, Georgia 30030

Undergrads: 530
Black Undergrads: 74
Faculty: 85
Black Faculty: 3
Tuition: $14,460
Total Expenses: $20,480

An awareness of black culture? Not enough, according to one undergrad: "A black student applying to Agnes Scott has to understand that this is a "white" campus, not just "predominantly white."

"Black culture is definitely lacking on campus," another student adds. "I think that because of the small number of students, there is not enough diversity."

Still, Agnes Scott, an all-women college that promotes academics as a top priority, is definitely a college for those who are serious about a first-rate education. Affiliated with the Presbyterian Church (USA), the school is located on 100 grassy, tree-filled acres in a residential community just six miles from downtown Atlanta. This private, four-year liberal arts college uses a highly selective admission policy. The majority of the students graduate in the top 20 percent of their high school class.

Black students participate in the recruitment process by serving as student ambassadors and admission volunteers.

Young women attending Agnes Scott receive a special privilege built around a code of ethics—the honor system. This system allows students social self-regulation and freedom academically. The system is based on standards of honesty and conduct specifically outlined in the *Student Handbook*. The benefits are self-scheduled exams, an open-room policy and unregulated quizzes. Over 30 fields of study are offered. These include double majors (e.g., liberal arts/engineering, computer science or management) through a program with Georgia Institute of Technology and an exchange program with Mills College in Oakland, California. Agnes Scott participates in the Atlanta University system, which allows students to take classes at Emory, Morehouse and Spelman, among others. Students with special preferences can also self-design a major.

A minor in Africana Studies is available. Most courses are offered in the history and sociology departments, but related courses are available in departments of religious studies, political science, psychology and Spanish. Classes include African-American History, Minority Politics and Psychology of Cross-Cultural Contact. Students can further enhance their African studies by using the general collection of over 1,200 books on African-American and Africana subjects in the campus library.

To supplement class discussions the college offers supportive class sessions in the math and language departments. Tutorial assistance is available at the Collaborative Learning Center. Study skills workshops and writing laboratories are also available.

Psychological, faculty and administrative counseling is offered. Students report that most of the women receive counseling from faculty and administrators. In addition, peer counseling is available through Witkase, an African-American student organization.

Racism-Free Zone seeks to improve relationships between black and white students. According to one respondent, "I think it is invaluable because it gives us the support that we as black students need on a white campus."

Witkaze provides cultural and social activities for the sisters. They sponsor a Black History Month convocation, an annual banquet, poetry readings and parties.

The Alston Campus Center is the general meeting place for most students. Most campus activities are held here, and plenty are available for interested young women.

One student says, "Blacks participate in intramural sports just as actively as whites do." Black participation also seems to be active in university-sponsored activities such as lectures, concerts and picnics.

However, black student participation in the on-campus social scene does not appear to be as high. "The on-campus social scene does not appeal to many of us black students," says one respondent. "The men that attend are usually white because ASC parties are not publicized on predominantly black campuses."

Some students also complain about the variety of music played at these parties. One students says, "Blacks at ASC tend to participate in social activities off campus."

Black/white student interaction receives average marks. One student says that the climate on campus is identical to that in the rest of society. "There are some nice blacks and some nice whites—these are the ones that get along," she says.

Students give mixed responses concerning relations with faculty. Although some feel that white faculty members are unconcerned about black students, one undergraduate reports that sometimes "strong bonds of communication form." Students consider black faculty to be very concerned and supportive. Other non-white staff members are also friendly, respondents say.

The President's Committee on Diversity deals with campus programs that will increase racial understanding and pluralistic appreciation. The committee schedules workshops, lectures and seminars designed to encourage racial sensitivity. In addition, the board of trustees has adopted a Policy Statement on Discrimination and Harassment.

Several students want to make sure that potential applicants consider the "lack of permanent black faculty members and the low enrollment of black students." Having warned prospective students of these problems, however, most respondents seem satisfied with their decision to attend Agnes Scott. One student says, "I think that the school's most attractive quality is the superior education it offers. The fact that Agnes Scott is an all-women school means that it promotes and supports women."

ALVERNO COLLEGE
Milwaukee, Wisconsin 53215

Undergrads: 2084
Black Undergrads: 313
Faculty: 199
Black Faculty: NA
Tuition: $8,978
Total Expenses: $12,748

Nestled in a 46-acre suburban area on the edge of Milwaukee, you'll find this gem: a relaxed and informal liberal arts college for women with a congenial mood toward the sisters.

Here you can find not only complete bachelor's degree programs during the day, but also a Weekday College for working women. There are 47 program areas and 25 majors. New this year: a major in international business and a master of arts in education.

Alverno is divided into eight academic divisions: integrated arts and humanities, behavioral sciences, business and management, education, information and computer studies, natural sciences and technology, fine arts, and nursing.

Courses related to the black experience include Race and Ethnicity in American Life, Bridging the Cultural Gap, The Minority Experience in American Life and Intercultural Communication. Alverno's special library collections pertaining to blacks include feminism, education, music, nursing and peace.

Recruiting is done several times per year by the minority counselor who visits high schools in the Milwaukee area. Multicultural Services gives presentations at high school as well as in the community.

The majority of the school's black students come to Alverno from Wisconsin, Illinois and Michigan.

Alverno offers tutorial assistance to all students in the areas of reading, writing and math, based on an enrollment assessment. A drop-in tutorial center is available to students having difficulty in math. Peer advisors assist students in selecting classes, and personal counseling is offered to students needing assistance with problems. The New Student Seminar is a freshmen course which includes a section on study skills.

Alumns are asked to participate in student panels at recruitment functions or in phonathons to call prospective students. Minority alumns are represented as marshals at commencement exercises. Alumns are encouraged to participate in all facets of the alumni organization, LITES. LITES encourages current black students to contact the alumns for any support needs, including counseling, tutorials and one-on-one activities. Black alumns also serve on many committees.

In addition to LITES, Women of Color and Concerned Black Nurses of Alverno are two other black student organizations on the case. Activities in the past have included Black History Month activities and special programs on multicultural issues. Alverno tries to encourage racial tolerance through various programs. Multicultural Services offers classroom presentations, lectures and other services. During orientation for all students, there is a session on multicultural perspectives.

Alverno has a complete fitness facility, spacious dorms, a friendly staff and two dozen student organizations. Minutes from downtown, students can visit museums, galleries, theaters, shopping centers, the Performing Arts Center and other entertainment attractions.

Alverno claims to have a high career placement rate thanks to its Career Development Center. In this combination library, classroom and counseling center, experts keep track of employment trends and work with students to help find the career for them. The Off Campus Experiential Learning program has all students, no matter the major, work for a semester in one of over 250 cooperating businesses, schools, health care or human services agencies. The Career Development Center's efforts pay off; within six months after graduation, more than 90 percent of Alverno graduates have jobs related to their college major.

For the career-minded black student who can appreciate the relaxed mood, Alverno could be a sleeper.

AMHERST COLLEGE
Amherst, Massachusetts 01002

Undergrads: 1,600
Black Undergrads: 128
Faculty: 200
Black Faculty: 6
Tuition: $21,065
Total Expenses: $26,625

"I'm satisfied, but not happy," reports a brother. "The Amherst College name will hopefully take me far, and that's what makes it most attractive."

Located in picturesque New England, 90 minutes from Boston, Amherst is the home of Emily Dickinson and Robert Frost as well as noted black graduates Charles Drew and William H. Hastie. It can offer real opportunities for African-American students. And it can take a lot out of you along the way.

This small, independent, coed liberal arts college is most selective, and for overall quality, it is ranked among the top 25 colleges in the country.

Admission officers visit about 600 schools a year. Amherst offers weekends in the fall for pre-freshmen, and a minority mentoring program has alumns linking current undergraduates with professionals.

From its beginnings in the early 1970s, the Black Studies Department at Amherst has emphasized cross-cultural and interdisciplinary approaches. About three dozen (count them!) courses pertaining to blacks and African Americans are listed, covering African and Caribbean history, race, literature and issues of gender.

Noteworthy: a cross-cultural psychology course compared childhood figures in Caribbean and African literary texts. And a junior year seminar examined the views of Alexander Crummell and W.E.B. Dubois. A special library collection has files on black graduates of Amherst—especially those who have made historical and social achievements.

Dissatisfied with the mainstream curriculum, a group of students is working to bring more ethnic studies to campus, and a Diversity Task Force last year hosted a symposium with prominent scholars.

A sizable number of black students are prep school graduates and therefore well prepared. For others, the going may be rough. Tutorial assistance is available for any Amherst course if approved by the instructor. However, one student describes this assistance as "reasonably effective." Reading and study skills help is provided for a modest fee. For general writing help, the Writing Counselor provides assistance for a variety of problems, like getting a paper started, editing, writing with confidence, managing time, and anxiety. A non-credit course designed to review math concepts is given by students majoring in math. Moans one senior, "There are not enough minority peer counselors; we have to rely upon ourselves to counsel each other."

Everywhere you turn, you find a student organization at Amherst. Of interest to brothers and sisters are the Black Student Union, which has as its foundation the seven principles of Ngozo Saba (Kwanzaa) and is the main outlet for the expression of black students' political concerns. At the biweekly Sunday afternoon meetings, spirited attention is directed at the grievances of the Amherst black community.

For Black History month, the BSU sponsored films, parties, artistic performances and forums in association with the Charles Drew House and the Affirmative Action Office. Last year's fare included a tribute to black composers—a semi-formal featuring the Amherst College Jazz Ensemble.

Look also for Straight Ahead, a group that brings a program of African-American speakers to the campus; the Black Business Association of Amherst College; and the Amherst College Choir, a black-run organization which has a "definitive religious bent." One student says the Black Business Association is "an active as well as an effective organization." And a Bible study group has a high percentage of students of color.

WAMH, the campus radio station, provides approximately 20 hours a week of prime broadcast time for the Minority Media Project. Forum is a lecture series that brings in distinguished Africanists to speak on various subjects. Every two years, Black Alumni Weekend reunites alumni to share their expertise and experiences. "It's the only contact we have with black alumns," says a respondent, "but we are trying to improve that. We have put many alumns on our mailing list to keep them abreast of our activities." Says another, "It is fabulous. We get to network with alumns, hear about their experiences which are always similar to ours, and just hang out."

Theme housing—living arrangements organized around a particular interest—is a popular option. The African-American Culture House residence is the Charles Drew House. Students have established a permanent collection of works by African, Caribbean and African-American artists.

For social life, Amherst will not rank in the top 25 for black students. "The social life is lacking," states one undergrad blankly. Relations with other students vary. "Most of us get along with white students, and many don't have much interaction at all," says one undergrad. Many white faculty have a reputation for disliking black students, but so do some black faculty. "Many have removed themselves from the black student body and feel no obligation to reach out to us," says a student about African-American faculty.

Assesses one student: "People are thoughtful enough...it is rare that you will encounter frustration...or racism. While the work is by no means smooth or easy, the rewards are there."

Overall, reports one undergrad, "I think I made a good decision to attend Amherst. It has fostered my intellectual growth without destroying my spirit, self-esteem or love for knowledge. You will receive support here from students—even if it means tutoring sessions, helping to ease the homesickness, or just deciding to skip the dining hall and get away to the nearby Caribbean Cravings."

ARKANSAS STATE UNIVERSITY
Jonesboro, Arkansas 72467

Undergrads: 8,740
Black Undergrads: 961
Faculty: 453
Black Faculty: NA
Tuition: $1,950; $3,600
Total Expenses: $4,540; $6,190

State supported, coed ASU sits on an 800-acre campus, 135 miles northeast of Little Rock. It offers a variety of degrees in agriculture, business, education, fine arts, liberal arts, and science.

Most of ASU's black students come from Arkansas, Tennessee, Missouri, and Mississippi. ASU's admission policy is not very selective.

How have ASU's black students adjusted to academic life? One student says that "about ninety percent" have made the adjustment well. Says another, "Some have made the transition successfully. Others still lag behind, either because of immaturity or simply because they can't measure up to the academic standards and pressures of college life."

For those who do encounter academic difficulties, "very good" tutorial services are provided by the Program of Academic Skills Services. Each student is assigned an advisor, and there is also an "excellent" professional counseling staff. Study skills workshops, according to one student, are "effective." Many special seminars and forums are offered—art exhibits and lectures included—but there are no special class sections. Unfortunately, fewer than a handful of black studies courses are given.

According to one respondent, "Quite a few" black religious services are available: "There are many black churches in the neighborhood. Almost any student will be able to find a church of his denomination." In addition to local church involvement, students get involved with the local community in other ways, as well: in high school tutoring, in political action groups like the Young Democrats, and in a "mass denominational choir." The school's fraternities also "have quite a bit of community involvement."

Of relations between black students and the local community—eight percent of Jonesboro's nearly 30,000 residents are black—one student says that they are "pretty good—no major problems that I've heard of."

Black and minority organizations at the school include the Union Board Cultural Enrichment Committee, The Black Student Gospel Choir, fraternal groups, and the Black Student Association. Black students gather at the school's Carl R. Reng Center which provides a place for meetings, lectures, and games. Black students do seem to hang out in groups, based on academic concentrations, geographical residences, fraternal groups, and religious groups.

"For people who like to party," one student says, "there are generally more than enough parties going on to suffice." Another calls the parties "very good," adding that they attract "a majority of black students." The same student mentions that intramural sports also play "a very big part in the lives of blacks around here. It's the biggest thing going next to dances."

The school's Cultural Enrichment Committee and the BSA do provide black-oriented entertainment as well as other social activities.

BARBER-SCOTIA COLLEGE
Concord, North Carolina 28025

Undergrads: 435
Black Undergrads: 431
Faculty: 33
Black Faculty: 21
Tuition: $1,950; $3,600
Total Expenses: $4,540; $6,190

Observes one undergrad, "Students should not try to find a school that they are going to have fun at because they are not spending their money for that. They should go to a place that is going to give them the education they came for. I am very satisfied because I'm getting my education and at the same time learning something about life."

Now coed, this very small, historically black, less selective Presbyterian college is big on personal attention.

It is the first black all-women's institution in the country. Most students are residents of North Carolina and graduates of public high schools. Others come from South Carolina, the Virgin Islands and Alabama.

Barber-Scotia provides a variety of support systems. The tutorial assistance programs include the Audio-Visual Tutorial Lab, Human Development Skills Center, Total Student Development, and the Living Learning Center. Counseling programs such as the Academic Advisement Program, Residence Advisors Program and the Peer Counseling Program focus on improving the quality of student life.

Seminars and workshops that focus on subjects such as test-taking and stress management are offered by some of the tutorial and counseling programs. There are also special seminars, in which outside companies come to the school and offer the students tips on career opportunities and interviewing techniques. One sister finds these seminars "helpful because they encourage the students to work harder."

The transition from high school to Barber-Scotia is not much of a problem for most. The college is small and the students can get a great deal of individual attention. One brother remarks, "I feel that the majority of students have adjusted to the transition very well. There are those that are having trouble, but most have made it with no problems." There are 10 active alumni chapters and a national association. Alumns offer recruiting assistance by attending workshops, providing housing for recruiters, and by sending interested students. Alumns participate in commencement activities as ushers and serve on the commencement committee. They also help out the director of Alumni Affairs in planning reunion and homecoming activities. In the opinion of a few respondents, Barber-Scotia could improve on alumn participation in career placement for seniors and in providing summer employment leads for undergraduates.

Fraternities and sororities play a large role in the social atmosphere at Barber-Scotia. One student states, "These are very helpful because they teach students togetherness and brotherhood. It also teaches them to work together in different activities." One sister reports that her sorority contributes to the community by participation in visiting nurse and children's homes organizations. The sisters bring presents to the members of the homes and spend time cheering up the residents.

The fraternities and sororities sponsor the usual social events like dances and parties. Student participation at these events is said to be enthusiastic, especially at the off-campus parties; a curfew puts a damper on the on-campus parties. One respondent remarks, "Everyone participates, except those that live near home. At times it gets boring because there are not enough people here, but that doesn't stop the others from having a good time."

Students report that the religious organizations at Barber-Scotia are quite useful. "These services are very helpful in that it helps a person expand herself spiritually and academically." "If you don't belong to a church, you can go to these services and find something for yourself," another student remarks.

Organizationally, students join the Staff, Science Club, International Club, Cheerleaders Squad, and many others. These groups also include each class as a group (e.g., Junior Class). Many events are sponsored by the different groups such as an Easter egg hunt for elementary school children, campus talent night, gospel choirs (from various colleges and churches), modern dance, and much more. The students are active in the university governance through the Student Government Association and one elected representative who speaks for the students.

One student says, "There is a lot of participation in student government. Most of the students are very active."

The attractive features of Barber-Scotia include the great history of the school, the special attention given to the students by the administration and faculty, and the family atmosphere. A sister mentions, however, that after classes the faculty are often not available. She would like them to participate more in events outside the classroom.

Some of the unattractive qualities are the lack of university-funded activities and the one a.m. curfew.

BATES COLLEGE
Lewiston, Maine 04240

Undergrads: 1,636
Black Undergrads: 33
Faculty: 165
Black Faculty: 3
Tuition: $26,300 (includes r&b)
Total Expenses: $26,300

"The hardest part here as a black student is leaving your past standards of excellence behind and pushing farther," says a brother, referring to the Bates challenge.

Some very impressive alumns have met it, including the great educator Benjamin E. Mays (for whom there are special scholarships named) and television personality Bryant Gumbel.

Located 35 miles from Portland and two-and-a-half hours from Boston, Bates College is settled on 125 acres of rolling land. This small, highly selective institution was the first coeducational college in New England.

Personal attention is the key phrase at Bates. Members of the faculty, not graduate students or teaching assistants, teach all courses. The small student-faculty ratio of 13 to 1 is certain to foster close relationships. The curriculum is divided into three parts: the humanities, the social sciences and the natural sciences. They encompass special programs such as freshman seminars and independent study projects. Courses relevant to the black experience are popular and tough to get into, particularly since 1991 when Bates first offered a major in African-American Studies.

Students find the academics very challenging but comment on the "excellent, readily available" (and free!!) tutorial assistance. The Writing Workshop is available on a regular basis to help ailing writers or those who just want to refine their skills. Special workshops include study skills, test taking and review workshops.

Faculty advising seems to be the most effective support system; each student is assigned an advisor at the beginning of freshman year who serves as a guide through course selection and as an objective counselor.

Bates College has no formal gathering center for brothers and sisters, and no black pre-professional societies; however, there are opportunities for blacks to find self-expression and direction. The African-American Society and Amandla! are key organizations designed to meet the needs of brothers and sisters of African descent, hoping to heighten black awareness both on campus and in the community. Says one student, "Amandla! has been very important for black students—it is a support group as well as a social and academic society." Similarly, Women of Color strives to promote a better understanding of their lives on the Bates campus as well as within the community and larger society. The college does not seem to play an active role in promoting black awareness, so many of the programs are sponsored by these groups.

These organizations sponsor Black Arts Week, poetry readings, plays, film festivals, dance ensembles, musicians and lectures. Last year's celebrations included a concert by the Bates Community Gospel Ensemble and in the Gannett Theater, Cheryl West's play, *Before It Hits Home*, about the effects of AIDS on a young black jazz musician. The Benjamin Mays Center was the site for a musical comedy by Sandra Deer of the Alliance Theater in Atlanta.

Members also work with the admission office on the special weekend visit for prospective minority students.

To aid with life after Bates, the Office of Career Counseling provides workshops on career planning, graduate school preparations and internship programs.

If weekly partying is your thing, then Bates is not the place for you. There are no Greek organizations (black or white) on campus. Picnics and happy hours provide occasional diversion from the heavy workload.

Off-campus opportunities are limited, probably attributable to the fact that Lewiston is 99 percent white. Individual motivation is a key factor in whether a student gets involved in the community. For the interested student, a Big Brother/Big Sister program is available as well as tutoring opportunities in elementary and secondary schools.

Although there are only a few black faculty members, they are cherished and respected by students. In addition, black alumns offer considerable support. They participate in informal discussions, recruiting and commencement activities.

On the whole, you can bet on Bates to provide a challenging environment. The small class size and tutorial assistance allow for personal attention. In no way do these alleviate fully the heavy academic demands, and the social life leaves much to be desired. But one can find a niche within the limitations. Says one respondent, "The key aspects in doing well at Bates are persistence and working with your educational tools to help you get over the stumbling blocks."

BELOIT COLLEGE
Beloit, Wisconsin 53511

Undergrads: 1,249
Black Undergrads: 50
Faculty: 128
Black Faculty: NA
Tuition: $17,544
Total Expenses: $19,612

Success and contentment at Beloit will depend a great deal upon attitude—and particularly your attitude about the importance of social life.

Highly selective and small enough to have fewer than ten students in 40 percent of its classes, Beloit College offers traditional as well as innovative programs of study.

All students are required to take a distribution of courses in the natural sciences and mathematics, in the social sciences, and in the arts and humanities. Degrees are awarded in business and education as well as in the arts and sciences. The geology and anthropology departments, offering field experience both in the U.S. and abroad, are considered among the best in the country.

Course participation through the urban studies program of the Associated Colleges of the Midwest (ACM) encourages study of the black American experience. History, anthropology, and sociology departments offer several courses concerning black heritage and contemporary black life. Beloit has a special Martin Luther King Peace Collection in its library.

In general, black students are recruited by alumns or admission officers at private and public secondary school visitations, Upward Bound and Talent Search agencies. The Charles Winter Wood Scholarships offer an attractive opportunity for motivated students to receive aid over four years. They come mainly from Illinois, Wisconsin, and New York. The transition from high school to college has been met with usual freshman difficulties, but as one respondent says, "there is help available for them."

Tutorial assistance, for example, is offered by the College Skills Center. Although it is designed to assist all students, it is urged upon students in the federally funded Educational Development Program which enrolls many blacks. This service is considered extremely helpful, but volunteer student services and departmental assistance are not as highly rated.

The small student-to-faculty ratio in the classroom allows for supportive relationships. And the relationship between black students and their professors is fairly good and getting better. Jinyosha is a black social organization offering educational programs to the campus. United Cultural Awareness (UCA) is a minority peer group, which is "a little productive, but there are so few black students," says one student. Most churchgoers attend Baptist service in town. For relaxation and entertainment, two hours a week on the campus radio are allocated for black programming.

The Black Student Union provides an outlet for students to discuss their political views, and participation is active.

The poor social life at Beloit distresses black students. Only a few blacks attend Beloit, and their parties rarely include white students. Likewise, invitations to parties given by whites are rarely extended to blacks. A few students are friends with blacks in the city of Beloit.

Jinyosha sponsors on-campus parties and speakers, but their resources are limited. University-sponsored professional and semi-professional entertainment geared toward blacks occurs once or twice a year.

Declares a satisfied respondent: "This small college atmosphere provides the student the opportunity to become acquainted with faculty, staff, as well as the student body. If I had to do it all over again, I would indeed attend Beloit."

BOSTON COLLEGE
Chestnut Hill, Massachusetts 02167

Undergrads: 8,896
Black Undergrads: 393
Faculty: 573
Black Faculty: NA
Tuition: $18,356
Total Expenses: $25,626

Overall, Boston College provides a challenging and worthwhile experi-ence to the open-minded student. Brothers and sisters say that the institution has much to offer black students. But don't be apprehensive, they say, about getting involved and asking many questions.

It is one of the oldest Jesuit-founded universities in the country, with four graduate and professional schools to its credit. The very selective, coed college is situated on two suburban campuses: Chestnut Hill and Newton. Both are within minutes of downtown Boston.

Most black students here come from Massachusetts, New York, New Jersey and Connecticut.

Founded in 1863, the college has undergraduate schools in arts and sciences, management, nursing and education.

The Black Studies department offers more than 20 courses to the interested student, including unusual offerings in American sport, business ethics and cultural diversity. The library system is one of the first in the country to offer a computerized public catalog of its collections.

Most respondents comment favorably on the tutorial and study skills services available. The Afro-American, Hispanic, Asian and Native-American Office (AHANA) supplies tutors and counselors. University Counseling Services as well as individual faculty and administrators also take respon-sibility for advising students. The AHANA office sponsors study skills workshops such as "Applied Learning Theory" and "Learning to Learn."

There are three black student organizations on campus: the Black Student Forum, the Voices of Imani and the NAACP-Boston College Chapter. Black pre-professional societies are non-existent, and there are no black theater or religious groups. But students get involved in organizations not specifically geared to blacks and also in the surrounding community.

According to one undergrad, "The gospel choir (Voices of Imani) has served as a uniting force between the Boston College community and the outside community." Moreover, the Black Student Forum promotes inter-action among clubs as well as participation in activities that enrich black students as well as show them diversity.

Socially, off-campus social affairs seem to be what's happening. Greek organizations have lost membership in the past few years because of the small black population and so are not able to provide large campus parties. College-sponsored activities are geared for the most part toward white students. At the same time, blacks are well represented in both intramural and varsity athletics.

Black alumns are looked upon very favorably by black students. They participate in Black Family Weekend, special dinners and black-tie affairs. They also give advice and job opportunities when available.

Programs to encourage racial tolerance are few, but students speak highly of the ones that do exist. Foremost is the Intercultural Awareness Program which sponsors forums during the orientation period for freshmen. It also arranges retreats and other activities throughout the year. In addition, AHANA provides merit awards and the Martin Luther King Scholarship to an outstanding minority junior. Several respondents mention the value of a course entitled The History and Development of Racism. Says one sister, "This class should be a core requirement of all colleges—it enlightens all to how both sides feel."

A black undergrad says that if you're an open-minded individual and interested in many things, Boston College will be perfect for you.

BOSTON UNIVERSITY
Boston, Massachusetts 02215

Undergrads: 15,097
Black Undergrads: 604
Faculty: 2680
Black Faculty: 28
Tuition: $19,700
Total Expenses: $26,800

A school with many golden opportunities is how one brother describes Boston University.

The institution is highly selective and offers a wide range of undergraduate and graduate programs. Situated in the nation's sixth largest city, Boston University has 16 colleges and schools.

Admission officers travel to both public and private high schools throughout the U.S. An admission officer attends the majority of NSSFMS College interview sessions, the Dream Jamboree in Atlanta, and Upward Bound programs during the summer.

Most black students are from Massachusetts, New York, New Jersey, Ohio, and Illinois.

The school offers bachelor's degrees in business, education, fine and performing arts, health sciences, language, math and sciences, philosophy, social sciences, and area studies (Russian and Eastern European Interdisciplinary Studies). The College of Liberal Arts provides a varied and extensive selection of courses relating to the African-American and African experiences. Some of those courses include psychology, West Indian literature, religion, and history.

The Graduate School of Arts and Sciences includes The African Studies Center, one of the first graduate programs to offer a multi-disciplinary African Studies curriculum. The center has achieved international recognition for its commitment to teaching, research, and publications, and the U.S. Department of Education has recognized it as a National Resource Center for African Language and Area Studies.

At the Mugar Memorial Library, you'll find the Africana Alcove and African Studies Library. A special collection contains papers of black Americans such as cartoonist E. Simms Campbell, poet Nikki Giovanni, and civil rights leader Dr. Martin Luther King, Jr.

The MLK Jr. Center for Career Educational and Counseling Services contains a minority library including tapes of speeches by Dr. King and his mentor, Howard Thurman. The center, along with the Office of Minority Affairs, is a division of Student Affairs.

The center and the Minority Affairs Office offer a kaleidoscope of services, programs, student activities, and educational opportunities. For example, an annual minority film series features black Americans. Also, every spring the MLK Jr. Symposium salutes the achievements of minority Americans who have distinguished themselves in civil rights, education, religion, or politics.

A component in the area of academics, the center's Learning Assistance Program sponsors workshops on test anxiety, increasing motivation, studying math and sciences, and stress management. In addition, there is a walk-in writing clinic for students who need help with basic writing skills.

The Career Planning and Placement unit of the center conducts workshops in resume writing and interviewing skills, and offers support groups for job hunters. Also, a Black Mentoring Program matches students with black faculty and administrative staff. UMOJA, the Black Student Association, has a fall picnic and peer mentors for freshmen.

Black students who wish to join organizations at Boston University have a wealth of choices. The heads of minority groups are on the AHANA Empowerment Council, which holds monthly meetings. The institution has a Black American Law Students Association, a Black Drama Collective, a Caribbean Club, a Minority Pre-Law Association, a Minority Engineering Society, a Minority Finance Society, a Minority Pre-Health Association, and a chapter of the National Association for the Advancement of Colored People.

There are also many other groups, fraternities, sororities, and associations. Financial aid program assistance by the Office of Minority Affairs provides part of the support for these groups and for annual events such as Kwanzaa, the Afro-American celebration of the harvest. Events last year included a discussion, "The History of Black History Month" and a talk by Eyes on the Prize producer Henry Hampton during the commemoration of Dr. King's birthday.

Race relations are considered to be civil, with only infrequent overt hostility. "The relationship between whites and blacks is usually pretty rewarding," declares one undergrad.

BOWDOIN COLLEGE
Brunswick, Maine 04011

Undergrads: 1,530
Black Undergrads: 31
Faculty: 162
Black Faculty: 5
Tuition: $20,555
Total Expenses: $26,500

It's cold and isolated up here in Maine, but you'll find a real commitment to diversity. And you don't have to submit SAT scores.

Bowdoin College employs a highly selective admission policy and looks for students from varying backgrounds. This small, independent, non-sectarian, co-educational undergraduate college is dedicated to a liberal arts education. In order to graduate, a student must take two courses in non-Eurocentric studies.

Brunswick is a town of 18,000 situated close to the coast, 25 miles from Portland and approximately 128 miles from Boston. Bowdoin was one of the first of the country's leading colleges to adopt a policy that does not require the submission of Scholastic Aptitude Test scores for admission.

Black American students who require financial aid qualify for John Brown Russwurm Scholarships, named after a 1826 Bowdoin alumn who was one of the country's first black college graduates.

The college combines a traditional approach toward a liberal arts education with innovations in programs and grading. There are 20 academic departments. Bowdoin does not prescribe specific liberal arts courses for all students. Instead, by their sophomore year, students must complete two semester courses in four areas of the curriculum: natural science and mathematics, social and behavioral science, humanities and fine arts, and foreign language studies.

Students then have the opportunity to choose from one of the 24 defined majors or to design their own major. Specialized programs include pre-professional training in health, legal studies, engineering, and teaching. Bowdoin recently expanded its Environmental Studies Program and established a Department of Computer Science and Informational Studies.

The Africana Studies Program is "an interdisciplinary program directed toward the areas of the African Diaspora—the United States, the Caribbean, South America, and Africa—in order to present a complete Pan-African perspective." At one point, a student may choose from over a dozen Afro-American Studies courses in history, economics, sociology, anthropology, and political science.

Perhaps the most noteworthy innovation at Bowdoin is the grading system. Rank-in-class compilations are now numerical grades with designations like high honors, honors, pass, and fail.

Bowdoin has student tutors in every subject and holds study skills workshops often. Faculty advisors counsel all freshmen and sophomores. The Dean of Students Office and the Counseling Center offer additional counseling.

Most of the black student-sponsored activities occur at the Russwurm African American Center, which houses a library with extensive materials relating to people of African descent. Campus events include Boothby Lectures, the Russwurm Lecture, and the Dr. King Celebration.

One black organization is the Russwurm African American Society. The organization sponsors public lectures, films, dramatic presentations, and the Annual Black Arts Festival during Black History Month. The Festival consists of activities including concerts, movies, and speakers, based on the theme of black achievement.

Last year the African American Studies department held a Senior Picnic. Other organizations and departments brought the following artists: Arrested Development (Student Union Committee/African American Society), Maria Hiojosa of National Public Radio (Latin American Student Organization), B. B. King (Student Union Committee), and poet Patricia Smith (Africana Studies/English).

BRANDEIS UNIVERSITY
Waltham, Massachusetts 02254

Undergrads: 2,929
Black Undergrads: 93
Faculty: 486
Black Faculty: NA
Tuition: $20,934
Total Expenses: $27,884

With a wide variety of support services available, and with five black organizations, several black administrators, and three special collections on the African-American experience in its library, Brandeis University appears to be a place in which black students can grow to their potential.

Liberal arts oriented and highly selective, Brandeis is regarded as one of the finest small, private research universities in the United States.

The university's Coordinator of Minority Recruitment travels extensively throughout the United States and Puerto Rico to attract minority students.

In addition to actively recruiting black students, the university also attempts to target various support services for them. Generally, black students adjust well to the transition with the assistance of advisors—black administrators.

Through the Dean of the College as well as the Math and Chemistry departments, students can utilize Brandeis' formal tutorial service, which is free for students on financial aid. This system is geared to the student body as a whole. Informal tutoring is provided by teaching assistants, while counseling is offered through the Office of Student Affairs. At the beginning of freshmen orientation, all students are assigned advisors who will be available for advice on a year-round basis. Students also find peer counseling for financial aid and concentration decisions helpful, "when they take advantage of it," adds one student.

Other support services at Brandeis include a series of study skills workshops at the beginning of each semester and a Psychological Counseling Center, which has two black psychologists. While study skills workshops offer topics ranging from time management to research techniques, the Counseling Center provides professional assistance to students who have personal and emotional problems. Many black students also utilize the Transitional Year Program, a pre-freshmen program which gives underprepared students a chance to build an academic foundation before entering their freshman year.

Afrocentric blacks can find an emotional cultural underpinning via Brandeis' Black Theater Group, its Gospel Choir and black radio show.

Many students enjoy the activities of the Black Student Organization which range from meetings, to parties, to lectures, to fundraising. University-sponsored entertainment has brought black entertainers. Although many blacks find them to be satisfying, events such as these need to take place more often, they say.

Intramural sports are very popular among blacks on campus.

Overall, it will be difficult to match the range of services available here for black students. The college even provides specially targeted literature for black seniors in its Career Planning and Placement Center.

BROWN UNIVERSITY
Providence, Rhode Island 02912

Undergrads: 5,942
Black Undergrads: 417
Faculty: 535
Black Faculty: 10
Tuition: $21,277
Total Expenses: $27,489

"Hopefully, I will make the Brown experience work for me," says one brother. "My experiences here are important, and I know the degree alone won't do it. It's important to know where you're coming from, to remain an individual and yet appreciate perspectives that are different from yours."

This private, coed "university-college," located in the residential setting of Providence, is renowned for its rigorous academic demands and innovative curriculum offerings. It is one of the two dozen most selective—and expensive—colleges in the nation.

Academically, Brown differs from its seven Ivy League counterparts by its flexible curriculum. Brunonians can register for independent and group independent study projects, independent concentrations (e.g., The Literature of the Black Mind) and satisfactory/no credit grade options.

The Brown curriculum has a healthy offering of Afrocentric courses in literature, sociology, history and music, most of which are taught in the interdepartmental Afro-American Studies program. Begun in 1970 with Charles Nichols as chairperson, the program features faculty like Rhett Jones, Lena Fruzetti and Fayneese Miller, director of Brown's new Center for the Study of Race and Ethnicity in America.

Support services are so plentiful that one is tempted to look for the dean of headaches. Components are the tutorial program, special support courses, study skills training, a writing center, minority peer counselors, faculty advisors and the Third World Center (TWC).

Still, many black students from public high schools have not been properly prepared for college-level work, and "it may be problematic for those trying to adjust to Brown when some departments are trying to weed you out in your freshman year," complains a respondent.

"It is stressful and quite a disservice to students who haven't yet learned the game to expect us all to be well prepared," declares another.

Most black students who matriculate at Brown are informed in September of all support services at a pre-orientation Third World Transition Program. "Every year, white students contest the need for the program," moans one undergrad. Receptions, meetings with administrators and faculty members, panel discussions, audio-visual presentations, parties, cultural "inner-attainment" (entertainment) and consciousness-raising skits are highlights.

Nevertheless, students maintain that those who need skills enhancement will not find much support at Brown. Tutorial effectiveness depends upon the relationship—"of how comfortable you are with and how you are perceived by your white tutor"—in the words of one. Career Services gets high marks, and faculty members are said to be approachable; but many of Brown's services are not advertised enough, say many.

"The student must take the initiative," says a sister, "to find out what's available."

In addition to the SSP (Student Support Program) faculty advisor assigned to Third World students upon entering, there are a host of other counseling services.

Where SSP programs fall short, other organizations, like the Black and Latino Pre-Med Society (BPMS), Black Pre-Med Society and the Society of Black Engineers, pick up the slack.

The pre-professional organizations are said to be "flourishing," with pre-law, pre-business and engineers heading the field.

A fair degree of activity for black students at Brown revolves around TWC (Third World Center), where they not only socialize but also "politicize themselves" by interacting with Asian and Hispanic students.

To foster unity among people of African descent, the African Students Association sponsors forums and cultural events.

Brown Sisters United is a support group for black women, offering Sista-2-Sista, designed to bridge the gaps between the classes by pairing, for example, seniors with sophomores. Moreover, they present an annual cultural show during Women's History Month, "And Still I Rise: A Celebration of Black Women."

Black radio programming may be in jeopardy as the station directors consider dropping the popular slot for black music. Still holding its own, though, is Rites and Reason, affiliated with the Afro-American Studies Program. It's a predominantly black dramatic arts group featuring students and Thespians from the community.

The Organization of United African Peoples (OUAP) has had a reputation for being more "political" than other groups. It seeks continually to get black students involved in university governance and recently spearheaded a 450-student takeover of the administration building to protest what they say are inadequate financial aid packages. OUAP not only publishes a newsletter, the African Sun, but also an art and literary publication, Uwezo (Swahili for "unity and strength"). Principal coordinator for Black History Month, they were instrumental also in establishing Harambee House, the African-American cultural dorm.

"Harambee House keeps getting bigger and better," says an activist. "When it first opened it only had 17 members; now it has 41. People used to stay for just one year; now they have members who plan to spend the rest of their post-freshman years there," he adds.

If you still can't find your ideological niche, check out the Students of Caribbean Ancestry (they sponsor Caribbean food events!), Onyx, for black seniors, or Voices of Inspiration who sing at Brown's black worship service every other Sunday. Friends of the Spirit, "more low-keyed than the others," is a religious group that has caught on.

Social life is dominated by the black Greek organizations which attract large numbers. Some mixing is reported with nearby Johnson and Wales students who may venture up the hill, but little movement in the opposite direction occurs. Only a few African-American students attend white parties.

"It's friendly and relaxed," assesses one student of the racial climate, adding, "but there is always some tension. But I guess there is no place on earth where there isn't some tension."

"It's not a bad place to be," reports another. "You can exist in several circles and find your niche."

Most, however, find relations with white students to be superficial if not plainly nonexistent. The same is said of relationships with white faculty: "Many of us are fed up with the way they downgrade us," says an undergrad.

According to one brother, Brown will either be your greatest experience, or you will hate it. "What you make of the resources and the people
here will either develop into a positive experience or the nucleus of
frustration," declares a junior.

BRYANT COLLEGE
Smithfield, Rhode Island 02917

Undergrads: 2,845
Black Undergrads: 46
Faculty: 246
Black Faculty: NA
Tuition: $13,900
Total Expenses: $20,600

According to most respondents, you can come to this small, rural New England college and get a top-notch business education.

Founded in 1863 and dedicated to the "educating of men and women for creative and responsible careers in business, industry and public service," small, private and coed Bryant is 12 rural miles from Providence and is a regular recruiting stop for hundreds of corporations.

The college offers ten major concentrations leading to the degree of bachelor of science in Business Administration (B.S. in B.A.). These programs include accounting, hotel management, and marketing. For courses relating to the African-American experience, check the history department.

Making the quantum leap from high school work to a Bryant College workload is not easy, and to aid in the adjustment, Bryant offers tutorial assistance (free of charge to minority students) and study skills workshops.

Bryant's black organization, Wantu Wazuri (Swahili for "beautiful people"), presents seminars and programs to offset any frustration caused by blacks assimilating into an all-white college environment by sensitizing both black and white students to race relations. Counseling is available through the Educational Opportunity Program on campus. Bryant also provides racial awareness training to its resident assistants and orientation leaders.

Black male students get involved in the community in the local Big Brother organization. Also, many students in their junior and senior years enroll in an internship in a local community organization to gain experience in the work world.

For good parties, go to Providence—as most blacks do. That sums up the responses regarding Bryant's social life. University-sponsored activities are usually sparsely attended by blacks.

Is there life after Bryant? The school's Career Services Office makes sure there is. Graduates of Bryant are, in the words of a black alumn, "coveted by most of the larger businesses and governmental agencies." In fact, every year over 100 corporate recruiters interview graduating seniors. Currently enrolled students use the highly successful Job Locator Service, which hooks up students with local businesses for summer jobs or internships during the school year.

BRYN MAWR COLLEGE
Bryn Mawr, Pennsylvania 19010

Undergrads: 1,193
Black Undergrads: 53
Faculty: 225
Black Faculty: NA
Tuition: $19,810
Total Expenses: $26,895

D espite—or perhaps because of—Bryn Mawr's intimidating program of studies, students seem to be convinced they made the right decision in choosing to pursue the Bryn Mawr degree.

The smallest and perhaps most feminist of the Seven Sisters women's colleges, Bryn Mawr is a tough school for everyone, but toughest for minorities: "No exceptions academically will be made for the black woman here," advises a sister.

There are few more selective liberal arts colleges in the country.

Located on 113 acres 11 miles west of Philadelphia, the school was the first college in the country to grant a Ph.D. to a woman. The campus is only one mile away from predominantly male Haverford College. Students may take courses at either school, major in any department on either campus, use the library of both, and even live and eat at either. Faculty also make an effort to plan curricula jointly so that duplication is avoided.

In addition to the arrangement with Haverford, Bryn Mawr enjoys cross registration and other privileges with Swarthmore and the University of Pennsylvania. Study abroad is encouraged—Bryn Mawr even maintains its own summer institutes in Madrid and Avignon.

There is a strict honor code because exams are self-scheduled. Courses do not include special class sections, because that would "not be in keeping with Bryn Mawr's philosophy." The result is a lot of pressure for Bryn Mawr women to succeed on their own. Although there is a six-week summer help session for those with poor high school backgrounds, tutorial and remedial assistance is generally described as "limited." Many black students have difficulty adjusting, largely because of the academics. Although there is an informal black alumn association and "valuable information" for pre-professional minority students, peer counseling is "almost nonexistent."

With the stress on academics and self-help, it is not surprising that the social scene at Bryn Mawr is less than scintillating. And Haverford's going coed hasn't helped. Athletic facilities are not that impressive, but intramural sports do get praise as "the only activity where absolute integration is achieved." Dorm life is "okay—although one or two blacks in a dorm of 80 people is often the norm." The Black Cultural Center offers "activities slow to start and badly organized." And there are no black religious services or black radio, and very little professional entertainment, black or white.

A weekly newspaper, The *News*, a strong Women's Alliance, the Black Theater Troop, and The Sisterhood attract the black women organizationally.

Black participation in university governance is described as "active, competent, and plentiful," perhaps because relationships with whites are generally "good." Some black undergrads think a strong black voice on committees is necessary. Interaction with the community is limited to a tutoring service (The Kids Connection) for inner-city kids.

But the lack of extracurricular activities doesn't seem to upset Bryn Mawr women. In general, they are occupied with their studies and don't miss the social commitments.

CARLETON COLLEGE
Northfield, Minnesota 55057

Undergrads: 1,752
Black Undergrads: 53
Faculty: 161
Black Faculty: 6
Tuition: $20,300
Total Expenses: $24,425

"I have grown in a healthy way at Carleton. My self-esteem has suffered a little in the process, but I will leave with a valuable education," assesses one brother.

Admission is extremely selective at this small liberal arts college where "classes are intense," yet "the campus is simply gorgeous, and the facilities are excellent." Minority students who require financial aid qualify for the Cowling Scholarship Program.

In addition to the concentration in African/African-American Studies, departments throughout the college offer similar courses. The Office of Multicultural Affairs provides paying programs for students of color whose career goals lie in teaching or science.

Black and other multicultural faculty and staff publish their office hours weekly. In addition, Carleton offers, among other services, a "peer counseling program for multicultural freshmen." One undergrad says, "These peer counselors are upperclassmen who advise freshmen on policies of the college and ease their adjustment into the Carleton environment."

Tutoring is available to all students free of charge. According to respondents, this service offers help from fellow students in any subject, for as long as necessary. Then the Learning Center provides one-on-one assistance to students who have difficulty writing, and it hosts study skills and reading skills workshops. For additional help with writing, undergrads trek over to the student-staffed Write Place. Also, says an undergrad, the Math Skills Center "instructs and helps students with all sorts of math problems."

The school does not have any closed groups like fraternities or sororities, but students of color have their own African-American Awareness

House and the Multicultural House. In addition, VOICE (Visions of Inspiration and Christian Enlightenment), a gospel choir, reportedly "takes trips to a black church in the Twin Cities at least twice a month."

There is a multi-format campus radio station, RLX. The black student organization SOUL (Students Organized for Unity and Liberation) sponsors parties and lectures. Last year, campus events included an art exhibit entitled "Diversity Enriches Our World," Black History Month, a Multicultural Retreat, an Ethnic Food Fest, and Women of Color Week.

One student describes the surrounding community as "withdrawn and reserved, but courteous." Another student states, "At least once a term there are workshops [whose purpose is] to encourage racial tolerance." Programs have included: Issues of Institutional Racism—Unlearning Learned Behavior, Building Community, and Vigil: We Are Together. The college has hired a race relations consultant to work with staff, faculty, and students. Last year there were six visiting professors of color.

In addition, the college annually sponsors four convocation speakers for the multicultural student groups. One year the speakers included Na'im Akbar, Floretta Dukes McKenzie, Ali Mazrui, and Samuel Proctor. Other speakers have been professional orator Patrick Russell-McLeod, J. D. and Cornel West.

"I am happy with my decision to come to Carleton," says one student, adding, "I did not realize what being a black minority female meant until I came here. It was a big adjustment my first term to go from a big city in the South to a small town in the North."

"The homogeneous Minnesota environment has caused me to think more deeply about my race and what it means to be black in the United States," assesses one brother.

CARNEGIE-MELLON UNIVERSITY
Pittsburgh, Pennsylvania 15213

Undergrads: 4,572
Black Undergrads: 183
Faculty: 747
Black Faculty: NA
Tuition: $18,760
Total Expenses: $24,610

A dvises one undergrad, "If a black student decides to come here, he should be prepared to work hard. Carnegie-Mellon is one of the most rigorous institutions in the nation." The university has excellent facilities, and students are exposed to the latest technology. But the tradeoff is hard work.

Carnegie-Mellon University is an independent, nonsectarian liberal arts and professional institution with colleges of science, technology, humanities and social science as well as one of the most prestigious fine arts and performing arts programs in the country.

This coed university, located four miles from downtown Pittsburgh on a 90-acre suburban campus, employs a highly selective admission policy. The majority of the university's black students come from Pennsylvania, New York, Maryland and New Jersey.

Students agree that Carnegie-Mellon offers a challenging academic experience. According to them, the university's programs in electrical engineering, computer science, robotics, drama and architecture are particularly outstanding.

The curriculum provides only a couple of courses that relate directly to the African-American experience.

To help students adjust to the college-level academic requirements, the university provides extensive support services.

For black and other minority students, the Carnegie-Mellon Action Project is the university educational unit that provides academic and nonacademic support in the form of tutorial assistance, counseling and study skills workshops. Most black students questioned describe CMAP support services as very useful. On the whole, respondents feel that black students adjust to Carnegie-Mellon in a semester or two.

Similarly, black students take advantage of the services offered by black organizations on campus. The National Society of Black Engineers (NSBE) gives special seminars and workshops for engineering students. NSBE also informs minority students of career opportunities in engineering and sponsors various lectures like "Blacks in the Business World," for example.

Black alumns assist black undergraduates in a number of ways. First of all, they help black undergrads gain summer employment. Second, they give career assistance to black seniors. Finally, they participate in special campus forums in which they share their knowledge and experience. Black alumns also help recruit high school students.

In addition to NSBE, two predominantly black student organizations, SPIRIT and the Gospel Choir, are active. SPIRIT sponsors cultural, educational and political events. Students hope that SPIRIT can reorganize itself and expand its efforts. Some students also participate in the local Upward Bound program. The Gospel Choir usually inspires students and facilitates "socializing" among different parts of the black community. Some black students attend religious services at local churches.

Black students describe their social lives in less than enthusiastic terms. In general, black students seem to feel out of place socially because they say most university-sponsored activities are aimed at white students. On the other hand, black students tend to be close to each other because there are so few of them on campus. Although few blacks play on varsity teams, they participate actively in intramural sports, and one respondent describes this active participation as an "important release mechanism" from social pressures.

A point to consider: Carnegie-Mellon graduates consistently receive good job offers.

CASE WESTERN RESERVE UNIVERSITY
Cleveland, Ohio 44106

Undergrads: 3,645
Black Undergrads: 255
Faculty: 1,936
Black Faculty: 35
Tuition: $17,235
Total Expenses: $22,095

For a thorough, varied experience at a predominantly white college, see what's up at Case Western. "The most attractive aspects are the clout of having a Case education and the big city location," says one undergrad.

This private, coed, highly selective school with diverse fields of study strikes a unique balance between technological concerns and liberal arts.

Case Western's recruitment for minority students begins as early as the seventh grade: they offer a pre-engineering program for seventh and eighth graders.

The majority of black students are from Ohio, New York, Michigan, and Pennsylvania.

To recruit minority students, an admission officer visits public and private high schools across the country as well as black recruitment fairs in Cleveland. Science and Engineering Outreach is a unique program that has faculty visiting high schools in several districts. They demonstrate scientific phenomena and conduct annual bridge-building and a mousetrap-powered car-racing competition among students.

Case also operates a year-round Upward Bound with an emphasis on pre-professional students in the Health Sciences, a college pre-preparatory program that is part of the federal program for potential first-generation, college-bound, low-income high school students. The target group is Cleveland and East Cleveland district high school students interested in professional health careers.

Wisely, the admission office works with local churches, community success organizations, and programs such as Inroads, Prime, College

Access, and One Voice. The office maintains a database of over 100 organizations whose locations are throughout the country. All admission counselors are responsible for this kind of vigorous recruitment in their jurisdiction.

At the same time that the Saturday Sampler, a program for all admitted students, is offered, black students may attend Celebrating Excellence, designed just for them. And then, a program entitled Share the Vision helps incoming freshman learn to appreciate differences.

The university application doubles as an application for financial aid. And the Office of Admission recommends qualifying minority students to the Office of Financial Aid. These students receive merit-based awards.

Looking for academic relevance to the black experience? Try courses like Race in American Cultural Thought; Culture, History and Mental Illness [Is there help for black writers?]; Modern African History; History of Black Women in the U.S.; Formation of African-American Culture; Psychology of African-Americans; Multicultural Issues in Human Communication, and Race and Ethnic Minorities.

The Writing Center and Educational Support Services (ESS) offer free tutoring; ESS also provides computer and writing/math labs. Learning assistants are assigned to each residence hall, and pre-freshman may work with peer assistants and mentors. ESS and the Minority Scholars Program (MSP) also provide study skills workshops.

It doesn't stop during the academic year. The Office of Minority Programs helps students obtain meaningful summer employment in industry. Minority programs serve African-American, Latino, Hispanic, and Native American students. Among these, the MSP recognizes and meets the social, academic, and intellectual needs of minority students. Its single goal is to ensure the success of capable minority students. Would you believe that MSP organizes a summer pre-freshman program, a summer internship for incoming freshmen, faculty mentors, and peer or professional support? In addition to university orientation, MSP sponsors a special reception and orientation to its programs. A Minority Round table gathers all minority undergraduate, graduate, and professional students.

Providing workshops in resume writing is one of the functions of the Minority Careers Awareness Program. Learning Assistants offer peer tutoring and support as well as workshops in time management, test-taking, and study skills.

Most noteworthy is the Minority Engineering Program, seeking to increase the number of minorities pursuing engineering careers. Ninth- and tenth-graders receive early exposure to engineering, and students may work as apprentices to the medical school faculty. Case Western helps teachers as well as their students by participating in a program to strengthen and to advance intermediate and high school math teachers in Cleveland public schools.

The Minority Engineers Industrial Opportunities Program (MEIOP) recruits students who have completed the eleventh grade. A five-week summer program includes special college-preparatory classes in math, physics, expository writing, and speech. Students are able to gain hands-on experience in a laboratory and perhaps to become apprentices in campus engineering and science labs.

More than figureheads, blacks hold the following positions: Assistant Vice President of Student Affairs, Assistant to the President for Minority Affairs, Assistant Director of Career Planning and Placement, and Chemical Engineering Chair. Two blacks are Assistant Directors of Admission.

Minority student organizations abound, and include the African-American Society, Black Women's Society, Careers Unlimited, Caribbean Student Association, CWRU Gospel Choir, Daniel Hale William Premed Society, MEIOP-SA (Student Association), National Society of Black Engineers (NSBE). There are no historically black fraternities or sororities on campus, but students have the option to pledge intercollegiate chapters at local colleges, most notably Cleveland State University.

Last year, campus events included the African-American Performance Arts Festival, Black Faculty and Staff Banquet for Graduating Seniors, Black History Month movies, Cultural Dance, Ebony Ball, and Minority Parents/Alumni Banquet.

There is a campus radio station, and Cleveland itself of course has black radio stations and black TV programming. Almost half of the city's population is black, so opportunities for extracurricular activities in the community are plentiful. You should be able to party. Says one respondent, "There is always a happy hour going on somewhere."

CHEYNEY UNIVERSITY OF PENNSYLVANIA

Cheyney, Pennsylvania 19319

Undergrads: 1,088
Black Undergrads: 1,044
Faculty: 112
Black Faculty: 89
Tuition: $3,729; $8,198
Total Expenses: $7,769; $12,238

There's something about Cheyney University's history that might surprise you: It's the first historically black college in America. Founded in 1837, this coed institution sits on 275 acres in southeastern Pennsylvania, an area halfway between suburban and rural. Cheyney prides itself on its long-time commitment to the inner-city student. It is part of the Pennsylvania State Colleges and University System.

Most of Cheyney's black students come from Pennsylvania, New Jersey, New York and Washington, D.C.

On the whole, students seem pleased with the supportive environment created for them by faculty and counselors. Cheyney's open door admission policy and support services provide an opportunity for the less than well-prepared student to enter college life and stay there. High school equivalency certificates are accepted and efforts are made to recruit students through visits to high schools and college fairs.

The school offers bachelor's degree programs in the liberal arts and sciences, business administration, industrial arts, home economics and teacher education. Highest enrollments are in business administration, special education and social relations. On microfilm is the renowned Schomburg collection of black history and literature.

Cheyney features an impressive array of services designed not only to prepare students for college level study, but also to support them as they continue. A special pre-admission course in study skills and academic basics is available to Pennsylvania residents, and a similar course, federally financed, is offered to out-of-staters. These confidence builders are supported by a counseling program and by tutorial services, both of which have earned high praise from students.

Respondents say that social life is vigorous despite Cheyney's rural setting and relative isolation. Students report that there are "numerous" parties, mixers and student center activities. The nearest black population center is in Philadelphia, 20 miles away. Cliques form around the usual factors—geography, academic concentrations and Greek societies.

Students credit the student government with effectiveness and a "strong impact" upon campus life. Students sit on all committees of the college and have influence on policies and procedures.

Major extracurricular activities include a growing theater department with its honor society, theater guild and black drama concentration; a student-run radio station; a choir of some renown; and weekly religious services featuring guest speakers.

Since most of Cheyney's white students are commuters (80 percent of the student body is black), some black students feel that interaction with them is difficult. There is some interaction with Cheyney's small, local community in the form of community tutoring and daycare center volunteering. Most students label relations between students and faculty, and students and administration "very good."

COE COLLEGE
Cedar Rapids, Iowa 52402

Undergrads: 1,312
Black Undergrads: 39
Faculty: 122
Black Faculty: 2
Tuition: $14,875
Total Expenses: $19,330

Academics at Coe are challenging but small classes and concerned teachers are what black students describe as principal advantages. They feel that they are getting a good education at Coe, which offers close contact with faculty, administration, and other students.

Small, private, liberal arts, and coed, Coe is located in a residential section of Cedar Rapids, Iowa. The college prides itself on the personal commitment of faculty and staff and has a very selective admissions policy.

Coe College concentrates its recruitment efforts of black students in the large Midwestern school systems. Admission officers visit Chicago, Minneapolis, St. Paul, St. Louis, and other areas. Their efforts pay off because most black students come from the Midwest. Others come from Southern states and the Virgin Islands. The college gives financial aid to 75 percent of the student body and to 98 percent of the black students.

Coe's offers a liberal arts curriculum leading to bachelor of arts, bachelor of music, and bachelor of science in nursing degrees. Also available are an interdisciplinary studies program and a major in Afro-American Studies. The college has pre-professional programs as well, in law, medicine, engineering, teaching, and community service.

Black students at Coe have high praise for the tutorial assistance, study skills workshops, and other support services. These are provided by the Center for Academic and Career Planning Special Services and by individual students and faculty members.

On the social and cultural side, the Black Self Education Organization (BSEO) provides programs for students, faculty, administrators, and the community. These are frequent and make the BSEO and its staff the center of black student life. The BSEO has a lounge, television, and meeting rooms, and is used as an informal gathering spot for black students. A literary journal called *Mwenlo* serves the black community and allows creative writing students to express themselves.

Black students take leadership roles in campus organizations and governance. Black Alumni Homecoming is an important weekend at Coe. Black alumns return to talk to the students and are in close contact with the BSEO. Alumns network and help the admission office in recruitment.

Black administrators and faculty are considered a tightly knit and supportive group. All faculty are given high marks for their accessibility and willingness to help on a one-to-one basis.

Since the school is relatively small, black students have frequent contact with white students. One student believes that if students choose to attend Coe, they will meet new and interesting people, but that it is very important to have a black student organization on campus to help students feel more at home and to promote black awareness and identity. The BSEO performs this function by providing space for parties, rap sessions, TV watching, and general get-togethers.

Relations with the surrounding community are good, and some students attend church and church-related activities in the city. Intramural sports offer black students another vehicle for interaction with the whole college community, and some blacks are members of white Greek-letter fraternities.

In sum, things are cozy way out here.

COLBY COLLEGE
Waterville, Maine 04901

Undergrads: 1,785
Black Undergrads: 36
Faculty: 155
Black Faculty: 6
Tuition: $20,990
Total Expenses: $26,640

Adjusting to academic life at the country's 12th oldest independent liberal arts college is relatively easy for most black students, according to respondents. "All of the blacks at Colby came to 'do business.' They know what it takes to make the grade and go on to graduate school or into the work force," asserts one student.

Another adds, "Many, if not all, were intensely prepared for the rigorous course work."

They'd better be, for Colby's highly regarded liberal arts curriculum is not to be played with.

It features over 500 courses and more than 45 defined majors and concentrations. A student is not limited to the defined concentrations, and one can choose to double major as well. Colby also offers an African-American Studies program which has courses in anthropology, English and history as well as economics, government, religion and music.

In light of the academic challenges, Colby makes sure that all students receive adequate tutorial assistance. A black undergraduate applauds the resources available. "There is a lot of support if you need it. You are encouraged to have a tutor, even if you are passing a class," she says.

Another student agrees: "Help is offered in all disciplines, and professors are concerned about a student's well-being." Respondents feel that the tutorial assistance is excellent and that the tutors are well-qualified. The Writer's Center helps students compose, edit and rewrite papers. Students also cite the orientation week and small discussion groups as beneficial.

Colby recruiters visit public and private high schools with large minority populations, participate in national and regional informational programs, and attend black recruitment fairs. Black Colby alumns assist with the recruitment process too. In addition, they help maintain the Ralph J. Bunche Scholars program which helps outstanding minority students defray the high costs.

Unfortunately, the social and cultural adjustment is not as easy as the academic one for most black students. In Waterville, the black population is less than one percent of the total. There are no campus theater, religious, pre-med or pre-law organizations targeted to blacks. Black sororities and fraternities are also noticeably absent from the campus since the college abolished the Greek system in 1984. Many black students participate in SOAR (Students Organized Against Racism) and SOBHU (Student Organization for Black and Hispanic Unity), an organization that "helps educate the rest of the campus," according to one sister.

In addition, peer counseling is available through dorm staff members and can be arranged formally through the minority counselor on the dean of students' staff or informally through SOBHU. Some black students rely on each other for support, guidance, counseling and recreation. "We get together and just 'bug,'" one student says. "Sometimes we watch movies, play cards or pool, and just basically hang out."

The black students at Colby are very much involved in school government through SOBHU and by serving individually on various committees. Some examples: Admissions, Educational Policy Committee, Financial Aid Committee, Cultural Life Chairperson, Ralph J. Bunche Scholars Committee, Black Studies Committee and the Student Judiciary Board.

Most of the black males at Colby participate in either varsity or intramural athletics; however, black women are not very active in the athletic programs.

Student opinions of the racial climate on campus are mixed. One student sees subtle and overt racism from white students. Other students speak of intolerance in broader terms. One sister feels that the school "doesn't celebrate the diversity it brags about," while another complains, "Colby is not very expressive of other cultures." But some black students think that the race relations on campus are fine and that students of every race interact on all levels. And one brother declares that he has "not encountered or heard of racial problems."

"In general, Colby is uncomfortable dealing with minority students," maintains one respondent.

Overall, blacks are happy with their decision to attend Colby—after making initial adjustments, because in the end, as one sister puts it, "Black students must be able to interact with all types of people."

COLGATE UNIVERSITY
Hamilton, New York 13346

Undergrads: 2,925
Black Undergrads: 117
Faculty: 254
Black Faculty: 6
Tuition: $20,650
Total Expenses: $26,415

Boonoonoonoos Hour? Yep, it's At Colgate. The Caribbean Student Association (CSA) hosts this event on a semesterly basis.

This small, selective liberal-arts school in upstate New York offers an innovative education and attracts intellectually and athletically active black students.

The year-round calendar is full of special programs, interdisciplinary freshman seminars, off-campus study programs and internships for credit. Admission is tough, and students seem to have a hunger for knowledge rather than grades. The new Grade Recording Option gives students the choice of accepting a letter grade or of taking courses pass/fail, depending on whether students receive the grade they have targeted for themselves.

One plus is that there are minors in African Studies and in Afro-American Studies. The other is that academic departments and the Office of Supportive Services offer peer, professional, and faculty counseling and tutorial assistance. The University Scholars Program for economically and educationally disadvantaged students provides counseling services and workshops before the students' first semester. And the Community of Color is a student-based committee concerned with helping students of color in applying and enrolling. One off-campus academic program makes it possible to meet students from African universities.

The college is residential, with 75 percent of the students living in campus housing. Created in the spring of 1982, the Harlem Renaissance Center (HRC) is one of three interracial living quarters aimed at students of color. The purpose of the HRC is to serve as a continuum for the social cohesion of black people and to promote cultural awareness to non-blacks. At the HRC, students learn appreciation for and awareness of the contributions of black Americans, and programming in the dorm celebrates their culture and heritage. The HRC holds a weekly Nia Gathering, and annually there is an Open House and a Valentine's Day dance.

Visit the Black Student Union (BSU) for social and cultural activities like lectures, parties, and films, for the black community as well as for the university at large The lecture series has brought in speakers like Maya Angelou, Dick Gregory, and Ambassador Andrew Young.

The Cultural Center promotes education about people whose origins are African, Latino, Asian, and Native American (ALANA). A gathering place for black students, the center has lectures, dance classes, a library, films, facilities for studying, a kitchen, and ping pong. A weekly ALANA general meeting is held.

Other organizational activities include the CSA-sponsored annual Caribbean Banquet. The African American Student Alliance annually holds a formal in addition to celebrations of Kwanzaa and African Women's Week, and the Cultural Dance Troupe promotes the culture of people of color through dance, music, and song. The Kuumba Dancers perform each semester. The Sojourners is a student gospel choir, which performs gospel music at University Church services and at semesterly concerts on and off campus.

The campus radio station, WRCU, offers a daily Night Flight show which "caters to the musical tastes of students of color," according to one undergrad. In addition, We-Funk is an organization composed of DJ's who provide musical alternatives at parties and campus events. We-Funk hosts a Fall concert, a Spring Party Weekend, and an annual talent show.

Overall, assesses one student, "I am satisfied because I've had the chance to open my eyes to see what the white world can be like."

COLLEGE OF WILLIAM AND MARY
Williamsburg, Virginia 23185

Undergrads: 5,480
Black Undergrads: 384
Faculty: 653
Black Faculty: NA
Tuition: $4,738; $14,428
Total Expenses: $9,110; $18,800

Students are content with William and Mary. Among its good points are its beautiful campus and the closeness a small school affords among students and faculty. "I would advise a black student to be prepared, mentally and scholastically, to deal with a predominantly white institution," says a brother, adding, "be open-minded and don't let color be a barrier. Others will accept you, and you will be able to deal with the academic challenge. Don't limit yourself."

Founded in 1693, the college is the second oldest in the United States and occupies 1,200 acres halfway between Norfolk and Richmond. William and Mary is state-supported and must enroll a majority of Virginians. Most black students are from New York, Maryland and New Jersey. In addition to liberal arts and sciences, the college offers pre-professional training and programs in business and education. Admission to the college is highly selective.

William and Mary makes a number of efforts to recruit black students. These include Weekend With Us visits for prospective black students, the Summer Transition and Enrichment Program (STEP) for entering black freshmen and high school juniors, and attendance at predominantly black recruitment fairs by the Dean of Students for Minority Affairs.

The admissions office also runs a program "Black-Student-White-College," which gives guidance counselors a chance to question administrators and faculty about recruitment of black students.

Despite the small percentage of black undergrads at William and Mary, the college offers a number of courses that pertain to the African-American experience. Among these are African and Afro-American history, black literature, jazz, and a course in African culture.

Adjusting to the academic environment at William and Mary has been easy for some black students and quite difficult for others. The main cause says one student: "Those who are sufficiently prepared adapt well; I'd say about 75 percent. Those who aren't from sound academic secondary programs don't fare so well." The many who have adjusted, according to another respondent, "have adjusted with help from faculty advisors and upperclass black students who provide a support network for incoming students."

A student will have to look around for those services, though. "We have very little hand-holding here," is one sister's way of putting it. Many of the counseling services are informal. Tutoring is available on a peer basis, through graduate student assistants in some courses, and through the Black Student Organization.

The BSO also provides "very helpful" peer counseling; students are encouraged to seek guidance and personal counseling from faculty and administration, although there is no formal program for such services. William and Mary does organize study skills workshops, which one student calls, "available, accessible and well-conducted," as well as career seminars in which students are given the opportunity to speak with representatives from various fields.

Because there aren't many black students at William and Mary, the college is unable to provide pre-professional societies for blacks. There is no formal black students' center. But blacks are very active on campus, particularly in college governance. The senior class president has been black, and black students also sit on all major student government committees. Student respondents stress the need for involvement in all aspects of campus life and cite opportunities for such involvement as one of the college's most attractive features.

William and Mary is not, however, devoid of all black-oriented organizations. The Ebony Expressions is a campus gospel group, and the Black Thespian Society, according to one student, is "an excellent medium for blacks interested in theater."

The BSO is active in promoting a Black Cultural Lecture series and in bringing black entertainment to campus. Students are unanimous in their praise of these activities, and they are well-attended. University-sponsored events receive mixed reviews. Although one student says that the events are excellent and frequent, black student attendance is low. "We do not take advantage of these activities as much as we should," admits a brother. Greek organizations are another source of campus activities, and play a large part in William and Mary's social life. Both black and white Greeks throw parties and "both are well-attended," according to one student, although another says that black functions attract more of the brothers and sisters.

Another respondent, however, has this to say about Greeks: "Here is where the segregation begins. Our social lives are basically black, although a few blacks join white organizations." Nevertheless, he agrees with other respondents that participation is dictated more by type of activity than tension: "Many black students don't see drinking and drunkenness as the only means of having fun."

On the whole, interaction between blacks and non-blacks on this campus is "extremely good." One student notes "a significant level of interaction" among students; another finds relations "very cordial and friendly."

The same holds true of relations between white faculty and William and Mary's black undergrads, although one brother makes this assessment: "Faculty members go out of their way to be helpful, some out of curiosity, some out of sincere interest and some out of fear." Black faculty/student relations are "distant, but strong." But "they are always willing to help" according to another respondent. All students questioned would like to see a larger percentage of black faculty and increased programs in black cultural awareness.

Black alumns are more visible on campus than they used to be. Two organized networks help with recruitment and admissions, and also contribute to undergrads' education financially (by donating to black student activities) and personally (alumns are available during some events for career advice and assistance).

William and Mary may lack a supply of black organizations and services, but it has plenty to offer to the black student who "will meet the challenge on his own."

THE COLORADO COLLEGE
Colorado Springs, Colorado 80903

Undergrads: 1,989
Black Undergrads: 40
Faculty: 203
Black Faculty: NA
Tuition: $18,084
Total Expenses: $22,646

For those who can deal with the color scheme, Colorado College remains "a good place for blacks because there is diversity in mind and excellence in academics," reports a senior.

Set one mile from downtown Colorado Springs, at the foot of Pike's Peak, this small, private, liberal arts college is ideally located for students who think and create best among snow-capped mountains. The co-ed college's admission policy is highly selective, and its track record for sending black students on to graduate or professional school is excellent.

Among the academic changes initiated by the college in recent years are honors programs, week-long symposia, a Southwest Studies Program, a Black Studies Minor Program, off-campus cooperative study programs, a wide variety of summer institutes, and most significant of all, the Colorado College Block Plan.

Many students find the unique academic structure to be inspirational. The Block Plan, which recently celebrated its 25th anniversary, divides the academic year into eight segments. During each three-and-one-half-week block, students concentrate on one course at a time. This structure allows for an emphasis on laboratory, field work, and seminar classes instead of the lecture as the primary mode of teaching. Other benefits of the Block Plan are the reduction of class size to an average of 15 students per class and the flexibility it gives students to participate in extracurricular activities without sacrificing their obligations to their studies.

Colorado College actively recruits qualified blacks. The Admission Office has a strong working relationship with the Office of Financial Aid to ensure that black students are funded sufficiently. A Minority Education Committee is responsible for developing and overseeing policies, both for faculty and students, that pertain to minorities.

The Black Studies Minor Program focuses on Afro-American religion, literature, history, sociology, economics, political science, and the arts. Courses on Africa are offered through the history and political science departments.

Most black students entering the college are already prepared for the college-level academic requirements. For those who aren't, free paraprofessional tutors are available in every area. Blue Key, an honor and service society, also provides tutors. The Writing Center regularly offers study skills workshops and programs to help students cope with stress, manage time more efficiently, and adjust to the Block Plan.

Counseling services are reportedly very good at Colorado College. Peer counseling is available through the Black Student Union. On staff at the health center is a black psychologist who is said to be very accessible, providing a great deal of support to the black community.

Programs designed to encourage racial tolerance are organized through the Student Center, the Career Center, and the Residence Hall program. One student remarks, "There should definitely be more of these programs," while another comments that faculty and student attendance is not very strong at racial awareness activities. Students feel that the administration is becoming more aware of the black community's needs and that more programs, such as black preprofessional societies, will evolve with time. Career placement assistance for black seniors is currently being developed.

There is room for black leaders at Colorado. A black person has been president of the student body and captain of the basketball team. There have been several black students who were officers in academic organizations such as Phi Beta and Blue Key. Brothers and sisters are involved in off-campus activities through the NAACP, Colorado Black Women for Political Action, the Urban League, and the Jolly Jills Civic and Social Club.

The Black Student Union plays the major role in addressing the social, political, and cultural needs of the college's black community. BSU activities are well-attended, but one student notes that because of the small percentage of blacks at the college, many feel that the organization cannot accomplish much.

Prospective freshman who place athletics or social life as their number one priority will be disappointed in Colorado College. While blacks who participate in sports do well, the high-quality education is still their strongest attraction to the college.

Brothers and sisters are more likely to attend off-campus parties (approximately one-third of the students live off campus) rather than the predominantly white fraternity parties. One can always count on the campus radio station's soul show.

The Minority Education Committee enacted a written policy that deals with racial harassment and discrimination. "It is not that we have had many problems with this type of thing," states a dean, adding, "the president simply feels more comfortable about having a form of procedure in writing."

White faculty and administrators try to help whenever possible, and are generally "tough" on all students alike.

The few black faculty and administrators on campus serve as excellent advisors to and supporters of black students' activities. Interaction with Hispanic faculty and professors (who compose a larger minority than their black colleagues) are also strong.

Colorado Springs is a city of 330,000, supported primarily by the electronics and aerospace industries and military installations. It is therefore a fairly young and transient community. The Black Student Union has enacted a Parent Sponsor program to get brothers and sisters better acquainted with some of the black families in the community.

Is four years at Colorado College a sacrifice for the African-American student? No, but it is a trade-off. You get a top-notch education and the individual attention that is only possible at a small school, all in an idyllic Rocky Mountain setting. What you miss out on is a large black support community. Any black student who enters the college unaccustomed to a white majority presence will be in for a jolt.

COLORADO STATE UNIVERSITY
Fort Collins, Colorado 80523

Undergrads: 18,136
Black Undergrads: 381
Faculty: 1,291
Black Faculty: NA
Tuition: $2,779; $8,782
Total Expenses: $6,931; $12,934

A ttending a predominantly white school—and you will definitely be outnumbered—brings positive thoughts from this career-bound brother: "I have no real regrets about my decision to attend CSU because I have already received word from prospective employers that they definitely favor a person with a degree from CSU." All this and the Rocky Mountains, too? This is Colorado State University, located at the foot of the Rockies.

CSU consists of nine colleges offering both bachelor's and advanced degrees. The colleges include the College of Agricultural Sciences, the College of Engineering, and the College of Veterinary Medicine and Biomedical Sciences. Teaching certificates at the elementary and secondary levels are also available.

The university offers almost a dozen courses that relate to the African and African-American experience.

Adjusting to the academic rigors at CSU is not easy; this is a very selective college that looks for only academically serious students.

However, once in, you will have several programs and services within reach geared to help you succeed both academically and personally. Noteworthy is the peer counseling program for black freshmen, offered through the Office of Black Student Services (BSS). According to one student, "The peer counseling for minorities allows freshmen to get adjusted to a predominantly white campus." CSU's Mentoring Program pairs black freshmen with faculty members in their major. Black Student Services also offers tutoring, study skills workshops, and personal counseling services.

Once you have made the adjustment to academics at CSU, then you ought to get involved in the student organizations on campus. CSU has over 200 clubs and interest groups, including about ten black organizations.

These include two fraternities, one sorority, a gospel choir, and the Congress of Afro-American Students.

For the artistically inclined, there are black dance and drama troupes "which portray positively the arts in the eyes of black Americans, Africans, and the like," says one student. If you are headed for a career in business or engineering, join the Society of Black Engineers or the Black Business Scholars Association. Black Campus and United Ministries, a religious group, is also active and well-supported.

No black community should be without a Big Brother/Big Sister Program, which allows black students to be role models for black children in the community.

On a Saturday night, you will do well to remember this advice: if it is Greek, it is going to be a good party. CSU's black fraternities and sororities have a good reputation. If you would rather shoot some hoops in the gym, expect to see some brothers and sisters there, too. As this student puts it: "Black students participate in intramural sports more than they do in any other organizations or events at CSU." There are only a few blacks on varsity teams, and the majority are on the football, basketball, tennis, and track teams.

If you want to get together with black alumns, head for the BSS office, which houses a Black Alumni Network.

"Know your priorities going into CSU," advises a brother. "This is not the place to come if you are not serious about school work."

COLUMBIA COLLEGE
New York, New York 10027

Undergrads: 4273
Black Undergrads: 422
Faculty: 571
Black Faculty: 12
Tuition: $20,262
Total Expenses: $27,126

"At Columbia, there is no middle ground. Either it is the place for you or it isn't; either it will screw your head on right, or it will blow it to smithereens," advises a brother.

The smallest school in the Ivy League enjoys one of its largest reputations. And with its most selective admission policy, the college would have to appear on any list of the nation's top schools. Part of Columbia University, it is a liberal arts men's college associated with Barnard College for Women.

Columbia draws most of its black students from New York, New Jersey, California and Maryland.

Columbia University has the nation's sixth largest library system, which includes the Alexander Gumby Collection of Afro-American materials. Alumni include poet Langston Hughes, actor and film maker Mario Van Peebles, lawyer and actor Paul Robeson, and Ford Foundation President Franklin Thomas.

Students must read deeply in major texts for the first two years as part of Contemporary Civilization and Humanities, two of the oldest courses. The purpose of this approach is to provide a broad base from which the student chooses a specialization.

Minority recruitment officers visit targeted cities around the country and attend college fairs. A committee of deans, professors and admission officers selects the freshman class. All applicants within a 50-mile radius of the school receive interviews. Pre-freshmen may enter an intensive summer program. During the regular year, the Higher Education Opportunity Program (HEOP) offers tutorial assistance to black students. The college also provides student advisors and faculty-student counseling.

Two black pre-professional groups, the Charles Drew Pre-Med Society and the Charles Hamilton Houston Pre-Law Association, are termed "very productive" and committed to "raising black consciousness." Both organizations provide study groups and counseling for black students.

Other groups include the Black Student Organization, Caribbean Students Association and Haitian Student Association. The United Minorities Board (UMB) sponsors social, pre-professional and political events. The Intercultural Resource Center supplements this work.

Last year, some of the campus events included Black Heritage Month, a Caribbean Conference, *Fame* and *Trouble in Mind* by the Black Theater Performing Arts Ensemble, a Kwanzaa Celebration, and a "Race Matters" lecture by Cornel West. Other campus visitors included U.S. Surgeon General Antonia Hernandez, historian and professor Manning Marable, Malcolm X's daughter Atallah Shabazz, and Children's Defense Fund founder Marian Wright Edelman.

Brothers have high praise for their academic experience at Columbia and feel that they have made the right choice in selecting the college. As one undergrad says, "This well-rounded education exposes black students to a variety of experiences and consequently prepares us to deal with a multitude of situations in the real world."

CONNECTICUT COLLEGE
New London, Connecticut 06320

Undergrads: 1,615
Black Undergrads: 65
Faculty: 163
Black Faculty: 5
Tuition: $26,325
Total Expenses: $26,325

Near the banks of Long Island Sound, small and very selective Connecticut College offers a liberal arts education and a liberal stance about the need for racial tolerance. A women's college when it opened in 1915, the school became coeducational in 1969.

Conn College sits on 721 acres halfway between New York and Boston (both cities are two hours away). The college is proud of the 445-acre arboretum on its campus.

An interdisciplinary Africana studies concentration allows students to examine the African diaspora through anthropology, sociology, history, literature, economics and religion. In addition, the library has an Afro-American collection of films, strips and books.

Admissions officers target high schools with large minority populations and attend black college fairs. Minority freshmen can attend an open house. Other efforts include a minority phonathon and minority internships through the admission office. Students come primarily from Connecticut, New York and Massachusetts.

For support services, look for tutorial assistance, skills workshops and counseling at the Learning Resource Center and the Career Development Center. Through the Crossroads program, which matches alumns with current students, alumns serve as an additional resource for black students.

Conn College is one of a few non-military and non-religious schools that has a student-run honor code.

The two black student organizations, UMOJA and South African Support Committee, hold gatherings at the Unity House. They sponsor activities like guest lectures on minority issues, minority awareness workshops and seminars, and curriculum development issues.

One of Conn College's goals for racial tolerance is to "enrich the diversity of our community and enhance common life." To accomplish this, they hold racial awareness workshops for faculty and staff, and offer initiatives to the faculty to develop courses in multi-culturalism.

COPPIN STATE COLLEGE
Baltimore, Maryland 21216

Undergrads: 3,007
Black Undergrads: 2,797
Faculty: 132
Black Faculty: 118
Tuition: $2,749; $5,963
Total Expenses: $7,389; $10,603

S tudents interviewed are generally satisfied with their decision to attend Coppin. They encourage others to apply. And one upperclassman notes that students coming to Coppin should want to better themselves and the community.

Located just west of downtown Baltimore on 38 acres, coed Coppin State College is a small but growing historically black college whose student enrollment has doubled in the last decade.

Coppin State has a less selective admission policy. Consequently, it grants admission to all applicants whose academic potential and personal qualifications indicate an ability to succeed in college.

Coppin offers over 20 bachelor's degree programs, including a nursing program.

Several programs reinforce student academic development. The Learning Skills Center assists freshmen who are inadequately prepared for college-level reading, writing, and math. For upperclass students who are first-generation college students, socio-economically disadvantaged or handicapped, the college provides free tutoring services and special workshops to enhance their skills. Undergraduates who simply want to improve their basic skills may participate, free of charge, in workshops given throughout the year.

On the whole, Coppin students describe their academic experiences as challenging and enjoyable.

As a non-residential college, Coppin has students of all ages and backgrounds. Students can attend day or evening classes on a full- or part-time basis. There is also educational, vocational, and personal counseling on a one-to-one or group basis through the Counseling Center and the

Career Development Center.

Student organizations are diverse. Fraternities and sororities are among the most active groups on campus. They sponsor scholarships, conduct educational workshops, and organize numerous public service activities like voter registration campaigns. The Gospel Ensemble and Inspirational Club go into the community for concerts, bible study, and church services. The TV and Video clubs inform students about on- and off-campus events. Respondents praise the Coppin Dancers, but note that the Theater department suffers from a lack of funds, faculty, and student participation. The various pre-professional societies are said to be excellent sources of information for those students interested in a particular career.

On a more social level, campus interaction between black and white students is "good" and "progressing." Black students also relate well to white faculty and administrators. Black students describe their interaction with black faculty and administrators as "very good" and "great." Despite the congenial campus relations, some black students want to increase interaction between the school and the community.

Throughout the school year, most students attend parties and other campus events at Coppin's I. Millard Tawes College Center. The center houses a bookstore, a multi-purpose dining hall, a faculty dining area, snack bar, TV lounge, a quiet lounge, and a conversation lounge.

However, respondents complain that high security and maintenance charges for using Tawes Center prevent them from having more activities. Although some students participate actively in student government, one student says that more students should become involved. Currently, students are voting members of the Student Activities Appropriation Board, the College Student Judicial Board, and other college committees. A Coppin upperclassman recently served as student representative with full voting power on the Board of Trustees of the State Universities and Colleges of Maryland.

Off campus, Coppin students can participate in the social, cultural, and political events in the Baltimore and Washington, D.C. areas. Many Coppin alumns live in this area and help recruit students. Undergraduate relations with alumns are usually very good, but one student comments that while most alumns are very helpful, more recent graduates tend to be apathetic.

CORNELL UNIVERSITY
Ithaca, New York 14853

Undergrads: 13,372
Black Undergrads: 535
Faculty: 1,586
Black Faculty: 34
Tuition: $20,066
Total Expenses: $26,828

Attracting brothers and sisters from around the country and the world, large, coed and Ivy League Cornell strives to provide quality support services for its hundreds of black students. Located in remote Ithaca, the school employs a most selective admission policy.

The campuses, stretching from Ithaca to the medical school in New York City, include 11 different colleges. The university operates the National Astronomy and Ionosphere Center in Puerto Rico, site of the world's largest radar-radio telescope; a marine biology laboratory off the coast of Maine (in conjunction with the University of New Hampshire); the Geneva, New York, Agricultural Experiment Station; and South American and Turkish archaeological sites.

The library's over five million volumes makes it one of the ten largest systems in the country, with more than five million volumes. Laboratories focus on atomic and solid-state physics, nuclear engineering, ornithology, radio physics, and space research.

Some of the undergraduate degrees are in area studies, business, fine and performing arts, and education. There are programs in peace studies, international population, and international nutrition. The school offers courses that professional programs require or recommend for entrance into dental, law, medical, and veterinary schools. The highly touted Africana Studies and Research Center offers more than 50 courses.

The university operates several special opportunity programs for minority and low-income students. COSEP (Committee on Special Education Programs) was begun in 1963, long before most major universities started admitting large numbers of black students. COSEP provides academic, financial, social, and personal support for minority students through recruitment, orientation, summer pre-freshmen programs, tutorial instruction, and counseling.

Each college has a COSEP admission affiliate who recruits and interviews. The university also sends representatives to annual minority student fairs and to fairs in selected cities where Talent Search groups exist. In the spring, a weekend program gives prospective students a feel for the campus climate.

For academic advising, preparatory course instruction, tutoring, and writing and study skills development, black students go to the academic support unit of COSEP, the Learning Skills Center. At the center, students have access to study carrels, chalkboards, typewriters, calculators, tape recordings of selected lectures, and a reserve library. Students, faculty, and professionals provide counseling services.

Student organizations like the Black Bio-Medical and Technical Association, Cornell Black Agriculturalists, National Society of Black Engineers, and the Minorities in Business Student Association try to offer solutions to academic adjustment problems.

Other black organizations include the African-American Students Worship Service, Black and Latino Greek Council, Black Student Union, Black Women Support Network, Festival of Black Gospel, Minority Industrial & Labor Relations Student Organization, and Pumoja-Ni Gospel Choir.

WHUC is the campus radio station. Ujamaa House, whose name includes the Swahili word for "cooperation," is a residential facility where students of African descent live. The house serves as a focal point for socializing and politicizing. For sisters seeking solidarity among their own ranks, there is Wari House, a women's cooperative residence. "These collective living arrangements are fruitful attempts to fight against the divisiveness of cliques," was one upperclassman's assessment.

Students have worked with organizations like the National Black Independent Political Party or the local Prison Project. Through the efforts of the Black Alumni Association, black graduates of Cornell try to make an impact on university governance. They exercise their influence by recruiting prospective black students, developing summer employment leads for black undergraduates, and contributing to the Scholarship Fund for Black Students.

Essentially, Cornell is a highly competitive institution with enough resources to fulfill the ambitions of most students. Black students who choose to attend can look forward to a full range of support systems.

CREIGHTON UNIVERSITY
Omaha, Nebraska 68178

Undergrads: 3,769
Black Undergrads: 113
Faculty: 1,310
Black Faculty: NA
Tuition: $11,562
Total Expenses: $16,110

Perhaps the most satisfying aspect of the black student experience here is that professors know your name and are available for assistance when you need it.

Coed, Catholic-in-the-Jesuit-tradition Creighton attracts students from 16 foreign countries and nearly every state. The university emphasizes individualized attention, and its admission policy is selective. The curriculum includes the liberal arts and sciences, professional and graduate divisions. Its campus is located in the birthplace city of Malcolm X.

Almost half of the undergraduates pursue degrees in the health sciences, math and other sciences. Business is a popular concentration. Seventeen courses in Black Studies are listed, but admission officers make few special attempts to recruit black students. Those that are here come mainly from Nebraska, Illinois, Kansas and Missouri.

Black students often need assistance to adjust to college life. Respondents agree that it is beneficial for them to get to know the predominantly white faculty and administration, but they feel reluctant to rely on these resources. Instead, students seek the support of tutors at Special Services—a program designed to aid minority and underprivileged students. Counseling services are especially popular in the beginning of the academic year. Advisors may help students list goals and desired grades, or provide a supportive atmosphere. Students show concern and encouragement for one another.

Creighton's administration has developed special financial aid packages to attract and retain black students.

Participants consider study skills workshops, special class sections, seminars and forums beneficial. Unfortunately, the consensus is that not enough black students take advantage of these services. Some respondents felt that lack of proper advertising may be a problem too.

Some black students find it difficult to adjust to the primarily white student population. Yet, in most extra-curricular activities, there is racial intermingling.

Mass on campus is held in the Catholic tradition. Faculty members offer students transportation to predominantly black Baptist and Methodist services in Omaha. Occasionally, Creighton's gospel choir performs at the campus chapel. They have also appeared on television.

Creighton University African-American Student Association (CUASA) sponsors slumber parties, mixers and movies. Entertainment has a personal touch: small ethnic theater is an example. CUASA sponsors all-black intramural teams. A black pre-med society exists, but students report that it is not very active.

The black student association's major problem is a lack of student participation. Even so, CUASA remains the political voice of black students. Black students, in the past, have not been very interested in university governance at large, but recently involvement appears to be on the upswing.

Black and white students get along with one another but on weekends tend to go their separate ways. All-black Greek organizations throw off-campus parties. Downtown dance clubs are popular. Some black students try to discourage all-black student cliques, and many undergrads are involved in fraternities and sororities that are not exclusively black.

A black alumn association exists, but students rarely interact with its members. Community-student interaction also offers room for improvement. Minorities in town do not seem to realize that there are black students attending Creighton. Located on a hill, the university is geographically isolated from Omaha. Students involved in tutoring, the Upward Bound Program and political demonstrations are among the few helping to shape community-student relations.

Although the social life is not especially exciting, black students at Creighton are satisfied.

DARTMOUTH COLLEGE
Hanover, New Hampshire 03755

Undergrads: 4,287
Black Undergrads: 300
Faculty: 488
Black Faculty: NA
Tuition: $20,910
Total Expenses: $27,039

At Dartmouth, adjusting to academic life is a matter of survival, not preference. "If we don't, we will fail," says one undergraduate. Her simple statement rings true since the academic load at coed, private, Ivy League Dartmouth probably surprises all of its students. But black students meet the challenge very well, according to respondents.

Nestled in the small community of Hanover, New Hampshire, this liberal arts-oriented college founded in 1769 employs a most selective admission policy.

In addition to its approximately 30 majors, Dartmouth offers African and Afro-American classes that include historical, economic, political, social and artistic experiences of people of African ancestry in the New World. Students may take classes in the African and Afro-American Studies Program for a certificate, as a modified major or as a minor. The program also offers specialized seminar classes for freshman.

Other programs of interest to black students are the Mellon Minority Academic Careers Fellowship Program, designed to encourage students to do independent research, the Ernest Everett Just Program for science majors and the Spelman-Morehouse exchange.

Dartmouth College provides its students with various tutorial services through its Academic Skills Center. Students say that these services are efficient and "widely available." Plus, they are free for any student who receives financial aid. One brother swears by the tutorial programs because "they make a difference between passing and failing." The academic departments on campus provide students with tutors as well.

Dartmouth College also offers its students a wide range of support services. The Intensive Academic Support (IAS) program attempts to make the student's transition from high school to college as easy as possible. The Career and Employment Services (CES) program assists students with career planning, arranging leave-term employment and finding internships.

Students also appreciate the attention and help they receive from professors. One undergrad says, "The professors here will tell you to your face that they are honored to have the opportunity to teach you, and they will often follow this up by giving out their home number in case a person has a question that can't wait."

The Afro-American (AAm) Society is probably the most important organization for black students. Founded in 1965, it sponsors a wide range of organizations and events including the *Black Praxis* newspaper and the *Spirit* literary magazine.

One of AAm's most popular organizations is the Black Underground Theatre and Arts Association (BUTA), which features diverse types of artistic and creative performances, including poetry readings and fashion shows. Often BUTA members write and perform plays depicting college life on Dartmouth's campus. One respondent says, "BUTA is one of the most enjoyable aspects of the Dartmouth experience."

Organizations not under AAm's umbrella also convey the black experience to the public. These include UJIMA, a dance organization founded in 1986, the West African/Latin American drumming ensemble, the Dartmouth Gospel Choir, the Student National Medical Association and the National Society of Black Engineers.

Students Organized Against Racism (SOAR) is active at Dartmouth as well. SOAR publicizes and protests racial discrepancies on campus. In addition, Dartmouth holds weekly sessions called "Rap on Racism" to discuss racial problems and issues. But according to one student, racism is not a big concern on campus. "White students are friendly, and there is hardly, if ever, any tension. Their friendliness initially surprised me," he goes on to say. Other respondents don't mention white students' friendliness. Instead, they say that black-white interaction is rare and limited to the classroom. And there have been nationally reported racial incidents.

The college is approximately 130 miles from Boston, the closest major metropolitan area. Being so far from a large city causes students to rely on Greeks and the AAm to provide most social functions. The student center also sponsors parties punctuated with culturally diverse music styles.

Brothers and sisters say they feel they've learned a lot about life while at Dartmouth. They are satisfied with their choice and feel academically prepared for the "real world."

And last but not least, advises one undergrad, if you choose to attend Dartmouth, "Consider the weather. It gets cold up here."

DAVIDSON COLLEGE
Davidson, North Carolina 28036

Undergrads: 1,616
Black Undergrads: 65
Faculty: 144
Black Faculty: 5
Tuition: $18,626
Total Expenses: $23,990

"**D**avidson," one black student asserts, "is a very positive place, very friendly, small, and conservative. I love the size. It enables students to know their professors."

It is conservative, so don't expect to find white students and administrators going out of their way to make your life comfortable.

Located 20 miles from Charlotte, prestigious, small, liberal arts oriented and Presbyterian, Davidson College employs a highly selective admission policy. The college's emphasis on teaching has led to its winning more Council for the Advancement of Secondary Education teaching awards than any other college or university.

Employing an honor system, Davidson requires completion of a core curriculum and a cultural diversity course.

One of the international opportunities is for students who wish to conduct environmental research in Kenya. The Dean Rusk Program in International Studies, which awards study grants, is named after former U.S. Secretary of State Rusk who graduated from Davidson in 1931.

Black American studio artists qualify for an award of $10,000 each year. Applicants must submit a portfolio for consideration for this four-year Bearden Scholarship which honors internationally acclaimed artist Romare H. Bearden. Other financial aid funds available for black students include the Davidson Scholar Award and the Duke Scholars Award.

For students with academic or transitional difficulties, students and private tutors charge a small fee for tutorial services. An annual Study Skills Workshop is also available for a fee. Professors arrange and seniors conduct special class sections at night, especially in math and science.

Look to faculty advisors for serious counseling, and for freshmen, dormitory hall counselors. The faculty advisors help with academic and personal problems. The hall counselors actively help their freshmen adapt to college life. The Assistant Dean of Students provides additional help, and students also help each other regularly.

Meanwhile, the Black Student Coalition (BSC) offers both tutoring and counseling, and provides special seminars and forums.

Students have the option of designing original service projects. Some have created and operate Reach Out, a group of over 20 Davidson and Charlotte projects.

The school has recently begun the Martin Luther King lecture series, which brings prominent black speakers to the school. The BSC also sponsors black theater and organizes various cultural and social activities, including a yearly Black Cultural Arts Festival and several parties. During the Black Alumni weekends, alumns return to the campus for special activities.

DELAWARE STATE COLLEGE
Dover, Delaware 19901

Undergrads: 2,902
Black Undergrads: 1,828
Faculty: 174
Black Faculty: 128
Tuition: $2,390; $5,872
Total Expenses: $6,700; $10,182

If you're seeking positive black faculty-student interaction, be advised that Delaware State won't let you down.

Small, state-supported, historically black and coed Delaware State offers undergraduate programs in over 40 areas, with the majority of students concentrating in accounting, business administration and education.

Its admission policy is not very selective: six out of ten applicants are admitted. Delaware State's 400-acre campus is two miles from the business section and 45 miles from Wilmington, whose black population is 36,000.

Delaware State conducts services to help students ease into college-level academics. The Tutorial Assistance Program matches students with students in a peer tutoring session, and the Special Services Program (SSP) arranges for students and professional tutors to help very needy students. SSP also organizes study skills workshops for students. Freshmen Orientation Classes are mandatory sessions which help students determine what is going to be important about their college education and then decide how to prepare for it.

Delaware State has two theatrical groups which present plays featuring the black experience.

The Wesley Foundation is a Christian organization and support mechanism for special student concerns. And Delaware State's choir, considered one of the top three college groups in the country, ministers to the musical as well as spiritual needs of the black community.

Although social activities are considered "only fair" at this institution, "parties make you feel like a part of Delaware State College," one student proclaims. "They are numerous and all people are welcome." Students release stress from academics through activities like bowling and card games.

"Basketball, tennis and track meets between different organizations are very popular at this school," points out one student. If these do not capture one's interest, the gospel festivals, picnics and happy hours may.

Off-campus involvement centers around a tutorial program, local religious services and community appearances by the gospel choir.

Most students feel that there are few problems between students and the local community. Black students consider their interaction with white faculty and students "fair." But relations with black faculty are "very good," says one student. Black students say they enjoy visiting black faculty because they communicate well with students.

The school may be affordable, but expect a limited social life. Yet, for those with specific concerns, this campus can be just what the doctor ordered.

DELTA STATE UNIVERSITY
Cleveland, Mississippi 38732

Undergrads: 3,276
Black Undergrads: 819
Faculty: 269
Black Faculty: NA
Tuition: $2,294; $4,888
Total Expenses: $4,474; $7,068

Regardless of the segregated community and the "invisible" status accorded to blacks at Delta State, blacks are adjusting well. "Most students adjust gradually. Others seem to think that they are in high school and can go without studying and achieve good grades," moans one student.

On the outskirts of Cleveland, a town of 20,000, Delta State awards B.A.'s and advanced degrees in the arts, sciences, education, business and nursing. Its admission policy is selective.

The school offers only one course, Black History, related to the African-American experience.

Delta State's admission officer primarily visits local public schools at least twice a year. There are no specially arranged campus visits for black pre-freshmen, and the admission officer does not attend black recruitment fairs. Some reasons: 50 percent of Cleveland is black, and 95 percent of Delta State students come from Mississippi. Black students also come from Tennessee, Florida and Georgia.

Respondents say the tutorial program is strong. Counseling is another strong area, if you can swallow your pride. But it is worth seeking, says a brother: "We have a very fine counseling staff. They are available at all hours of the day or night, ready to render assistance."

Delta State also offers health care, career and psychological counseling. One study skills class is available. Every department has a pre-professional club.

Only two black student organizations exist for 700 brothers and sisters: the Black Student Organization and Ebony Women. There is no black student center. And there is little black participation in the student government. The story is the same with sports, although Delta State has intercollegiate and intramural football, baseball, softball, track and field, and tennis.

Delta State also has a theater producing "first-rate plays," but few black students attend the performances. Religious organizations play an important role to many on campus. The Baptist Student Union and the Wesley Foundation supplement the services offered by the university chapel. Again, not many blacks attend.

Why? Observes one brother: "Everything is centered around the white students." With 20 percent of the student body being ignored by the university, it is not surprising that their involvement is low.

Black-white student interaction is just as low: "Socially, there is not very much interaction, but within a class setting one would probably find more." The quality of interaction with white faculty depends on which professor you get: "As a whole, the white faculty and administrators get along with the students. But you will find a 'bad apple' or two in the bunch." Black faculty are few, but worth seeking out: "The few black faculty and administrators that we have on campus get along very well with the students and the students enjoy working with them," reports a respondent.

Interaction with the local community is sparse. "The university gets involved politically on campus and off during political rallies and campaigns." Religious organizations also sponsor community-based projects.

Another complication: the community itself is segregated, so don't go walking on the wrong side of town. According to one student: "The community here is really segregated. Two high schools—one all-black, the other predominantly white. Blacks live on one side of the major highway, whites on the other side."

Things are not exactly fair at small, coed Delta State University, which offers a liberal arts education but curiously has few black-oriented courses for its large enrollment of brothers and sisters.

DENISON UNIVERSITY
Granville, Ohio 43023

Undergrads: 1,995
Black Undergrads: 80
Faculty: 163
Black Faculty: 8
Tuition: $18,630
Total Expenses: $23,570

One student reports, "Being black at Denison is an individual experience. Some blacks can't fit into the mainstream of life here because of
other experiences they've had, but Denison has a lot to offer if you use it in
a constructive way." Coed, and privately endowed, Denison is liberal arts
and sciences college sprawling over 1000 acres just 27 miles east of
Columbus.

In a mark of distinction, Denison requires that every student take at least
one course in Minority/Women's Studies.

Students come from various states, with the majority from Ohio,
Maryland, and Georgia. Denison is committed to enrolling highly qualified
students regardless of their financial means and will assist a student in
obtaining financial aid.

Denison offers a black studies program with 24 courses a year, and
students can major or minor in black studies. Some course offerings:
Introduction to Black Studies, Ethnic Literature, and Black Religion and
Theology.

The Black Student Union serves as a support group, academically and
socially, for black students. It helps incoming students adjust to college life
by teaching them how to study and manage time. BSU members counsel
new students and help them meet with appropriate administrators/faculty for
further assistance. The Big Brother and Sister Program gives freshmen the
opportunity to meet people quickly and to make friends. Students say it is
a political voice and an educational stimulus.

Happenings on campus include Black Student Orientation, Black
Student Retreats, the Black Student Science Support Group, a Black
College Visitation Program, Black History Week in February, the Vail Arts

Series, the *Black Student Newsletter*, the International Student Association, the Martin Luther King Jr. Birthday Celebration, the Black Arts Festival, the Black Alumni Speakers Bureau, DARE (Denisonians Against Racism Everywhere), and Amnesty International.

"This is a place where black students can really blossom and find out a lot of things about themselves," says one brother.

DICKINSON COLLEGE
Carlisle, Pennsylvania 17013

Undergrads: 1,840
Black Undergrads: 18
Faculty: NA
Black Faculty: NA
Tuition: $19,750
Total Expenses: $25,020

B ecause of its small size, faculty, counselors and the Office of Multicultural
Affairs can work individually with students who request assistance in
meeting the academic hurdles.

Liberal arts-oriented Dickinson, with its small town setting and handful
of black students, will definitely test your capacity for learning to think,
being challenged, getting involved and developing confidence.

Dickinson's admission policy is selective, and its academic program is
demanding. Most of its black students come from Pennsylvania and New
York.

There are five multicultural student groups on campus. Of particular
interest to black students is The Congress of Afro-American Students
(CAAS), which serves as a support group for black students and promotes
cultural awareness and enrichment for the entire Dickinson community.

The CAAS maintains the Martin Luther King, Jr. Library as the focus
of cultural and social events in Strayer House.

Two members of CAAS, along with two members from each of the
other multicultural groups, two independent students and the coordinator for
multicultural affairs, belong to the Multicultural Advisory Board. This
board develops programs and entertainment for the campus in general. The
Board sponsors the Multicultural Fair which brings in speakers and entertainment from a variety of cultures. Speakers have included Dr. Ralph
Abernathy, Martin Luther King, Jr.'s successor as president of the Southern
Christian Leadership Conference.

The board also created Multicultural House, where everyone involved
makes a commitment to promoting multicultural awareness through various
programs.

DUKE UNIVERSITY
Durham, North Carolina 27706

Undergrads: 6,264
Black Undergrads: 501
Faculty: 2,122
Black Faculty: 33
Tuition: $20,004
Total Expenses: $26,324

"My greatest source of education has been my fellow students—I have learned more about different races, religions, and personal convictions from a wide variety of individuals than I ever could have learned from any other environment," says a brother.

If you're looking for academic excellence and a good support system, nationally reputed Duke is a good choice.

Located in Durham, just 26 miles from North Carolina's capital city of Raleigh, Duke University is highly selective, private, and coed. Eighty-eight percent of the students live on campus, and freshmen must live in university residence halls.

Seven new minority students receive Reginaldo Howard Scholarships. They are four-year awards with a minimum GPA requirement. The late Howard was the first black American president of the Student Government.

Duke offers degrees in either the School of Engineering or the Trinity College of Arts and Letters. Students can pursue one of two undergraduate paths: Program I allows students to explore the liberal arts. Program II allows the student to draw up an individual plan of study.

Duke's African and Afro-American Studies department has added Paula Giddings to teach an undergraduate course on black women in the civil-rights movement and a graduate course on race, gender, and social theory.

Formidable as they may seem, academic hurdles are not insurmountable at Duke. The Office of Minority Affairs (OMA) administers many of the counseling programs that help with these problems. Duke's Summer Transitional Program helps make that leap from high school to college a bit easier. OMA assigns personal counselors once brothers and sisters arrive on campus, to guide them through the rough spots of freshman year.

Academic support services are available throughout the four years at Duke, from special study skills seminars and tutoring in introductory math and science courses, to peer counseling through the Black Student Alliance. Individual academic departments also offer tutoring.

Lauded as particularly useful is the advice given by the Counseling in Social and Academic Affairs (CASA) division of the Office of Minority Affairs.

Various campus organizations also provide valuable support for students. There is a black pre-law society, and the black pre-med society, according to one brother, "provides essential means of relieving tension that comes from the rigor of the pre-med grind." There are religious groups on campus, and the Modern Black Mass Choir performs both on and off campus. Duke also has black fraternities and sororities.

Intramural sports, as well as university-sponsored activities like lectures and concerts can be forums for interaction. Black Student Alliance sponsors Black Solidarity Day and voting drives, among other activities. Recent visits included the Alvin Ailey Dance Company, Maya Angelou, Mary Frances Berry, Jesse Jackson, Spike Lee, Wynton Marsalis, Leontyne Price, Cornel West, and Andrew Young.

Race relations are cordial, with little interaction as a whole between blacks and whites. But black students have immersed themselves in the university's heterogeneous community as a foundation for personal growth. One student explains: "Such a wide spectrum of individuals gives a student a realistic view of society as a whole."

"The intense academic environment will more than prepare you for graduate work at any institution," says one respondent. The flip side is that adjusting to the rigid demands of Duke's regimen can be frustrating.

EARLHAM COLLEGE
Richmond, Indiana   47374

Undergrads: 1,017
Black Undergrads: 71
Faculty: 102
Black Faculty: NA
Tuition: $17,160
Total Expenses: $21,465

One student's assessment: "I would tell a black student, 'If you're serious... then, yes, come here.'"

Founded in 1847 by the Society of Friends (Quakers) and located on 800 acres of woods, fields, and farmland, Earlham provides an environment that fosters appreciation of cultural diversities. The liberal arts institution has a selective admission policy and a tough curriculum.

Earlham enjoys a low student-to-faculty ratio, making for a comfortable, informal atmosphere. Professors are accessible and approachable. This open environment helps students and teachers relate to each other and overcome misconceptions.

But the curriculum does have some pleasant surprises. Students can major in African Studies or black/African-American studies. Courses offered include, "African-American Literature," "African and African-American History," "Topics in African/African-American Studies," "Sociology of Black Religion," and "Afro-American Biography." There is even an off-campus study option to do biological or cultural/anthropological research in Kenya.

The college encourages black students who have applied for admission to visit the campus to attend classes, talk with faculty and students, and stay overnight in a residence hall. This gives pre-frosh the chance to decide if Earlham is for them.

For academic help, the Student Development Program offers individual tutoring in all subjects and courses. In August of each year Supportive Services leads a program for selected students who need strengthening in writing, study skills, and math.

The Associate Dean of Minority Affairs serves as an advisor to the college on minority issues and is a counselor and problem solver for individual students. The Associate Dean works with a faculty advisory committee which has black members of the teaching and administrative faculty on board.

Black Leadership Action Coalition (BLAC) is a student organization which sponsors cultural and educational programs on campus including lectures, workshops, films, and concerts. BLAC informs the campus about black concerns, contributions, and perspectives.

The Cunningham Cultural Center promotes a better understanding of black culture and contributions to society. The center has a resource library and serves as a residence for six students and as a meeting place for BLAC and other student groups. The center also sponsors events for the campus.

"You can't help but be perceived as a black person on campus, but it's up to the individual to decide how he wants to participate in the community," says a brother about Earlham.

EASTERN COLLEGE
St. David's, Pennsylvania 19087

Undergrads: 2,155
Black Undergrads: 216
Faculty: NA
Black Faculty: 4
Tuition: $11,750
Total Expenses: $16,786

S mall and committed, Eastern has a special flavor that may fit your palate.

Small, coed Eastern College, located just eight miles from Philadelphia, provides an environment that is big on commitment to racial fairness.

Eastern admission officers visit all Philadelphia city schools and minority college fairs in Philadelphia, Washington, D.C. and New York. Most black students come from Pennsylvania, New York, New Jersey and Maryland. To encourage them to enroll, the college holds a visitation day for African-American students which is hosted by the Coordinator of Minority Student Recruitment and Retention.

Courses related to the black experience include "Historical Survey of Black Civilization" and "Human Diversity." A few of Eastern's anthropology, social work and sociology courses relate to black studies as well.

Eastern offers tutorial assistance, counseling, study skills workshops and seminars for students needing help with the heavy academic load.

For cultural enrichment, look and listen for Black Student League activities on campus and the Angels of Harmony, the gospel choir. Black students meet in the student center for organizational activities.

Among Eastern's programs to encourage racial tolerance are a required campus assembly dealing with race relations on campus, a multicultural task force and a special anti-discrimination statement.

Blacks hold a couple of administrative positions and one black person is on the Board of Directors.

Alumns have formed an African-American Alumni Association and attend homecoming activities.

EMORY UNIVERSITY
Atlanta, Georgia 30322

Undergrads: 5,200
Black Undergrads: 520
Faculty: 2,404
Black Faculty: NA
Tuition: $19,000
Total Expenses: $25,710

Where can you hear the Modern Jazz Quartet a month after attending rapper Chuckie Dee's concert? Try Emory, a university that can satisfy the black student wanting both to attend a very selective, private white college and to stay in touch with a black community.

With 76 areas of study, Emory is a liberal arts college and a national teaching, research, and service center. All students enrolled in Emory College's coeducational undergraduate arts and sciences school must complete distribution requirements. Favorite majors are psychology and biology.

Emory's recruitment drive for black students stems from its association with two well-established support organizations—A Better Chance (ABC) and the National Scholarship Service and Fund for Minority Students (NSSFMS).

As a member of the ABC program, Emory encourages applications by sending out 2,000 letters annually to prospective students. In addition to visiting targeted public and private schools for the past three years, Emory has sent representatives to NSSFMS recruitment programs.

The African-American and African Studies program includes 11 departmental offerings of relevant courses ranging from music to literature to history. The catalog also lists a number of complementary courses in related areas. The archives of the Independent African Orthodox Church of South Africa contain the personal papers of its founder, William Daniel Alexander. There are also papers relating to the civil rights movement, Peace Corps workers in Africa, and other missionary materials focusing on Africa. Also, the library has numerous current subscriptions to African periodicals and newspapers.

Emory provides a wide variety of services to help its black undergrads adjust to academic life. Black students and their parents may meet and talk with black upperclassmen, faculty, and administrators during a special orientation reception. Orientation programs include the seminar "Campus Life for Black Students."

Usually, academic departments offer tutorial assistance. Many students ask upperclassmen for academic help because they major in the pertinent subjects and are more accessible than faculty members.

Additionally, the Division of Campus Life organizes study skills workshops that cover procrastination and poor time management. There are also special seminars and forums on sociopolitical events as well as on academic topics.

Black student organizations on campus include the Black Student Alliance and black fraternities and sororities on the undergraduate level. The Black American Law Student Association (BALSA), Student National Medical Association, and the School of Theology Black Caucus are on the graduate level. Four black Greek organizations have chapters here. The college stresses the importance of the integration of its alumni association programs, and some alumns earmark their contributions for black scholarships.

The Career Planning and Placement Center and the Atlanta Area Emory Club hold an annual Career Day when they seek young black alumns to counsel black undergrads about career opportunities. Also, the center conducts a search program to find meaningful summer employment opportunities for black undergraduates.

The campus events last year included Dr. King's Birthday, and some of the visitors were Maya Angelou, actor Charles Dutton, actor and director Spike Lee, and Cornel West.

Many black students socialize in metropolitan Atlanta. Some students get involved in the surrounding Atlanta community through their work with the Campus Ministry, the United Way organization Volunteer Emory, or an internship with the Department of Political Science or Sociology.

Black students at Emory seem to have adequate support from the university. And they have unique opportunities to contribute to community activities in this black Southern capital.

EVERGREEN STATE COLLEGE
Olympia, Washington 98505

Undergrads: 3,410
Black Undergrads: 102
Faculty: 169
Black Faculty: NA
Tuition: $2,442; $8,295
Total Expenses: $6,912; $12,765

You'll find evergreen here all right: 1,000 acres of pine forests and evergreen trees and 3,000 feet of beach on Puget Sound where this liberal arts college sits with the promise, according to one First People's student, "of unity among us all."

Just minutes away from the state capital of Olympia and an hour away from Seattle, Evergreen State seeks to achieve a diverse student body, and gives special recognition to applicants of color. Black studies courses include "Political Economy and Social Change," and courses in the core curriculum include "Cultures in Collision" and "Problems Without Solutions." The library houses the Schomburg Collection of black literature.

Evergreen generally recruits by visiting private and secondary schools within the state of Washington. The First People's Recruitment Office arranges campus visits for sub-freshmen. The college welcomes visits from interested students.

Looking for help? Try the Learning Resource Center (LRC), a tutorial service for writing, reading, and study skills, including time management and English grammar. Individual tutoring, writing groups, and a writing improvement module are available through LRC. Students can drop in or make an appointment with a tutor.

In addition, the Math Skills Center provides help in math and related areas.

The Student Advising Center (SAC) provides up-to-date information on programs, workshops, and academic resources. SAC includes the offices of Academic Advising, Career Development, Cooperative Education, KEY-Special Services, the First Peoples' Coalition, and five student organizations, including the black organization Umoja and the Women of Color

Coalition. KEY-Special Services provides personal and academic skills development. Finally, the First People's Coalition provides peer support to students of color.

An administrative office, The First People's Coalition of Color tries to make sure that all students of color have complete access to equal educational opportunities at Evergreen and to provide assistance with any problems.

The Umoja Society encourages development and reinforcement of black consciousness. Black students can meet and talk in a friendly atmosphere. Umoja provides cultural and educational activities throughout the year.

The Women of Color Coalition is a female support group designed to meet the needs of women by ensuring their representation at any First People's or women's events on campus. The group recognizes International Women's Day in March and brings activities to campus which are of interest to children of color.

The Upward Bound program offers job opportunities for junior and senior students, and is not limited by race or color. It is an opportunity for college students to work with low-income or minority students in offering support for high school students with academic potential, by increasing motivation and performance to complete high school and pursue higher education.

Parties seem nonexistent, but recreation is plentiful.

Evergreen students are active in intramural sports in soccer, swimming, diving, basketball, volleyball, tennis, softball, track and field, frisbee, sailing, and skiing. Students can grow their own crops on the school's farm, flex in the weight room, work at KAOS, the campus radio station created by students and community volunteers, or participate the black-box Experimental Theater. Many other student organizations (over 30 in all) are available for student involvement.

Activities during the year include Day of Absence, Black History Month, Conference for Black Students in the State of Washington, Ethnic Food Days, Martin Luther King, Jr. Day, and Indigenous Peoples Day.

Evergreen encourages racial tolerance by training its student staff to increase multicultural sensitivity. The Affirmative Action office sponsors training for staff on multicultural issues.

Says one student: "Our dean of student development is a leader, and in this category we have programs but need more."

Another student encourages black students to attend Evergreen to "gain a good education and learn to grow in an environment that will help them gain a world view on education and life."

Says another, "Most of the faculty is great. I feel okay attending an all-white school, but some black students here have felt alone until they become active in the campus community."

FAIRFIELD UNIVERSITY
Fairfield, Connecticut 06430

Undergrads: 2,956
Black Undergrads: 59
Faculty: 388
Black Faculty: 2
Tuition: $16,340
Total Expenses: $22,940

For the outnumbered students of color here, this school founded by the Jesuits offers a reasonably comfortable environment where interracial relations are "open and casual."

This small, coed school means combining campus life with access to the city, since its 200-acre wooded campus is an hour from New York and three hours from Boston. The university offers B.A. and B.S. degrees and an interdisciplinary International Studies major that qualifies for either degree. There is also a Caribbean Studies Program and Schools of Business and Nursing.

Black students at Fairfield feel that the academic environment is a challenging one, but a smooth adjustment from high school to college may be possible. Fairfield has strong and impressive support programs including study skills workshops and a Career Planning Center. Tutorial assistance is under the direction of a counselor who is assisted by a black student to help organize the program.

The African American student organization, UMOJA, organizes concerts, plays, lectures, and socials, and helps to organize the annual Cultural Horizons weekend.

The campus annually invites black alumns. The school's minority counselor keeps up with their achievements and informs the black undergraduates of all alumn accomplishments.

The Visiting Black Scholars Program consists of lectures and informal discussions by black scholars. Past lecturers included Maya Angelou, civil rights leader Julian Bond, and playwright Athol Fugard, who discussed South African apartheid. The list continues with NAACP Director Benjamin Hooks, and Dr. King's daughter Yolanda, who spoke during the celebration of his birthday.

FLORIDA A&M UNIVERSITY
Tallahassee, Florida 32307

Undergrads: 8,957
Black Undergrads: 7,882
Faculty: 678
Black Faculty: 613
Tuition: $1,873; $6,669
Total Expenses: $5,051; $9,847

A proud sister puts it this way: "When black America needs education, black America comes to Florida A&M."

With more National Achievement Scholars than any other school except Harvard recently, historically black FAMU must be doing something right to attract the best and the brightest.

Although Florida A&M University (FAMU) has three colleges and five schools, it is best known for its highly acclaimed School of Business and Industry. Its 112 buildings are spread out over 408 acres, and it has the largest women's athletic program at any historically black institution. This is also the first and only historically black university to have an accredited journalism program. And for those who don't recognize such academic distinctions, FAMU is renowned for its athletic trademark—its 300-member marching band.

FAMU is one of nine schools in Florida's state university system. It offers bachelor's, master's and doctoral degrees in most of the natural sciences, social sciences areas and humanities.

Outside of paying dues as "neophytes," most frosh adjust to FAMU quickly and easily. Those students who don't score too high on SAT tests are encouraged to attend a summer preparatory program that provides basic courses in math and English.

Under Operation Student Concern, professionals and faculty members offer free tutoring services to students. For peer tutoring, students turn to the Satellite Tutorial Program. Students consider both programs "effective." The organization holds workshops on subjects such as test taking, time management and stress management early in each semester, and it sponsors seminars by alumns and other invited guests on a monthly basis.

The School of Business and Industry is successful in bringing black professionals to campus. A bi-annual Professional Development Seminar allows students in all concentrations to meet people working in their field of interest.

Both student counselors and faculty advisors address student's academic and personal needs through the University Counseling and Assessment Center. Also, students have access to the Student Hotline for jobs, internships and career plans at the Career Communications Network Resource Center. For daily struggles, most students rely on the resident assistants located on each dorm floor.

Many pre-professional organizations exist at FAMU. The pre-med, pre-nursing, and pre-veterinarian groups schedule seminars; the pre-law club works closely with the student government's judicial branch, and the Public Relations Student Society of America sends representatives to conferences regularly.

The FAMU Playmakers Guild and other Thespian groups on campus perfect the craft of drama. For entertainment, information or just a sedative, students turn to WAMF, the campus-based radio station which features music, news and sports. At other times, students frequent Rattler's Den or the Student Union.

On the weekends, parties are abundant; the university tries to promote week-long social activities through the Lyceum Committee, made up of students and faculty. As a result, the local Civic Center has been home to many major concert performances. However, one of the most treasured social events, the All University Picnic, only comes once a year.

Black and white students don't socialize much at FAMU, but the little interaction that does occur is considered healthy. Black students describe their relations with white faculty members and administrators as "no different" from interaction between black students and black faculty and administrators. Some students get to know faculty and administration by sitting on various university committees. And it is generally agreed that this system allows students to play a significant role in university governance.

Other than internships and direct independent studies, students don't seem to be that involved in non-academic work off campus. It seems quite apparent that the School of Business and Industry has created a "strictly business" atmosphere.

FLORIDA INTERNATIONAL UNIVERSITY

Miami, Florida 33199

Undergrads: 19,184
Black Undergrads: 2,686
Faculty: 1,198
Black Faculty: NA
Tuition: $1,905; $7,182
Total Expenses: $8,161; $13,438

D espite being greatly outnumbered, black students find the FIU international atmosphere and progressive curriculum quite attractive.

Florida International is the newest of the nine universities of the State University System of Florida and offers day, evening and weekend courses to accommodate working students and residential undergraduates. Its goal is to become a major center for international education and to create greater understanding among the peoples of the Americas and the world. Most students come from Florida, the Caribbean and Central and South America, as well as a few other states.

The college shows another aim of its goals, to meet the needs of the greater Miami area, in certain educational centers. A Drinking Water Research Center and an English Language Skills Center reflect some of the unique needs of the surrounding communities, while an International Affairs Center, Latin American Center, International Banking Center and an International Institute for Housing and Building are part of the stated goal of becoming a major center for global concerns.

The FIU student may study at the College of Arts and Sciences, the College of Business Administration, the School of Education, the School of Hospitality Management, the School of Nursing, the school of Public Affairs and Services and the College of Technology. In addition to courses at the two campuses and 80 off-campus sites, FIU offers opportunities for work-study-travel programs and hands-on internships.

Programs are often geared to the special needs of those from other cultures. The Development Education and Retention Program at Florida

International is specifically designed to help black students make the adjustment and remain at the university. Blacks find assistance through remedial work, tutorials, study skills enrichment and other programs. The program also publishes a black student newsletter which spotlights distinguished alumns, and offers hints on studying and making the most of textbooks. It also reports on black history celebrations, offers tips on financial aid and highlights outstanding black students.

Clubs are responsible for most out-of-classroom activities. Many of them attest to the international flavor of the school and include a Brazilian Club, a Colombian Student's Club, a Federation of Cuban Students Club, and a Latin American and Caribbean Student's Club. There is a Black Student Life Committee.

Intramural athletic events are well-received, and there is some involvement in the basketball, baseball and soccer varsity teams. University events—lectures, music, dances—during Black History Month are well attended, as are others, "depending on the emphasis."

Activities for students are available in the greater Miami area, and year-round swimming, snorkeling, tennis and sailing make outdoor activities attractive for all students. Over 80 student organizations offer a chance for participation and social activities, but most gear themselves to the educational goals of FIU.

FLORIDA STATE UNIVERSITY
Tallahassee, Florida 32306

Undergrads: 22,554
Black Undergrads: 2,255
Faculty: 1,671
Black Faculty: NA
Tuition: $1,798; $6,700
Total Expenses: $6,298; $11,200

Most black respondents seem content about their choice of schools. One student says, "I am happy with my decision to attend Florida State. I have fun here."

Florida State University prides itself on its outstanding reputation for commitment to minority students. They not only actively recruit minority students, but they also provide them with a variety of support services to keep them comfortable once they get there.

Concerned about adjustment? Here's a typical response: "The students that I know all seem to be adjusting very well," says a sister, adding, "they all seem to be happy at the university and tend to motivate one another."

The large state university provides a full range of bachelor's, master's and doctoral degree programs. Florida State also offers its students the opportunity to study the history and culture of black Americans in addition to its required curriculum. Its Black Studies headed by Bill Jones, a combination of the culture, politics, economics and history of African-Americans, is considered top notch.

The Office of Minority Affairs is one of the first contacts black students should make when they get to FSU's campus. The Office of Minority Affairs dedicates itself to the smooth adjustment and retention of minority students. The office provides workshops to improve adjustment and communication skills. The office also publishes a newsletter to keep students informed of the services and activities offered at FSU.

In addition, most of the academic departments at Florida State offer tutorial services for their students. FSU even offers some tutorial services free of charge. One student states that the tutorial program on campus is readily available for anyone in need of it several days a week. "The tutorial program on campus is widespread and available to anyone needing assistance," she says. "There are even ads published in order to make the services known."

The Horizons Unlimited Program, designed for incoming freshmen, consists of counseling and tutoring. Students participating in the program are usually nominated by high school counselors and admitted to the program even before they arrive on campus. The Horizons Unlimited Program helps disadvantaged students by providing special classes in English, history, math and speech.

Florida State also provides its undergraduate students with labs in the areas of reading, writing and math. The Reading/Writing Lab helps entering students increase their level of proficiency in reading and writing. The lab helps the student to identify and improve specific areas that need enhancement. The Mathematics Lab provides assistance (on a walk-in basis) to students who are having difficulty comprehending mathematics.

Black students at Florida State actively participate in many facets of collegiate life. Blacks fervently participate in student government, pre-professional and social organizations. Several black students at FSU have held positions in the student senate. Florida State University has even had a black student body president. One student says that both the Black American Law Students Association and the Black Criminology Society are "very useful" for those planning on practicing law.

Students who are looking for a creative outlet during their college careers are sure to find one at Florida State. FSU has a black actor's group and choir that will allow its students the freedom to express themselves. The Black Players Guild and gospel choir give black students the opportunity to creatively express themselves through words and song.

One of the most unifying and popular black organizations on FSU's campus is the Black Student Union. Formed in 1968, the BSU sponsors a variety of programs and support groups for minority students. The BSU sponsors a support program for freshmen and transfer students called "Helping Hands." The BSU also sponsors movies, lectures and seminars during Black History Month. The NAACP, Minority Business Association, Ladies of Distinction and the Caribbean Club are other predominantly black organizations on FSU's campus.

The social life for black students at FSU is largely supported by the black Greek organizations. One student says, "Black Greeks hold a lot of parties, and they are almost always full." Yes, the black Greek organizations do an adequate job of providing black students with social outlets, but some students express the desire for the university to sponsor more black functions. "Some blacks go to these functions, but not many," one student says. "The functions seem to be designed with the white student in mind."

When there are not any parties to go to, black radio and television both provide entertainment to FSU's black students. The campus radio station, WFSU-FM, broadcasts contemporary black music on its radio show, "Black Expression." The Office of Minority Affairs also co-produces a program for WFSU-FM called "Vibrations."

Interaction and communication among various facets of FSU's campus needs to be improved, says one student. "Black and white students interact fairly well as long as they don't have to live together," she says. Another student says most black and white students are very courteous to one another, but there is not much personal interaction between them.

Each year, Florida State sponsors the program, "Communiversity," to provide the students and the community the opportunity to communicate with one another. The university hopes the program of films, lectures and performances will also prompt communication among the students.

FORDHAM UNIVERSITY
New York, New York 10458

Undergrads: 5,795
Black Undergrads: 290
Faculty: 765
Black Faculty: NA
Tuition: $15,084
Total Expenses: $22,257

Some black students find the transition from high school to college-level academics to be difficult. However, several say that the transition is managed "impressively." One respondent places the success of the transition on the students' prior education at "either parochial schools or good suburban high schools."

Fordham's location in one of the five boroughs of New York City makes it a place where different kinds of people come together, adding another dimension to its already dynamic academic and social atmosphere.

The moderately sized, private Jesuit institution has a very selective admission policy and offers a wide selection of bachelor concentrations designed to meet the needs of its diverse student body. It is surrounded by a predominantly black and Hispanic community.

New York and New Jersey are the home states of the majority of the black students who attend Fordham.

With a staff of 25 full-time black faculty members, Fordham's curriculum offers 12 courses relating to the African-American experience.

For those students having difficulties, Fordham's counseling center provides peer and faculty-to- student counseling, and also offers courses on developing study skills.

Additionally, students belonging to the Higher Education Opportunity Program (HEOP) can obtain free tutorial assistance. And for a small fee, all other students have access to tutors too.

Aside from a black pre-medical society, which many judge to be beneficial, no other black pre-professional or pre-graduate school societies exist at Fordham University. Likewise, there is no black theater. Black religious services are in the developing stage. A campus-based black radio program "gives students a chance to get experience, while at the same time do something socially rewarding for the black population."

The absence of a black student center where social events could be organized adds to the limited social life for blacks at Fordham. The university gears its professional entertainment to the majority of students, and for this reason, the concerts don't always appeal to the black population.

For those interested in intramural sports, Fordham can be very fulfilling. One student comments: "They have almost every imaginable sport."

Interaction between black and white students is said to "be very limited on a group level, but possibly a little better on individual levels."

Says another, "Immediate reaction is one of culture shock, but eventually everyone adjusts."

Most of the respondents detect the presence of cliques on Fordham s campus. Defined as "not being cliques in the true sense," the groups revolve nevertheless around whether the students involved are commuters, in the same classes, or of the same ethnic background.

Contact with both black and white faculty and administrators is good. A few students mentioned that "black students tend to interact with white faculty on the academic level," while their interaction with the black faculty and administrators is "very good because it is on both a professional level and a personal level." Community interaction is very limited, and there are no programs that place black students in the local community.

African-American students play a minimal role in university governance. On the other hand, Fordham does have a significant number of black administrators. Contact with black alumns usually occurs during an annual alumn wine and cheese hour sponsored by the Afro-American Student Club.

One respondent sums it up: "College is what one makes it. If one is enthusiastic and open-minded, Fordham will be a lasting experience of beneficial importance."

FORT VALLEY STATE COLLEGE
Fort Valley, Georgia 31030

Undergrads: 2,431
Black Undergrads: 2,261
Faculty: 152
Black Faculty: NA
Tuition: $1,920; $5,130
Total Expenses: $4,695; $7,905

S tudents point to the attractiveness of the buildings and grounds as one of the school's major assets. Students are proud to have chosen a black school, and many are satisfied. This traditionally black liberal arts and teacher's college, located 32 miles from Macon, draws most of its students from Georgia. Others come from Florida, Alabama, Michigan and New Jersey. Fort Valley State is coed and less selective than most schools.

As well as liberal arts, Fort Valley offers degrees in agriculture and in business, and has master's programs in counseling. Although it does not have a major in black studies, this college keeps with its heritage by providing a number of courses that deal with political, cultural and historical aspects of the African-American experience.

The library houses the Homer Regulus Black Heritage Collection, which includes books, periodicals, clippings, paintings, records and cassettes relevant to African-American concerns.

Fort Valley's Counseling Center offers several study skills workshops for students having difficulty, and trains as well as provides peer counselors. There are also tutorial sessions for freshman courses and special classes for those who need to bring their basic skills up to required levels.

In addition to basic skills programs, this school emphasizes career development and placement workshops. One student also praises the Lyceum Programs which "give disadvantaged students a chance to enjoy cultural programs to which they would not otherwise be exposed."

Students do join the Fort Valley community for such activities as voter-registration drives and church functions. There are also a few tutorial and counseling outreach programs. But for the most part, students complain that the town offers little and that it is one of the major drawbacks of the college.

Social life is restricted to the campus, but it is fairly active. Parties are "great" and well-attended, hosted mainly by the numerous fraternities and sororities. There is also active participation in student center activities and in such events as picnics and happy hours. There is less participation in such cultural events as lectures and music programs.

Although there is a student government and there are student members on all standing committees here, political involvement is low. Sports, both varsity and intramural, are big on campus. Varsity football is especially prominent. Other organized activities, such as drama and the radio station, are available but are not as heavily emphasized.

Overall, response to this college is mixed. "The most attractive feature of this school is its history," says one of its undergrads.

FRANKLIN AND MARSHALL COLLEGE
Lancaster, Pennsylvania 17604

Undergrads: 1,866
Black Undergrads: 56
Faculty: 175
Black Faculty: NA
Tuition: $25,630
Total Expenses: $25,630

"Ifyou are concerned about your social life, don't come here. Academics should be the sole priority here, and with that in mind, I would strongly recommend this institution to any black who would apply," one student writes.

Franklin and Marshall is a small, private, coed, liberal arts and highly selective college that stresses its sense of community.

Admission officers visit private and public secondary schools. These officers also participate in spring NSSFMS College Fairs in New York, Philadelphia and Washington, D.C. F&M also recruits at fairs sponsored by high schools, community civic groups and community colleges. Alumns are active, with one program, Alumni-Admissions Associates, assisting the admission staff by identifying prospective students, conducting interviews and bringing students to campus.

F&M offers a Black Pre-Freshman Weekend, when accepted black pre-freshmen visit the campus and sample college life.

Course offerings of special interest include special classes in English, history, music, religious studies, sociology as well as offerings in anthropology, including "Sub-Saharan Africa," "The Cross-Cultural Study of Women," "The Culture of Poverty," "Comparative Urbanization" and "African Art and Culture."

Courses in American studies, comparative mythology, and government supplement these offerings. Academics are rigorous, with a distribution requirement in certain areas.

Tutorial assistance is available through a Study-Buddy program. Through the Black Student Union's tutorial service, upperclassmen assist underclassmen. In the Mentor Program, each freshman pairs with an upperclassman who serves as counselor, assisting the freshman with academic assignments and social adjustment. Professors and guidance counselors back up these supportive efforts.

A student adds, "You'll find that if you are willing to make an effort, you can receive a tremendous amount of support; but you have to be responsible enough to look for it." Both the Black Student Union and the Counseling Office offer study skills workshops. An English writing workshop is available.

The College Center sponsors various seminars and forums for the black student. These include religious programs, psychology and sociology groups, NAACP meetings and guest speakers.

The Black Cultural Center is one gathering place for black students. It provides not only academic programs, but also social and cultural events. A student reports that these activities are "very good, but usually poorly attended by blacks."

The social life? F&M is isolated and the social life particularly leaves much to be desired for the black student. One student writes, "F&M satisfies my intellectual needs, but the college does nothing to stimulate my cultural interests as a black person."

Another student says, "F&M has had no activity in which there has been much black participation because none of the events is designed to appeal to minorities."

The most popular activities for blacks on F&M's campus seem to be intramural sports and the Gospel Choir. The Black Student Union sponsors roller skating and bowling. The Black History and Black Cultural months also rate highly with black students. Although the social life for blacks is limited on F&M's campus, blacks can find entertainment at nearby Millersville College. Millersville offers membership in black fraternities and sororities, in addition to various parties.

Intramural sports are strong. "I played on one of the football teams, and the unity sensed as players, friends and blacks was the experience of a lifetime," one student says.

Interaction between black and white students is reportedly good, as is the black student-faculty relationship. One student notes, "The black faculty and administrators are extremely helpful and supportive to the black student particularly since they have been here for a number of years and can offer a wealth of information about the campus and its resources."

Black alumns also participate in Homecoming and Black Weekends, career forums and lectures; they recruit for their employer firms and participate in annual gift-giving campaigns for the college.

Administratively, blacks hold positions in admissions and student affairs, and a black trustee serves on the college corporation.

Students describe black alumns as, "a tremendous resource for the black student. They are extremely supportive of the Black Student Union and are always willing to give of their time and resources whenever possible."

Another project undertaken by the BSU is "New Direction," a volunteer-based community service which has undergraduates working as student interns with local junior high school students to provide them with cultural experiences they otherwise would not enjoy.

A black F&M student sums up: "The most important thing is to come here ready to give your very best effort and be willing to work harder than you ever have before."

"I feel that attending this school has been a rewarding and worthwhile experience. The career-oriented will find many open doors after graduation," another black student advises.

FURMAN UNIVERSITY
Greenville, South Carolina 29613

Undergrads: 2,417
Black Undergrads: 97
Faculty: 198
Black Faculty: 2
Tuition: $14,576
Total Expenses: $18,744

Several respondents report that they are pleased with their decision to attend because of "Furman's strict standards of academics and morality."

A coed, residential college committed to Christian ideals, Furman is located in the foothills of the Blue Ridge Mountains, five miles outside of Greenville, South Carolina. Furman has a very selective admission policy.

This university's mission is "to develop individual excellence and to prepare students for living as well as for a livelihood." While the emphasis at Furman is on a liberal arts education, the university also offers professional programs to prepare students for entry-level positions in the fields of music, business administration and education.

The school awards the bachelor of arts degree for two interdisciplinary majors—Urban Studies and Asian-African Studies.

Furman also requires attendance at a certain number of cultural events under the Cultural Life Program (CLP). A student enrolled at Furman for all four years would be required to attend 48 events.

Despite the interdisciplinary majors mentioned above, there is very little opportunity for students to learn more about their African-American heritage at Furman. The Asian-African Studies Program, however, lists several courses related to Africa.

Students report that with the exception of some black athletes, most black students are successful in making the academic transition at Furman. (Black athletes reportedly participate in a special study program administered by the athletics department). Students describe the Special Service's tutorial assistance program as "very helpful." They complain, however, that free tutorial assistance and study skills workshops are available only to freshmen.

Although counseling is available through the Office of Counseling and Testing, black students bemoan the absence of any black administrators or staff and the presence of only two black faculty members.

The only two black student organizations at Furman are the Student League for Black Culture (SLBC) and the Furman University Gospel Choir. The SLBC is especially important to the black students. In addition to serving as "a forum where black students can discuss issues of importance to blacks," SLBC is also the vehicle for black student participation in most campus activities such as intramurals and student politics. The Furman University Gospel Choir is very active and "gives students a chance to belong to something black-oriented."

Nevertheless, the social life for black students at Furman is bleak. The recruitment of black male athletes has resulted in a large disparity between black men and women on campus. Students report "very limited participation" in on-campus activities sponsored by white organizations. Off-campus parties are rare. Although students are required to attend university-sponsored cultural events under the Cultural Life Program, black students "often attend with reluctance since most of the programs reflect white culture."

Race relations in the New South do not hold any surprises. Black students describe interaction with white students as cordial, but they contend there is little interaction outside of the classroom. The white faculty is described as "very helpful when approached." However, programs sponsored by the administration to encourage racial tolerance are noticeably absent from student reports. Fortunately, black students enjoy "a good relationship with the surrounding community." This contact is facilitated by community-based programs run by the Student League for Black Culture and the Collegiate Education Service Corps.

GALLAUDET UNIVERSITY
Washington, D.C. 20002

Undergrads: 1,298
Black Undergrads: 147
Faculty: 260
Black Faculty: 14
Tuition: $5,610
Total Expenses: $12,920

"The school's attractive features are its grassy properties and lovely statues recalling deaf history at Gallaudet," maintains a senior.

Gallaudet has grown from a small school of five students in 1857 as the Columbia Institution for the Deaf and Dumb and the Blind to a world-renowned university specializing in deafness and the education of deaf students.

Its history almost parallels the country's sleepy progress toward equal opportunity. Twenty-three years after being chartered in 1887, its president, Edward Gallaudet was criticized for allowing six women to register. In 1894, students and alumns helped change the name from the National Deaf-Mute College, which they thought was inappropriate, to Gallaudet College. And then, in 1988, students mounted a successful Deaf President Now (DPN) movement to protest the selection of a non-deaf president. Within 10 days the Board of Trustees had reversed itself and selected an alumn, I. King Jordan, as the school's first deaf president.

Located in Washington, D.C., the small, coed, specialized school uses selective but flexible admission criteria.

Applicants are evaluated on the basis of their standardized test scores, Gallaudet English Language Sample score, grades from previous schools, at least two letters of recommendation from school personnel and/or employers, and their interest in college studies.

If you need an application and are outside the Washington, D.C. area you may call toll-free: (800) 995-0550.

In addition to regular transfers, Gallaudet has articulation agreements with 20 two-year institutions. The result is easier transferring of credits toward the Gallaudet bachelor's degree. Participating schools:

Bryant and Stratton Business Institute, Buffalo, NY
California State University-Northridge, Northridge, CA
Camden County College, Blackwood, NJ
Flagler College, St. Augustine, FL
Hinds Community College, Raymond, MS
Houston Community College, Houston, TX
Howard County Junior College, Big Spring, TX
Johnson County Community College, Overland Park, KS
Los Angeles Pierce Community College, Woodland Hills, CA
Miami-Dade Community College, Miami, FL
Montgomery College, Maryland, all campuses
Mt. Aloysius Junior College, Cresson, PA
National Technical Institute for the Deaf (School of Business Careers),
    Rochester, NY
Northern Essex Community College, Haverhill, MA
Northwestern Connecticut Community College, Winsted, CT
Ohlone College, Fremont, CA
Seattle Central Community College, Seattle, WA
Waubonsee Community College, Sugar Grove, IL
Western Piedmont Community College, Morgantown, NC
William Rainey Harper College, Palatine, IL

To orient yourself, you can start with the New Signers Program, offered
to freshmen and transfer students who have little or no signing skills. It's a
three-week total immersion program. By the time fall classes begin, you'll
be able to communicate with other Gallaudet students, staff, and professors.

A full range of support services then are available, and include tutoring
as well as workshops on time management and stress. "In general, they give
lots of positive reinforcement to students who need counseling," assesses
one undergrad.

For information on visual aids, directories, and events, the University
Center is the place to go.

The Black Deaf Students Union is in the words of one respondent, "an
active, politically aware group for black students."

Although Gallaudet offers special lectures on diversity, one student
states, "I'm still struggling to get along with them." In the case of white

faculty, "Not many of them acted as role models for black students," says a sister.

So Gallaudet, a campus for a special population, may present a double set of challenges for black students who represent the double whammy of being a minority in more ways than one.

GEORGETOWN UNIVERSITY
Washington, D.C. 20057

Undergrads: 6,316
Black Undergrads: 442
Faculty: 2,114
Black Faculty: NA
Tuition: $19,402
Total Expenses: $26,868

Highly selective and highly regarded, demanding academically, and located in an affluent, predominantly white residential area, Georgetown still leaves much for black students to complain about socially. It is the country's oldest Roman Catholic college.

Academics are of primary concern here, although Georgetown is known for its high-powered basketball team. Two courses in theology and philosophy are required.

Its black-oriented course offerings include African Politics, Cultures in Conflict, and Women in Labor in Africa.

The majority of Georgetown's students come from the East—principally New York, New Jersey, Pennsylvania, and Washington, D.C. Admission officers visit both private and public schools in efforts to recruit students. In many areas where large numbers of minority students live, a representative from the office of Minority Student Affairs accompanies the admission officer. The university adheres to a policy of not attending recruitment fairs that charge fees for participation, but admission officers attend all others, like NSSFMS College Fairs, for example.

Black alumns participate in the recruitment of black students by attending recruitment functions whenever possible. Georgetown also sponsors a Minority Pre-Freshman Weekend to facilitate a smoother transition to the academic and social atmosphere of the campus.

In addition to participating in college fairs, black alumns attend reunion weekends and activities during Black History Month. The Center for Minority Affairs and the Career Planning and Placement Office offer assistance for black seniors and summer employment leads for black undergrads.

The Community Scholars program provides personal counseling and free tutoring in all academic subjects for all minority students. Its student assistants aid incoming freshmen in adjusting to both the academic and social environments.

In the summer, the Community Scholars Program offers a program for incoming freshmen, which provides a chance for the student to become acclimated to the academic and social atmosphere of Georgetown. Moreover, the University Counseling Center provides study skills workshops for all undergraduates. The university itself offers basic courses in mathematics and English to all students requiring preparatory courses before entering the regular curriculum, and a writing center assists the students with specific assignments.

The Center for Minority Student Affairs helps students in easing the transition from high school to college. The Center has instituted both the Educational Community Involvement Program, a community outreach to students in the District of Columbia, and the Upward Bound Program, offering academic counseling and non-academic services for high school students. There is also a varied array of black student organizations, including the Black Student Alliance, the Black Theater Ensemble, the Georgetown University Gospel Choir, and the NAACP.

Located in 75 percent black Washington D.C., where activities geared to the black student are practically unlimited, social activities for blacks at Georgetown seem to be lacking. And there are no intramural sports programs particularly geared toward blacks.

"The black faculty express extra concern for their black students," says one student in assessing the advantages. "Unfortunately, the number of black faculty members are too few by comparison to the number of whites."

GETTYSBURG COLLEGE
Gettysburg, Pennsylvania 17325

Undergrads: 2,000
Black Undergrads: 60
Faculty: 174
Black Faculty: NA
Tuition: $20,834
Total Expenses: $25,356

Dedicated to diversity through its Think Tank and Intercultural Resource Center which offers genealogical research facilities, Gettysburg is a liberal arts college that has taken an innovative approach toward attracting and retaining more black and minority students.

Perhaps no college in the country will do as much to help you find your roots.

Founded in 1832, Gettysburg College is within easy access to Baltimore and Washington, D.C. although it is located in rural Gettysburg, site of the Civil War battle.

The annual Think Tank sessions provide a means for students and scholars to discuss and promote a better understanding of racial and cultural diversity. The Intercultural Resource Center provides students with a meeting place, a center for both academic and personal counseling and guidance, and a facility for genealogical research. The center is a source of cultural and historical information about diverse ethnic groups with emphasis on the contributions of blacks.

The Center also sponsors educational, cultural and social programs.

The Intercultural Resource Center encourages students to trace their family roots. It isn't easy to find one's ancestors if they were slaves—they were not counted in any census and many changed their names after the Civil War. However, the center offers resources, including more than 500,000 names from passenger lists, and an index to the records of the 186,000 men of the U. S. Colored Troops from the Civil War. It also houses information and teaches genealogical research skills to students who wish to have a firm sense of their identity. There is no other center in a college that offers African-American genealogy.

In addition, the center contains a library of books by important African and African-American writers, along with biographies of black historical figures.

The Minority Youth Educational Institute (MYEI) offers minority school children the chance to receive academic and cultural enrichment at the Center. After-school activities designed by staff and students help the children with their class work and help teach them about their heritage. Gettysburg students and the MYEI children enjoy entertainment programs, such as "Step Shows," or share a meal with other students in the college dining room.

Blacks are active in the Black Student Union and in any number of clubs, activities or programs, such as fashion shows at the center or the yearly "Step Show."

Another example of Gettysburg's quest for diversity is their published and widely distributed brochure on little known achievers of African descent, compiled by the Office of Minority Advancement. Among the notable people are Matthew Henson, Dr. Daniel Hale Williams, Charles R. Drew, Elizabeth Taylor Greenfield and Alice Coachman.

GRINNELL COLLEGE
Grinnell, Iowa 50112

Undergrads: 1,261
Black Undergrads: 63
Faculty: 161
Black Faculty: NA
Tuition: $16,628
Total Expenses: $21,410

One sister's assessment is that attending Grinnell makes you appreciate every opportunity you have: "We don't take anything for granted." Very selective and coed Grinnell College is a rare find. Located in a small Iowa town an hour from Des Moines, it is the first college west of the Mississippi to grant a liberal arts degree to an African American. It has, on average, 50-60 black students at a time, yet it offers more activities and programs for them than larger schools do. Black students may complain that the school is "reclusive" and "isolated," but you can't say Grinnell doesn't try.

Founded in 1846, Grinnell is committed to the recruitment and retention of minority students. The college goes all out, visiting schools, agencies and college fairs as well as places of worship to find black students. Black alumns call, write and interview prospective students, and Grinnell offers bus trips for black students from nearby metropolitan areas. Accepted black students are invited to the campus for a spring visit.

This top-ten liberal arts college offers an interdisciplinary concentration in black studies with more than a dozen courses, including The Tradition of Islam, African Cultures and The Jazz Tradition in America. Students who want a more hands-on approach to black studies can look into Grinnell's exchange programs with Howard University and Spelman College.

Other programs for black students are the Alumni Sharing Knowledge (ASK) Program, a mentor program between junior and senior students and black alumns; Pathfinders, a monthly program that brings black professionals on campus to discuss life after graduation; and a Multicultural Student Graduate School Conference sponsored by alumns.

According to students, academics are top-notch here, and support services are plentiful. Even better, they are free. One student says, "Tutors for most departments are paid by the college at no cost to students." Another undergrad refers to the tutorial services as "excellent." A variety of labs—reading, math, Spanish, writing— assist student study efforts.

A peer assistance program matching returning black students with incoming ones is available too, and some black students find their support from black staff members. According to one sister, "Black students often look to black faculty members for academic support and as mentors. Many also develop strong relationships with black administrators." Another student commends black faculty for "being receptive to our experiences and trying to help whenever possible."

Despite the small number of brothers and sisters, the campus offers many organizations, activities and performing groups to keep them busy. Some options: the Young, Gifted and Black Gospel Choir; a Black History Month Soul Food Bazaar and Talent Show; Concerned Black Students (the governing body of the black community); Black Awareness Week; a Kwanzaa celebration; and an annual Civil Rights Symposium. The Kimbo Cultural Center is home to many of these events. Furthermore, black students are active in Grinnell's student government association. One sister thinks the size of the black community here is the reason why a "higher percentage of black students are involved than on most larger campuses."

What are race relations like on a campus in *Iowa*, you may wonder. Not bad, according to respondents. One student says that interaction between black and white students is extensive and frequent, but it depends on the person. "Different students have different patterns of interaction," she continues. One brother's perspective is that blacks and whites interact informally most of the time but formally (only in class) sometimes.

To keep communication open, the Student Government Organization sponsors an open forum and a discussion group of Grinellians from multi-racial backgrounds. A role play and simulation workshop is called "Undoing Racism."

Although Grinnell does well in other areas, socially it falls flat for most black students. "This kind of environment tests one's will," a student moans. Depending on the extent of your involvement with the white community, Grinnell can be a "heaven or a hell," theorizes another undergraduate. For those not familiar with predominantly white social activities, finding a party on campus will be difficult. "Most of the black community feels uncomfortable or unaccepted" at parties on campus, one student says. One sophomore's experience: "Personally, I am still trying to adapt; this may be a process that continues until I graduate."

On the bright side, the size and location of Grinnell can be a positive thing. One sister says, "Because our community is small, we are closer to each other. We're more aware of ourselves as a black community because we are constantly surrounded by other types of people."

HAMLINE UNIVERSITY
Saint Paul, Minnesota 55104

Undergrads: 1,504
Black Undergrads: 44
Faculty: 96
Black Faculty: 4
Tuition: $14,182
Total Expenses: $18,880

Overall, it has been a good decision, say respondents. "The academics are good, and the liberal arts focus is fine," says one sister.

Small, private and coed, Hamline is a liberal arts and sciences university located in the heart of Minnesota's Twin Cities, halfway between the downtowns of Saint Paul and Minneapolis.

Academically top-notch, it employs a highly selective admission policy for students seeking a liberal arts experience and career advantages. Its Hamline Plan for developing skills and knowledge is nationally regarded.

All students must take three courses emphasizing diversity issues. Courses relating to the black experience are in various departments and include African Music and Cultures, African Philosophy and African-American Literature.

Hamline's African-American Admission Officer recruits primarily within the Twin Cities and in the Washington, D.C. metropolitan area. At last year's annual Students of Color luncheon, 161 students turned out during the largest snow storm of the year for information, a tour, and contact with students and faculty. In addition, the office uses hand-written postcards and telemarketing to assist their recruiting efforts.

Most brothers and sisters here are from Minnesota, Wisconsin and the Washington, D.C. metropolitan area.

For a solid orientation and exposure to goal-setting, time management, note-taking, test-taking, study behaviors and reading approaches, you'll enroll in Fresh Start, a six-week program given each fall.

To help you in handling the challenging academic load, a Study Resource Center provides tutoring and study skills classes. Peer tutors there are trained to help clear up foggy notions. Having trouble organizing your thoughts?—try the Writing Center.

"I found the support services pretty adequate," is one respondent's rating.

Black students can obtain additional support through the Office of Multicultural Affairs and through organizations like PRIDE—Promote Racial Identity and Dignity and Equality. Both are geared to making your environment comfortable. Reports a sister, "The black woman in charge of the office made me especially comfortable."

Noteworthy is Hamline's cultural diversity policy—an outgrowth of the school's belief that the different needs of individuals in the university must be respected, and that these cultural differences should be valued.

Black-white relations seem without tension, although one undergrad remarks, "I did not have good relationships with white students outside of my organizational interests. "The faculty and staff adhere to diversity issues," says one respondent, "but most of the white students are ignorant about cultures different from theirs."

Socially, it's what you make of it, they declare. "Most of the action is within the organizations themselves," says one brother. "The theater group will tend to party with each other regardless of color."

"But applicants should know that this is not a party place," says one respondent. "You must be strong enough to separate the two—academics and social life. They never mesh."

HAMPTON UNIVERSITY
Hampton, Virginia 23668

Undergrads: 5,711
Black Undergrads: 4,854
Faculty: 389
Black Faculty: 303
Tuition: $9,062
Total Expenses: $12,756

"I have grown in many ways through academics, and I have learned about myself and my race. I would encourage students of any race to attend Hampton," declares one sister.

Small, prestigious, coed and liberal arts oriented Hampton, sitting on the bay, is one of the hottest black colleges in the country. Insiders say its application pool is increasing while Howard's is slipping. It may not offer its students everything, but respondents are not complaining about paucity.

Its admission policy is selective, and it has had a no-nonsense attitude about education since it was founded in 1868 "to educate the newly freed slaves."

Hampton's five colleges cover just about every possible interest: arts and letters, business, education, nursing, and pure and applied sciences. Degrees on both the undergraduate and graduate levels are available in most departments.

Students wishing to find out more about their heritage can choose from over 50 courses, but many grumble that, for a black college, there should be more.

Hampton students—mostly from the Northeast and Southeast—are the first to admit that it is not easy to adjust to college-level demands. "Many of the students don't take Hampton seriously enough to understand that high school is history," says one observer. "Their immaturity just adds a high school atmosphere to the campus."

Not to worry; Hampton's got help for your poor study habits. Every department has a tutorial program, combining faculty and student help. "My tutor saved me from failing statistics," declares a senior. Hampton even offers a course— Reading 101—which contains a special seminar on good study habits. For writing help, go to the Writing Center, where faculty—including the department chairperson—will assist you with anything from an outline to refining a thesis. Peer counseling in the dormitories is also available, and faculty are known to call *you* in for counseling if you get too slack.

"Faculty are like surrogate family," declares one sister. "They give you plenty of encouragement, have high standards and make it clear that they expect you to live up to your potential."

For students who need more than just classes and homework, Hampton has student organizations. The major ones are the Student Union Board, the Student Affairs Committee, two college newspapers and the yearbook committee. Every department has its own club which offers pre-professional information. There are also various honor societies, choirs, drama groups, and social clubs, including fraternities and sororities.

Hampton's FM radio station is one of the most progressive in the country and is located in the same building where students produce a daily cable news show in the fully equipped television studio.

On the social side, no complaints. The town itself may be a sleepy haven, but the school's on- and off-campus parties are "plentiful and good," says one brother. The Musical Arts Cultural Society, a group run by faculty and students, organizes most of the entertainment on campus. The list of social activities is also impressive—from bazaars, receptions, picnics and art exhibits to boat rides, feasts, ice cream frolics and block parties. The main sites of these activities include the Williams Student Center, Ogden Hall, the museum and the conference center.

You could catch Lou Gossett, Doug Wilder, Ernest Gaines, Nikki Giovanni or Dr. Samuel Proctor addressing students in Ogden or eating with them in small groups. "I know that eventually every black leader in America will have to visit Hampton," assesses one senior, "so I'll get to meet them."

Hamptonians also have strong ties to their alma mater. "Many of the administration are Hampton alumni," reports one sister. "My parents went here, along with many of their co-workers and friends." The National Hampton Alumni Association (NHAA) has 93 chapters nationwide.

Not only do alumns lend a hand in recruiting, but they also hold campus forums during the year, march during commencement and give out scholarships. Every five years the organization publishes a directory. And every five years they also hold a reunion, complete with picnics, banquets and individual class activities. The NHAA gives each senior a "Black Family"—a kit including an alumn contact number to call for advice and employment suggestions.

Community involvement is plentiful. Teaching in the community is mandatory for education majors. Students from the community visit the campus regularly for recreation. Other activities include spring cleaning for senior citizens, a high school writer's workshop, a minister's conference, a foster grandparents program, Girl Scout activities, and Christmas projects for low-income families.

The question of racial interaction is almost irrelevant, since there are so few whites on campus. A large percentage of the faculty, however, is white. But according to one sister, "Color doesn't matter."

Students realize that life at Hampton isn't perfect. "The administration is sometimes hard to deal with, and registration is often a nightmare," complains one. Says another, "I'd like to see cleaner dorms for the amount of money my parents are paying." But most would agree that Hampton comes close enough to perfect. "We could use more books in the new library facility," moans an undergrad.

The bottom line, though, is that Hampton, like FAMU, Morehouse, Spelman and Howard, must be on your list if you're thinking black college.

HARVARD AND RADCLIFFE COLLEGES

Cambridge, Massachusetts 02138

Undergrads: 6,643
Black Undergrads: 531
Faculty: 2,106
Black Faculty: 11
Tuition: $20,865
Total Expenses: $27,575

Many respondents feel good about their decision to come to Harvard. "I'm happy with the racial atmosphere here," says one student. "I think there is a black community here, but people have other things going on and other issues in their lives."

Despite its reputation for elitism, the oldest and perhaps most prestigious college in the country has its advantages. For the black student here there are many: the world's largest college library, a renowned faculty, an incredibly diverse student body and the cultural riches of Greater Boston. Located on the Charles River facing Boston, this independent, coed institution employs one of the most selective policies in the country. Big Brother/Big Sister programs send volunteer tutors and counselors into Cambridge and the surrounding area. Students also have broad recreational opportunities in the Boston area.

Harvard admits students from every state and 45 foreign countries and has extremely high academic demands. One student describes the school as "full of pressure," but believes blacks who were good high school students make the transition to college successfully and remain "on par" with their fellow students.

Concentration possibilities range from East Asian studies to visual studies to astronomy; half of the undergraduate degrees are in the social sciences. The Afro-American Studies department and the Dubois Institute have special library collections pertaining to Africana and African-Americana. The Dubois Institute also sponsors colloquia, visiting scholars, a speaker series and research opportunities for black scholars.

Harvard has committed itself to "enrolling minority students in significant numbers." Recruitment of black students centers around visits to private and public secondary schools, participation in black student fairs, and help from an "extensive" alumn network.

Harvard administers advising and counseling services without focusing on particular racial groups. Students may seek assistance from their teaching fellows or attend seminars on study habits or on memorization and reading techniques. Counseling is available to those who seek it. One undergraduate stated, "Support groups won't find you. You have to find them." Groups, counselors, and psychologists help students with topics such as stress management and adjustment to college life.

For freshmen, "each dorm has an adult proctor who is available for academic advising and counseling. Faculty in the department for your major are always available for counseling on courses and research. There are also tutors from different majors in each house who are available for help." The Bureau of Study council and Radcliffe offer study skills seminars, and the writing center helps with papers.

Student organizations aimed at blacks include the Black Students Association, Caribbean Club, and Minority Student Alliance. Blacks are the majority in the acapella and gospel groups, such as Kumba and Brothers. There are no fraternities, and in order to avoid cliques, there is random housing.

An undergraduate describes interaction between black students and white faculty and administrators as good. "The professors here are usually from all over the world, and there is a pretty good range of ethnicity. Teachers are usually accessible to everyone." The same is true of black faculty and administrators. "I think that there is some kind of minority mentorship program, but you have to apply to get in it. They then assign you a professor who mentors you."

Harvard, said one respondent, "has more resources than you could ever use—all you need is initiative."

HAVERFORD COLLEGE
Haverford, Pennsylvania 19041

Undergrads: 1,115
Black Undergrads: 45
Faculty: 116
Black Faculty: 5
Tuition: $20,075
Total Expenses: $26,625

"Support from white faculty and administrators is fantastic," reports an undergrad, describing one of the best features of Haverford.

This elite liberal arts school's credentials are that it is one of the most selective colleges in the country, small, and coed. You will be close enough to Philadelphia for some cultural high life, but far enough away to think. Members of the Society of Friends (Quakers) founded Haverford in 1833, and it continues to be one of the best choices a black student can make.

Haverford considers all black and Hispanic students for the merit-based Ira Reid scholarship.

Once accepted, you will have to pledge yourself to the Honor Code students have monitored since its 1896 origin. The code allows students the freedom to arrange their own exam schedules, and it requires mutual respect and concern among all students.

You will have 26 majors to choose from, offering B.A. and B.S. degrees. If you are ambitious, there are independent study programs. Haverford undergrads may also register for courses at Bryn Mawr College, Swarthmore, and the University of Pennsylvania, through a cooperative arrangement.

Furthermore, Haverford has a cooperative arrangement with Bryn Mawr. Being only a mile apart, both schools reap the benefits of shared library facilities, course offerings, coeducational classes, dormitory living, and extracurricular activities.

A concentration in Africana Studies offers courses in more than 30 topics.

Haverford offers special programs called the Minority Science Scholars Program and the Minority Humanities Scholars Program, providing students with a pre-freshman summer session covering math, writing, and computers, and term-time seminars focusing on science and nature. A pre-sophomore session prepares students for courses in physics, biology, and chemistry.

The Black Students League (BSL) is a factor in maintaining and nurturing Haverford's black population. Their cultural events include seminars, workshops, and lectures at the Black Cultural Center named the Ira De A. Reid House, honoring the school's first black professor. The center has housing facilities for four students.

Most would probably agree that it's hard to top Haverford.

HOWARD UNIVERSITY
Washington, D.C. 20059

Undergrads: 7,668
Black Undergrads: 6,901
Faculty: 2,021
Black Faculty: 1,612
Tuition: $8,510
Total Expenses: $13,510

It could be exhausting naming the titans associated with this mecca: alumns like Toni Morrison and Andrew Young; faculty like Thurgood Marshall; deans like Howard Thurman; presidents like Mordecai Johnson; trustees like Vernon Jordan and Colin Powell. In terms of national and international influence, no black school comes close.

People affectionately refer to it as the "Mecca" and the black man's Harvard for intellectual thought in this country. The faculty represents the largest concentration of black scholars in any single institution of higher education in the world. "Howard is something you have to experience," says one satisfied undergrad. "I came to a black school to learn more about myself."

Through its 17 colleges and professional schools, various research centers, and over 75 major undergraduate programs, the university—which has a selective admission policy—produces a high percentage of America's black professionals.

Howard has a wide array of counseling services, with tutorials receiving the highest grades from students. "There is great help for you if you take advantage of it," declares one sister. The university tests students for deficiencies before enrolling them and offers study skills programs throughout the year, and the Center for Academic Reinforcement (CAR) helps those who are weak in certain areas.

In addition, "There are always special programs," reports one student, "from proper diet to date rape to Afrocentricity. Howard has everything you can think of."

A psychological counseling center gives students a chance to talk to professionals about problems such as relationship troubles, homesickness, or rape. The counselors meet with a student at the student's convenience, but some students find solace elsewhere. "Teachers are your best sources for counseling," says one.

"Howard has really bad advisors," one student complains. "I was told in mid-semester of my senior year that I needed one more class to graduate."

Howard has an organization for every interest. Many future politicians and lawyers hone their skills with HUSA, the Howard University Student Association. HUSA "makes it their business to stay informed about the issues." They took over a university building to protest the appointment of Republican leader Lee Atwater to the governing board several years ago.

Although most of the fraternities originated right on this campus, some earned suspension for overly aggressive hazing. Currently, all four sororities and two fraternities are active on campus.

Pre-med students consider the Health Careers Club valuable, while talented musicians make music with the jazz ensemble. The many choirs of Howard often go on national and even worldwide tours, and one, the Howard Gospel Choir, recently recorded a CD.

WHUR-FM, a 24-hour station reaching most of D.C. and parts of Maryland and Virginia, is one of the best in the nation and the originator of the "Quiet Storm" format. In addition to this station, WHBC, a student-run station, gives students hands-on management experience as well as a chance to dazzle audiences over the airwaves.

Other organizations include the respected weekly newspaper, *The Hilltop*, the Howard University Film Organization, National Society of Black Engineers, and the Student Cluster Big Brother and Big Sister Program.

Parties on campus are rare, so students usually travel to local clubs for weekend fun.

Changes? Students want to see more support from alumns. "Many within the city will help you," says one undergrad, "but it appears as if most got a great experience at Howard and forget what helped them to get where they are. The areas reserved for them at the football games are only filled up at homecoming."

Another sore point is the administration. One student says, "They just seem as if they don't care."

"The administration is unbelievably disorganized," echoes another, calling them "rude and uninformed." Complaints like these prompted new university president H. Patrick Swygert to call for an evaluation and overhaul of the school's entire system to make it more effective and—most students hope—more pleasant.

Other complaints: students say financial aid packages should be more generous and that the dorms are "horrible."

But respondents laud the faculty for going beyond the call of duty. "They're always available to help you and are really supportive," declares an undergrad. "Most give you their home telephone numbers and even get angry with you for not doing your best."

The local community of D.C. is overwhelmingly black, but students have mixed reviews about the community. "The area is not conducive to studying," declares one student. "Watching crime on a daily basis puts a damper on school." What doesn't help matters, one undergrad adds, is the condescending attitudes of some Howard students. "They make all of us look bad, and it strains the fragile relationship with the community."

Overall, students are happy with their choice. "Why go to a white school when you know the school doesn't want you there?" asks one contented sister.

At Howard, they say, you know someone cares about you. You're not just a number.

Declares one brother, "It's a close school. The teachers are working hard for you to get out. You'll never be able to go to a college to learn so much about yourself and your culture. This school loves you."

ILLINOIS STATE UNIVERSITY
Normal, Illinois 61761

Undergrads: 16,663
Black Undergrads: 1,500
Faculty: 949
Black Faculty: NA
Tuition: $3,544; $8,073
Total Expenses: $7,171; $11,700

Many respondents feel that the administration here could lend a more sympathetic ear to their concerns. The oldest state university in Illinois, it appears to have definite potential for black applicants. Yet it can be a difficult place for blacks who have come from predominantly black high schools where preparation may not be top-notch.

The rural campus located 40 miles from Peoria and 130 miles from Chicago has at least 40 percent of its students living on campus. ISU's black population is drawn predominantly from Illinois, Missouri, Indiana, and Michigan.

The school offers a range of courses relating to the black experience, and the library maintains an entire African-American reference department.

The jump from high school is difficult for black students, and therefore it may take two semesters before the black student is settled at ISU. One student points out, "Black high schools don't prepare us for college work."

In spite of the difficulty, there are over three dozen black student organizations, a Black Student Union, and a well-developed tutorial program as well as a Study Skill Center aiding students in note-taking, time management and test-taking.

Black students eat and party together, but when they describe interaction between black students and the faculty, both white and black, they give ratings ranging from poor to fair.

Every school is a setting for personal enterprise and growth, and the enterprising black students at ISU seem to find ways of bringing their talents to the university. The radio station plays jazz and soul and is a forum for current happenings. Black religious services also play a vital role in the social life of the black community. Further, black student input in the student government is high.

INDIANA UNIVERSITY
Bloomington, Indiana 47405

Undergrads: 15,773
Black Undergrads: 631
Faculty: 1,628
Black Faculty: NA
Tuition: $3,582; $10,770
Total Expenses: $7,730; $14,918

A black student says, "I'm pleased at the amount of inner growth that has developed for me as a result of my experiences at this institution."

Selective in its admission and located in Bloomington, about 55 miles from Indianapolis, the school draws most of its black population from Indiana, Illinois, Pennsylvania, and Michigan.

A black student here can find the academics to be culturally rewarding. Among the programs offered by Indiana are an interdisciplinary Afro-American Studies major.

Black students who do not choose this major can find minority-oriented supplements to other areas of interest.

Even with all of these encouraging black-oriented groups and programs, a black student's transition to life at IU can be tough. "There is a visible difference between those who are able to grasp and understand concepts and those who memorize facts as they probably did in high school," says one sister about adjustment to life at the university. Another respondent adds, "Too many black students do not possess good study habits. The ones that adjust are the few who have found outside sources to help them along."

But there is an abundance of support services available to IU's black undergrads. They consider tutoring assistance very helpful. Basic skills sections help students with poor backgrounds fulfill fundamental requirements.

Indiana also provides career and personal counseling services. "Other programs," according to one student, "are too extensive to mention. Almost anything you are interested in will be the topic of programming at IU." Another warns, however, that any student must take an active role in seeking assistance and special programs.

Out of the classroom, Indiana University offers just as many opportunities. Indiana hosts five black fraternities and three black sororities whose parties draw dedicated gatherings.

Blacks maintain high visibility in other activities as well and particularly at the Black Student Center.

In varsity sports, the heaviest black involvement is in track and football, then basketball. Black team members are "treated fairly." Participation in intramural sports is heavily Greek, according to some respondents, but enjoyed by all.

With some reserve, respondents describe relations between black and white students here as good, but without a great deal of interaction. A sister speaks of black faculty/black student relations in terms of family closeness although she finds it difficult sometimes to meet with them.

A more general complaint about the campus atmosphere is the feeling of isolation or impersonality some students experience, on campus and in the community.

"The band of blacks who do attend is very tight and very supportive," says a sister.

"Requirements are high, and the classes are tough at large Indiana. Be prepared to face the challenge of academics here as well as the challenge of remaining an individual," advises one undergrad.

JAMES MADISON UNIVERSITY
Harrisonburg, Virginia 22807

Undergrads: 10,503
Black Undergrads: 630
Faculty: 717
Black Faculty: NA
Tuition: $4,014; $8,294
Total Expenses: $8,694; $12,974

JMU is providing an environment for black students that is not only supportive but also inspiring. As one African-American male puts it: "Judge me for what *I am* instead of what *you* want me to be. If people judge me for what I am, then the true man that I am—a proud black man—will emerge."

A public liberal arts institution whose students are mostly from the Shenandoah Valley, James Madison offers an environment where interaction between blacks and whites is, in the words of one sister, "unusually successful."

Six colleges offer academic programs in business, education and psychology, fine arts and communication, health and human services, and letters and sciences.

An interdisciplinary minor in Afro-American studies enhances appreciation of the black experience through a study of Africa and black America.

Black students are adjusting to the rigors of college academics rather well, according to respondents. Says one: "The first year is always the hardest. After that, I feel that they adjust better than many white students."

Another view: "I think that we adjust well. We tend to stick together and bond closer when we need help."

When they need help, students may visit the Counseling and Student Development Center staffed by psychologists, counselors and a study skills coordinator. "It's always open to help students that may be mentally stressed for whatever reasons," declares one observer. The center sponsors a Peer Helper Program consisting of specially trained upperclassmen who help students with study skills, time management and class scheduling.

One student complains that there are few minority counselors and administrators. "I'm sorry to say that the ones that we do have don't go out of their way for the minority students," she states.

On the other hand, another reports, "Most faculty will help black students. You must show interest by going to a teacher to receive help."

Few students are said to take advantage of tutorial assistance offered by the reading, writing and math labs which one student says is "very good." According to respondents, most instructors and many departments hold outside class sessions to help students. Greater publicity for the study skills workshops is necessary says one brother.

Organizationally, key groups at JMU are the seven Greek organizations; "Ebony in Perspective," a campus radio show geared "to the tastes of the black community," and the 180-member Contemporary Gospel Singers which sponsors an annual gospel extravaganza.

According to one radio announcer, the push is to get more time than the few hours allotted to it on Sunday evenings.

Providing for growth religiously is a Sunday night service with nearly three dozen members.

Black theater is only a few years old, but black students are said to be active in JMU theater as well as other radio and television programming.

No black pre-professional or political clubs exist at James Madison.

Socially, brothers and sisters stay busy in their quest to "wind down from the weekly classes," as one scholar put it.

It doesn't matter who throws a party—Greeks, fellow students, dormitories—JMU students will attend and enjoy.

The Black Student Alliance has innovative and popular programming that benefits black and white students. Their picnics, happy hours and socials usually pull.

The University Program Board brings a "wide variety of lectures and concerts to JMU," according to one undergrad, and the list includes Maya Angelou and Spyro Gyra.

Participation in intramural sports is very high, and includes tennis, swimming and basketball.

Says one observer: "Varsity sports at JMU are dominated by black athletes. JMU has also provided black coaches in every major sport geared to help the black athlete."

In university governance, black students are just as active. Blacks have served as president, vice president and secretary of the student government, and they serve as senators and committee heads.

"I am proud to say that blacks do play a great part in the student government," declares an upperclassperson.

Contact with black alumns has been encouraging and helpful, say respondents. "They have been willing to assist in any way possible, and they want to give back to JMU some of what they received from it," declares an undergrad.

On the racial front, students consider interaction quite comfortable. "Prejudice does rear its ugly head," suggests one respondent, "but the newer generation tries to beat it down."

"We seem to be at a university where people are willing to help each other regardless of color," says another.

Exudes an upperclasswoman, "We are very fortunate to have great support from the white administration."

And with black administrators and faculty, there is a special closeness students say they feel: "The students know that the black faculty and administrators will try to assist them in any way possible so that they can succeed," declares a brother.

"I am very proud to be a student here at JMU," reports a brother. "The university has shown me both the good and the bad sides of life. It's taught me how to deal with racial incidents and made me aware of my heritage as well as my future. I've been given the opportunity to grow at my own pace and be myself," he adds.

THE JOHNS HOPKINS UNIVERSITY
Baltimore, Maryland 21239

Undergrads: 3,444
Black Undergrads: 172
Faculty: 413
Black Faculty: NA
Tuition: $19,700
Total Expenses: $26,750

Of small, coed and expensive Johns Hopkins, a brother states, "I have truly benefited from my undergraduate experience at Johns Hopkins. The school has allowed me to grow in ways I never would have thought I was able to grow."

Situated on 140 wooded acres in north Baltimore, its liberal arts school is one of the most selective in the country.

Black students here point to the college's reputation and small size as the most attractive features. Most students' home states are Maryland, New York, Virginia and Pennsylvania.

But according to respondents, many black freshman, particularly from all-black high schools, find the road leading to college-level academics to be much rougher than expected. "They may have been at the top of the class," says one student, "but they may still be under-prepared for what Hopkins demands." Still, respondents agree that by the end of the sophomore year, most black students here are managing well.

Certainly the wide range of support services makes the transition easier. Qualified tutors are readily available. Moreover, the Office of Advising and Counseling hands out packets on study tips. Large classes invariably have short discussion sessions conducted by teaching assistants. "Incredibly invaluable" is an exam file kept by BSU (Black Student Union) to serve as study tools. And professors run review sessions which can lead to student success "if the student is prepared."

As with academic services, faculty and students handle counseling. "The best advice comes from upperclassmen," declares one brother, "but faculty are helpful also." Peer student advisors will discuss old exams and help freshmen with course scheduling, and health peer counselors hold clinics on subjects including birth control. Moreover, students are allowed 10 free visits per year for psychiatric and psychological counseling.

Hopkins offers more than a dozen undergraduate courses related to the black experience, including seminars on political and cultural aspects of Africa and the Caribbean. But academically, Hopkins is what you make it, say respondents.

In addition to the BSU, one fraternity and two sororities serve as the principal organizations for black students' extra-curricular involvement.

Principal campus events include the February cultural festival and the usual round of Black History Month lectures and activities. In addition, the school sponsors an annual African heritage dinner and a spring Martin Luther King lecture. Serious partying does occur here, but, in the words of one black observer, "Hopkins keeps you busy academically." He continues, "People don't party every night or every weekend, but when we get together, we really party."

Others insist that the university's failure to bring more professional black entertainment to the campus keeps black students' social options limited. But BSU is on the case, sponsoring lectures and cultural activities including a dance troupe and a gospel choir. A few black DJs add rhythmic color to Hopkins' radio programming. And for spiritual uplift, students go off campus to attend black church services. "These services help maintain the balance between the university and reality," reports one student.

Most, however, seem to have few qualms about Johns Hopkins. One sister says that she is satisfied and would do it again if she had to. "I already know what it's like to be black—I have comfort in my identity," she says, adding, "but here I've been given the opportunity to see how other cultures operate."

"You get the feeling that you're not swallowed up by everything," says one sister.

JOHNSON C. SMITH UNIVERSITY
Charlotte, North Carolina 28216

Undergrads: 1,398
Black Undergrads: 1,384
Faculty: 88
Black Faculty: 69
Tuition: $7,538
Total Expenses: $10,168

Students express satisfaction with their decision to attend Johnson C. Smith specifically, and a historically black college in general, because "it gives you a chance to become a real person."

"I'm satisfied with my decision. But tuition is really kicking my behind," reports one respondent, adding, "we're paying too much for so little." Moreover, students suggest that the administration does not strive for physical upkeep and reasonable fees at coed, privately supported, historically black Johnson C. Smith.

Echoes another: "I wanted to attend a historically black school, but the tuition at this school and other black colleges is simply ridiculous unless the school is state-supported."

Still, for those looking for a family-oriented campus whose alumns are committed to staying in touch, JCSU on the outskirts of Charlotte, North Carolina (where the black population is 98,000) deserves a serious look.

Admission policy is less than selective with an acceptance rate of approximately 70 percent. Most students hail from North Carolina, South Carolina, New York and New Jersey.

JCSU offers 26 programs of study leading to one of three degrees: bachelor of science, bachelor of arts or bachelor of social work. The two-step curriculum requires that all freshmen participate in a general education program, and in the sophomore year, begin course work oriented toward a specific major. JCSU participates in a consortium with other area colleges.

Individual courses with an African-American orientation include Sociology of the Black Community, The Afro-American Press and Afro-American Art History. The university library, which houses more than 100,000 volumes, has the Alice Tate/E.A. Johnson collection.

Students needing more proficiency can find help at the Writing Center, Reading Lab, Computer Lab, Science Labs and Foreign Language Lab. Faculty and peer mentors work together to bring these services to freshmen.

Additionally, resident advisors provide counseling in the dorms, and the Counseling and Testing Center is professionally staffed.

Performing at your peak qualifies you for honors sections. And residence halls hold special seminars and workshops regularly as part of convocation programs and as part of the Student Government Association offerings. Topics are varied, including leadership development, test anxiety and male-female relationships.

Noteworthy is their Lyceum program which brings persons of national and local reputation to campus.

Upperclass students still complain that despite the wealth of counseling, many of their colleagues "have still not matured." Another puts it this way in describing the transition from high school to college: "Some are still childish."

JCSU allows for plenty of student input in institutional governance. Undergrads sit on the president's advisory council—a meeting with the university's president and the presidents of student organizations—and three students serve as full voting members of the university's board of trustees. In addition, they are "heavily represented on several of the university's judicial boards."

Religious associations are strong, among them the Student Christian Association and a Gospel Choir. Religious Life Programs offer activities including worship, seminars and workshops to "facilitate an environment in which persons in the campus community may realize as fully as possible their potential for spiritual growth."

A campus radio station affords those students interested in communications the opportunity for first-hand experience. However, students' comments on the quality of the station range from "fair" to "very weak."

Student participation in the university theater group is good and the reaction to theatrical productions is enthusiastic. JCSU participates in the Central Intercollegiate Athletic Conference. The intramurals program includes volleyball, basketball, badminton and swimming.

At the Memorial Student Union, activities include homecoming, the Bullfest (named after the school's mascot, The Golden Bulls), the annual

Valentine cabaret, convocations, receptions, special dinners and events.

Parties are the focus of the social life at Johnson C. Smith University. The four fraternities and four sororities on campus attract approximately ten percent of the student population. The extensive social activities available in the university's host city, Charlotte, provide students with ample opportunities to fill their leisure time.

Students would like to see more music and dance concerts, however, and rate varsity athletics as "poor" to "fair."

Alumni involvement in university affairs is considerable at Johnson C. Smith. Look for BEEP, the Black Executive Exchange Program as well as the Alumni Career Day program at homecoming. Currently an annual giving program called Million Dollar Year is stirring up enthusiasm.

In general, brothers and sisters at JCSU do not seem to feel tension in their interactions with the local community although one reports that whites have a superior attitude.

On their wish list is a desire for an improved physical plant with greater attention to grass, paint, pavements and ceilings.

KANSAS STATE UNIVERSITY
Manhattan, Kansas 66506

Undergrads: 17,014
Black Undergrads: 681
Faculty: 1,102
Black Faculty: NA
Tuition: $2,199; $7,484
Total Expenses: $5,569; $10,854

Although some students say Kansas State could stand some improvement, they have still benefitted from their experience here. One undergrad says that attending a predominantly white university has made her become a stronger person. She says that the diversity of people has given her insight and knowledge about the real world.

There is no disputing among brothers and sisters that they are receiving a quality education from competent professors at Kansas State, which enrolls over 17,000 students in seven undergraduate colleges. There is also no disputing the lack of black courses and black professors.

"Many of the professors...seem non-receptive to black students, especially in lower-level classes," explains a sister.

The limited number of black awareness courses disheartens many of the students who complain that the offerings in black American literature, Kansas City jazz, the black family and Afro-American music are taught about every two years.

Given this sparse cultural diet, black students here say they need more support services in order to survive. They judge tutorial services to be "pretty good" for general classes but still far from excellent. Students say that they benefit from the tutorial services when they need help in basic classes, but tutoring services become less than average when students need them for specific majors.

"Most of the tutoring is done in groups," reports an undergrad, "which does not allow for the individual student who may need extra attention."

Many say workshops are beneficial, but wish there were more seminars and workshops available. Suggests one student: "KSU needs to have more workshops and not limit them to special occasions such as Martin Luther King, Jr.'s birthday or certain months."

Several organizations center around minority students, with the Minority Engineering Study Center, the Minority Assembly of Students in Health (MASH) and the National Society of Black Engineers (NSBE) getting most of the play. The center is open 24 hours and its services are free.

MASH encourages and advises minorities who would like a career in the health professions. They bring students and resources together.

NSBE advises youths about engineering as a career.

For social life, students here rely upon the United Black Voices (UBV) Gospel Choir, the nationally recognized Ebony Theatre Company and the black Greeks. UBV provides a social outlet as well as a spiritual anchor for black students.

On the weekends, the seven black Greek organizations sponsor parties. On other occasions, educational and community service projects are their focus.

But respondents say that although the organizations and services existing are adequate, there is still a need for more.

"Kansas State is in need of more black clubs," says one student. "Currently blacks are becoming more involved with the senate, which is a step in the right direction. A separate political club for blacks may even be a good idea," she muses.

Students say that racial prejudice exists openly and that many brothers and sisters have had bad experiences with white faculty members. "I personally know some students who have come across racist professors and administrators," reports one informant.

Another says that the low percentage of black faculty is the main reason for the lack of mentoring opportunities. And many black students don't come into contact with a black professor in their entire four years.

"I have not had a black professor since I've been here, and I don't come into contact with enough black administrators," complains an upperclasswoman.

This lack of black faculty fuels the belief that the university does not really care about them. Further, some question the commitment of black faculty and administrators.

Still, there is resilience. "My decision to attend a predominantly white school benefitted me because it gave me a taste of what the real world would be like," one undergraduate explains. "I think everyone should be able to adjust to any situation."

KENNESAW STATE COLLEGE
Marietta, Georgia 30061

Undergrads: 11,114
Black Undergrads: 778
Faculty: 484
Black Faculty: NA
Tuition: $2,058; $4,986
Total Expenses: $2,058; $4,986

Good things come in small packages. Kennesaw College, a small, community-oriented college that promotes friendliness between the faculty and the student body prompts—appropriately—this response: "This is the main reason I chose to attend Kennesaw in the beginning."

Admission is not overly selective at the coed, public institution, and the curriculum is fairly traditional.

For those who need to develop their study habits, the tutorial assistance program and counseling services at KC are "readily available," says one student.

Black students' adjustment to the transition from high school to the academic requirements of Kennesaw, according to one student, is "kind of hard for most." Some students have a hard time adjusting because "college requires a great deal of effort, and a majority of the students have to work as well as go to school. Nevertheless, most of them are doing well."

For those who need a little extra help, the college has tutorial assistance for mathematics, English and reading. Developmental learning labs assist students in need of special attention. "This program helps a lot because it works on a one-to-one basis and helps students to discover their weaknesses," reports one satisfied student. On the other hand, one student feels that more black tutors should be on hand to assist black students who need help.

Most respondents feel that the counseling services available at Kennesaw are supportive and motivating. "I find the counseling services to be very supportive and a major resource for freshmen and seniors," says one student. Another program that helps new students adjust to college-level requirements is the Black Collegian Advisement program which offers "counseling and advisement services to black students."

According to another student, support services like the Black Collegian Advisement program are necessary and crucial for motivating students so that they can adjust to college course work.

The social and college life on the Kennesaw campus is rather limited since it is a small commuter college. Because of its size, Kennesaw is not equipped with dormitories, Greek organizations or other social organizations on campus. Many of the students who attend the college believe that Kennesaw is a good school academically, but lacks social outlets. Another student feels that because Kennesaw is a commuter college, and the students have to work and have families, they cannot participate as much as students on residential campuses can. The campus does, however, have an athletic program, and many blacks play on the basketball team.

The campus benefits from an "outstanding group of role modes" who come in order to motivate and encourage its students.

One student describes the interaction between white students and black students on the campus as "cordial" and "friendly," but another believes that the white students keep themselves isolated from the other students, especially outside of the classroom.

Most of the respondents report that the faculty is easy to talk to and willing to work with the students. Other students also feel that the non-black faculty and staff "try their best to help the students."

The academic relationship between the students and the black faculty is positive. The students and the black faculty at Kennesaw get along famously. "They try to help students out in any way they can," reports a senior. Another student feels that it is encouraging for black students to see a black staff on a college campus.

The interaction between the local Marrieta community and students is quite beneficial to the campus, according to one student. A local church, Mt. Zion, even has a Kennesaw College Recognition Day, which is dedicated to recognizing the students and faculty on the campus.

"A very strong bond exists between the college and the community in a concentrated effort to recruit and retain minorities," says one student. More blacks are migrating to the local community, thereby bringing a heightened awareness of cultural differences with them.

KENT STATE UNIVERSITY
Kent, Ohio 44242

Undergrads: 16,222
Black Undergrads: 973
Faculty: 1,329
Black Faculty: NA
Tuition: $4,084; $8,168
Total Expenses: $7,918; $12,002

On the whole, respondents feel that Kent State has much to offer the black student, but only a unified group of African-American students can take advantage of the opportunities here.

Large, state-supported and coed, Kent State seeks to combine the resources of a major university with the friendly atmosphere of a small liberal arts college. The university's main campus covers more than 1,200 acres in the center of northeastern Ohio. It has a less selective admission policy.

Kent State students enjoy a great variety of academic offerings, and the Department of Pan-African Studies offers more than two dozen courses related to the African-American and African experience. Students who major in Pan-African Studies analyze through various disciplines the theoretical and practical issues of black community organization and development.

Counseling services for individuals and groups are available on test-taking anxiety, goal setting and interpersonal relations. The Career Planning and Placement Center provides students with career counseling, and regularly schedules resume-writing and interview technique workshops. Through the Minority Mentor program, black alumns assist students with similar career interests.

The Center of Pan-African Culture is the base of activities for Black United Students, The Black Greek Council and the Pan-African Women's Association. Black undergraduates also support the NAACP and the National Black Independent Political Party. They express their views further via the campus black radio program and the weekly black television show.

Socially, brothers and sisters here enjoy parties and dances regularly, participate in intramural sports and stay involved in campus politics.

Students agree that while there is "very little" interaction between black and white students outside of the classroom, there may be even less interaction between black students and white faculty.

KENTUCKY STATE UNIVERSITY
Frankfort, Kentucky 40601

Undergrads: 2,505
Black Undergrads: 1,227
Faculty: 149
Black Faculty: NA
Tuition: $1,860; $5,040
Total Expenses: $4,844; $8,024

Kentucky State University has a friendly general climate and small student body to give new students a feeling of closeness and personal attention. One sister satisfied with the school and its atmosphere says, "If I had to make the decision all over again, I would do the same thing—choose KSU."

KSU is a small public university located 25 miles from Lexington, Kentucky. Admission at this liberal arts school is nonselective.

Although the student body of Kentucky State has changed, the campus, for which the school is well-known, has not. "The most attractive thing about KSU is its beautiful campus and the friendly, warm administrators," says one pleased respondent.

"KSU is losing its black tradition," complains one undergrad. "This is not even a predominantly black school anymore. Blacks are a minority." For a historically black university, the student body is indeed relatively mixed— more than half of its undergraduates are white.

Kentucky State offers a wide variety of Black Studies courses like Directions in American Art, The Black Ages, Geography of Africa, Sub-Saraha Regions, and Afro-American Politics.

For students who need added attention and help with their studies, KSU offers developmental studies classes in communication arts, mathematics, reading, science, and composition. Other special courses include television classes "which are helpful to students who are not used to a traditional classroom setting."

The adjustment to college life at KSU is difficult for most because of the drastic change in the environment from high school to college. A KSU student believes that many incoming freshmen have a hard time adapting because they arrive at KSU expecting a "black college" and instead find a school that is troubled by a lack of black awareness.

To help students adjust, KSU assigns each freshman a mentor, who is responsible for advising the new student about all aspect of college life. The director of public information at KSU says that even after freshmen declare a major they still have their personal mentors, as well as their academic advisors, to help them throughout their academic careers.

In addition to the mentorship program, KSU provides psychological, career, and financial aid counseling, as well as individual and group counseling sessions on social and health topics. One undergrad says, "The counseling department is exceptional. All counselors are available when they are needed." Other students, however, say that improvements are necessary, including the hiring of more black male counselors and the creation of a peer counseling organization.

The alumns of Kentucky State offer supportive services and assistance to the students on the campus by participating in school activities, maintaining contact with the counseling and placement office to help graduates find jobs, and serving as mentors to KSU students. One respondent says, "They are terrific! After so many years, they still care about their university." About 15 percent of the alumns of KSU contribute financially to the university each year. That rate is among the highest of historically black colleges.

Forty campus organizations are available to students. Several respondents are impressed with the Kentucky Players Theater Club, "which provides students with some cultural change and entertainment." Religious services, reportedly a fast-growing area, are popular. One respondent praises the Greek fraternities and sororities, which "instill a sense of brotherhood and sisterhood, show unity, and give freshmen someone to look up to."

According to one undergrad, "The students here love sports and are always ready and willing to support the teams." However, students complain that intramural sports are too male-oriented. Other problems mentioned are poor organization, bias, and lack of concern at the athletic department. "We definitely need more coaches who care about their players," says a sister.

The social aspect of college life at Kentucky State is enjoyable and eventful. The Greek parties at KSU tend to draw the most people, but respondents complain that they are limited in time and that the administration is too strict in its regulation. "We are treated like high school kids," says one student.

Activities such as picnics are fun, according to one respondent, but hard to get to because they are located off campus. Others complain that university-sponsored activities do not encourage enough participation because they are not well-publicized.

However, one undergrad describes the student center activities as "exceptionally well put together. The student life officers have the students' best interests at heart." Another respondent says that movies, bowling, and parties are the most popular student center activities.

Student-faculty relationships at KSU are reportedly smooth. However, one student feels that black students "are able to communicate a little better with black faculty than with white faculty." Another reports that although most white faculty demonstrate an understanding of black students, others "seem to fake their concern." Another complaint: there are not enough black faculty members.

Interaction between black and white students is not really visible, according to respondents. Most feel that relations are positive in class but that students isolate themselves from other ethnic groups outside the class.

One undergrad offers this opinion about the local Frankfort community: "The people in general are very friendly and accept all of the students, although most of the community here is white." On the other hand, some respondents believe that the community's attitude needs improvement and needs to include the students more.

KNOX COLLEGE
Galesburg, Illinois 61401

Undergrads: 1,127
Black Undergrads: 59
Faculty: 102
Black Faculty: 8
Tuition: $17, 571
Total Expenses: $22,440

Black students are appreciating their stay here. As benefits, they cite the curriculum, which teaches them to "think critically, write well, develop good study habits," and the lessons learned about themselves and others. How bad can things be if, according to one sister, the most unattractive feature of the school is the cafeteria food?

Located on a 70-acre campus, and employing a selective admission policy, Knox, small, with special strengths in the sciences and creative arts, is about three hours from both Chicago and St. Louis. Even closer are Peoria and Quad Cities, which are about 45 miles from Galesburg. Most blacks are from Illinois, Texas, New York, and Missouri.

Academic life at Knox centers around the Preceptorial Program. After they learn to pronounce it, freshman are introduced to a liberal arts curriculum through intense, intimate classes (no more that 15 students). Juniors and seniors take an advanced preceptorial that encourages them to extend and synthesize information.

Further, the college requires all incoming students to attend an orientation on the value of intercultural life on campus, and it sponsors forums and workshops on racism. While Knox does not offer a major in African-American Studies, it has almost 20 courses relating to the black experience. Students interested in studying on their own can find editions of the collected papers of Marcus Garvey, Martin Luther King, Jr., and Booker T. Washington in the library. A special Civil War collection includes information on slavery, the abolitionist movement, and the life of African-Americans during the war.

Recruiters welcome interested students to visit the campus, where they can attend class, take a tour, and meet professors. Recruiters venture off-campus to attend black college fairs in Oklahoma, Chicago, Atlanta, Dallas, and Missouri, as well as at predominantly black high schools. Current students get involved by phoning prospective students.

Support at Knox comes from peers as well as a structured center. Peer counseling stems from ABLE (Allied Blacks for Liberty and Equality), which matches freshman with upperclass students. The Learning Center offers help in reading, writing, and math. It also sponsors workshops on effective time management, improving study skills, and coping with stress. Students have another resource—the black professors. One grateful undergrad applauds black faculty members for "making every attempt to be there for the black student." The Office of Intercultural Life offers counseling as well.

Respondents give high praise for tutorial services but have a less enthusiastic response to the counseling services. One student is convinced that she is successful because of study skills workshops. A recent graduate says the counseling is "outdated" because counselors merely listen to problems without providing solutions.

Organizations of interest to black students include the Umoja Gospel Choir, the Black Culture Center Committee, *Indaba* (literary magazine), and the Intercultural Council. The ABLE Center for Black Culture is equipped with computer facilities, a library, a conference room, an art exhibit, and offices for black student groups. The center allows black students to study, hold meetings, and relax in a supportive environment.

Respondents have few gripes about the social life on campus, although one brother remembers that it took a while to adjust to the small-town atmosphere. Most blacks attend parties on campus, and they create fun when none is provided for them. "Black students attend, host, or co-sponsor the majority of parties on campus," one student boasts.

Perhaps because of Knox's emphasis on diversity and tolerance, racism is not a big problem on campus. However, black students note that there is little social interaction between whites and blacks.

If you think it is a struggle for today's black student to make it to Knox College, imagine what it must have been like for a slave in the 1850's when Knox was a refuge for fugitive slaves en route to Canada. It's been a long time since Knox's abolitionist days, but it still claims to embrace diversity and equality.

Knox stands out as a healthy and supportive place for a black student.

LAFAYETTE COLLEGE
Easton, Pennsylvania 18042

Undergrads: 2,219
Black Undergrads: 89
Faculty: 232
Black Faculty: NA
Tuition: $19,621
Total Expenses: $25,621

Adapting to Lafayette may be a difficult task for a black student. Most agree that the experience is "worth it if you can adjust" because the school offers a good education.

"Lafayette is a unique school," says one black student to describe this small, private, coed, highly selective college located just north of Philadelphia. "If you want to party all the time, don't bother coming!"

Lafayette's black student population is primarily from Pennsylvania, New York, New Jersey and Washington, D.C.

The school boasts of giving students the opportunity to do the "out-of-the-ordinary," offering special academic programs, unconventional courses, community outreach projects and dozens of student organizations.

Its curriculum offers B.S. and B.A. degree programs in engineering, math, the sciences and liberal arts. Students may also choose an interdisciplinary concentration or a five-year dual degree program.

Some of the black students at Lafayette find it difficult to adjust to the school's challenging academic environment. Those unfamiliar with predominantly white environments may be uncomfortable here, a feeling which often interferes with academic performance.

The shift from high school to college may be eased by the academic support services offered by the dean's office. The program offers tutorial assistance, study skills workshops and peer counseling. Professional counseling services and several study skills workshops per semester are provided by the health center, and faculty-student counseling is available through individual faculty advisors.

Black students say their interaction with white students on campus is limited, and they attribute this situation to a lack of communication and understanding. In general, black students consider relations with the faculty and administration to be cordial.

The non-academic life leaves real gaps. Social contact is extremely limited, with small black populations both on campus and in the community. Black parties at Lafayette are infrequent and somewhat monotonous because of the small number of blacks here. "If you are used to partying on a large scale, you may be disappointed," warns one student. Other outlets include attending a nearby, predominantly black Baptist church, intramural sports and black programming on the campus radio station.

Says one black student, "Lafayette will always be a white institution, but the challenges are here for those willing to meet them." And another adds that despite its drawbacks, "It's possible to be a name and a face rather than a number at Lafayette."

LAKE FOREST COLLEGE
Lake Forest, Illinois 60045

Undergrads: 1,028
Black Undergrads: 62
Faculty: 113
Black Faculty: NA
Tuition: $19,000
Total Expenses: $23,400

To determine whether Lake Forest College is the right choice, one student recommends, "Visit the college, and stay at a time other than minority weekends in order to see what the college is really like."

"Unless one has been exposed to a mostly white environment before, it may be a shock," says one student about this small, selective liberal arts school located 35 miles from Chicago. "However, when it comes to individualized attention from your professors, Lake Forest is second to none."

However, it's not for everyone. Classes are taken seriously, and students may find themselves in over their heads if they are not able to handle the workload.

If they stick it out, though, they will have the opportunity to sample an impressive array of classes relating to the black experience. Thirteen courses are available at least once every two years. In addition, Lake Forest offers an Urban Studies program.

"I think students have adjusted relatively well," says one undergrad. "Many were properly prepared in high school." However, others disagree. "For many black students, the transition is not an easy one," a junior says. "Most black students came here not knowing how to study for these types of classes. They did not go to school in this kind of environment. Most high school programs are not geared toward helping a black student succeed on a campus such as this one."

To deal with under-preparation, Lake Forest holds workshops and seminars for their minority students. But some say timing is a problem. "There are good seminars here," a freshman says, "but many were held only during Black History Month. We're working to have more all year long."

Study workshops, conducted usually during the midterm and final exam periods, are usually provided by professors in individual classes, based on students' needs. Professors teach the sessions, and teaching assistants will work with them occasionally.

Counseling is a Lake Forest asset. The campus counseling center program provides assistance for all students, faculty and staff. In addition, "The Dean Team," composed of all the deans, the campus activities head and the career planning and placement head, advises and counsels students.

A campus writing center offers tutorial assistance, and professors offer one-on-one tutorials or small group sessions on special-interest topics upon request.

The Black Student Forum is a minority peer counseling group, and peer counselors are available to all students in every dorm.

A nearby black church and a campus gospel choir offer religious opportunities. In addition, the Interfaith Center is available for all students of all religious affiliations.

There are no black radio stations, but MXM, the campus radio station, caters to many different tastes in music and is open for all students. The station features some black programming, and a few of the DJ's are black.

The principal gathering place for black students is House of Soul, a dorm lounge used exclusively for black student meetings and social activities. Some of the most recent activities of House of Soul include a multiethnic and cultural awareness workshop, the organization of a black student support group, guest speakers and the assisting of the Admission Office in recruitment weekends.

Since Lake Forest is a predominantly white institution, black-white relations play a key role in whether black students will feel comfortable with the social scene.

Formerly known as BUCS, ACCESS (African-Americans and Others Committed to an open Community for Equality, Sensitivity and Service) is an organization on campus which sponsors programs to encourage racial tolerance.

Black freshmen and sophomores usually attend white fraternity parties or dorm functions, but as time goes on these functions can lose their appeal because of cultural differences. Blacks may simply find these get-togethers boring after a while. "Social life can be a bit limited," admits one student, "but remember that a certain responsibility lies with the student to become involved and find ways to have fun while maintaining a positive attitude."

Another student adds, "On an individual basis, interaction is very good. Blacks are accepted on the same basis as anyone else, according to their individual personalities and friendliness. As on any campus, though, there are racists and people from both sides who choose not to interact with the other groups on a personal level."

The white teacher-black student relationship at Lake Forest is extremely tight, and most black students at Lake Forest have expressed satisfaction. "The white faculty really and truly care about the black students," a freshman says. "They are always checking to see if you need any assistance."

Another student mentions that white faculty members have been excellent participants in black-sponsored events on campus and are genuinely interested in black concerns.

On the other hand, the community surrounding the campus is a white, conservative area that many black students say is a racially biased town. However, some blacks have mentioned that administrative, grocery and even babysitting positions can be found rather easily.

"The campus in general is a very personable one," reports another student. "Much is done to try to ensure that the students are not just numbers."

LANE COLLEGE
Jackson, Tennessee 38301

Undergrads: 664
Black Undergrads: 664
Faculty: 46
Black Faculty: 37
Tuition: $5,196
Total Expenses: $8,398

Most Lane students are satisfied with their academic experiences, listing Lane's sense of community as its greatest advantage.

Historically black Lane College, a tiny, coed, less selective liberal arts school with a Christian Methodist Episcopal heritage, offers B.A. and B.S. degrees in business, education, English, fine and performing arts, math and sciences, philosophy, and social sciences.

Most students here are black, Protestant and very religious: "Without God it is impossible to succeed," says one.

Sixty percent of Lane's students are from Tennessee, but a good number also come from Mississippi, Florida and Alabama. Half live on campus, where all unmarried freshmen and sophomores must stay.

Students can design individualized majors, and participate in cooperative programs in computer science at Jackson State University and in physics at Howard.

Two national honor societies have chapters on campus, and Lane offers its students several avenues of academic support. Remedial programs are available in English, reading and math, and a writing lab offers programs geared toward the needs of individual students.

Social life at Lane revolves largely around religious activity; there are services almost every day, and chapel every Wednesday. Students frequent community churches, and they often use the vans provided for this purpose. One student complains that there is "little or no social life," but another says, "It's what one makes it." Parties are held in the dorms each month and are generally not standing room only. But, says one brother, "There's always a party off campus."

Popular on-campus activities are church services, intramural and varsity athletics, and school picnics. Greek organizations also sponsor occasional social activities.

Students and administrators alike make reference to the "Lane family," and campus activities (picnics, community church services) reflect this theme. The Lane family extends to embrace alumns, who maintain close ties to campus and students, supporting the school and helping in recruiting efforts. Says one student, "It's important for a person to have a sense of belonging or fitting in."

LANGSTON UNIVERSITY
Langston, Oklahoma 73050

Undergrads: 1,120
Black Undergrads: 1,105
Faculty: 128
Black Faculty: NA
Tuition: $1,212; $3,274
Total Expenses: $3,792; $5,854

L angston's atmosphere is appealing to most black respondents. An accommodating environment eases the adjustment process, which allows more students to focus on academics. And the academic setting is not an especially rigorous one since Langston emphasizes practical training and seems to focus on instilling pride and confidence in its students as they prepare for the real world.

Langston is less selective in its admission policy, accepting some students whose academic records are not outstanding. This small, private institution views its mission as one of preparing students for new and challenging careers. Therefore, the curriculum focuses on general and specialized education. However, the school makes efforts to ensure that all students reach their full academic potential. The majority of Langston's students come from Oklahoma, Texas, Illinois and Michigan.

The university offers bachelor of arts and bachelor of science degree programs in the arts and sciences and education. A student may also obtain a bachelor of science or associate's degree in business or applied science, or a certificate in business management.

Students can enroll in courses on various topics in black studies.

Most adapt easily to their college environment. The ease of adjustment depends largely on the students' efforts since many sources of support are available. Among the resources that may facilitate the transition are a pre-college orientation course, freshman development program, learning resources center, tutorial assistance program, counseling services and study skills workshops.

The university incorporates the tutorial assistance program into the residence hall system, with student tutors in each dormitory providing free tutorial sessions in the evenings. Student tutors, who receive high praise from the residents, prepare to help in all courses. Langston students speak highly of its counseling services. Each student pairs with a faculty advisor who provides academic counseling and a list of students available for peer counseling.

The Office of Student Affairs also helps with academic adjustment, offering workshops in reading, math and speech, as well as in courses where a large percentage of students have difficulty.

Students say that black faculty are especially supportive, and that there is a considerable amount of interaction between the students and the all-black community surrounding the university.

Pre-professional organizations are scarce at Langston, and the number of students that participate in university governance is small. Black alumns play a very active role in the school's affairs, sponsoring a career fair, campus forums, homecoming events and Founder's Day activities.

Most brothers and sisters here deem the social life acceptable. Greek letter organizations are an integral part of the social structure, and they sponsor picnics, parties and happy hours. The student center, the William H. Hale Student Union, has a game room, several dining rooms and a ballroom. It hosts banquets, faculty-student gatherings, dances, performances by professional artists and serves further as a meeting place for student groups.

Langston competes in intercollegiate basketball, baseball, football and track. An intramural sports program is "very popular" among the students. Parties are frequent during the beginning of the school year and "very satisfying."

Black students seem pleased with their decision to join the predominantly black, "family" atmosphere of Langston University.

LA SALLE UNIVERSITY
Philadelphia, Pennsylvania 19141

Undergrads: 4,073
Black Undergrads: 407
Faculty: 324
Black Faculty: NA
Tuition: $13,160
Total Expenses: $19,130

"I suppose every school has its problems," says one, "but I feel that compared to others, La Salle has fewer."

La Salle University is a commuter school with almost 75 percent of the black students attending the evening division program. Because it's located in Philadelphia, a relatively active city with a sizable black population, it does have something to offer college-bound black students—especially those who can appreciate the merits of a Roman Catholic educational institution with a selective admission policy. Most black students are from the surrounding states of New Jersey, Maryland, and New York.

La Salle offers a few sociology and history courses dealing with the African or Third World experience. Academic support services are reputed to be reliable and rewarding at La Salle, and although there aren't any formal programs geared toward black students, one black La Salle undergraduate notes: "The support systems for blacks are very good at helping students to work toward their goals."

General tutorial and counseling services for students with lower-than-average admission credentials are offered.

La Salle doesn't have many organizations that appeal to black students. The Black Students of La Salle serves the day-time students, and the Black Students of La Salle Evening Division serves those attending night school. The success of social events sponsored by these black student organizations depends largely on the attendance of blacks from the surrounding community, because there aren't that many black students on campus.

With only a few black faculty members and black administrators, black students at La Salle are on their own.

Most of the La Salle students are older than the average college student.

It's not unusual to find mothers, military veterans, and other resumed-education students at La Salle, so the level of maturity, at least among the evening division students, may intimidate a young freshman. At the same time though, the atmosphere can be quite challenging for the serious black student perceiving college as more than just an academic holiday.

Says one student about the La Salle environment: "It's easy to talk to professors and administrators about academic or personal matters. They care about the students."

LEHIGH UNIVERSITY
Bethlehem, Pennsylvania 18015

Undergrads: 4,357
Black Undergrads: 131
Faculty: 504
Black Faculty: NA
Tuition: $20,500
Total Expenses: $26,520

What does it take for a black student to make it at Lehigh University? According to one experienced undergraduate, you must be "a very strong individual who is open-minded and willing to accept failures but learn from them as well."

Located on a 700-acre wooded campus overlooking the Lehigh Valley in southeastern Pennsylvania, the small, private, coed school is 60 miles from Philadelphia and 90 miles from New York City.

Highly selective Lehigh offers over 60 majors in its three undergraduate colleges. Students can obtain B.A. and B.S. degrees in the arts and sciences, business and economics, and engineering and physical sciences. African-American studies is available as a minor.

Regardless of your major, expect some hard studying—and readily available counseling. Lehigh offers study skills workshops and free tutorial assistance. Special seminars help with math and English as well as with overall study habits.

These services are quite needed. According to one student: "It seems as though black students have difficulty making the transition. They tend to struggle at first." As a solution to this problem, Lehigh offers the Challenge for Success Program, an intensive six-week summer opportunity designed to acclimate pre-freshman to a college environment. Minority students take English and math courses and attend seminars on computers, personal development and career exploration.

Recognizing the unique career development needs of black students, Lehigh has a Minority Career Development Program that offers career planning, internship and externship opportunities and mentoring.

Approximately 17 formal organizations exist for black students. These include a gospel choir, the National Society of Black Engineers, the Black Student's Union and Umoja House, a residence hall for black students. In addition, two black fraternities are active on campus. Although there are no black sororities, female students can join sisterhoods of the fraternities.

Lehigh is far from being the ultimate party school. One sister sums it up this way: "Socially the atmosphere is lacking. For students who need more of a social outlet, this is not the place." And if you are coming from a predominantly black environment, be prepared for a "culture shock" one student warns.

"Racism is definitely a factor," says one respondent. She describes the relationship between blacks and whites as one of "tolerance rather than acceptance." Other students feel that developing friendships with members of other races is possible, but it depends on individual students.

It is probably a good idea to build a relationship with black faculty and administrators. "They offer much support to black students," says one undergraduate. "They encourage academic progress, individual growth and social unity— not only amongst ourselves but with the community at large too." Another student agrees: "We look to them for support and for guidance." Lehigh alumns are also an important resource, and undergraduates interact with them through LUBLAC (Lehigh University Black and Latino Alumni Council). According to one sister, "A number of black alumns have given me ways to channel myself. It is good to get to know black alumns so that you can see where a Lehigh degree can take you."

LINCOLN UNIVERSITY
Jefferson City, Missouri 65101

Undergrads: 3,083
Black Undergrads: 802
Faculty: 202
Black Faculty: NA
Tuition: $2,046; $4,032
Total Expenses: $4,722; $6,708

"A love affair." That's what one student affectionately titles his relationship with Lincoln University. "If a student has a need to find and appreciate his heritage," he continues, "Lincoln University is the place. You can find, appreciate and know yourself here. Lincoln is a family."

Although it is a historically black college, founded for the special benefit of freed blacks after the Civil War, Lincoln's student body is now more than 50 percent white, making it a most integrated black institution.

Lincoln has since grown to state-controlled Lincoln University, offering a wide variety of undergraduate programs in the arts and sciences, business, agriculture and pre-professional areas.

This small, non-selective university situated on 52 acres draws most of its students from Missouri and the neighboring Midwestern states.

Lincoln awards most of its undergraduate degrees in business and the arts and sciences. Among the business concentrations are accounting, industrial relations, marketing and secretarial sciences. A School of Applied Science and Technology offers degrees in agriculture, natural resource management, computer science, data processing and others. In the School of Arts and Sciences, students study biology, art, history, philosophy and mathematics as well as communication disorders, criminal justice administration and mass media.

Seminars and workshops and tutorial assistance are readily available at Lincoln. One program helps incoming freshmen adapt to college life. Special Services help students deal with financial, academic or personal problems. Academic departments and dormitories offer study skills workshops.

Lincoln hosts four local and three national fraternities and the same number of sororities. Despite the fact that only a small percentage of the students belong to them, these groups are apparently influential in student life. Various academic departments and majors have clubs such as the Criminal Justice Club. Several active religious ministries draw student support.

All of that and a good social life too? Yes, it's true. Students describe the social life in glowing terms, and Student Union parties attract heavy numbers.

Students at Lincoln report that relations between white and black students could stand improving. They say that many white students do not participate in campus activities. Relations with both black and white faculty are generally good.

According to respondents, some tension exists between the black and white communities in Jefferson City. Most student reporters say the black community is supportive of Lincoln black students but that the white community isn't as positive.

Students are unqualified in their praise of Lincoln. "Its pride, history, faculty and administration are most attractive," says another. "It is a place you can find and appreciate yourself in...I wouldn't change it!"

LINCOLN UNIVERSITY
Lincoln University, Pennsylvania 19352

Undergrads: 1,296
Black Undergrads: 1,218
Faculty: 138
Black Faculty: NA
Tuition: $4,431; $5,044
Total Expenses: $8,181; $8,794

"It's knowing that Lincoln gives everyone a chance, and a chance to take advantage of its services," says one of its students.

Established in 1854, Lincoln sits on 422 acres of rolling hills 45 miles south of Philadelphia. Small, coed and state-related, this liberal arts institution is the first historically black college in the country, and includes Thurgood Marshall, Langston Hughes and Kwame Nkrumah among its graduates. Its admission policy is less selective than most schools.

In addition to offering the usual bachelor's degrees in the humanities and sciences, Lincoln also offers associate's degrees and a three-two program in engineering through a cooperative effort with Drexel, Penn State, Lafayette and New Jersey Institute of Technology.

Students may alternate academic study with career-oriented employment through the school's cooperative education program.

The study abroad program offers students a chance to visit the People's Republic of China, Russia, Taiwan and other nations.

Respondents say that Lincoln students' adjustment to college life is moderately successful. In one brother's words, "It's a process of learning independence."

Respondents speak highly of both the academic and personal counseling services offered here, terming them very well-organized, with dedicated tutors. Counselors are "interested in whatever problems you have" and "a big help," although students agree that they must take the initiative in seeking aid.

SPEED offers tutorial and counseling assistance for frosh and sophomores, while TIME boosts basic writing, reading and mathematical skills.

Help and advice also come from Lincoln's black alumns, who appear to be very active in school concerns. One undergrad says, "They are a large part of my being here. They lead you the right way."

A new pre-college science, engineering and math program recruits Philadelphia high school students. It features a four-week summer bridge program focusing on career orientation, field trips and workshops.

Outside of the classroom there is plenty going on at Lincoln. The college sponsors a drama group, a chorale, and a gospel group, as well as varsity and intramural sports.

Lincoln hosts a number of fraternities and sororities, as well as seven independent non-Greek organizations. Black students support the weekly parties wholeheartedly.

Students are satisfied with faculty relations, especially with black faculty, but some point to a gap between students and administrators. "They need to communicate more with us."

On the whole, respondents seem happy at Lincoln and proud of its history. "The attractive part of Lincoln is knowing what a rich heritage it has," says one. Another student sums it up: "A black student can get more than his money's worth by attending Lincoln."

LINFIELD COLLEGE
Mcminnville, Oregon 97128

Undergrads: 1,562
Black Undergrads: 20
Faculty: 118
Black Faculty: 1
Tuition: $14,976
Total Expenses: $21,138

L infield College offers black students a quiet campus, a solid liberal arts education and—you probably never would have guessed—a prime location. Just 40 miles from the Pacific Ocean, Linfield is also less than an hour's ride from Portland. Several respondents cite the school's proximity to fun areas (and to home, since most black students hail from Oregon or California) as assets. Still, a few find it hard to adjust to the small-town setting.

Linfield students choose from 37 majors, which range from accounting to physics to creative writing and theater. The International Exchange Program is extremely popular; more that half of all students participate. But one sister warns incoming students to research the program before jumping in head first because "looks can be deceiving."

Linfield doesn't have a major in African-American Studies, but several departments offer courses of interest to black students. Some examples: Twentieth Century South African Literature, Race and Minority Culture in the U.S., Civil Rights and Liberties in America.

Recruiters visit public and private schools as well as a college fair for black students. Prospective students can visit the campus to experience what life is really like for minorities.

The Black Alumni Association gets in on the recruitment process too, hosting a reception for accepted students and their families.

Students can receive tutorial services at no charge—that's right, free! Some departments go a step further, providing a list of tutors for students. One respondent lists the pros of the tutorial program: "Its easy to get, fits into your personal schedule, student run. It's great."

What about race relations on a campus with only 20 black students?

Surprisingly, not bad, according to respondents. One sister says that blacks and whites get along "great" despite the discrepancy in numbers. According to another student, interracial friendships and relationships are not unusual. Although racism does not appear to be a problem, Linfield has a student panel on diversity. The school also holds diversity lectures every month; recent speakers include Lou Gossett, Jr., Anita Hill and Cornel West.

The lone black faculty member, obviously under great pressure, apparently does her job well. A student describes her as "very helpful and supportive."

The social scene is better than one might think. The black population of McMinnville is a scant four-tenths of a percent, so don't look for the Elks Home. One student describes campus parties as "good," adding that "People are well-adjusted, involved and accepted."

The Black Student Union is the only organization geared toward black students.

MACALESTER COLLEGE
Saint Paul, Minnesota 55105

Undergrads: 1,768
Black Undergrads: 71
Faculty: 208
Black Faculty: NA
Tuition: $16,686
Total Expenses: $21,661

The school claims that it can offer aid to every admitted student who demonstrates financial need. That plus the positive reports on the campus environment should be enough to captivate any college-bound black student who is considering a predominantly white school.

Small, coed and very selective Macalester College confers B.A. degrees in English, performing arts, languages, math and sciences, philosophy and the social sciences. The school allows students to design their own majors and to participate in exchange or combined programs. A large percentage of Macalester's students also participate in overseas study or travel programs.

Most of the students are from Minnesota, yet undergrads represent every state and about 40 different countries. A solid Third World community includes black, Hispanic and Native American students.

The black student population commands a large percentage of the university's support services. Each Third World student works with a faculty advisor and student counselor of her nationality. Tutorials and study skills workshops on topics spanning speed reading to understanding mathematical concepts to note-taking strategies also exist.

According to one student, it usually takes blacks about two years "to get used to the system" at Macalester.

Still, there is enough help to weather the storm. "The overall feeling among black students is that the black faculty and administrators are like substitute families all working for the betterment of each other," declares a respondent. Black students also feel close to the other non-European administrators and faculty members. To reinforce these ethnic allegiances academically, black students can enroll in courses on African civilization and other area studies.

Many of Macalester's black students go on to graduate school, and others secure meaningful jobs. Yet, the alumns don't forget to pay their dues to the black community at Macalester once they've graduated. Some return to campus to speak about their careers or to recruit; others hold "interest meetings" in their homes and serve as community liaisons.

Says one student, "I am very satisfied I attended a predominantly white school, because you learn a lot about how the real world in America is."

MARY HOLMES COLLEGE
West Point, Mississippi 39773

Undergrads: 405
Black Undergrads: 405
Faculty: 27
Black Faculty: 17
Tuition: $4,169
Total Expenses: $7,990

If you want a small school and a short stay, this may be just the place for you. A predominately black two-year college, Mary Holmes offers its students a quiet environment and a student-faculty ratio of 20 to one. Founded by the Board of Freedmen of the Presbyterian Church in 1892, the school is still influenced by these origins.

Students can obtain associate of arts or associate of science degrees in 21 areas of concentration. These include a variety of subjects—education, communications, natural science and liberal arts. Many students (over 75 percent) go on to complete four-year degree programs.

The typical yearly enrollment is 400-600, and most students hail from Mississippi. Sizable representation is from Illinois, Tennessee and New York.

Most respondents feel that adapting academically to Mary Holmes is not difficult. One undergraduate says, "Students know that they really have to work hard." Another feels that the administration puts a damper on the adjustment process: "It could be better if they treated us like adults," he says.

For students who do find the shift from high school to college difficult, the school offers tutorial groups and workshops. One student calls the tutorial assistance "beneficial and rewarding." Students who do not meet basic competency requirements must enroll in developmental courses until they meet the college's standards in reading, math and writing.

The Learning Resources Center, a two-year facility that houses the library, computer lab and media center, is an important asset for students, faculty and staff. In addition, students may obtain library resources from nearby Mississippi State University.

For entertainment, you'd better like intramural sports. Student opinions about the available athletic activities range from "excellent" to "poor." The formal sports teams are women's basketball and softball and men's basketball, soccer and baseball. Other organizations include the Student Government Association, the Masquers Drama Club, a Gospel and Concert Choir, and the Student Christian Association. Students also sponsor a pageant each year.

Located approximately 150 miles from both Jackson, Mississippi and Memphis, Tennessee, Mary Holmes is tucked away in a rural area. Students say that they enjoy parties, but because of distance, they just don't have much of an opportunity to attend them. As one student puts it: "Even more students would attend social functions, but they don't have transportation."

Despite this inconvenience, this small, religious-based school fits its students like a glove. One future alumn says, "I am proud and glad to have gone to Mary Holmes."

MEMPHIS STATE UNIVERSITY
Memphis, Tennessee 38152

Undergrads: 7,851
Black Undergrads: 1,178
Faculty: 835
Black Faculty: NA
Tuition: $4,405; $8,568
Total Expenses: $8,405; $12,568

Says one undergrad, "For a black student here, it is important that he or she put studies first."

Located in a city with a predominantly black population, this large, coed, less selective state institution enrolls students mostly from Tennessee, Arkansas, Mississippi and Missouri.

In addition to a wide variety of majors, programs for certified and continued education are available in almost any field.

Academics at Memphis State require that students apply themselves to the work. Study skills workshops are arranged informally through the Education Support Office. Minority peer counseling has reporteldy improved tremendously. In addition, the Black Student Association (BSA) provides special seminars and workshops concerning policy awareness, job availability and preparing for the job market.

Six black organizations direct most of the activities: Black Student Association, Black Society of Engineers, Black Business Association, Black Journalistic Association, High Rise Dimension and the Pre-Law Society.

Greek organizations are also very active on campus. They provide many parties and step shows. They also sponsor a picnic during the spring semester in conjunction with the BSA.

University-sponsored concerts and dances do not draw as well as intramural sports.

Black alumns meet at least twice formally during the semester and serve as support members of the BSA. They also participate in recruitment fairs, sponsor Snack 'n' Rap sessions and Unity Conference workshops and provide scholarship assistance.

The racial climate on campus is described as just cordial and unstrained, and BSA-sponsored mixed social functions attempt to aid race relations. In comparison, interaction between students and black faculty members is described in positive terms, though students express a great need for more blacks in meaningful positions.

Says one brother, "Race relations in the city are not what they should be. It has stifled the growth of our community, but we are working to help improve the situation."

Memphis State University requires that "students are academically sound and confident about their abilities," according to one respondent. Although the lack of black faculty, administrators and black studies classes are listed as disadvantages, students seem satisfied with their decision to matriculate and note that "exposure to a variety of cultures and ethnic groups is one of the most interesting situations on the campus."

MIDDLEBURY COLLEGE
Middlebury, Vermont 05753

Undergrads: 2,041
Black Undergrads: 41
Faculty: 251
Black Faculty: NA
Tuition: $27,020
Total Expenses: $27,020

The strong sense of identity remains with the black students even after leaving Middlebury. As alumns, some have kept in touch and most of them are helpful, students say.

With its small student body and flexible liberal arts curriculum, highly selective Middlebury fosters intimacy and individualized attention.

Most of the students at Middlebury come from New York, New Jersey, Massachusetts, and Washington, D.C. Six out of ten attended public schools. Meanwhile, the town of Middlebury is rural and predominantly white, thereby presenting a challenge to black students accustomed to inner-city life.

Nevertheless, there are resources like the BSU and academic support services which help blacks survive academically and personally.

A pre-enrollment program for students interested in academic enrichment prior to entering college takes place in August. Each year the program has a different theme that focuses on contemporary social or political events.

Minority recruitment efforts include a weekend visit in January for students interested in Middlebury. Thirty high school juniors and seniors come to campus free of charge to attend classes and special seminars.

Middlebury provides academic support services in the form of study skills workshops, held in the winter and summer sessions, and tutorials. A full-time professional tutor helps with writing problems. Also available are departmental tutors in math and science and, most importantly, peer tutors.

The BSU, which represents Hispanic students too, coordinates speakers, films, cultural affairs and social events. Many BSU activities take place in the John Coltrane Lounge, which houses a special African book collection, the Twilight Library.

Despite BSU-sponsored political and cultural functions, social life at Middlebury seems to be lacking something for black students. Although there are jazz and reggae concerts, "Good parties are few and far between," complains one brother.

Another comment, "The school's most attractive feature is its beautiful location. One of its most unattractive features is a certain clannishness among some students who have operated in a rather exclusive world."

There is said to be moderate interaction between the black students and the white students—and usually for academic reasons rather than social.

On the other hand, relations between black students and white faculty are "commendable and friendly," respondents say, probably because "both the black students and the white faculty members make a genuine effort to understand one another."

Since Middlebury is relatively isolated and has no black residents, the "only contact with whites in town is through business, as in the stores." This confinement to an overwhelmingly white campus can intensify the comradeship within the black community on campus.

Things have changed dramatically since the college was founded, but one black woman student insists that to be successful at Middlebury has always required self-confidence.

"I think black students adjust well to the academic requirements," says a sister, "but not as well to the other, more personal aspects of college life—like living in Vermont."

MISSISSIPPI STATE UNIVERSITY
Mississippi State, Mississippi 39762

Undergrads: 11,115
Black Undergrads: 1,778
Faculty: 828
Black Faculty: NA
Tuition: $2,591; $4,816
Total Expenses: $5,806; $8,031

You get varied reactions here about the good and the bad, but most importantly, the black students here seem to have settled on finding the attractive features and running with that.

Mississippi State University is state-supported and coed. Bachelor of science and bachelor of arts degrees are offered in departments spanning business, mathematics, engineering, psychology, history and education. Almost half of the degrees conferred are in education or business.

Almost all of the black students at MSU come from the state. And most don't sound intimidated at all about matriculating at this predominantly white university, especially since the support systems seem quite adequate for many of the university's black students.

The curriculum includes a bevy of courses pertaining to the African-American experience, and the school has several special library collections related to African-Americans and Africana—especially on black authors of the South.

Making the switch from high school to college academics is rough for some brothers and sisters. Yet for the most part, black students experience very few "growing pains" here.

Incoming freshmen have an orientation period to help them make the transition. For those black students who have difficulty in dealing with Mississippi State's academic environment, the school has a Learning Skills Center and an Outreach Program.

The Learning Skills Center is basically tutorial in nature, while the Outreach Program for Student Development is primarily devoted to counseling students. The Learning Skills Center provides special class sections for many of its students, while the Outreach Program offers special study skills workshops.

Many organizations and activities keep black students busy, with cultural and social activities such as art festivals, dinners, fashion shows, parties, and lectures and forums on issues which range from civil rights to the eradication of poverty.

Most significant is Black Awareness Week, held during the second week of February and focusing on the contributions blacks have made in the shaping of America.

The Council of Black Student Organizations works in the interests of not only black students but also the entire student body.

For scientists, there is the Black Engineers Society, and for singers, there is Black Voices, a chorus that sings on campus and in churches in the general area. A weekend radio program is called "The Black Experience." And blacks participate actively in the school's intramural program.

Respondents say that almost all of the university-sponsored concerts are geared toward MSU's white student population.

Interaction between black and white students is characterized by cordiality and few incidents of open racial hostility. Rapport with black faculty and administrators is termed "very good," and students report that they can turn to most of the black faculty and administrators when they are in need of help.

While some black students feel that their interaction with the white faculty and administrators is good, other brothers and sisters have expressed reservations.

It helps to enjoy the small-town life say brothers and sisters here who seem happy with their choice.

In sum: it ain't all bad, and it ain't all good.

MOREHOUSE COLLEGE
Atlanta, Georgia 30314

Undergrads: 2,992
Black Undergrads: 2,932
Faculty: 178
Black Faculty: 149
Tuition: $10,430
Total Expenses: $16,200

You can always tell a Morehouse Man, they say, but you can't tell him much. Well, you'd have a superiority complex too if you walked around on a campus that had a legacy which included Benjamin Mays, Martin Luther King, Jr., Edwin Moses and Lerone Bennett.

This is the House, they explain, known for its heavy hitter list of alumns, known for its dynamic Afrocentrism and known for its unshakable pride. Morehouse has to be one of the most satisfying collegiate experiences an African-American youngster can encounter.

"Any school can provide academics, but Morehouse College builds character," one student says about this all-male, historically black, selective liberal arts college.

The college's national student body is best represented by the states of Georgia, New York, Florida and Michigan.

To begin, all freshmen must take a history course which includes information on African-America and Third World countries. Non-required courses related to the black experience include Survey of Afro-American Literature and Swahili. "However, students must be disciplined because Morehouse has a lot of distractions," notes one student.

"A little over half successfully make the transition from high school to Morehouse. The others don't—due to social life and personal adjustment problems," notes another.

To help students stay on top of things academically, Morehouse offers a healthy supply of support services.

Morehouse men can find free student-to-student tutorial service and counseling at the Counseling Center.

The Summer Pre-Freshmen Science Program, the Brazeal Williams lecture series and study skills workshops are services designed to lower the attrition rate. In addition, the Pre-Med Program "provides seminars and speakers, visits to medical schools and informational meetings on medicine in the community." Students also find the pre-law, pre-business, English, history, math, human sciences and physics societies helpful.

There are three religious campus chapels, but the Martin Luther King, Jr. Memorial Chapel is where the action is, sponsoring a dizzying series of performances and lectures that are intellectually, spiritually and ethnically invigorating.

"If it's happening at King Chapel," declares an undergrad, "then you know it's serious."

Further, intramural sports and black theater are alive and well. For actors and actresses, the Morehouse Spelman Players put on plays by writers as diverse as Shakespeare and Ntozake Shange.

Parties sponsored by Greek-letter organizations are "frequent, popular and entertaining," proclaims one brother. But students sometimes spend "too much time at the Frederick Douglass Student Commons," points out another.

Since Spelman College is across the street, there are few complaints about the social life. "We do have access to the most beautiful young sisters in America," boasts a freshman. "I'm looking forward to my years here."

Student representatives are on the college's Board of Trustees, although it is "not active enough due to a lack of participation," points out one student. However, political and sociology internships as well as a tutorial program in the local community allow students to exhibit their leadership abilities.

There is some pouting going on. The administration could be more sensitive, and the dormitories aren't the most luxurious. Despite the fraternal organizations and appearance of cliques ("*Vogue* for women and *GQ* for men" comments one student), Morehouse College still has much to offer most students who apply.

"If you are willing to work, you can reap many benefits from the College. Morehouse needs students with foresight," concludes a brother.

MORGAN STATE UNIVERSITY
Baltimore, Maryland 21239

Undergrads: 5,601
Black Undergrads: 5,153
Faculty: 340
Black Faculty: NA
Tuition: $2,832; $5,750
Total Expenses: $7,672; $10,590

State-supported with a liberal arts emphasis, famed Morgan State offers black students the opportunity to gain a college experience at an affordable price.

Historically black Morgan State may be best known for its "smoking" track-and-field team and its "smoking" fraternity parties. But nationally, educators know the school as the leader among all public institutions in awarding bachelor's degrees to black students who eventually get doctorates.

Throughout the year, Morgan's admission officers visit private and public secondary schools, as well as special college fairs. However, Morgan stretches its hand a little farther than most schools by reaching out to junior high schools and local youth organizations, to make black youth aware of college at an early age. During the month of April, prospective students and their parents attend an open house. These efforts make Morgan well-known among young people in the Baltimore area.

In Baltimore, which is five miles from the campus, residents know Morgan well for its community involvement, the loyalty of its alumns and its vigorous recruitment program.

Along with the B.S. and B.A. programs in the natural sciences, social sciences and humanities, there are special programs for undergraduates in gerontology, urban studies, African and Afro-American studies and religious studies. In addition, the School of Engineering offers majors in civil, electrical and industrial engineering.

A Connect Program, through a collaboration with community colleges, offers students the chance to transfer to Morgan by automatic admission after they complete 24 credit hours with a 2.0 GPA.

The Soper Library houses special collections dealing with Africa south of the Sahara, Emmet P. Scott (one-time secretary to Booker T. Washington), and the relationship between the Quakers and slavery.

A mandatory freshman orientation for incoming students informs them of the existing support services such as the peer counseling program and faculty advisors. An official welcoming convocation follows freshman orientation.

Students and staff at the Learning Resource Center (LRC) provide tutoring sessions free of charge. The LRC also provides counseling services and organizes study skills workshops. Almost all departments sponsor special workshops and forums as well as participate in "University Hour," a weekly slot for students and faculty to meet informally.

Even with these support services, some students agree that the adjustment to Morgan can be a real struggle "because of the other social and emotional distractions." Since the resident assistants constantly monitor the single-sex dormitories, most students socialize in places like McKeldin Center, a facility for nearly 80 different activities. On the weekends Greek organizations throw parties, yet many students opt to go off-campus to clubs.

So many Morgan students come from mid-Atlantic states other than Maryland, such as Virginia, New Jersey and Pennsylvania, that geographical clubs form along these "home lines." For example, Caribbean students formed the "Society for the Advancement of Virgin Island Students."

Dramatists can shine in the black theater group, The Little Theater, and Christians can worship at the Christian Center. To ensure that all students can be included in some organization, departments sponsor clubs which attempt to personalize academia.

To supplement the Baltimore-based radio stations and to provide broadcasting experience for students, Morgan has a well-respected radio station, WEAA. It also acts as a voice for student organizations, such as the Student Government Association (SGA). This group sponsors social functions like the annual picnic and appoints student representatives to the Board of Regents so that students can express their concerns to administrators.

Students assert that the SGA has no real influence in university governance.

Although the number of white undergraduate students amounts to seven percent, there is almost an equal number of white and black graduate students at Morgan. The white student presence is so minuscule that racial interaction is negligible. As for interaction between students and faculty, one brother believes that "the relationship between black students and black faculty and administrators is stronger than the one existing between black students and white faculty and administrators." The difference may relate to numbers: "I've never had a white teacher at Morgan," reports one undergrad.

Morgan's alumns seem to be relatively active. Not only do they get involved in commencement by giving awards at senior ceremonies, but they also make financial contributions to the Alumni Scholarship Fund and the emergency student loan fund. They work with the Career Center in funding summer employment for undergraduates and participate in the "Adopt-A-Student" program by calling incoming students.

Morgan encourages community outreach. Fraternal organizations are quite active. Morgan's students provide free academic help to Baltimore youth through the Umoja (Swahili for "unity") Tutoring Program. Many brothers and sisters work with local community organizations. Twice a semester, community interest meetings are held to bring students and local residents together so that they can inform each other of their activities.

MORRIS BROWN COLLEGE
Atlanta, Georgia 30314

Undergrads: 1,897
Black Undergrads: 1,726
Faculty: 125
Black Faculty: NA
Tuition: $8,210
Total Expenses: $13,160

Most respondents are happy with their choice of a black college, and some with Morris Brown College in particular.

But MBC's most attractive feature is its history, according to all respondents. One sister sums it up: "I'm very proud to be able to attend MBC. I'm proud because it was founded by our own black people. It means so much, and I am grateful."

When you enroll at Morris Brown College,"you are enrolling in the world's largest consortium of black colleges," boasts one of this school's brochures. Small, private and coed, Morris Brown shares faculty and courses, as well as cultural events, with Clark, Spelman and Morehouse Colleges, Atlanta University and the Interdenominational Theological Center. The group make up the Atlanta University Center.

Located in downtown Atlanta, Morris Brown is less selective than most colleges and draws the majority of its students from Georgia, Florida, South Carolina and Alabama.

As a historically black college, Morris Brown offers a relatively small group of African-American related courses; a larger Afro-American Studies major is offered through the University Center. This school emphasizes its liberal arts and pre-professional programs.

At Morris Brown, the transition from high school to college is usually painless. In fact, several respondents find this a point to criticize, feeling that it gives students the choice not to make that transition, or be challenged. "In my opinion," says one, "the students can only go through the transition if the instructors teach on a college level, and many instructors at this college do not."

Others, however, disagree; and one student claims that the transition is easier "partially due to the departmental tutorial assistance and special skills programs" provided through Upward Bound and the Special Services programs.

The Counseling Center affords personal assistance, and faculty and administrative counseling is available although some students seem not to be aware of or take advantage of it. Dedicated students can seek out special skills workshops and class sections.

Morris Brown undergrads describe their relations with faculty and administration, black and white, as good. "The student interaction with these groups is healthy, positive and unlimited" proclaims one respondent. A brother adds, "Everyone enjoys each other's company." A third is more cautious, saying that sometimes the faculty and students get along, and "sometimes they don't."

Out of the classroom, activities at Morris Brown are not only available, they are policy. "MBC recognizes the need for leisure time and promotes and makes available to its students a full social life," asserts its brochure. In addition to its pre-professional groups and its active student government, Morris Brown hosts a healthy number of fraternities and sororities, which play a large role in campus social life. Participation in Greek-sponsored events is high although one student complains, "We don't have enough dorm parties, and we have too many Greek parties." Involvement in other activities, especially sports, is enthusiastic as well.

Morris Brown commands loyalty from its alumni. Not only do graduates of the college assist with recruitment, campus forums and employment opportunities, but also, one student says that he has had extensive contact with alumns because "many Morris Brown administrators are former students."

A brother warns that the dorms could stand some improvement and cleaning, and wishes that the "overall running of the college was handled better." MBC's location in the heart of the city is a positive feature.

MOUNT HOLYOKE COLLEGE
South Hadley, Massachusetts 01075

Undergrads: 1,946
Black Undergrads: 78
Faculty: 213
Black Faculty: NA
Tuition: $20,290
Total Expenses: $26,240

Holyoke women are usually genuinely satisfied with their choice of college. "For all the negatives that may exist, the vast educational opportunities are worth it."

This independent, liberal arts institution for women is located 90 miles west of Boston and 150 miles north of New York City.

Founded 1837, it is the oldest continuing college for women in the United States, with one of the most selective admission policies in the country.

Be prepared for four years of diverse and challenging academics. Competency in a foreign language, six credits of physical education, successful completion of two four-week winter terms, and courses from at least seven different disciplines are all requirements for graduation. Another requirement is for all students to take at least one of over 65 courses that focus on non-Western cultures. The faculty's rationale: "The legacy of racism in our country is so deeply rooted and so entrenched in our mores, habits, and languages that it too, like our understanding of foreign cultures, requires an extensive re-examination."

Fortunately, assistance is available in the quest for a successful education at Mount Holyoke. "Tutoring is available for all students in any subject upon request," says one student, "and deans are available along with faculty." Students also have peer and faculty advisors for counseling in both personal and academic matters. Says one upperclasswoman, "Personally, I have found my academic advisors to be very helpful, inspiring, and extremely interested in my academic life."

If study habits are a problem, the college's Association of Pan-African Unity (APAU) sponsors study skills workshops whereby upperclasswomen are available to answer questions and tutor freshmen and sophomores. "By and large, there is no real adjustment problem on a major scale from high school to college academics," claims one student. One senior says, "I can look back and say that black frosh and sophomores worry too much. Most of them do just fine academically and socially. I must say that if you can make it through here academically and emotionally, then you can make it just about anywhere."

Mount Holyoke students find ample opportunity to involve themselves in seminars and forums relating to minority concerns. Seminars on racism designed "to make the campus aware of existing racism and the feelings of the whole community" are student-initiated. Recently Mt. Holyoke offered a Workshop for Third World Students on Personal Identity, and sponsored *A Celebration of Life*, a two-day series of minority theater, readings, and dance.

Alumnae play an active role; black alumns hold a triannual conference on campus which includes panel discussions and workshop sessions with faculty and students. The college keeps a list of black alumnae who have expressed their willingness to advise students about their fields of employment. Students also explore career possibilities during Mount Holyoke's winter term, when students may opt to participate in a four-week Career Exploration Project.

A leading organization is the Black Pre-Medical Society. Explains one future physician: "Our pre-med program is competitive and blacks need that extra support. There are no Third World faculty in the sciences; that contributes to the lack of support."

"The campus-based radio station, although not all black, has programs that are produced by black women for black listeners," reports one woman. Adds another, "Living in an area like this you can feel that the white world is closing in on you. Having the radio station play the music of my people gives me that needed lift."

APAU plays an important role in the uplift process by organizing poetry readings, dramatic productions, dinners, and parties. "Often these are the best opportunities to interact with the sisters on campus." One senior cautions, however, "There are a lot of activities that APAU offers which don't get much participation."

APAU representatives telephone newly accepted students to offer words of encouragement. All black applicants also receive a letter from minority students during the admission process.

Opinions vary about race relations at Mount Holyoke. Says one woman, "Friendships can be as extensive as you like."

Another disagrees: "In most cases relations are strained because of the ignorant and racist attitudes held by white students."

Reflects one senior, "I don't feel like an outsider, but I am aware that this is not my community. I enjoy being here most of the time, but I do not fool myself by thinking that this is my world because no matter how look it, it just isn't."

Black students' views of relations with white faculty members vary. One senior says that the white administrators and faculty are a bit overprotective, yet helpful. "Sometimes it comes as a surprise to the underclasswomen," the senior adds, "when an administrator whom they have never known personally walks up to them and knows who they are."

One student sees members of the local community as racists. "They expect blacks to steal, and follow you around like you are going to take everything in sight. I have stopped shopping in the area except for emergencies." One black student, however, is trying to organize an off-campus Big Sister and counseling program for pregnant teenagers.

If an active and varied social life is very important, Mount Holyoke may not be right for you. "Parties are definitely not the highlight of one's experience at Mount Holyoke," says one upperclasswoman. "This is not to say that Mount Holyoke is a nunnery, but that if one wants to meet men, one definitely has to take the initiative to go out to parties to find them." Students point out the lack of entertainment that interests black students as another drawback to Mount Holyoke's social life.

"Mount Holyoke will provide a challenge to you that is not only academic, but social; not only individual, but collective with other black women," says a sister. Concludes another, "Mount Holyoke is a good place to grow up and become independent."

MURRAY STATE UNIVERSITY

Murray, Kentucky 42071

Undergrads: 6,777
Black Undergrads: 339
Faculty: 358
Black Faculty: NA
Tuition: $1,960; $5,060
Total Expenses: $5,060; $8,160

A student writes, "I am happy with my decision to attend school here because it is truly challenging. Even though there are not many programs geared toward black students, most people are really nice."

A coed state university with a less selective ranking, Murray State is located in the residential, lake country of west Kentucky, and focuses on undergraduate, graduate, professional and continuing education instruction. Most students come from Kentucky, Tennessee, Illinois and Missouri.

The six colleges of the university are the College of Business and Public Affairs, of Creative Expression, of Environmental Sciences, of Human Development and Learning, of Humanistic Studies, and of Industry and Technology. While there is no black studies program, Murray State does offer a number of courses related to the African-American experience.

Pre-professional programs are plentiful. But courses geared to the black student are not a strong point at Murray State.

Black students have made favorable adjustments to the college environment, reports one student, although another claims, "the majority have not adjusted well and have withdrawn from the university after the first year."

One sister feels that some black students "do not realize the importance of taking an education seriously." There are a myriad of support services available. Tutorial assistance and counseling are among these, but one student says that most students go to their academic advisors for counseling. MSU offers study skills workshops through its Freshman Orientation, required of all freshmen. The Office of Counseling presents study skills workshops, remedial class sections and open labs for some courses. One student labels the university's frequent seminars and forums "very informative."

There is a Special Service program for students who may be economically, academically or culturally deprived of those characteristics necessary for a successful college career.

There are no black pre-professional societies, but students say they are sorely needed; so is a black theater group. There is, according to a sister, a black theater group in the community, but "few students know about it." There seems to be very little interaction with the local community. The Black Ecumenical Ministries holds black religious services on campus which, according to one brother, is one of the "most visible outlets for blacks on campus."

The campus radio station has a program called "Soul Flight," which entertains "blacks on campus and in the surrounding community."

Social activities include well-attended parties usually given by the black Greek societies. One student complains that there is "too much participation" in these events. There are also black activities and general services sponsored by the Black Advisory Committee and the Minority Awareness Committee. There are also some black-oriented mixers. But almost all respondents feel that cultural activities and participation need to be more frequent.

"MSU does not offer very much professional black entertainment," reports one student, adding, "in the course of a year, the university might come up with one good black program." The popular intramural sports program attracts black participation.

The general atmosphere between blacks and whites seems to be civil, whether on a student-to-student level or a student-to-professor level. White faculty are concerned and helpful, according to respondents, and all black faculty "try to maintain some sort of cohesiveness." The cliques that form on the campus are usually fraternity- or sorority-based. Some revolve around mutual interests rather than purely insular congregations.

"Coming to a predominantly white institution really prepares a black student for the real world; for if you can make it here, you've just about got it made," a Murray State student says.

NORFOLK STATE UNIVERSITY
Norfolk, Virginia 23504

Undergrads: 16,150
Black Undergrads: 1,130
Faculty: 1,693
Black Faculty: NA
Tuition: $4,060; $8,300
Total Expenses: $9,336; $13,576

Those who are not particularly satisfied with Norfolk State cite the lack of challenge and motivation as keys. On the plus side, new curriculum programming and the family-like atmosphere elicit positives. "I know people care about me at Norfolk State," assesses an undergrad.

The third largest black college in the country, coed Norfolk State comes out on the short end when compared to nearby Old Dominion and Hampton Universities; in comparison it is often cited as having a "high school" atmosphere.

Nevertheless, the university serves a purpose, primarily educating and encouraging a host of African-American youth whose potential may not be realized elsewhere.

Its admission policy is not very selective, yet it is affordable, and in addition to its liberal arts curriculum, it offers vocational—and technical—education. Business, communications, technology and nursing are the strongest areas, say students, and its new program in hospitality holds the promise of enhancing its respectability. To spur more blacks into the sciences, Norfolk State's new Dozoretz Institute features a special curriculum, two-week summer session and internships.

It also offers accelerated study, cooperative education and programs with Old Dominion and Tidewater Community College.

NSU has an "open door admission policy," which means almost anyone who wants to enter the school can. Most students are Virginia residents. While this policy can be seen as a desirable means of providing higher education for all, one student remarks, "Most people here are not serious about their education, and some use it just to get the government grants."

A few students complain about the "high-school-type courses that can be frustrating." Yet for the academically poor, the university does have the state-funded TRIO program, which provides student counselors for such classes as math, accounting, economics, English and French. Remedial courses and summer sessions are also available.

Freshman Orientation Week, which familiarizes students with the university's services, is mandatory. Faculty are assigned to advise freshmen, but after that most students seek advice from their own special instructors. Sports coaches too are popular counseling sources.

The ROTC program here is well known and enrolls the second largest ROTC female population in the country. One student says, "ROTC definitely attracts many, many students to the school."

Many students at Norfolk tend to join the departmental clubs. These clubs offer social and educational programs open to all, but most students become "departmentalized and will not attend any other department's social activities," according to one student.

The gospel choir and theater group are seen as "good, solid organizations." NSU has a newspaper and its own radio station, WNSB, which reportedly features the only jazz format in Norfolk.

White students at NSU represent about ten percent of the school's population. According to one respondent, "The number of whites is growing largely due to the cheap tuition and the country's current economic situation." Another student reports: "White students and faculty are most accepted and liked."

Nevertheless, most administrators and faculty at Norfolk are not only black but also alumns. Student reaction to faculty is varied. Another asserts that some instructors view students as a threat. Another feels that the professors "can be extremely helpful on a personal level."

Norfolk, a city near the ocean, is approximately 35 percent black and is said not to have too many racial incidents. The university maintains an anti-crime center within the community, the first of its kind in the country. Student organizations like the seven sororities and eight fraternities provide tutoring and other service projects to the community. Students have also been active in voter registration drives.

"NSU's social life is good. If you want to party, you've got it here," says one brother. However, some social activities are hampered by the liquor regulations on campus. Consequently, most parties—including the cabarets and Greek functions—are held off campus. Fraternity parties are the most popular, and one respondent assesses: "Right now, the Deltas are the most popular, while the Ques draw crowds."

The student center is often the location for dances, concerts, forums and tournaments. The center also houses the dining halls, the mail room and various student organization offices.

Football is the biggest sport at Norfolk. Women's basketball is very popular. Intramural sports are also well-attended.

The usual cliques exist at Norfolk, and one respondent describes the student body as a "mixed bag."

Apathy is the problem most often cited as the crucial campus issue. "It seems like many students have mixed-up priorities," declares an undergrad. Apathy seems to extend to the faculty and administrators. A respondent reports: "The common attitude among the faculty is, 'I have mine so you have to get yours.' "

Norfolk State University also has to face the problem of constant and unfair comparison to its white neighbor, Old Dominion University. One student complains, "ODU is always good, yet Norfolk is inherently bad."

NORTH CAROLINA AGRICULTURAL AND TECHNICAL STATE UNIVERSITY

Greensboro, North Carolina 27411

Undergrads: 6,854
Black Undergrads: 5,963
Faculty: 668
Black Faculty: NA
Tuition: $1,632; $8,474
Total Expenses: $4,812; $11,654

One brother offers a firm and important observation for black high school seniors considering A&T: "A black student who wishes to apply to my school must have his or her priorities straight. The purpose for being here is primarily to get an education. but you also want to enjoy yourself."

Still, this environment is troubled by animosity toward non-black professors who hold higher standing in the academic scheme at A&T. "I do not appreciate high-ranked non-black administrators," a student says, "but I feel that in a predominantly black institute we should have qualified blacks to make decisions that will affect our black students."

A&T is a small, nonselective university located 30 miles from Winston-Salem, North Carolina. Most of the students come from the Middle East Coast region (the Carolinas, Virginia and Washington, D.C.). There's definitely something for everyone here—the athletic program is considered exciting and the academic program solid.

Courses relating to the black experience include the History of Africa, U.S. Slavery, History of Black Culture in the United States, and Modernization in Africa from 1920 to the Present. Other opportunities to learn about black culture include exhibits at the Taylor Art Gallery, the 1500-volume Black Studies Collection at Bluford Library and an African Heritage Center.

The adjustment to a new way of life is hard for most new college students. Some Aggies are divided on the subject of high school students' adapting to life at A&T. "I feel that the students here are very well-adjusted," one student says, adding that the students are able to interact in a mature manner.

On the other hand, another student feels that Aggie freshmen "have not fully adjusted to the transition from high school to college-level academic requirements, failing to realize that time for studying needs to be scheduled." To aid students academically, workshops, counseling and tutorial assistance are available.

The Freshman Advisement Center and academic departments sponsor study skills workshops during orientation week and periodically throughout the year. In addition, special seminars and workshops are organized each month by the administration. Career planning and development and scholastic competition are just a few of the topics discussed.

"Counseling is effective, especially to freshmen because each one is assigned a counselor," a senior says of the center. "Appointments can be made to discuss any problems the student may have."

Tutorial assistance is also readily available. Students may seek help at the Learning Assistance Center, the Special Services tutorial Assistance Program, the Honor Society tutorial group or individual academic departments.

There are over 100 student organizations and a variety of school activities at A&T. The Nigerian Students Association, the Pre-Vet Club, (veterinary students), the Brothers in Christ Fraternity and the Digit Circle (math organization) are just a few of the many A&T offerings. There is even a Philly's Finest, a club for students from the city of brotherly love.

Religion is important to many in the black community. A&T offers plenty of opportunities to express religious faith, including the gospel choir and several denominational student organizations.

"Our university offers regular Sunday and Wednesday worship," a student says. "Our students actively participate in these. We also offer religious counseling and societies." Another student adds, "Morning prayer service is available each day for all interested parties."

The student government is an active voice at A&T. The students are represented by the Student Union Advisory Board and the Student Government Association, and there are students on all of the major university committees. "The SGA enables students to take part in making decisions concerning governing affairs such as the Senate and the Judiciary Council," one student explains. "The university provides ample opportunities for students to become active and be an important factor in decision-making."

One of the most important aspects of black college life is the Greek scene. Most of the students seem to accept the fraternities and sororities as a way of life on campus. "Students are enlightened by the many activities sponsored," says one sister. "Some programs include talk sessions, tutoring, movies and many social events."

Some respondents think that campus interaction between races is positive, with no major problems resulting. One believes that many "have overcome their prejudices." Others feel there may be some tensions on campus but none that they have seen in the open.

A common student complaint at the university seems to be the school's administrators. One student reports personality conflicts with some professors, both black and white, while another "dreads going to the administration building." Other opinions include that certain school officials and faculty are "very rude," and that they do not always "function in an organized, professional manner."

The language barrier between students and foreign professors is a challenge. "They don't seem to be able to communicate with their students," complains one undergraduate.

However, other undergrads report that faculty members "interact well in a classroom setting" and try to be helpful.

"A&T offers a quality education, as well as a black environment in which to grow and develop," says one student. "Such an environment is important because well-rounded people require an awareness of who they are."

Another says that A&T encourages students to work closely with one another and lend a hand when necessary. "Overall, A&T is a great school because the students come together as one."

NORTH CAROLINA STATE UNIVERSITY

Raleigh, North Carolina 27607

Undergrads: 18,821
Black Undergrads: 2,259
Faculty: 2,623
Black Faculty: NA
Tuition: $1,686; $9,848
Total Expenses: $5,542; $13,704

Says one student, "I am satisfied with my decision. If one can graduate from this university, it's definitely an accomplishment." Large and coed NC State has a selective admission policy and a leading reputation for scientific research. The state-supported school gets its black student population mostly from North Carolina, Virginia and New York. Its curriculum covers the liberal arts and sciences, business and education.

"Overall, blacks have a moderate problem with the transition from high school," notes one student. "Because it is predominantly white, some blacks feel intimidated at first, but most take advantage of tutors."

Tutoring is provided by the Special Services Program and the Learning Assistance Center. In addition to their services, there are several student organizations, such as the Society of Black Engineers, a black athletes tutorial program and peer tutorial assistance, which offer academic aid to needy black students.

The Counseling Center offers professional service on personal and academic matters, while "a mentor program provides black students with black faculty and staff who can serve as role models." In addition to the above services, the Counseling Center also offers weekly study skills workshops throughout the year; there are also reading skills workshops and films on stress available. The Learning Assistance Center provides audio-visual equipment and slides on good study habits.

Other service programs offered by the university include the Career Planning and Placement Center, the Resident Advisors Council and "Pan African Week," in which a career day is offered.

If academic and peer counseling do not serve a student's needs, perhaps the Black Student Fellowship, a religious group, will. "It is getting better organized and even the campus minister is black," proclaims one student. The 200 members also work closely with the campus black choir, New Horizons. Its singers bring gospel music "alive." Additionally, black students can "jam" from 1:00 p.m. to 6:00 a.m. on weeknights on the university's radio station.

Finding a social life at North Carolina State is usually not a problem for most black students. With five black Greek-letter organizations, Dance Visions, The Society of Afro-American Cultures and the Black Student Board, there is always something going on. "Greeks sponsor parties every weekend," one student notes, adding "and there are parties in dormitories and in student apartments. Intramural sports are also entertaining because, according to one student, "Some of the teams are all-black."

Black Greek-letter organizations also sponsor picnics. The big one is the Black Student Board's annual affair, the Pan African Picnic. These events are complemented by those given by the Cultural Center, which handles Black Awareness Week, the Martin Luther King Birthday Commemoration and Black History Month at North Carolina State.

"Essentially," one student notes, "most of the black leaders on campus are the heads of Greek-letter organizations." These also sponsor blood drives, tutorial sessions and cleaning days in the local community. "Yet most students are isolated from the surrounding community," points out one observer.

With a ratio of 20 whites to every black student, most blacks on campus "choose to separate themselves" from white students. Interaction with white faculty is similarly less frequent. As one student puts it, "interaction is filled with tension." However, relations with black faculty are more cordial. "Most are willing to help; they don't give us special attention," claims one student.

North Carolina State appears to be an environment in which a young black person can grow both intellectually and socially. "My advice is to come prepared to work hard because there will be covert racism," one student proclaims.

NOTRE DAME COLLEGE OF OHIO
South Euclid, Ohio 44121

Undergrads: 653
Black Undergrads: 196
Faculty: 101
Black Faculty: NA
Tuition: $10,000
Total Expenses: $13,215

Founded in 1922, this private, liberal arts school still exists as a women's college. Although small and selective Notre Dame College is located 14 miles from downtown Cleveland, one sister notes that "college life for a black student here is boring. There is nothing to do, and no activities are planned with a black person in mind."

"Most blacks have adjusted well," says one student, "but there are others who need to improve their writing, typing and studying skills." An undergrad also advises that high school students who consider applying to this college "should concentrate on their college prep." To help the underprepared, Notre Dame College offers a tutorial program as well as a Mentor Program providing one-to-one support for all entering freshwomen. "The Life Skill Development Center also offers many workshops for students needing help in study skills," notes one student. "If you need special class sections, all you have to do is ask."

The principal black organization is the Black Scholars Group, which is not very active on campus.

"Most sports and activities are geared toward white people," says one sister. Another notes, "There are no parties here that involve black students. Some parties are given, but they don't take into account the way a black person parties." Another reports that on an individual basis, "most white students are alright. But others ask stupid questions about food, your hair, etc."

However, despite some tension with whites on campus and in the local suburban community, black students do some academic counseling in the local schools. In addition, the degree of prejudice which black students encounter at Notre Dame is lessened by the attitude of the white professors there. "White faculty seem very willing to reach out and help a black student, just as they would a white," states one woman.

Nonetheless, another student notes: "The only positive aspect at this college is that a Black Scholars Group was formed. I only hope that blacks after me will keep this group in full force. Maybe then, some of the black students' needs will be met."

In contrast, another sister concludes, "I am very satisfied here. It is small, select and efficiently run." A third, who says she is "completely satisfied," may offer the best advice for prospective black students: "Give the black students a chance to know the campus better before asking them about black interests."

OBERLIN COLLEGE
Oberlin, Ohio 44074

Undergrads: 2,823
Black Undergrads: 226
Faculty: 217
Black Faculty: 14
Tuition: $20,746
Total Expenses: $26,716

"I will never regret choosing Oberlin," declares one satisfied respondent. The admission policy is highly selective at this campus of Gothic buildings 35 miles from Cleveland. It consists of the College of Arts and Sciences and the famed Conservatory of Music. One of the first schools in the nation to admit blacks and women, Oberlin remains a front-runner in improving policies for minority life.

Course offerings include ethnomusicology, and The Black Studies Department offers a major or minor concentration. The library has one of the largest collections of printed matter on slavery and the abolitionist movement of the 18th and the 19th centuries.

Support services include labs for reading, math, writing, and tutoring, academic advisors, career development specialists, and minority counselors. There is an association between the Black Studies program and the Afrikan Heritage House. This is a "dormitory for black students who wish to live together, work together, eat together, research their history together, and prepare for their future together." The house provides a library of African sources, a series of lectures or films, exhibits, readings, and performances. Abusua (clan) is the black student organization.

According to one student, the activities of the black student center "have proved to be very important, setting the political tone for the whole campus. These activities have induced the hiring and tenuring of black faculty, in addition to improvements in admission and financial aid of black and minority students."

Other organizations in which students may participate include theater and the radio station WOBC. One undergraduate speaks of the black theater as "a tool for promoting social awareness," explaining, "important messages are often relayed loudly and clearly through the arts."

"Oberlin is not the haven of social life," says one sister. "Most of the time, students use their spare time to form lasting friendships, attend cultural events in Oberlin and Cleveland, or attend the various campus parties."

Reports one undergrad about race relations: "The interaction between blacks and whites is no different here than it is at other white campuses. Some white students socialize with us on all levels, and some do not seek interaction with us."

OCCIDENTAL COLLEGE
Los Angeles, California 90041

Undergrads: 1,580
Black Undergrads: 95
Faculty: 197
Black Faculty: 3
Tuition: $17,992
Total Expenses: $23,652

"I love this school," explains a sister, "but I think it would definitely improve if more black students came here."

Highly selective Occidental, in the northeast section of Los Angeles, is a small, coed liberal arts institution close to all of the cultural and social offerings of the big city.

It offers distinguished programs in diplomacy and world affairs through an interdisciplinary curriculum and a core academic program. The most popular majors are English, history and fine arts.

Occidental's recruiting efforts show strong support for black students. Recruiters visit over 500 public and private schools nationwide. Admission representatives attend national recruitment fairs. Alumns get in on the act, too, and so does the Black Student Alliance. For local minority high school students seeking an overview of the college, the annual Campus Visitation Day is a good bet.

The college offers a wide range of degree programs and provides an excellent springboard for graduate study. And its success rate comes with strong academic support services. Professors and departments tutor. Seminars in time management, study skills, and test-taking are available at the Counseling Center. A writing specialist works with students. Interested in medicine? Occidental offers a Health Professions Preparation Program that exposes students to a whole summer's worth of science, math, and writing training. This program is available to all accepted students, before or after their freshman year.

Occidental's Career Placement Center provides a file of alumn contacts and of internships for various community and state agencies. Through Occidental's Academic Advising Program, each freshman has faculty and student advisors to help plan the student's educational program and lay the groundwork for a career. One respondent reports, "Students help students plan class schedules and adapt to college life."

Encouragement and acknowledgment of academic achievement come at the annual Minority Scholarship Dinner.

The Black Theme House is an off-campus, student-run, residential facility. Kappa Alpha Psi fraternity has a chapter on campus, and there is a Gospel Choral Ensemble.

Ujima, the black student caucus, works to increase cultural awareness. Their admission committee has hosted a reception for all accepted black students in the southern California area. They also conducted a phone-a-thon to congratulate each black student accepted and to answer any questions about the college.

Last year's events included comedian and actor Franklin Ajaye's Black History Month performance, Maya Angelou, Dr. Willi Coleman's presentation on "Women in the Civil Rights Movement," and Bill Cosby. 1968 alumna Rear Admiral Marsha Evens, the third-highest ranking woman in the U.S. Navy, spoke about "Women in the Military." Dr. Joseph Graves' lecture was "Biological Aspects of Racism." The Los Angeles Theater Center performed *Angels On Fire*, about people in the Los Angeles riots. Also, Cornel West gave the lecture "Beyond Euro-centrism and Multiculturalism."

Apparently, for black students, it is still not accidental to choose Occidental.

OHIO STATE UNIVERSITY
Columbus, Ohio 43210

Undergrads: 35,475
Black Undergrads: 2,483
Faculty: 3,724
Black Faculty: NA
Tuition: $3,273; $9,813
Total Expenses: $7,941; $14,481

Take note: you can be easily intimidated and discouraged by a university this large. But the word here is that the impersonal can be turned into the personal if you have a strong support system of black students, black faculty and administrators. Of course instances of commitment on the university's part—and there are sufficient examples at Ohio State—don't hurt either.

With the main five campuses at Columbus—where one out of five residents is black—famed Ohio State offers bachelor's degrees in a variety of areas including Black/Afro-American Studies, international business, medical communications, Arabic and zoology. It is a non-selective public institution whose black students hail primarily from Ohio, Indiana, Michigan and Illinois.

Expect to find an abundance of support services that receive high grades from the respondents of color: "Counseling is exceptional, especially for coping with black-white relations," assesses one undergrad. The Office of Developmental Education, the Office of Minority Affairs and the Office of Black Student Programs direct tutorial assistance, counseling and study skills workshops. "I have had a few teachers hold extra classes before midterms and finals," says a respondent. For professional counseling, a fourth of the psychologists on staff are black.

Many students participate in study groups and peer counseling warrants accolades.

The list totals more than 35 when black student organizations are tallied. You'll find MWANAFUNZI for those inclined toward social work, the Black Undergraduate Engineering Council, Black Students in Home Economics and the Council of Black Students in Administration. Black Studies airs a radio program, and they sponsor theatrical productions in the absence of a full-scale black Thespian organization. The non-denominational Black Student Fellowship is said to be the most representative black religious group. "The black engineering organizations have provided students with an avenue to reach corporate America," declares one sister, adding, "and they are channels through which students can share concerns." Not many are bored on the weekends. "Social activity is plentiful!" reports a witness. "You have to be careful and not party too much," is one warning, while another wonders if black partying has an effect on what he sees as low retention.

Off campus, you'll find most blacks at the Mineshaft Bar. The popular strip is High Street, "the happy hour joint" every Thursday, Friday and Saturday.

Yet it's no secret that the majority of students tend to party on and nearby campus. And few attend functions unless they are sponsored by black organizations and offices. "It seems that most blacks don't frequent the campus bars that mostly white students attend," says one upperclassman.

One of the most partying fraternities is Alpha Phi Alpha, while Kappa Alpha Psi has earned fame for its three-week intramural basketball tournament. Not to be missed is Alpha Kappa Alpha Sorority's "Greek Scene," and the annual semi-formal hosted by Alpha Phi Alpha is said to be "really nice."

Many blacks participate on the varsity and intramural level, especially in basketball, football and track and field. Ohio State has dozens of black varsity football players.

No outright hostility is observed, but there is little interaction between the races, to hear respondents tell it. One student's view: "Many blacks and whites will socialize through common interests." Offers another, "Overall interaction is positive, but there are many white students who are having their first contact with black students."

Brothers and sisters find black faculty to be quite supportive, especially in their attendance at non-class-related activities. With white faculty, relations seem to be unstrained.

Communication with the black community—spearheaded by a Black Studies Community Extension Center run by Black Studies and housed in the heart of black Columbus—appears to be solid. "The black community seems very supportive, especially the black church," says a student.

But look forward to infrequent black involvement in university-wide governance. On the other hand, blacks contribute long hours to the Black Greek Council and the Office of Minority Affairs Student Advisory Council.

Respondents speak positively of their contact with black alumns, many of whom live in Columbus. "Enlightening and helpful," is one rating. Black alumns return for commencement and Homecoming Weekend. Many contribute to special projects like the Minority Scholars Program.

Black students agree that the principal advantages of attending Ohio State are the resources and facilities. "Minimize social activities, use resources, be determined and get to know instructors," advises one respondent.

What Ohio State may lack in personableness may be compensated for in effort. The university has set the tone for affirmative action through policy statements, and high-level blacks hold positions in the administration.

OHIO UNIVERSITY
Athens, Ohio 45701

Undergrads: 16,271
Black Undergrads: 619
Faculty: 1,109
Black Faculty: 41
Tuition: $3,796; $8,035
Total Expenses: $8,056; $12,295

L ooking for a big college in a small town? Get to know Ohio University; it may fulfill all your expectations.

Seventy-five miles from Columbus, Ohio University offers 335 majors through nine colleges: arts and sciences, business, communication, education, engineering and technology, fine arts, health and human services, honors tutorial (25 specialized majors) and university (for students with undeclared majors).

Black students can use the major in African-American Studies to learn more about their culture and history. The major features almost 30 courses that cover art, literature, language, geography, history, philosophy and political science. Advanced courses include Images of Blacks in the American Mind, and Gandhi and King: Nonviolence as Philosophy and Strategy.

To help students adjust to the academic life, Ohio University allows all multicultural students to enroll in the LINKS program free. LINKS consists of two phases. The first includes a three-day program the summer before the freshman year where students meet upperclass students and participate in workshops on multicultural issues on campus. In the second phase, students receive an upperclass mentor to guide them through the first year.

Tutoring is free for LINKS students and for some freshman-level courses, a source of contention for at least one student. "Once you get so far into your major you start having problems finding tutors," she complains. Another student feels that tutoring should not be available free for certain students (i.e., those in LINKS) and on a fee basis for others.

Despite the tutoring and peer-counseling elements of LINKS, and a similar Pre-Engineering Program (PEP), most respondents complain that not enough programs exist to help black students adjust to academic life. According to one sister, "Freshmen have a hard time adjusting, especially in math and science." One brother ties the lack of support services to the retention of black students: "Many don't adjust well and leave after the first two years."

Those students that do manage to stick it out seem to be visible in many campus organizations. A respondent notes that blacks play a role in the student senate, and another points out that a recent president of the student council was black. Some organizations targeted to black students include the Black Student Business Caucus, the Society of Black Engineers, the African Student Union, the Caribbean Scholars Association and STARS (Students Teaching About Racism in Society). Two black sororities and three black fraternities are active on campus.

What about the social life on campus? Students say that participation at fraternity and sorority parties is lively. One brother views parties as a chance for black students to bond and relieve stress. The most popular parties are on-campus ones, as students don't venture out into the city much. Happy hours are a popular activity for black students.

Blacks don't attend functions on campus that are not "black-oriented." They complain that out of the many events sponsored by the university, very few cater to blacks. In one student's words, "I believe that there should be more diverse events on this campus for African Americans."

Interaction with white students rarely occurs outside of class, respondents say. The result: a segregated but peaceful campus community.

Overall, students give mixed reviews of Ohio University. Their ratings range from wonderful to terrible. The only way to find out if the school is your dream or your nightmare is to check it out for yourself!

OHIO WESLEYAN UNIVERSITY
Delaware, Ohio 43105

Undergrads: 1,712
Black Undergrads: 68
Faculty: 161
Black Faculty: NA
Tuition: $17,569
Total Expenses: $23,445

One student has found that in "my own personal experiences, I have found white students at OWU to be warm, friendly and open." Others look upon OWU as a unique educational experience. "Here you are being educated and also doing the educating," says a sister. "You have to enlighten your classmates on 'mythconceptions' they may have."

Coed and private, Ohio Wesleyan draws most of its students from Ohio, New York, Pennsylvania and Connecticut.

OWU's curriculum includes a major in the Black World—an interdisciplinary program focusing on "the integrity, continuity and development of black experience" from a historical, political and cultural perspective.

Classes are small, and individual attention is the norm.

Students here agree that adjustment to college life can be difficult, especially for those who "haven't quite moved out of the high school mentality." There is a fairly small percentage of black students here, and one of them points out, "For a person coming from a predominantly black neighborhood, adjustment may take some time." On the whole, though, students make the transition "as well as can be expected from anyone, black or white."

Academic life at OWU provides a strong incentive for students to make that transition, according to responses. One sister states, "Although this school has some drawbacks, the excellent academics, faculty and university community more than make up for the few negatives." Both faculty and administrators are "very helpful" and "always accessible." Black faculty, one student says, "are very few, but they are the best!" Both black and white faculty, according to others, are "supportive—professors want to help!"

For those who have difficulty, there are several support services. There is a Writing Resource Center which provides individual tutorial sessions. The Counseling, Advising and Placement Center (CAP) provides psychological and academic counseling.

For black students in particular, the Black Student Advisory Network can assist students in adapting to life at this predominantly white university. In addition to the regular academic advisors, there is a black student advisor. Peer counselors and special skills workshops during the year round out the support services menu.

SUBA, the Student Union on Black Awareness, is the most active black organization on campus. This group also provides tutorial sessions for students who need help. In addition, SUBA arranges for guest lectures and holds bi-weekly meetings to discuss campus issues and political, social and cultural awareness. SUBA's Alumni Committee arranges for alumns to visit and speak at some of these meetings; otherwise, there seems to be little black alumn activity at this school.

Other special programs are Sisters United, which emphasizes black women's issues and provides a support network, and the Student Y Committee, which offers workshops on racism for both black and white students.

Social life and extra-curricular activities for blacks at OWU do not get very high marks. This is a small school in a small town, and there is little interaction with the community. On campus, the black fraternity, Alpha Phi Alpha, has a chapter, and a few brothers belong to some of the other predominantly white fraternities. While blacks participate in "almost all forms" of social activity, says one student, "There aren't many to begin with," and most of these are for the general community.

There is a good deal of energy and participation in intramural sports, which one student describes as "very competitive." Except for track, blacks are not as visible in varsity athletics. Again, students feel that the few enrolled blacks and the small sports program account for this lack of representation.

Other cultural activities, mostly music and drama, are available to the black student. The campus radio station has two programs directed by black DJ's. The singing group, the Gospel Lyres, performs in various churches and at campus functions.

OWU also allows its students to play a very active role in political life on campus. "The student has a great deal to do with how this school is run. We can make things happen," claims a respondent.

Whatever its drawbacks, black students are satisfied with OWU. One "strongly recommends Ohio Wesleyan to any prospective black student." This is a predominantly white university, but students view this positively.

Comments one undergrad about this small liberal arts college 20 miles from Columbus, "It's a good place for a black person to come if he wants to be able to deal with society as a whole, not just one aspect of it."

POMONA COLLEGE
Claremont, California 91711

Undergrads: 1,402
Black Undergrads: 70
Faculty: 164
Black Faculty: 7
Tuition: $18,880
Total Expenses: $26,380

"If you want an excellent education and preparation for the professional world, Pomona is the place," says a brother. "But before accepting, know yourself and your priorities."

Pomona is the founding member of the five colleges making up the Claremont College system, modeled after the colleges making up England's Oxford and Cambridge universities. Thirty-five miles east of Los Angeles, private, coed and liberal arts-oriented, Pomona is most selective.

Each of the Claremont colleges is an autonomous institution, but the school encourages students to make use of the academic offerings of the sister schools.

The effort to recruit minority students has many stages. When possible, a current student accompanies an officer who attends a black recruitment fair, either locally or out of state. The Partnership Program sends admission officers to AP and Honors classes. The Claremont Scholars Program involves the entire high school system. Representatives discuss private colleges. Both programs focus on high schools with large numbers of students of color.

Most black students are from California, D.C., New York, or Washington.

The Claremont schools' Black Alumni Association helps at introductory receptions in areas with traditionally high application rates. They also conduct interviews with nearby students. Pomona students conduct phone-a-thons to invite prospective students to visit the campus. An additional recruiting bonus is the Fly-in Program, which makes a visit possible for students with financial need.

The Intercollegiate Department of Black Studies offers a multidisciplinary curriculum focusing on African, African-American, and Caribbean experiences. Examples of these are Arts of Africa, African-American History 1860 to Present, Black Psychology, and Politics of Race.

Orientation workshops and seminars serve as a forum for discussion of topics such as diversity and cooperative living. These inspire students to inject culture into film and lecture series and retreats.

Pomona is an academically rigorous school. If you're seeking academic help, there is tutoring, study skills workshops, and special class sections as well as peer, minority peer, faculty, administrative, alumni, and psychological counseling.

The school offers internships for students, who get stipends to work in the community.

The Office of Black Student Affairs organizes tutoring, support groups, and events such as Kwanzaa and Dr. King celebrations.

Black student groups include the Third World Christian Fellowship, Pan-African Student Association, and Claremont Gospel Choir, which has performed off campus. There are also intramural sports such as basketball, flag football, and coed softball.

Plus, black students participate on the student council's Committee for Campus Life Activities. The Dean of Campus Life, Coordinator of Student Activities, and two admission officers are black.

One satisfied respondent says that Pomona must be a consideration if "blacks are looking for a high-quality education."

PRINCETON UNIVERSITY
Princeton, New Jersey 08544

Undergrads: 4,609
Black Undergrads: 323
Faculty: 886
Black Faculty: 8
Tuition: $22,000
Total Expenses: $28,325

Although the challenge is tough at this small, coed institution that is one of the 25 most selective colleges in the country, Princeton attracts hundreds of black students who want to sample the challenging liberal arts curriculum at a national research university.

With faculty like Toni Morrison and Cornel West, 23 libraries with six million books, outstanding engineering, liberal arts and architecture programs and a highly regarded Afro-American Studies program, it's not difficult to see why.

Princeton offers a core academic program, and its most popular majors are history, political science and government, and English.

The science-oriented student can find academic aid through the Imhotep Society (black pre-meds) and the Society of Black Engineers (SOBE). There are peer counseling services at the college's Counseling Center and the Educational Opportunity Program.

Seeking spiritual guidance? Explore the Black Theater or the Black Gospel Choir. "People with or without drama experience can perform in the theater," one student points out. The gospel choir has frequent on- and off-campus concerts.

Black students can also find social activities through other black organizations, ranging from the Organization of Black Unity to the West Indian Students' Association. The college has a black literary publication as well as a time slot for black radio.

The Third World Center not only provides social and cultural activities, but also resource counseling and tutorial services. It hosts speakers and forums on third world issues as well. The center sponsors some trips abroad for those who want to expand their cultural horizons. Through Community

House, black students tutor black high school students in the local area. There is a Big Brother/Big Sister program and local church services.

Despite Princeton's overwhelming credentials, one student believes the college experience centers on the student rather than on the school. This student concludes, "I've gotten where I've gotten because of me, not because of Princeton."

No respondent regrets going to Princeton; it offers an excellent education, "top-notch students, faculty, the prestige of the Princeton name, and a strong black community."

RAMAPO COLLEGE

Mahwah, New Jersey 07430

Undergrads: 3,940
Black Undergrads: 394
Faculty: 286
Black Faculty: NA
Tuition: $3,521; $4,878
Total Expenses: $9,033; $10,390

In the world of colleges and universities, Ramapo is just a baby. Formed almost 25 years ago, it is a public liberal arts institution dedicated to developing students who are active both on campus and in the larger world community.

The college offers more than two dozen majors and is divided into five schools: administration and business, American and international studies, contemporary arts, social science and human service, and theoretical and applied science. A minor program in African-American studies features classes such as African-American Culture and Civilization, Black Experience Through Theater, Civil Rights, and Third World Women, among others.

Adjusting to academics is apparently a breeze—for about half of the black students. The rate of successful transition is "about 50/50," says one respondent. "Some either stick with college or drop out and never return," she adds. Other responses range from the more negative ("There are too many minority students that are failing out of school") to the more positive ("I have adjusted well thanks to the summer programs").

Students give mixed responses to questions about Ramapo's support services. Evaluations of the tutorial services range from "average" and "adequate" to "very helpful." Most agree, however, that the counseling services could be better. In one sister's opinion, "Ramapo is lacking in this area because we need more positive counselors to help the minority population." Another feels that the counselors are "no good."

The school sponsors an Educational Opportunity Program, a six-week summer session designed to help disadvantaged students ease the transition from high school to college.

Black students on Ramapo's campus are active. They support black clubs such as Ebony Women For Social Change, Brothers Making a Difference, and Organization of African Unity. One respondent commends them for being helpful and for providing a place for minorities to support one another. A brother feels that they are "excellent at getting information out" to black students. Black students are also extremely visible in the student government association. One respondent estimates that minorities represent 80 percent of the organization.

Students have few complaints about the social life. A student mentions that there is "great involvement and support" for all kinds of parties. A sister adds, "You will see a lot of African Americans at these functions whether they go here or not." And Greek-sponsored parties are possible too, as chapters of Kappa Alpha Psi, Delta Sigma Theta, and Alpha Kappa Alpha are active on campus.

Although one student mentions that white students are friendly if given a chance, several others describe race relations as tense, both with white students and white faculty members. One respondent suggests that white faculty members attend a workshop to make them more sensitive to the needs of minority students.

Some final thoughts from a current Ramapo student: "I don't recommend that African Americans come here because Ramapo doesn't offer anything for us. In order to get something we have to fight for it."

REED COLLEGE
Portland, Oregon 97202

Undergrads: 1,276
Black Undergrads: 13
Faculty: 126
Black Faculty: NA
Tuition: $20,760
Total Expenses: $26,510

R eed's exceptional dedication to quality education and its resolve to extend its resources to a larger share of black students makes it an outstanding candidate for those seeking a small, liberal arts college.

"Reed College is not for everyone: it's for a self-motivated and intellectual student, who both enjoys and respects freedom," claims one of its black undergrads.

Located in Portland, whose black population is 28,000, Reed is an independent, highly selective liberal arts college. Three-quarters of the students hail from beyond the Pacific Northwest, and 40 percent are from east of the Mississippi River.

Reed College is determined to recruit black students. An admissions staff visits approximately 350-400 high schools each year, with 20-30 schools especially targeted for black recruiting.

Alumns assist in school visits and follow-up. In the past, Reed has helped pay expenses for some accepted black applicants who visit. Special mailings have been sent to A Better Chance participants and to students on a Talent Roster of Outstanding Minority Community College Graduates.

Most notably, Reed College guarantees financial aid according to need to all black students admitted.

Reed offers an intimate educational atmosphere, dedicated to intensive student participation in the arts and sciences. Classes are conference style, and laboratory work in the science courses is extensive.

Reed, according to one student, does not emphasize grades.

"Courses are extremely intense," she notes, "They want students to do their best, and the important thing is to learn." A thesis requirement completes Reed's commitment to a thorough education.

Course offerings geared to the black student are extensive, considering the size of the school, and include "The History of Southern Africa," "Urban Poverty and Government Policy" and "The Politics of School Desegregation and Affirmative Action," among others. The sociology department is in the midst of revamping its offerings and has offered courses of particular interest to the black student in the past.

Reed's library collection is outstanding, with the largest solely undergraduate collection in the Northwest. Of note are collections of African History, the Black Experience in America, Black Literature and other traditional topics in the social sciences and literature.

The library also subscribes to the *Journal of Negro History*, the *London Times* and other journals especially helpful for senior thesis research. Reed possesses the rare holdings of original theses and documents relating to the British Colonial Office, the *Collection on Exploration and Colonization of Africa 1794-1844*, and it possesses the Irish University Press, a multi-volume series of documents relating to the slave trade in the nineteenth century.

In addition, Reed recently has obtained access to an extensive data bank for the social sciences which will support research in a variety of fields.

Various academic support systems are available to all students, including study skills workshops, tutoring, informal writing workshops and counseling. Tutorial assistance is arranged by departments on a limited basis, but a sister reports that it is adequate: "if one needs help, all one has to do is ask."

The college does not offer many specifically black-oriented societies, although there is an active Black Student Union. Black undergrads participate in general activities both social and cultural. One student reports that blacks "take a more active role in school governance than their white counterparts," although others believe that blacks do not play any part in this area. There are no varsity sports, but plenty of intramural events.

As a rule, social life is limited for both blacks and whites, but interaction is unlimited. One undergrad writes, "Because of the social make-up of Reed, it is impossible for me to judge the school by racial standards. I find myself writing and thinking of individuals, rather than groups." He goes on to say, "As a student, I am glad that I chose Reed. As a black man, I feel as though I am missing a valuable part of my educational experience. But Reed has taught me a great deal about myself; I have developed a sense of pride in being a black American."

"But remember," cautions one student, "Reed represents a whole different way of life: Not only is one left to do pretty much what one wants to do, but one is also exposed to unique and unconventional ideas. One's individuality may be stripped away just as easily as it is gained if one does not have an idea of who he truly is and what he wants to be."

RENSSELAER POLYTECHNIC INSTITUTE
Troy, New York 12181

Undergrads: 4,360
Black Undergrads: 174
Faculty: 342
Black Faculty: NA
Tuition: $18,555
Total Expenses: $24,710

One student writes, "I think the environment is a model of the real world...I am attending school to learn, so I feel that the number of black social activities is more than adequate."

Rensselaer Polytechnic Institute is the first school of engineering and applied science in North America. It maintains a highly selective admissions policy in its major disciplines of engineering, science, management and architecture. And one student relates, "I have heard from graduates that having a degree from Rensselaer is very helpful in getting a job. This makes all the hard work and little social life more than worth it."

Recruitment activities are extensive in keeping with the institute's desire to increase minority student enrollment. Each year RPI visits 150 secondary schools which have provided applicants in the past. A prospective Minority Student Seminar is held on campus each April. Alumns provide information on RPI to students and recommend qualified students to the institute. Academics are all-important at RPI, and classes are rigorous. The institute boasts placing some of the first successful blacks in industry. It maintains its dedication to enroll increasing numbers of African-Americans, as well as Hispanic Americans, students from the South Pacific and those of Native American descent.

The academic support services are extensive and well-founded. The Office of Minority Student Affairs (OMSA) is professionally staffed and provides a wide variety of assistance to minority students, including a Higher Education Opportunity Program with specialized support for disadvantaged New York State residents.

The Bridge Program, funded by Exxon, IBM, Union Carbide and RPI, helps students to complete Chemistry I and Computer Fundamentals I during the summer prior to the freshman year. OMSA also offers services in expository writing, study skills, leadership training, scholar incentive grants, summer employment and interface seminars.

Counseling is provided through Big Brother/Little Brother, OMSA and the Black Student Alliance (BSA). One student writes, "The Alliance has been very successful in indoctrinating the freshman to campus life."

Special recitation sections are established for freshman-level courses in physics, calculus and chemistry. Seminars and forums are offered by students, OMSA and industry, and various programs abound for academic, professional and social development.

Though small, RPI's chapter of the national black pre-med society participates in local and national events. An award-winning chapter of the National Society of Black Engineers is active at RPI. The organization sponsors the annual school job fair, organizes field trips and sponsors workshops on career development and interviewing. One member states, "The organization provides me with a means to get summer jobs and provides a service to the community. The organization is politically active too."

Black religious services are provided through the local community. Campus-based black radio is strong, with extensive programming catering to the minority community. The BSA also promotes the social and cultural interests of the minority community. One student writes that in recent years, black participation in student government has been effective, with the minority community reaping many benefits.

Relations between black students and white students, black and white faculty, and with advisors, are good. One student writes that the only problems encountered tend to come from administrators, not faculty. Tension exists within the local community of Troy, although black students at RPI have sought to aid the citizens through tutoring, attending city-sponsored events and the distributing of food baskets.

Parties are "infamous in the area and usually have a heavy turnout of campus minority students," a student says. There is a black fraternity and a sorority, but no housing for them. RPI is located near Russell Sage, Skidmore, Albany State and Siena, and communication among blacks is continual.

RPI gives large disco parties in the fall and spring. Small parties are given in the Black Cultural Center, which also sponsors study break parties and spur-of-the-moment get-togethers.

Mixers are held during the job fair and awards banquet; they are formal and well-attended. University-sponsored entertainment is top-notch and quite varied, from tap dancing exhibitions and well-known entertainers to jazz concerts. Basketball and football are popular intramural sports. The Black Cultural Center also holds picnics, though "not nearly as often as necessary," one student comments.

"Rensselaer is much more of a challenge academically than I ever thought it would be, but I feel that I am really learning something," states one student.

RHODE ISLAND COLLEGE
Providence, Rhode Island 02908

Undergrads: 7,500
Black Undergrads: 225
Faculty: 395
Black Faculty: NA
Tuition: $2,969; $6,996
Total Expenses: $8,069; $12,096

One student says, "I'm satisfied with my decision. I feel it is a chance to have many experiences that will be useful to me later on in life. It's also a chance to interact with white students and a chance to prepare yourself to work in a predominantly white world."

Rhode Island College, the state-run, liberal arts and education college on a 125-acre campus three miles from downtown Providence, will certainly challenge you. RIC is selective in its admission policy, and most of the students are Rhode Island residents who commute to school. Only about 14 percent of the students live on campus.

Recruitment of blacks—who come primarily from Rhode Island, Massachusetts, Connecticut and New York—is done mostly through visits to private and public secondary schools. Most RIC students have graduated from public high schools. RIC does have specially arranged campus visits for black sub-freshmen.

Black students have mixed reactions on the subject of making the adjustment from high school to RIC. One sister believes "Adjustment for half [of the blacks] has been successful, but the other half may never adjust if they do not change their attitudes and become more serious." Another student says, "Black students have adjusted well, but I feel they need more social and ethnic-related stimulation as far as programming of events geared to promote racial tolerance."

There are only a few courses related to the African-American experience, usually under the headings of anthropology and sociology.

Tutorial assistance and study skills workshops are free of charge and available to any student who needs help. While some respondents did not know these services existed, others find these services "adequate and helpful." One student states, "The Writing Center and Math Center have helped me a lot." The counseling programs, including personal counseling, academic advising and special services, are considered "very helpful, especially for incoming freshmen," by one black undergrad.

Students agree that black participation in the campus radio station is "outstanding."

No formal or informal black alumn associations exist at RIC. One student says, "Those blacks that come back to RIC are very supportive of today's black students. The contact is good." However, other students have had little or no interaction with black alumns.

RIC has made efforts to provide programs that encourage racial tolerance. An average of two or three lectures per month are sponsored by various departments and organizations. Many local and national speakers come to the school during the academic year.

Black participation in the student government has improved over the last few years. One sister feels, "Active participation in student government [among blacks] has been increasing steadily over the past four years." Another student states, "At RIC, blacks have recently been acknowledged for participation in university governance."

Black participation in activities such as parties, athletic events and black student center events varies. One student says there is very good participation at the black parties both on and off campus. The black student organization is called "Harambee."

One student feels that black student participation in student center activities is somewhat low and could be better if more people were willing to get involved. Basketball games is the varsity sport most attended by blacks at RIC, mainly because this is the sport with the most blacks on the varsity squad. Black participation in other varsity athletics is low, and therefore, black support of these sports is minimal.

The interaction between black and white students at this predominantly white college is not always the best and is a subject of concern among some of the brothers and sisters at RIC. One student reports that blacks associate with other black students and that there are few white students who associate with blacks. Says another: "White students do not understand the needs of minority students. They also have a hard time understanding that Spanish, Cape Verdean and African Americans are not all one culture."

Interaction between black students and white faculty members and administrators is without tension. "They seem to treat all students equally, regardless of color," one student declares. The interplay between black students and black faculty members and administrators is rated very good.

One student maintains that they don't try to prove anything to the students by acting either black or white, but are very fair to everyone. Several administrative positions at RIC are held by blacks.

A senior declares: "For the most part it has been a good experience. Coming to a white school gives me a challenge to become a well-respected member of the community as well as an important role model for other minority students."

RHODE ISLAND SCHOOL OF DESIGN
Providence, Rhode Island 02903

Undergrads: 1,815
Black Undergrads: 36
Faculty: 302
Black Faculty: NA
Tuition: $17,780
Total Expenses: $24,398

Do you want to have fun or do you want to "take your art to the next level?" That's the choice that black students feel they have to make to attend Rhode Island School of Design.

Although RISD may be, in one student's opinion, "socially horrible," the academic opportunities are excellent. RISD is recognized as one of the best art schools in the country. It offers B.A. and M.A. degrees in art and architecture with specialization in art history, drawing, painting, photography, sculpture, fashion design and film.

Small, coed, with a selective admission policy, "RISDY" (pronounced *riz-dee*) is located deep in the residential east side of Providence, down the hill from Brown University.

Freshman students participate in Freshman Foundation, a year-long program that introduces them to visual language with studio experiences in drawing and two- and three-dimensional design. Foundation courses also include art history, literature and composition.

The school offers three courses that relate directly to the African and African-American experience—Literature of Black America, African Art and Aesthetics and African Culture. Additionally, some broad courses (Freshman Art History, for example) include references to African and African-American culture. Students are able to cross-register for classes at Brown.

The Multicultural Affairs Office serves RISD's students of color. A minority counseling program in which upper-class students advise frosh is considered by at least one student to be ineffective. Interaction between black students is low he says, because "most black students tend to be very individual and don't want guidance from others."

RISD recruiters visit high schools, especially ones with art specialization, attend National Portfolio Days in 25 cities and using College Board listings, send target mail to minority students interested in art and design. But statistics show that these efforts are not getting results. Black students are about 2.5 percent of the total student population. One brother warns incoming freshmen to expect to be the only black student in most of their classes. And despite RISD's national acclaim, the majority of its black students come from nearby New York, Massachusetts and New Jersey.

Three multicultural organizations exist on campus: the Third World Coalition of Artists, which sponsors social and cultural events; Common Threads, which sponsors student forums and deals with political issues; and the Muticultural Student's Association. The President's Committee on Diversity was founded in 1994 to recommend programs and policies to the President.

Although the number of black faculty and administrators is small, it is possible for students to develop nurturing relationships with them. One student finds her instructor to be "supportive, aware and active." Other students are not as pleased. One feels that black faculty members don't reach out to black students enough, which "gives the idea that they don't want to be bothered."

As for social events, one brother says, "We create our own parties." When that gets tired, students can travel to Brown or nearby Johnson and Wales to party. RISD undergrads can pledge at sororities and fraternities on Brown's campus as well.

Campus racism seems to be less of a concern than social livelihood for the black students surveyed. One student says, "Most people are open-minded and embrace ethnicity and culture, although instances of ignorance and stereotyping occur sometimes." Another student adds, "Most white students and faculty are eager to learn about black students and culture." Bemoans a third student, "I honestly feel like they can appreciate the difference but will never understand it."

Although several students expressed a desire to visit a historically black college or university, they do not regret choosing RISD. What is the attraction? According to one student, "It provides an environment that is about the development of the student as an artist/designer." Another applauds RISD for its openness. "Most classes allow students to be creative with their ideas." But as a seasoned student warns, "Maturity, exposure and personality are all relevant to how you will adjust to RISD. You must know what you are about."

RICE UNIVERSITY
Houston, Texas 77005

Undergrads: 2,645
Black Undergrads: 175
Faculty: 449
Black Faculty: 8
Tuition: $12,800
Total Expenses: $19,206

"Iam very satisfied with this school," contends an undergrad, "because I have made friends with people of all races. The mood here is one of acceptance and tolerance of other races."

"Being a member of the Rice Community has been a learning experience, to say the least," writes another. "Rice teaches many things well, but it teaches humility very well."

Coed, private, and very, very well endowed, Rice offers the small college advantages with the resources of a large research university. Set on a 300-acre academic park in Houston, our fourth largest city, the university offers an interdisciplinary curriculum and a core academic program.

To recruit, Rice visits secondary schools in 35 states, attends recruitment fairs, uses alumns for interviewing and letter writing, and offers overnight visits. One program for minority candidates, Vision, flies in 50 students for a campus visit.

For outstanding African-American applicants, Rice provides merit scholarships (Presidential Scholars, Honor Scholars and Leadership Scholars) with maximum values of $12,000 per year.

Most of the brothers and sisters here are from Texas, Louisiana, New York and California.

Areas of study include schools of humanities, social sciences, architecture, music, natural sciences, engineering and interdepartmental majors. Engineering and science are nationally ranked programs.

For courses in the black experiences, go to the departments of history, English, anthropology, religious study or sociology, where you will find offerings like Metropolitan Africans, Comparative Slavery and Race Relations in the Americas, and Race and Ethnic Relations.

Their library collection includes a special database of African-American poetry from 1760 to 1900 which provides a unique portrait of early America.

Support services feature tutoring, counseling and special workshops. Tutoring is offered through the Office of Academic Advising, the Office of Multicultural Affairs, academic departments and the residential college system.

A range of academic, psychological and special issues counseling is available also.

Referring to the arduous adjustment from high school to college, one undergrad states that there are a number of programs that "can help ease the transition." Supplementing the formal Rice tutoring, "There are course-organized study sessions and impromptu study groups that offer further assistance," she explains.

Says an undergrad, "There are always workshops on many different subjects, such as interracial dating, peer pressure and a lot of other interesting topics."

To encourage racial tolerance, Rice produces a role-playing workshop during orientation week and sponsors a Unity Through Diversity Week. A month-long celebration of Martin Luther King's Birthday and black history takes place in February.

Rice has an affirmative action policy that seeks to recruit minority group members.

For organizations set up to meet your concerns, check out the Black Student Association, the National Society for Black Engineers and a group called Advocating Diversity and Assisting Career Exploration (ADVANCE).

A black pre-med group has created a valuable support network for blacks, reports an observer, adding "I'm sure that these connections will last as the members spread across the country. It is also lets members know that they are not alone in their struggle to do well in a difficult curriculum."

Interracial relations are passable. "I can't think of any instances of blatant racism," says a respondent. "There seems to be a feeling of acceptance between the races, but there is rarely any sharing of cultures. Just walking into the cafeteria sometimes...the self-segregation makes it seem like we are from two different worlds."

Reports another about relations with white faculty: "My black friends often feel that they are being discriminated against, and I feel that they are sometimes right."

For parties, most black students attend those in dorms or off campus thrown by friends. "Blacks here most often come to a party sponsored by the black organization because it is generally accepted that the DJs at other campus parties will play relatively few songs which appeal to blacks," explains a brother.

"By taking full advantage of the education Rice is offering, you can pave the way for others like you. The minority situation in this country is bleak, particularly at the collegiate level. It's up to us to change it," declares an undergrad.

How come so many advantages? It helps if your endowment of more than a billion dollars ranks you fourth of all colleges in the country.

ROCHESTER INSTITUTE OF TECHNOLOGY

Rochester, New York 14623

Undergrads: 10,552
Black Undergrads: 528
Faculty: 1,095
Black Faculty: NA
Tuition: $14,937
Total Expenses: $20,835

One student summarizes RIT this way: "The common tie for most black students here is their lack of unity." Another student adds, "It's pretty easy to lose your sense of self entering a place such as Rochester Institute of Technology."

"If you have the desire to change things that are wrong or support things that are right, Rochester Institute of Technology is a good place to be," says another about the 150-year-old privately endowed, coed, non-sectarian school; its principal task is preparing students for technological competence in a world of change.

RIT also awards bachelor of science degrees in business, criminal justice and the graphic arts. In addition, RIT offers a variety of B.S. degrees in business, graphic arts and photography through the National Technical Institute for the Deaf. There is also a College of Fine and Applied Arts including the School of Art and Design, and the School for American Craftsmen, which offers a junior year abroad with full credit.

Most of the brothers and sisters at Rochester Institute of Technology come from New York, New Jersey, Pennsylvania and Massachusetts, with emphasis for minority recruitment largely confined to New York City, Buffalo, Syracuse and Rochester.

The curriculum features nine courses relating to the African-American experience.

The move from high school to college-level academics has been fairly smooth for most black students here. Commenting on the transition, one sister says, "Students must be encouraged to meet the challenge which they have the potential to overcome."

Those experiencing academic problems can go to the Higher Education Opportunity Program and the Office of Special Services. It is within these two programs that black students find tutorial and counseling assistance. Moreover, the university has a Learning Development Center which helps black students with study skills. In cooperation with the Special Services Program, the LDC conducts various workshops.

Additionally, the Rochester Institute of Technology has a special co-op program in which many of the school's black students participate. Under this arrangement, students alternate quarters of study with quarters of paid work experience in business or industry directly related to their major. According to some black students, this program is RIT's most attractive feature. "It is required of most majors and gives the student a perspective on what working in the real world is all about," reports one respondent.

Interaction between black and white students is minimal at best. One student describes this relationship as "not that strong, but there seem to be signs of improvement." While some black students rarely communicate with the few black faculty and administrators, most brothers and sisters queried feel that contact between the two groups is "pretty good." Evaluations of interaction between black students and white faculty and administrators range from "fair to poor," according to one student. But a Minority Task Force has been developed to allow black students to discuss their problems with white faculty and administrators, and another respondent describes relations as "good and improving."

Because of their small numbers, blacks rarely participate in student government. "However, we now have two to three active blacks in the school student directorate. This is the first time," adds one undergrad.

Most of Rochester's black students have had no contact with black alumns. Furthermore, no formal black alumn program exists.

Although most black students are satisfied with their courses, most of them agree that the social life at the university is unexciting. Many brothers and sisters say that the campus parties are usually well-attended. Others add that parties are the only activities that black students can or want to organize. Moreover, the absence of black fraternities and sororities and the lack of a center for black activities contributes further to the dismal social life for RIT's black students.

The Black Awareness Coordinating Committee (BACC) is the school's only organization geared directly toward brothers and sisters at RIT. Yet most students feel that this committee is inadequate for their needs. Also, there aren't any black pre-professional societies, nor is there any campus radio or television programming specifically designed for RIT's black community.

The university reportedly never sponsors acts by black professional entertainers.

The only extracurricular activities geared specifically for blacks are their religious services and some intramural sports.

"I feel as if I'm missing out on a great deal of cultural growth that I could have received at another school," declares one student about his stay at RIT.

ROCKHURST COLLEGE
Kansas City, Missouri 64110

Undergrads: 2,140
Black Undergrads: 150
Faculty: 224
Black Faculty: NA
Tuition: $11,240
Total Expenses: $15,730

In the long run, most black respondents are satisfied with Rockhurst. "In all," a senior concludes, "a stay at Rockhurst can be very rewarding."

Situated in the middle of the Kansas City metropolitan area, small, coed and selective Rockhurst is a Catholic institution established in 1910.

Over 60 percent of entering black freshman come from parochial high schools, primarily from Missouri, Kansas, Illinois and Nebraska; approximately 80 percent of all students are Catholic.

Rockhurst College confers bachelor's degrees in arts, sciences, nursing and business administration. There is an evening division which offers many of the same degree programs as the day college.

The bachelor's degree in business administration is limited to students in the evening division. Rockhurst's Cooperative Education Program allows students to alternate semesters of full-time study with semesters of full-time employment. The student's earnings from the employment helps them defray some of the high costs of a college education.

As far as adjustment is concerned, black students agree, "After they begin to buckle down and study, the majority of blacks adjust fairly well." One adds that one learns to "separate studies and free time" and sees "no serious problems" for those who do.

Support systems offered by RC include tutorial assistance, counseling, some study skills workshops and special class sections. The tutorial services are arranged by the Tutoring Center. Peer tutoring is the form of tutoring most commonly utilized by the students. One student says, "Rockhurst has a very good program to aid students who need help in a certain subject."

The counseling services are organized by the Counseling Center. Although these services are for the general population, one black student notes, "The Counseling Center takes interest in blacks and their futures." Another declares "Rockhurst has good counseling procedures. One just has to use them." The Black Student Union also offers informal counseling and tutoring by its upperclass members. Study skills workshops are operated by the Learning Center. Special class sections are arranged by the Freshman Incentive Program, which is designed to assist academically marginal students.

The Black Student Union is the only black student organization on campus. Participation by black students in the BSU is very good, but support by the white students in BSU-sponsored activities is minimal. Each year some of the principal activities organized by the BSU during the academic year include interracial forums, social functions, a BSU Annual Retreat and Black History Month activities. There are no black fraternities or sororities on campus, but there are white fraternities that do have a few black brothers.

A great deal of social life for the brothers and sisters at RC takes place off campus. Off-campus parties given by black fraternities attract decent numbers. There is also some participation in predominantly white on-campus activities. "We try not to alienate ourselves," says one brother. However, one student says that one of the white fraternities is reputed to be prejudiced, and therefore, blacks don't attend parties given by that frat.

The climate, as far as racial tension between black students and other members of the university is concerned, is "generally good." One student on the subject of interaction between white and black students at RC states, "We all get along pretty well. There is really no racial problem, but there aren't enough of us to have a problem."

One issue which concerns a few students is the extremely low number of black faculty members and administrators. The BSU is making efforts to get more hired and is also pushing for a stronger voice in campus governance.

One student's advice: "Most black students should know that Rockhurst, and campus activities, center around whites," adding, "this should not discourage blacks from coming. Blacks should be part of a situation that is more challenging; it makes success more meaningful."

ROGER WILLIAMS COLLEGE

Bristol, Rhode Island 02809

Undergrads: 2,230
Black Undergrads: 45
Faculty: 202
Black Faculty: NA
Tuition: $15,100
Total Expenses: $21,960

Some black students find Roger Williams attractive because it has a "beautiful campus, freedom, respect for ideas and no cliques." One student responds, "Yes, I am satisfied because the school is what you make it."

Founded in 1948, small, private and selective Roger Williams College is "one of the few seaside campuses in the Northeast." A liberal arts, coed institution, the college offers various support services for its students.

"Tutorial service and counseling are available at the Counseling Office," one student notes. "But sometimes you have to wait a long time before receiving help," says another. Yet administrative counselors help students from a professional view, and peer counselors offer advice or refer students to other sources. Students also find academic and emotional relief at the Career Development Center as well as through different college workshops ranging in topic from interviewing to stress.

"The transition from high school to Roger Williams depends upon a student's ambition and determination," points out one student. To ease that adjustment period, the United Minority Coalition (UMC) provides pre-professional information, seminars, political awareness materials and social activities.

However, one student notes in dismay, "The only parties geared toward blacks are given by blacks. We only have one fraternity and no sororities." There is no black student center, nor radio, nor theater. However, mixers are "numerous, very successful and helpful in meeting other students and faculty," and students are very active in the "Battle of the Dorms"—intramural sports.

However, relationships with white faculty "lack a personal touch," another notes.

Opinions vary on the interaction with the local community. While one student finds the community "prejudiced against the college," another feels "community interaction is very good. For some reason, they respect the black students more than the white."

In conclusion, black students must adjust to being a minority. "Not many things are geared toward blacks here," states one student.

RUTGERS UNIVERSITY
New Brunswick, New Jersey 08903

Undergrads: 27,655
Black Undergrads: 2,338
Faculty: 1,763
Black Faculty: 123
Tuition: $4,837; $8,757
Total Expenses: $9,772; $13,693

Its long history of minority education goes back to 1892, when James Dickson Carr, its first black student, graduated. Then in 1919, Paul Robeson was elected valedictorian. If only Robeson, All-American, Phi Beta Kappa graduate and the most outspoken black leader of his day, could see the place today.

One thing is certain: Rutgers is motivated. It has more black faculty than any other predominantly white university. And its president has spearheaded the Committee to Advance Our Common Purposes, a program against racism, homophobia, and sexism.

Known as the State University of New Jersey, coed Rutgers combines the advantages of a large public university with those of a small-to-medium-sized college.

The New Brunswick campus consists of four liberal arts colleges: Douglass, Livingston, Rutgers, and University. The four professional schools are Cook College, Mason Gross School of the Arts, College of Engineering, and College of Pharmacy.

Admission officers visit private and public high schools to conduct interviews, and both they and black alumni attend minority recruitment fairs. Blacks join one of the 18 alumni groups, the 6,000-member African American Alumni Alliance (ALANA), or the worldwide Regional Alumni Club network. Both black alumni and current students are Alumni Admissions Representatives. In addition to these efforts, academic departments arrange for black middle and high school students to stay on campus.

Most black students at Rutgers come from New Jersey, New York, Pennsylvania, and Maryland.

While each college sets its own selective admission standards and degree requirements, students in any of the colleges may, under certain faculty guidelines, take courses at any of the other colleges. Consequently, Rutgers offers a broad range of courses in over 90 major fields of study. If you're looking for your roots, you'll find them here.

Africana Studies can be a major or a minor, and includes African languages and literatures. African history courses include African Labor and Cultural History, Ancient Africa, and Modern Africa. The interdisciplinary African Area Studies curriculum offers as many as 19 courses. And within Women's Studies are courses like The Black Family, The Black Woman, Black Women Writers, and Third-World Women.

Douglass provides African languages, and Mason Gross has a jazz major and courses like Jazz Dance and Evolution of Jazz. Other Mason courses are African-American Music, Black Theater History, Ethnic Dance, Introduction to Non-Western Music, and Third-World Artists.

The university supplements these course offerings with a strong academic support system. Students receive tutorial assistance from the Learning Resource Centers. The special Gateway courses are in biology, economics, history, psychology, sociology. Minority students may also take courses for help with studying and to prepare for the GRE, LSAT, or GMAT. "I've had excellent results," reports a brother, "but you have to be patient."

Approximately 2,600 students from low-income families may receive personal as well as academic counseling from the state-funded Educational Opportunity Program. Students who wish to be health professionals receive help from the Office of Minority Science Programs.

Members of the alumni alliance act as mentors to black students and provide them with internships. There are two career days for minorities, and career center counseling. Blacks may look for jobs in such publications as *Black Collegian*, *Minority Engineer Magazine*, and *The Daily Targum*. Each semester, job opportunities look for them; students find the ALANA newsletter in their mailboxes.

The school collected 1,400 ALANA resumes for internship openings with 30 employers. INROADS also makes it possible for students of color to be summer interns.

Now minority students can apply for the hefty James Dickson Carr Scholarship fund—available for 100 black and Puerto Rican students at any of the three campuses: New Brunswick, Camden, or Newark. Further,

Rutgers has instituted a $5,000,000 Cross Cultural Campaign for minority students. For life after Rutgers, the university hosts the annual Minority Exploration Committee on Careers Associated (MECCA), a career development program that provides workshops and career placement assistance. Representatives from over 40 major corporations throughout the United States come to meet minority students.

Black alumni are active, performing community service with the Citizenship and Service Education Program. They also sponsor a black alumni reunion, an African art exhibit, and a reception during Homecoming Weekend.

For academic and non-academic support, most black students utilize the Robeson Cultural Center (considered "too damp and too small" by one respondent). It sponsors special programs and speakers series. The center works with communities on a local, regional, state-wide, national, and international capacity.

There are more than three dozen black student organizations, including black Greek sororities and fraternities. At least 145 black students play on intercollegiate teams. The list of recent visiting performers and lecturers includes A Tribe Called Quest, A Salute to Africans in Russia and the Soviet Union, and current President Bill Clinton.

"There are plenty of parties," says one undergrad. Blacks also take advantage of church service on campus, considered exceptionally inspirational, and black radio programming.

Race relations are viewed as "okay" and "passable." Each group stays out of the way of the other, is the bottom line.

An undergrad offers this advice: "When choosing a school, one shouldn't consider whether it is good for me as a black student only, but rather is it good for me educationally." And since Rutgers is a huge university, "you have to be self-motivated," he declares.

ST. JOHN'S COLLEGE
Santa Fe, New Mexico 87501

Undergrads: 379
Black Undergrads: 4
Faculty: 54
Black Faculty: NA
Tuition: $18,720
Total Expenses: $24,775

B lack students desiring an education based on classics and focusing on much independent thinking should check out St. John's curriculum. Tiny St. John's College is an independent, highly selective college with no religious affiliations. Its unique educational experience is based on a study of great books; its four-year curriculum concentrates on the written monuments of Western civilization, from Plato to the present. This is truly a "classical education."

Because the college runs identical programs on campuses in Annapolis and in Santa Fe, St. John's students can choose the location they prefer; many split their time between the two.

There are twice-weekly discussions of the great books, supported by daily tutorials in language and mathematics and twice-weekly laboratory periods for natural sciences. Music is included in the first two years.

Students are also expected to attend a formal Friday night lecture on some topic pertaining to the Great Books. St. John's stresses that its students learn through tutorials, in discussion, translation, demonstration, experimentation and writing. It is an almost purely non-elective educational policy. Transfer students are accepted on a limited basis.

The college offers additional course work for students planning to continue in technical fields, and extracurricular courses in art are offered. No special interest groups and activities are black-oriented.

The education at St. John's appeals to only a very few students. The director of admission states that St. John's has tried and failed at special recruiting attempts for black students and other minorities. Necessarily, "a small budget and limited staff means that all recruiting efforts are for all interested students."

ST. JOSEPH'S UNIVERSITY
Philadelphia, Pennsylvania 19131

Undergrads: 2,790
Black Undergrads: 148
Faculty: 354
Black Faculty: 2
Tuition: $18,720
Total Expenses: $24,775

If they had to do it all over again, would blacks at St. Joseph's go to a predominantly white college? Most would answer yes, based on the responses.

St. Joseph's, a dynamic, coed liberal arts university that is in touch with the needs of black students, pursues a very selective admission policy.

For the academically hungry student, St. Joseph's offers a veritable smorgasbord of degree programs. The College of Business and Administration houses one of six nationally recognized programs related to the food industry. The Food Marketing Program, which is wholly industry-supported, prepares students for careers in food retailing management, food service management, sales advertising, or research management.

You will have to do some digging to find the handful of courses on the black experience, but what black students might miss in the classroom, they get from the Black Culture Program (BCP) and the Black Awareness Society.

Both were formed to meet the needs of the growing number of black students at the university.

BCP provides a resource office for all aspects of university life for the black student culturally, educationally, and socially. "The BCP gives one a sense of self-awareness, confidence, and respect," declares one student. "It provides assistance on referrals to whatever your needs may be."

The tutorial assistance offered through the BCP is described as "readily available, with qualified students who are knowledgeable in their field."

Another student sums up his experience with the BCP this way: "It was there when I needed it."

Depending on whom you are asking, the amount of racial unity in campus party life is either "limited" or "good." Another student puts it this way: "There is great participation of blacks on and off campus at the parties, especially if the group or persons sponsoring it are black."

St. Joseph's has an abundance of athletic activities: varsity intercollegiate sports, six club teams, and intramural programs. Despite this wide range of choices, black representation in sports is generally low, except in basketball.

Similarly, black representation in university governance could stand some improvement. One student rates participation as "good—we try, but we need support."

Black alumns give their support. "Alumns have returned to take part in Black Culture Week, to give lectures, to participate in parties and other black culture program events," notes a respondent. Another adds, "I have had discussions with several black alumns. They were encouraging and supportive of your goals."

"I like learning about different cultures, but the white students do not make things easy for you because of their preconceptions of blacks," complains one respondent. These preconceptions are being dealt with by the Committee for Interracial Affairs, which is part of the BCP. The committee, billed as "the only committee of its type in all the nation's colleges and universities," is composed of a small group of black, white, and foreign students.

Through lectures, workshops, and rap sessions, the group seeks to "educate students and the university in the area of interracial affairs." According to one student, the committee "is a profitable endeavor to unite students of all races."

"The main issue is to study and achieve high grades in addition to socializing; both can be done with white students and black students," is one assessment.

"Because of its size, there can be more frequent one-time contact with faculty and administrators. I am very satisfied with my decision to attend a predominantly white school," reports one undergrad. "The attractive feature here is its very high academic standing."

SAINT XAVIER COLLEGE
Chicago, Illinois 60655

Undergrads: 3,353
Black Undergrads: 302
Faculty: 261
Black Faculty: NA
Tuition: $11,600
Total Expenses: $16,400

One student sees it this way: "Understanding oneself before attending a predominantly white school is important. I feel I have given myself a challenge, but I can fight it out."

Saint Xavier College is a small, Roman Catholic, liberal arts college established by the Sisters of Mercy. SXC is largely a commuter school, and is located in southwest Chicago. About half of its black students are in a continuing education program. SXC is selective in its admission.

Some of the strong academic fields at SXC are health sciences, education, business and social sciences. All students must complete core courses, and undergraduates can earn either a bachelor of arts or sciences degree. SXC boasts a 13-to-1 student-to-professor ratio.

The Continuing Education Program is open to men and women 23 years or older. To accommodate those who have other commitments, classes are offered during the day, at night or on weekends in the Weekend College.

Those who have been out of school for some time feel that most blacks adjust quite well, although for some it takes more time. However, for blacks entering SXC straight from high school, adjustment is difficult if they don't take school seriously.

A brother states, "Black students enter this school and form cliques. They identify with these same people throughout their stay here. Sometimes they don't identify with anyone at all. In this case, they isolate themselves from all students and may even drop out when things get tough."

SXC provides various support systems for the student body. Tutorial assistance is offered primarily in the areas of math, science, business and, on a limited basis, in English. Black students rate the tutorial services highly; they are easily accessible to those in need of help. Many different kinds of counseling services exist, including peer, minority peer, psychological, faculty, administrative and religious. Study skills workshops are given "at least twice a semester," according to one university official.

There are also special class sections in math, English and chemistry. Special seminars and workshops in such areas as academic advising, continuing education and adult education are sponsored by individual departments. Special seminars and workshops are offered each year.

The Black Student Organization (BSO) sponsors activities and events which are designed to encourage racial tolerance. The principal activities sponsored by BSO during the school year are Gospel Night, an Ethnic Food Festival and Black History Week.

The social life among the brothers and sisters at SXC is limited. The fact that most students commute tends to have an effect on campus activities. There are no black fraternities or sororities at SXC. One student's view on the participation of blacks in on-campus and off-campus parties: "They only attend black parties, and there aren't many of those on campus."

The interaction between black and white students is minimal, but the two groups get along "fairly well." Students say that they have not had any problems with either black, white or non-white faculty members or administrative officials.

On the other hand, watch out for the community. One black resident declares, "Blacks are despised in this neighborhood."

One respondent warns, "I would tell a black student not to expect a rose garden." Some attractive features of SXC are on-campus residency, the business, nursing and education programs, the financial aid awarded to blacks and the academic program. Some of the unattractive qualities are the cafeteria food and the relationship between the black students at SXC and members of the local community.

SAM HOUSTON STATE UNIVERSITY
Huntsville, Texas 77341

Undergrads: 10,886
Black Undergrads: 1,306
Faculty: 514
Black Faculty: NA
Tuition: $1,638; $6,660
Total Expenses: $4,798; $9,820

One brother's beginning criticism: "Black students on campus need to find some source of unity. Black faculty and administrators need to make themselves more visible to more students, and the BSU needs more support from both."

Between Houston and Dallas, two of the largest cities in the state, the less-selective SHSU is situated in Huntsville, a small community surrounded by beautiful lakes and camping areas. About 95 percent of the students are from Texas, and 98 percent of the entering freshmen come from public schools.

SHSU was established to prepare teachers for the Texas public school system. Pre-professional preparation and liberal arts education are also offered.

The university confers bachelor's degrees in many areas including applied arts and sciences, arts in criminal justice, business administration, radio/television/film, and social work. The curriculum also has pre-professional programs including dental hygiene, pharmacy, and physical therapy.

Only a few courses relate to the African-American or African experience.

Black students think that most of the blacks at SHSU have adjusted to the transition from high school to college level academic requirements very well, while another believes that the brothers and sisters need more encouragement.

Various support systems are available to the brothers and sisters at SHSU including tutorial assistance, counseling, study skills workshops, special class sections, and special seminars and workshops.

Some respondents have mixed reactions to the tutorial assistance programs, and most think greater publicizing is needed. The Counseling Center offers peer, faculty, and administrative help. One black student says that the counseling by faculty members is pretty good. Study skills workshops are offered mainly through fraternities and sororities. One brother on the subject of study skills workshops declares, "There are a few, but they are not publicized very much campus-wide."

Special seminars and workshops are offered in the College of Criminal Justice. Several students mention that these seminars and workshops are quite valuable.

SHSU sponsors a number of non-academic activities geared toward the black student. There are six predominantly black fraternities and sororities at SHSU. The Black Student Union and the Soul Lifters, a gospel singing group, are also popular black organizations. All of these groups sponsor social, cultural and service activities during the academic year.

Participation level of black students in these organizations is considered excellent. Frats and sororities also organize service projects in the local communities, so there is some opportunity for off-campus activities.

Black student participation in university governance, however, is low. One undergrad states, "There is virtually no participation from blacks in the university governance." Another feels, "They don't seem to realize that it's one of the strongest voices they have." A few students agree that the black religious groups are a source of unity. One sister says, "They offer a very strong bond for a great many students."

SHSU does not provide many programs that are designed to promote racial tolerance. The students confront this issue mostly through class work. The interaction between white and black students is, on the average, good. One respondent notes that the school is small enough to encourage interaction, and there is little tension among students.

Black undergrads get along with white faculty members and administrators fairly well. One student says that they are "helpful at times, but like anything else politics takes over." Relations between black faculty and administrators and students are (generally) smooth. The only complaint one students voices is: "There are not enough of them."

Responses to the subject of the interaction between black students and other non-white faculty members and administrators range from average to worthless. One respondent says, "They don't relate to us."

Some black students have not had any interaction with any of the residents of Huntsville. Those students who have had contact with the community have found the local residents to be "very involved." One student finds that the people in the community "are nice to college students and seem to be interested in the life of students."

Although student response about SHSU, located deep in the heart of Texas, is not overly enthusiastic, it is usually positive. One sister says, "Sam Houston has always been the school I have wanted to attend because of its business and education programs."

SAN DIEGO STATE UNIVERSITY
San Diego, California 92182

Undergrads: 23,182
Black Undergrads: 1,391
Faculty: 2,228
Black Faculty: NA
Tuition: $1,902; $7,380
Total Expenses: $7,526; $13,004

The adjustment to SDSU is not all that easy—and some never make it: only one-third of freshmen go on to graduate from the school. Certainly SDSU's academic and personal counseling helps alleviate many difficulties. And the beautiful beaches and sunny southern California weather must also go a long way toward picking up gloomy spirits.

If you have a surf board, like Mexican food, desert air, and business studies, then check out San Diego State. Located just a half hour from Mexico and two hours from Los Angeles, San Diego State is the biggest and most southern campus of the California State University and Colleges.

Established as a teachers' college in 1897, it now offers a variety of bachelor's degrees.

Of course all is not paradise at this beachhead university, despite the extensive support services for minority students. Relations with white faculty and students are described as "neutral" rather than good. "Many students feel alienated," a brother suggests, explaining the lack of black involvement in university governance.

Yet San Diego State seems to have a strong commitment to minorities. The Office of Student Outreach Services makes presentations at high schools with high percentages of minority students, and through its two affirmative action divisions, it both recruits minority students and offers specially tailored counseling services to them once they have matriculated at San Diego State. The school consists of several colleges and offers a wide variety of majors including Asian Studies, Mexican-American Studies, Counselor Education, Urban Studies, and Social Work.

The Afro-American Studies program features courses like The Psychology of Blackness and Ethnicity and Social Competence. Its professors "are like friends," according to one brother. There is a special ethnic library collection for research and supplemental reading in the field.

To help freshmen adjust to college-level academics there are study skills workshops offered throughout the year. These workshops as well as a special summer session for skill building are highly praised by brothers and sisters at SDSU. In addition, the Educational Opportunity Program (EOP), a minority recruitment project, maintains an advising center and has a staff of tutors. The various academic departments have tutors also.

Additionally, there is the Institute for Cultural Pluralism, which coordinates research and schedules training programs that will lead to the improvement of educational opportunities for minorities. It sponsors bilingual and multicultural educational projects.

Each freshman is assigned an upperclass "mentor" with similar academic interests and ethnic background. "The mentor is a tutor, counselor, friend, information resource," one respondent explains. This advising network gets high praise from most students.

Nine out of ten SDSU students are commuters looking for career-oriented professional training. About 15 percent major in business administration.

For pre-professionals at SDSU there is the Black Business Students Association, a black pre-med society, and a black science organization. For the liberal arts major there is the Afro-American Majors/Minors Association. All these organizations sponsor forums and provide information of special interest to blacks. In addition, there are Career Placement Department seminars for blacks, and other workshops and lectures are organized not only through the various colleges and departments, but also through the Black Student Union.

A Black Student Council oversees all other black organizations on campus, sponsors picnics and parties, and brings a few black professional entertainers to campus. Yet, "More black music and theater is desperately needed," a brother notes.

There is a black television program, but no black radio. The Black Repertory Total Theatrical Experience offers acting and dance exposure. Black churches are plentiful in the community. All-black intramural sports teams get their share of undergrads, but "you will not find many blacks on mixed teams," according to a brother.

Participation in varsity sports, especially basketball, is good except for the football team where there is said to be "noticeable racism." The "strong" Black Student Union with offices and entertainment space in the Aztec Center sponsors seminars and other activities.

But sports and dances constitute black social life for the most part, according to respondents. While fraternities are not very big at the school, they are an important part of black social life, students say, even though they are said to generate cliques when greater unity is needed. "Turn-outs are not so good unless it's a major issue," a respondent states about political rallies and cultural activities.

And another cautions, "Black students need to know that if they decide to attend any predominantly white school, they need to be prepared to deal with racism. . . . Don't lose your identity. Get to know black resources on campus and the black faculty."

SANTA CLARA UNIVERSITY
Santa Clara, California 95053

Undergrads: 4,100
Black Undergrads: 123
Faculty: 555
Black Faculty: NA
Tuition: $14,772
Total Expenses: $21,294

The zesty partying atmosphere of Santa Clara's campus life may appeal to the majority of students, but black students are not terribly happy with their environment. The concerns of the black student population at the University of Santa Clara seem neglected despite an educational philosophy centering around religious values. One respondent explains, "Most white faculty, and especially the administrators, try to show concern for black students, but still, there is a lot lacking."

Situated just 45 miles from San Francisco in the fast-growing city of Santa Clara is this coed, Catholic, independent institution. The University of Santa Clara is open to students of all faiths, and admission is selective.

Californians make up the majority of the black student population. Still, the University of Santa Clara attracts black students from Arizona, New York, Alaska, Pennsylvania and Illinois.

Degrees in business, math and science are most often pursued, but the university remains committed to the humanities and theology. Three courses in religious studies and one in ethics are required. The curriculum is diverse, but a student interested in developing an understanding of the African-American experience will be disappointed to learn that these courses are rarely offered. Their Da Vinci program is an interdisciplinary approach to the humanities, science, business and engineering.

The workload here is heavy, but the transition from high school to college-level requirements is, for the black student, no different than it is for anyone else. Says one upperclassman, "It's rough in the beginning but tapers smoothly in later stages."

A black student organization, Igwebuike, and two principal black student centers, Iaamont W. Allen and the Black Affairs Office, sponsor cultural activities and counseling programs. These are enjoyed and appreciated by a few students. Unfortunately, not only are most white students not willing to participate, but attendance by blacks is also reportedly poor for these activities.

"The biggest role black students play is in black organizations," responds one student when queried about the role black students play in university governance. "We are not involved in larger governance."

By contrast, students do, through recruiting assistance, reunion activities, special campus forums, career placement and summer employment, have good connections with black alumns.

Less can be said about their interaction with people in the local community. Even though the university upholds values that tend to be other-oriented and community-based, programs that involve students with the local community are almost impossible to find.

Black students relate especially well to the black faculty members. One student explains, "Because there are so few blacks on this campus, the interaction between those groups is a special one; we all try to get to know each other, we participate in each others' activities and we have a friendship." When questioned about their relationships with white professors, black students give a range of responses, from "not well" to "good."

Social activities seem geared toward the white student. Nevertheless, white students are friendly, and interaction is positive. Although self-segregation is more often the norm, some students have developed friendships which extend across racial lines. The pressure perceived by some as a message to assimilate hinder them from crossing such boundaries.

Says one student, "The whites are easy to get along with as long as they don't have to acknowledge that we are black and not just students." The scarcity of university-sponsored black professional and semi-professional entertainment, the relatively few campus wide activities that appeal to both whites and blacks, and a feeling expressed by an intramural participant that there may be some discrimination in the athletic sphere suggest further that black heritage remains somewhat unappreciated here.

Most live off campus. Over all, these students are not altogether dissatisfied. Concludes one respondent: "On a scale of one through ten, I'd give this school a six."

SAVANNAH STATE COLLEGE
Savannah, Georgia 31404

Undergrads: 3,211
Black Undergrads: 2,761
Faculty: 155
Black Faculty: NA
Tuition: $2,406; $5,175
Total Expenses: $5,106; $7,875

Students describe the campus as "very beautiful," and the faculty and administration are generally supportive. In fact, many instructors are SSC alumns, and many students, the children and grandchildren of alumns. These factors make for a sense of warmth, continuity and tradition on campus.

Sprawled across 136 acres in suburban Savannah, this state-supported, coed college boasts a 94-year heritage as the oldest institution of higher learning in Georgia founded specifically for the education of black students.

One student explains that attending a school like Savannah State "further identifies the black student with his race while preparing him to relate to other races and real world situations."

It is still a predominantly black school; whites make up 16 percent of the student body, and most of the faculty are not white. The majority of SSC's students are from Georgia, South Carolina, and Florida, and many are from the Savannah area itself.

About half of SSC's students live in university residence halls (four of which are fully air-conditioned). All students whose parents do not live in Chatham County, or who have not established legal residency there, are required to live in the dorms as long as space is available.

Admission requirements at SSC are not stringent, but once accepted, students are expected to perform to their full capacity. Many no-nonsense restrictions include obtaining documentation for missed classes and notifying instructors about missed classes.

SSC makes every effort to keep a vigilant eye on the academic endeavors of each student. Each freshman who is not sure of his major is assigned an advisor with whom to meet periodically and discuss his program of study. Several grade evaluation periods are held during each term. And students whose scores do not meet admission requirements, but who show some academic promise, are enrolled in the college's Developmental Studies Program, which offers remedial course work in English, reading and math.

Academic support is available on several levels at SSC. The Comprehensive Counseling Center offers academic, personal, social and career counseling, as well as test information. The Center employs both staff counselors and peer counselors who work on a student-to-student basis and offer tutorial services. One brother claims that peer counseling is "the most effective tutoring" at SSC.

In addition, each academic department sponsors tutoring programs, and most classes in one's major hold special meetings to discuss career opportunities in that field. However, some criticism is leveled by students at SSC's academic support system. It is noted that assistance is not offered in all subjects, but tends to concentrate on math, English, reading and the technical fields.

One student feels, "Tutorial assistance is not widely available," and another complains that counseling at SSC "lacks continuity." Several respondents feel that counseling and tutorial services are not well-utililized by their peers.

Savannah State College's degree programs in the humanities, social sciences, and business administration are augmented by internships in the local community and by membership in various campus pre-professional organizations. The college has several publications and communications clubs; a pre-med society which is deemed "quite useful" by its members; a pre-law society; and business organizations which, says one of their members, "expose students to business owners and experiences they would not ordinarily be exposed to during college."

The Department of Biology and Life Sciences offers two Ph.D. preparation programs, known as the Minority Biomedical Research (MBR) Program and the Minority Access to Research Careers (MARC) Program.

For students bitten by the broadcasting bug, and others with varying degrees of interest in radio, the campus station offers great experience and a chance to bring jazz, reggae, gospel and educational programming to the community. There is also a well-regarded theater company, "The Players by the Sea." But the group's facilities are lacking. Says one sister: "For a student enrollment of nearly two thousand, a theater that seats a maximum of two hundred and fifty people is useless."

But never fear; there are other things to do at SSC. Students are active in both intramural and varsity sports, and religion and religious groups are alive and well on campus. Students are not, however, very active in student government, and often such roles are repeatedly filled by the same people.

Fraternities generally play a sizable role in decision-making processes at SSC and provide a good source of social activity. One student explains that "most students aspire to become a member of one of these organizations." Another agrees, adding that Greek membership often increases competition in academics and leadership, providing an incentive to keep one's grades high. Most students agree that fraternities and sororities are an important part of the college community although one brother warns that their pledging procedures "sometimes get out of hand."

Interaction between SSC's black and white communities is minimal. Whites are not socially active on campus, says one brother, but are "welcome and well-respected by most of the black population." Relations between black students and white faculty and administrators are also cordial, but one sister objects to the white faculty's "informal manner" with black students, deeming it "not for real."

Most black students, say respondents, prefer black teachers to white; one explains that she feels black teachers "care more about the direction their students choose in life." A fellow student offers another explanation: "Some students feel intimidated by white instructors when there's really no need to be."

Says one senior: "SSC doesn't give their students any chance at all to communicate with or visit members of the opposite sex." Indeed, dorm life at SSC has its restrictions: no cooking equipment is allowed, and all residential students must be on meal plan.

SSC students are happy with their decision to attend a black institution. Says one senior: "Attending a historically black college has helped me find myself, and now I can relate more to my culture." As for Savannah State College in particular, most agree that it offers a pleasant environment for four years.

SEATTLE UNIVERSITY
Seattle, Washington 98122

Undergrads: 3,294
Black Undergrads: 132
Faculty: 334
Black Faculty: NA
Tuition: $13,635
Total Expenses: $18,174

The general limitations of the school's social life seem to be compensated by not only an active community close to the campus, but also by the black student organizations. And nearby University of Washington offers additional social options. If you can enjoy these particular advantages of the urban atmosphere here, then you will probably find Seattle University attractive.

Most of the black students attending Seattle, which is within walking distance of downtown, come from Washington (over 75 percent), California, and New York.

Recruitment of black students is limited, and occurs mainly in Washington high schools.

The curriculum includes a wide variety of disciplines such as nursing, education, business administration, engineering, and the liberal arts. An Institute of Public Service offers majors in human resources and public administration. Early admission to the college after the junior year of high school is possible for students with a GPA of 3.3 or above.

Many students comment that the transition from high school to college has been comfortable.

Some are dissatisfied with the effectiveness of the Learning Resource Center—especially when it comes to the needs of black students. One student comments, "We really have no assistance that is adequate to help black students." The center offers weekly workshops in note-taking, writing research papers, study skills, and taking exams, and provides tutoring services.

Yet the counseling services appear to be a valuable asset. Freshmen are scheduled to meet once a week to discuss academics and other matters. One student says, "I feel that this is one of the positive things we have going for black students on campus." The counseling office also promotes peer counseling through PACE (Peer Advising on the Collegiate Experience), designed to make the transition to university life easier. Teams of upperclass students are trained as peer advisors and meet with freshman during the fall quarter to discuss student concerns.

"The student must take the initiative in this situation," offers one student. Some students do not rely on the formal program at all, and look to black organizations for support. "Our Black Student Union is a source for advice for those beginning college." Faculty-to-student seems to be the weakest area in the counseling program.

Further, black students can find guidance and support through the Minority Student Affairs Office (MAO). This office coordinates ethnic-cultural programs and aids in the academic growth of students by setting up study groups and providing counseling services. Additionally, community resources are identified, and special seminars relevant to minority concerns are sponsored.

Working in cooperation with MAO, the Black Student Union (BSU) plays a central role in providing campus social activities. The BSU plans parties, picnics, and other activities of special interest to the black student. Both BSU and MAO support a radio station, run with another college.

Unfortunately, there are not many blacks involved in some of the more important functions of the university. The staff has very few full-time black faculty members.

A number of concerns are on the minds of black students here. "A stronger union between upperclassmen and the incoming students is what is needed to make black students feel more comfortable," observes one undergrad. One student complains about both the core requirements and a lack of understanding from the professors. Another student comments, "Those who stay on campus have a difficult time because dorm life here is not conducive to the learning process."

Interaction with white students is limited, but "non-hostile." There is contact within the classroom, but seldom in the social realm. One student explains, "Many white students on this campus are insensitive toward ethnic group cultures."

Feelings toward the white faculty are mixed. Some students feel they cannot or will not take the time to understand the black students' needs. The social life of the black student is usually tied to the BSU although students do get together to throw their own parties. There are no Greek organizations on Seattle's campus, but many students go to the Greek functions offered at the nearby University of Washington. Usually, entertainment groups and mixers sponsored by the university are not attended by black students. Intramural sports are popular with some black students and provide a valuable social outlet

The nearby community and the black student body interact positively. The city has a black population of over 45,000. Students find support through various predominantly black church congregations.

One resource is the Paul Robeson group, a community-based black theater project in residence at the University of Washington. Programs which place students in other community activities include the Sidney Miller Clinic, which provides tutoring to elementary students, and the politically oriented National Black United Front. Black politicians often visit the campus.

Describing the black presence, one student says this about small, selective, liberal arts, and Jesuit-influenced Seattle: "The pressure to succeed in a predominantly white school is great." It seems that most students come well prepared to tackle the academic demands, but other circumstances may affect one's performance."

SKIDMORE COLLEGE
Saratoga Springs, New York 12866

Undergrads: 2,129
Black Undergrads: 43
Faculty: 262
Black Faculty: NA
Tuition: $19,950
Total Expenses: $25,840

L ooking for an intimate, small campus with a liberal arts curriculum as well as cooperative programs in engineering, business and architecture? You might find Skidmore appealing. However, repondents say look for chilly town/gown relations and the occasional need to explain to white students what your needs are.

Located in scenic upstate New York, in a residential area 30 miles from Albany and originally a college for women, Skidmore has a very selective admission policy.

Government and English are considered to be two of the best departments, while a combination of business and economics with other courses is possible. Skidmore's theater and music programs are highly respected also.

Courses in the black experience include African-American Literature, History of Jazz in America, and Race Relations and Minority Groups.

Most black respondents agree that the transition from high school to college has been comfortable. One student comments, "At first, it is difficult to get used to the heavier load of work, but once they get organized, they usually don't have any major problems."

The smoothness of the transition may be attributable to the Higher Education Opportunity Program for New York state residents. This program includes supportive services such as counseling, pre-freshman academic work, tutoring and special class sections.

A full counseling service is available, as well as study skills workshops. Both Career Planning and the Minority Affairs Office (MAO) help black students find summer jobs, and MAO plans to publish a black alumni directory.

BAM, the Black Action Movement, meets every two weeks, and they plan discussion grops, forums and social activities including parties.

Last year's celebrations included Black History Month, Black Solidarity Day, Ethnic Meals Fest, Kwanzaa and Dr. M.L.K., Jr. Week.

SMITH COLLEGE
Northhampton, Massachusetts 01063

Undergrads: 2,668
Black Undergrads: 107
Faculty: 292
Black Faculty: NA
Tuition: $19,814
Total Expenses: $26,484

Although blacks at Smith are a small minority and the college is located in a small white community (one percent black population), the black presence is strong. Respondents seem to agree that personal strength is important for those aspiring to attend Smith. Creativity and flexibility are part of planning one's program of study at Smith College. This small, private liberal arts college for women offers a variety of academic programs leading to a bachelor of arts degree, a master's or a doctoral degree. One of the seven sister schools, Smith has a highly selective admission policy.

In addition to the traditional majors in the arts and sciences, Smith offers non-traditional majors such as Afro-American Studies, Theater and Education, and Child Studies. There are various interdepartmental majors including American Studies and Ancient Studies. Pre-medical and other pre-health professional programs can be arranged with advisors.

Smith participates in a five-college cooperation program with Amherst, Hampshire, Mount Holyoke and the University of Massachusetts in which faculty and other resources are combined to offer students more extensive educational opportunities. Smith also participates in a 12-college exchange program, intended primarily for the junior year. Other exchange programs include junior year abroad, a semester in Washington program and a year's study at one of several historically black colleges.

Students who encounter difficulty with their work have access to a Center for Academic Assistance, where they are directed to peer tutors. Tutorial help is also available in developing and improving writing skills.

Extensive counseling services are available to Smith students. In addition to professional student counseling services, Health Services offers a peer support hotline which is "completely anonymous." The Career

Development Office sponsors several study skills workshops throughout the year and provides excellent career counseling services, including bringing students and alumnae together. "They keep the alumnae connections strong all over the U.S. and internationally," one student advises.

A pre-orientation workshop for incoming minority frosh called the Bridge Program is scheduled "to promote cultural and racial awareness and to help minority students ease into a predominantly white institution." A lecture series entitled "Bridges to Pluralism" is conducted throughout the year and is aimed at specific minority groups. Racial awareness workshops are presented by students to "promote or encourage racial tolerance in the houses and on campus."

Although there is no separate black theater on campus, black student participation in theater is very strong. Several plays are produced each year that relate to the black experience. These plays are well-attended by both black and white students; so are performances by Genesis, a black gospel choir. Sustained black participation is seen also in the pre-med and pre-law societies on campus.

Considering the small number of blacks on Smith's campus, the black voice in student government is very strong.

Black-specific organizations on campus are the Black Student Alliance, which sponsors numerous lectures and activities, and the student chapter of the NAACP, which is "a very strong group on campus."

Smith supports its intercollegiate athletic teams including basketball, gymnastics, swimming and track. Black participation in varsity sports is "not too good" at Smith although participation in intramural sports is "better," according to reports.

There are no sororities at Smith. House (dormitory) parties are not well-attended by black students although "the Five College Program gives the Smith student an opportunity to go to parties beyond the house parties." Parties sponsored by the Black Student Alliance are very well-attended, both by Smith students and students from neighboring towns and colleges. In general, however, black women at Smith have a complaint: "a lack of social life."

The relationship between black students and white students on campus is described as "fairly good." One student comments, "Interaction between the races could be improved, but it is not a situation where one could become alienated." Interaction with white faculty and administrators is "very smooth." Ties between black students and black faculty are seen as especially strong, particularly in the Afro-American department.

"I think black students applying to Smith must have a strong sense of self and a strong black identity," declares one undergrad. Echoes another: "The smoothest transition only happens for those who are secure with their race and culture and who possess an open mind."

SPELMAN COLLEGE
Atlanta, Georgia 30314

Undergrads: 1,961
Black Undergrads: 1,922
Faculty: 209
Black Faculty: 159
Tuition: $8,875
Total Expenses: $14,765

"At Spelman, you learn to become sure of yourself without the added factor of racism," asserts one undergrad. "I've never received a grade and wondered if it was because I was black."

The college traces its beginning back 115 years as the first American college for black American women. The namesake of Mrs. Harvey Spelman (John D. Rockefeller's mother-in-law), the school began in a Baptist church basement. The overwhelming sense of pride in Spelman is one of the keys to the sense of sisterhood found here.

Situated on 32 magnolia-shaded acres in the heart of Atlanta, the college offers a diverse liberal arts curriculum leading to a B.A. or B.S. degree. Together with its "brother" school, all-male Morehouse College, Spelman is a member of the Atlanta University Center (AUC) of seven black institutions on adjoining campuses.

The consortium includes four undergraduate schools: Spelman, Morehouse, Clark, and Morris Brown. The three graduate facilities are Atlanta University, Interdenominational Theological Center, and Morehouse College of Medicine.

Spelman features majors in African and Afro-American Studies, with a supplementing special library collection. There are also pre-med, pre-law, and education humanities offerings. In conjunction with Georgia Tech, there is a 3-2 liberal arts/engineering program. Internships and placement in community agencies can supplement academics and provide valuable professional experience.

To help smooth the switch from high school to college-level academics, Spelman offers a variety of support services. The AUC Student Crisis Center offers counseling, special seminars and course sections, tutoring, and writing and study skills workshops.

For the undergrad seeking advice about careers, Spelman maintains an Office of Life Planning, and offers workshops in both résumé writing and business and leadership skills. There is also a Health Career Office and Club.

Spelman alumns participate in everything from recruiting to commencement exercises, and a number of members of the black faculty are also Spelman graduates.

Organizations include the Student Government Association, yearbook, the newspaper, the Institute on Third World Policy, the Library Club, the Society for International Students, and Sisters-In-Blackness.

Intramural sports include flag football, bowling, basketball, softball, cross country running, and gymnastics. The Atlanta University Morehouse-Spelman Players "run the gamut of culturally enriching performances." The Drama Department, Center Dance Theater, Morehouse-Spelman Glee Club, orchestra, and an award-winning debate team form a broad spectrum of extracurricular "performing" arts.

The social life at Spelman seems to be a bustling variety of cultural and social activities. Sororities have been on the Spelman campus since 1978. They too offer a form of socializing through mixers and various other activities.

One student asserts, "This school makes me realize that my education is my responsibility, not the school's, and that conclusion would apply at any school, anywhere."

"Spelman not only motivates you to reach higher goals, but it also gives you the equipment to reach these goals," boasts one sister.

STANFORD UNIVERSITY
Stanford, California 94305

Undergrads: 6,577
Black Undergrads: 526
Faculty: 1,455
Black Faculty: NA
Tuition: $19,797
Total Expenses: $26,851

"D on't use college as an opportunity to change. Use it as an opportunity to grow," advises a senior. "Whether it's at a black college or predominantly white college, one should know oneself and maintain his or her true identity."

Stanford, 29 miles south of San Francisco, is a liberal arts institution awarding both undergraduate and graduate degrees. It is also one of the most highly selective colleges in the U.S. Stanford has an exchange program with Howard University as well as opportunities to participate in international living through its Stanford Overseas Studies Office.

Senior respondents agree that black students adjust to Stanford well. "It takes them almost their entire first year to make the social and academic transition," says one. For students who have trouble making the transition, there are many tutorial and counseling services.

Says one brother about tutorial assistance, "I would grade Stanford an A+ in this area because not only are the teaching assistants accessible, but so are most upperclass students, who are willing to take other students under their wings." Plus, Stanford provides a tutorial network. And student willingness to work in groups "makes the university great."

As for counseling, one student mentions the "excellent resources" at the Bridge, which has 24-hour peer counseling. The list continues with Counseling and Psychological Services, and Cowell Health Center. Writes one senior, "The main counseling comes from student advisors, who do a great job." Also, "The black faculty are very supportive," according to another respondent.

The Center for Teaching and Learning offers reading and writing workshops. "They are good but focus mainly on self-help, with the student setting an individual pace," says one undergrad. "Some students might need more structure."

Outside the classroom, social, and political organizations abound. The Black Community Services Center, for example, houses the various black student organizations and publications. It also sponsors social events and serves as an all-purpose "hang-out." Students who want to learn more about the African or African-American culture on a day-to-day basis apply to live in coed Ujamaa House. Ujamaa provides a comfortable living environment and it facilitates cultural exchange through speakers, plays, soul food dinners, and rap sessions.

Black organizations include the Black Community Yearbook, Black Society of Graduate Students, Stanford Black Music Association, various fraternities and sororities, and the Vision newspaper. One student describes the black pre-med society as "very useful." Another says it is "excellent" because the members "provide the support necessary for each other...in such stressful majors."

The Black Pre-law Society, however, is variably "useful" and "not so useful." The first respondent complains, "Students do not participate as vigorously as they could." Declares another, "Over the years I've attended Stanford, this organization has not been functioning well." The National Society for Black Engineers is considered "excellent." The members tutor each other and organize trips.

Students audition for the annual production by the Committee on Black Performing Arts. Stanfunk "features acting, singing, and dancing. Almost everyone is able to perform." Says one listener: "Top-notch. It generates widespread interest in its activities." And the campus radio station, KZSU, "has the best black programming in the Bay area," according to a sister.

Every Sunday night, the school holds black church services. One student believes this is "a great way to foster a sense of community." Stanford's students also interact with the surrounding community. The gospel choir has visited the nearby black community of Palo Alto. The Society of Black Engineers has tutored elementary and high school students in the general area. Black fraternities and sororities sponsor the off-campus tutoring programs, The Guide Right, School America, and Operation Chill. Students also volunteer at nearby counseling organization Free At Last.

One student writes that parties are unsuccessful as the years go by, but many blacks participate in these and in intramural sports. Meanwhile, few blacks participate in black center or university-sponsored activities. Still, some students praise the quantity and quality of all these activities.

Assessing black student involvement in school government, one says, "We have a lot of representation on university student committees, but the committees themselves have limited power." A conflicting perspective is that black activity is "fair to low, but maybe from lack of trying." Another says that black students have held a number of leadership positions including Senior President, Associated Students of Stanford University senators, and Council of Presidents member.

Student assessment of racial interaction varies. Black and white students are "polite, but not intimate," say most respondents. There is little overt racial tension. "Mostly, however, we all try to coexist," reports a student leader. Another view is, "I have not experienced any strife. I think most Stanford students are able to respect differences."

One brother finds his relationship with white faculty and administrators "positive for the most part. I wish I was more comfortable talking with them. I could have made my experience better by being more assertive." As for contact with their black counterparts, a student reports, "There is a very close-knit relationship here."

Contact with black alumns is "one of the most positive aspects of Stanford." Says another, "The alumns I have had contact with are mostly successful. Some are engineers; some are Wall Street traders; some even play in the NFL."

A senior's advice: "I chose Stanford for its academics, as I feel all students should choose universities for academics. A predominantly white school is good for learning how to deal with different attitudes and understanding where they come from...all things that you'll meet in the 'real world' and have to confront. I think a homogeneous environment...is insulated from these things and provides no 'preparation' for the post-graduate world. Stanford's academics and professors are excellent and, from my experience, genuinely interested in relations with students. These types of contacts become useful after school and may make a difference in where you go and how far."

STATE UNIVERSITY OF NEW YORK

Albany, New York 12222

Undergrads: 10,197
Black Undergrads: 918
Faculty: 1,039
Black Faculty: NA
Tuition: $3,956; $8,300
Total Expenses: $8,792; $13,136

Overall for blacks, it is not very sunny at SUNY. Improvement in the racial environment at The State University of New York at Albany (SUNYA) may be still in the future but, as this student explains: "It is three times as hard for a black student here which is why so many drop out. But my ancestors never stopped fighting, and neither will I."

SUNYA is the oldest of the 64 campuses composing the SUNY system and employs a very selective admission policy. Its 500-acre modern complex is located within Albany, the state capital.

"Its most attractive features are expenses, location, reputation, and academics," says one student. Another student agrees, but adds, "A black student entering SUNYA must be aware not only of the racist environment, but she must also realize the academic and competitive excellence available here."

SUNYA offers 45 majors leading to a bachelor's degree. These programs include African/Afro-American Studies. Students can also choose from 63 second fields or minors including journalism, religious studies, and urban studies. Self-designed majors are available as well.

But remember, SUNYA is not easy: "If blacks realize this fact before mid-terms, they can receive help by obtaining tutors and attending workshops to better their study skills," according to one student. Academic counseling, tutoring, and study skills workshops are offered through the Educational Opportunity Program (EOP) and the Office of Minority Student Services.

For career counseling, there is the Minority Business Association or the Minority Science Club, as well as the programs available at the EOP office. Cultural support organizations, such as the Albany State University Black

Alliance (ASUBA) and the Pan-Caribbean Association, are active and "excellent."

Race relations on campus, however, earn poor reviews by virtually all respondents. One student describes interaction with white students as "distant." White faculty and administrators are "insensitive." Explains one student: "The superficiality that white students function with is carried over into the almost lily-white administration." With black faculty and administrators, there is "not enough interaction."

According to a respondent, there is a deep level of understanding from black administrators and faculty, "but we still need to capitalize upon this."

Racial tensions seep into SUNYA's social life as well. One student puts it this way: "The campus social activities are geared toward white students. Emphasis is placed on rock music and big beer bashes." Another student notes, "Most parties given by black fraternities and sororities have a great amount of participation by blacks." A third student gives this sad commentary: "Parties are the only social outlet for blacks on this campus."

In varsity athletics, the story is the same. "Too much discrimination exists; therefore, blacks either do not try out or try out and are turned down." Despite intercollegiate teams, "Blacks can be counted on three fingers," says one student. Another is optimistic: "SUNYA varsity sports are known for their racism, but with some help things will eventually change."

It looks as if things are changing already. SUNYA sponsors a two-day "multicultural awareness workshop" each year before school begins.

According to a university official, the "student participants include the leaders of organized minority student groups as well as student government leaders, the student newspaper editor, radio station manager, etc." The workshop aims to promote cultural awareness and understanding through discussions, group exercises, and films.

On the admissions front, the university has recently formed a Minority Recruitment Program to address the underrepresentation of blacks as well as other minority groups. There is also an active Minority Alumni Association, which has activities for enrolled students, assists in recruiting, and plans reunions for minority alumns.

STATE UNIVERSITY OF NEW YORK
Buffalo, New York 14260

Undergrads: 16,150
Black Undergrads: 1,130
Faculty: 1,693
Black Faculty: NA
Tuition: $4,060; $8,300
Total Expenses: $9,336; $13,576

The university is happy about recruiting black students, say respondents, but loses enthusiasm for their social needs after they enroll. This lack is the main reason why many of the university's black students are unhappy with SUNY Buffalo—a large, public, selective institution located five miles from downtown. Complains one respondent, "Everything is geared toward the white students."

The curriculum offers bachelor's degree programs in business, education, engineering and liberal arts. The curriculum does allow a student to pursue a degree in African-American Studies.

Most of the university's black students come from New York, New Jersey and Pennsylvania.

The move from high school to college-level academics is easy for those blacks who are prepared well, and "rough" for those who aren't. One student states, "Often black students cannot adjust to the transition from high school to a big university. Most blacks transfer or flunk out. Only a few graduate."

For those blacks who have trouble with the university's academic environment, the college offers many tutorial and counseling programs. Tutorial assistance is available at the Learning, Reading and Writing Centers. Study skill workshops exist also.

The University Counseling Center and Buffalo's "Drop In" Center are the major resources for counseling.

Most brothers and sisters join the Educational Opportunity Program (EOP), a healthy mixture of counseling and tutoring, with an emphasis on counseling.

Yet this particular program has not been accepted by all of Buffalo's blacks. As one student observes, "Students get turned off by the humiliation counselors put them through. Most counselors discourage your ambitions and career goals if your grades are not acceptable."

Interaction between black students and white students is usually "tolerable," but one student states, "There seem to be many racial conflicts between blacks and whites in the dormitories." Black student-faculty interaction is minimal at best simply because there aren't many black faculty and administrators at the university. Relationships with the white faculty and administrators are practically non-existent. Many brothers and sisters feel that white faculty and administrators are, "Uncompassionate, strict and very impatient."

Communication with the local community is infrequent. Many black students who live off campus feel that their landlords are racist and, therefore, dislike renting to black students.

Some blacks complain about the small percentage of black students in student government. Contact with black alumns has been limited for all students. Some students make efforts to keep in touch with recent graduates, but the university still has no formal alumn program.

Many brothers and sisters at the university feel that the social life is "alright" but that it could be better. While the university does have a few fraternities on its campus, there are no black sororities. A majority rate the parties on campus highly. The word is that the fraternities usually throw the best functions.

The Black Student Union is the university's main black student organization, but students give it mixed reviews. Some feel that the BSU is strong; others feel that it doesn't do enough and suffers from lack of black student input. They agree, however, that if black student organizations don't sponsor cultural or social events for themselves, then the university will not "pick up the slack."

The Black Engineering Society is the only black pre-professional organization for the university's black students. Moreover, there is no black theater program or black religious services on campus. Intramurals are fairly popular with the university's black students, with basketball being the sport in which most blacks participate.

Any student not willing to work hard here is in for a long four years—and maybe more—at SUNY Buffalo.

STETSON UNIVERSITY
DeLand, Florida 32720

Undergrads: 1,950
Black Undergrads: 58
Faculty: 197
Black Faculty: NA
Tuition: $13,700
Total Expenses: $18,500

It appears that Stetson's black students are paying more than tuition to obtain the education they respect so highly.

"If you are looking for a small, private institution for quality education, then come here, but also be prepared to pay for it and study hard," says an undergrad about Stetson, located in sunny Florida, 25 miles from Daytona Beach.

Founded in 1883, Stetson is an independent, coed college with a student to teacher ratio of 13:1. The university offers academic diversity in an uncrowded, personal environment. The four schools within the university are arts and sciences, business administration, music and law.

Stetson recruits by visiting predominantly black high schools, attending NSSFMS fairs and other minority recruitment fairs. In addition, a relationship with Upward Bound has been established, and seminars are given in churches on choosing a college. The home states of the black students here are mostly Florida, Georgia and South Carolina.

Although Stetson does not offer a major in black/African-American studies, it does offer related courses like Race and Ethnic Relations, Multinational USA, Geography of Africa, Introduction to Islam and other courses where the African/African-American experience is an important component.

To make life easier, tutorial services and counseling are available, especially in math and English. "Professors," says one student, "have flexible office hours," and student tutors are available in most departments. In addition, study skills workshops are offered three times a semester by the counseling center. And fraternities and sororities offer study skills workshops. Peer counseling is available along with most other counseling for other problems.

Also available are special honors classes, and religious and leadership seminars.

Stetson's Faculty Senate has endorsed a policy designed to actively increase racial diversity. All official university policies are non-discriminatory, and many encourage racial tolerance.

There don't seem to be any black student organizations, but the university says that an African-American organization is in formation.

For cultural enrichment, black students must wait for special events like the Coalition of Student Responsibility's sponsoring tributes during the month of February to Martin Luther King, Jr.

University-sponsored events are not generally attended unless it is of direct interest, or if speakers or performers are black.

Social life has serious gaps too. One student says, "Most black students party off campus if they are not in a Greek organization."

"The Greek system is dominated by the white students," says another student. Still, a different respondent declares, "There are certain fraternities/sororities that seem to be more open to blacks."

Intramural sports, another outlet, are basically Greek-oriented, and as one student puts it, "Since there aren't many blacks in the frats or sororities, very, very few blacks participate." However, the men's basketball team is mainly black, with only one black each on the women's basketball, soccer and volleyball teams.

The opportunity for blacks to have an active role in the university governance is there, but as one student says, "Many black students neglect to take the opportunity."

Students report that the transition to college is handled well. One student concludes, "Blacks that are accepted are outstanding, and only some have expressed minor problems." Another student says, "The adjustment is smooth since most of the black students who come to Stetson know that the academic pressure is high." Another student suggests that adjusting academically is easier if the social aspects go well.

STILLMAN COLLEGE
Tuscaloosa, Alabama 35403

Undergrads: 842
Black Undergrads: 834
Faculty: 73
Black Faculty: NA
Tuition: $5,200
Total Expenses: $8,300

Students are positive about their choice of attending Stillman. "Come academically well-prepared," advises one student about small, Presbyterian Church related, coed and definitely black Stillman College.

Founded originally as a divinity school, the college still requires five semesters of religion and regular attendance at chapel, assemblies and convocations. It offers bachelor's degrees in sciences, business, elementary education, communications and computer science, among others.

The African-American experience is integrated in the curriculum, and courses include history (African and American) oral traditions and Hausa.

Admission counselors visit several high schools in Alabama, Mississippi, Georgia and Florida throughout the academic year. Alumni too participate in many ways including attending college fairs in their areas and visiting high schools on behalf of Stillman.

Campus visits are encouraged for sub-freshmen, either individually or in groups.

Once on campus, students will discover that tutorial assistance—considered "very helpful"—is available through the Student Support Services Program and the Cordell Wynn Honors Program, which has teaching assistants.

Further, the Student Development Center provides individual and group counseling services. A respondent notes that the counseling is "very helpful for grades, career planning and for depressed moments." Other psychological or social services not available on campus are referred to local agencies.

For improved academic achievement, study skills workshops are held periodically, usually in groups. The Freshman Basic Studies course focuses on study habits. Seminars and workshops on graduate school, Career Day and test-taking are held continuously.

To stay busy, Stillman students can participate in activities of the Student Government Association, Pan-Hellenic Council, seven Greek organizations, Masonic Lodge, Chancellorettes and Chancelors. Students can also organize at the Samuel Burney Hay College Center and take advantage of the art gallery, snack bar, bowling, billiards, dancing, health fairs and other activities.

Students rate the participation in the student center as good. Parties are rated favorably, but one student complains that more activity is needed in the dorms. Gauges another: "There is good participation for university-sponsored activities from both students and faculty."

Intramural sports received mixed comments. One student remarks that "There are more guys participating than girls," but another suggests that the program still provides a major recreational outlet for students.

Stillman students are active in the college governance, with undergrads on almost every committee and students are represented on the Board of Trustees.

Alumns have assisted in providing job leads for students and serving as consultants for programs involving placement and co-ops. Alumns attend Homecoming, Founder's Day and various alumn meetings.

All respondents report positive interaction between blacks and whites. There are not many white students, but interaction is good. Faculty and student interaction is also reportedly good. One student says, "Most of the whites on the faculty I know are very nice and try to help."

"I am very satisfied attending a predominantly black college. It enhances my self-esteem and cares about me," says one undergrad.

Concludes another: "I have been given a chance to accomplish a dream."

SYRACUSE UNIVERSITY
Syracuse, New York 13210

Undergrads: 10,097
Black Undergrads: 909
Faculty: 1,343
Black Faculty: NA
Tuition: $16,280
Total Expenses: $23,430

You should know that Syracuse emphasizes the integration of all students into all aspects of university life. The school does not exalt the special interests of minority groups. So, say respondents, learn to deal with your white peers, be serious about your career goals, and use the help that is available when you need it.

Syracuse is a comprehensive university, providing for study in many professional areas as well as in the traditional liberal arts field. Large, private, and coed, it has a selective admission policy.

The Afro-American Studies program offers more than three dozen courses through an interdisciplinary approach including the culture, litera- ture, history, and socioeconomic parameters of Afro-Americans and the linkage with continental Africa and the Caribbean areas.

University libraries house extensive collections pertaining to African- Americans, Africans, and Afro-Caribbeans.

When you apply to Syracuse University, you do not apply to the university as a whole, but to one of its more than 16 individual schools or colleges. Some highly recommended degree programs are housed in the S.I. Newhouse School of Public Communication, the School of Management, the College of Visual and Performing Arts, and the School of Architecture.

Other attractive features include specialized programs such as the Division of International Programs Abroad, the Community Internship Program, the Honors Program, and a Gerontology Center. Brothers and sisters have, with effort, adjusted well to the college-level academic requirements at Syracuse. As one student puts it, the university "does not tolerate anyone who is here merely to play games. The professors, admin- istrators, and staff are more than helpful to students and are willing to provide you with what is necessary to be a successful student."

Non-departmental courses designed to help students improve their educational attitudes and their reading, writing, and study skills are offered for credit. Study skills workshops and tutors are available in most subjects. The Office of Minority Affairs pays for 10 hours of tutoring for freshmen and sophomores. Black pre-professional societies are said to provide moral support, academic motivation, and a link to the "real world" for students interested in law, medicine, engineering, and business.

There is no black student center on campus, but rather a variety of organizations which support black culture. The Black Celestial Choral Ensemble, which produced an album several years ago, is very influential in the black community and important to students with any kind of religious background. A black theater organization provides another medium for the proud portrayal of black culture.

Brothers and sisters are active in the Campus Urban league and the Student Afro-American Society, which brings speakers and movies to the university and works with the general Student Government Association. Meanwhile, campus-based radio programming catering to blacks has some limited time slots.

Though one student asserts that blacks and whites at Syracuse get along well because: "We're all here for the same thing—to get that SU degree," others attest to the lack of racial interaction. Perhaps most telling is the comment: "Most whites seem nice." While there is little or no hostility, there also seems to be little or no personal communication between blacks and whites.

Though limited in number, students find black faculty and administrators very helpful.

Relations with white faculty and administrators are "good" on the whole: a student states that there are "a handful who are truly willing to help." One undergraduate observes: "Since the university is so big, you have to make a real effort to get to know faculty and administrators—whether you're black or white."

Black students may find themselves in a double bind with the local community in Syracuse. First, a communication barrier exists between locals who think that students "up on the hill" are haughty, and students who think the "townies" are troublemakers.

Second, blacks have to cope with the racial prejudices of the predominantly white city. According to one undergraduate, "The whites in the local stores treat blacks differently when they find out they are SU students, i .e., their vocabulary exceeds a fifth-grade level."

While student/community interaction is generally low, there are several positive ways for blacks to get involved in off-campus activities. The Afro-American Studies Department offers a course that is a supervised internship with a local community agency. Black fraternities and sororities have worked with community centers on after-school programs and reportedly do participate in local political events. The Black Celestial Choral Ensemble, mentioned above, sings in community churches. During Black Expressions Month in February, students add to the political and cultural activity of the community.

Students express mixed opinions about extracurricular activities on campus. Though a number of black students are actively involved in university governance, it is "not as much as we all would like." The Student Afro-American Society, according to one undergraduate, is "good, but has little cohesiveness."

Students do, however, voice unanimous enthusiasm for the black choir, the Creation Dance Troupe, the varsity athletics program, and a career day, sponsored by the Office for Minority Affairs, which gives students an opportunity to discuss the career world with black alumns.

Most black students attend the parties given by black Greeks on campus. One student remarks: "There are no problems between black Greeks and white Greeks." For many blacks the problem with campus-wide social events, such as the bi-annual picnics, is that they tend to cater to the tastes of the white majority. Some note that kegs of beer and rock music aren't their idea of a great time. Says one student, "There is usually no alcohol at black parties, just good rhythm and blues music." Another claims: "Blacks are not known as drinkers on campus."

For students who seek the academic depth and diversity that a large university has to offer, and who make the effort to participate in the many offices, services, and organizations available, Syracuse can be a rewarding college experience.

TALLADEGA COLLEGE
Talladega, Alabama 35160

Undergrads: 786
Black Undergrads: 778
Faculty: 67
Black Faculty: NA
Tuition: $6,084
Total Expenses: $9,048

Students seem happy about their decision to attend a historically black college. All respondents agree that the most attractive feature about Talladega is its beautiful campus and the historical buildings. One student declares, "It's most unattractive feature has to be the same as many academic institutions—the food is terrible; but you are here for an education."

Located in the foothills of the Blue Ridge Mountains, independent, coed and liberal arts Talladega College is Alabama's oldest historically black college, established in 1867. Its bachelor's degree offerings in business administration, biology and English are most popular, and it also offers the bachelor of music degree. Pre-professional programs exist in engineering, allied health, and legal and civil professional studies.

Talladega's programs combine study in and out of the classroom, and on and off campus, including opportunities at Los Alamos National Research Laboratories, AT&T Bell laboratories and dual degree programs with five other universities.

Afro-American History, Survey of African History, The Rise of African Nationalism and Central Themes in African Studies are some of the courses related to the black experience offered at least every two years.

Talladega admissions officers visit private and public high schools, and are active in arranging visits for black sub-freshmen. The Alumni Affairs Office has a plan whereby every alumn, faculty staff and student of Talladega will recruit at least one student for enrollment at the college. Students come from Alabama, Georgia, Illinois and Florida to attend Talladega.

Says one student about the adjustment to college-level academics, "The majority of the students have adjusted very well. They are taking up the responsibilities needed on a college-level program."

Still, tutorial assistance is offered by the Office of Special Services, the Department of Business and Finance, and other departments. Students say they that the assistance is helpful. One student proclaims, "It helped me to improve my overall grade-point average."

"There is a sufficient amount of counseling; someone is always there for you to turn to," reports one undergrad. Seminars and workshops are on-going and offered through various departments, in particular through the Department of Business and Finance.

The Career Planning and Placement Office offers special seminars and workshops also, including the Business Olympics, where students compete in job interviewing contests.

There are enough organizations and clubs to keep students socially active too. Among the 20 are the Student Government Association, Students in Free Enterprise, Business and Econ Club, Kennon Investment Group, Pre-Law Society, Society of English Scholars, Talladega College Dance Company, 10 Greek organizations, National Honor Society, Little Theater, Talladega Jazz Band, Biology and Chemistry clubs, Cheerleaders, Choir and Spanish and German clubs.

Students usually gather at the Callanan Union Building, where "most students are when they are not in class or studying."

Greek organizations play an important role at Talladega both for students and the community, through various work such as raising money for UNCF, for instance. One student says, "They could do more if they were organized and didn't take things so in stride."

Parties are generally viewed favorably. One respondent notes, "Students get involved with these activities and hold them in high regards." Another student says, "There is a lot of participation in parties that are Greek, off campus, or in dormitories."

Students report that interaction between black faculty and students is close. "Interaction seems to bring about a bond between the two." Another declares: "Interaction between students and white faculty and administration is also close; about the same as with black faculty." Relations between white and black students "is casual."

Students are quite active in university governance. Students are elected to serve on the Board of Trustees, College Council and Judiciary Review

Committee. Respondents report that Stillman brothers and sisters are active and "try to stay updated on the institutional situation." However, one student argues that the students at Talladega have very little to say about the process of the college and other matters.

Alumns also attend Alumni Weekend once a year, and attend reunion and commencement activities. In addition, several alumni return during the year to discuss their careers and assist students in obtaining summer internships. The alumni association sponsors a Welcoming Dance and picnics.

Advantages of attending Talladega? One student says, "It not only helps me to learn about my culture and heritage, but it also helps me to become closer to my brothers and sisters. Black schools are provided to help black youths further their education."

TEXAS WOMEN'S UNIVERSITY
Denton, Texas 76204

Undergrads: 5,783
Black Undergrads: 867
Faculty: 763
Black Faculty: 14
Tuition: $1,648; $7,408
Total Expenses: $4,818; $10,578

Overall, students seem satisfied with TWU. They like the relaxed atmosphere of the university being predominantly women. This allows for "a warmth and openness...an atmosphere that has been supportive and nurturing."

Texas Women's University, 35 miles from Dallas, is a teaching and research institution primarily for women. Sitting on a 270-acre campus, it emphasizes liberal arts and health sciences.

Black students attending TWU come mostly from Texas, Louisiana and Mississippi. TWU has an admission counselor who specifically recruits minority students through NSSFMS fairs and NAACP ACT-SO student competitions, and black alumns are involved in the Alumnae Admissions recruitment program.

TWU also schedules open houses at the TWI Houston Center and provides chartered buses so minority students from around the state can visit the Denton campus. Other efforts at recruitment include phonothons, scholarship programs for minority students, visiting two-year colleges, and a direct-mail program which involves the purchase of names from Student Search and other organizations.

Transition seems to go smoothly. One student says, "The academic requirements are stated specifically for each student, and the majority of students apply themselves to these requirements." Support systems are rated favorably by the undergrads. One remarks, "The school has a good tutorial system of professors and students. They are sure to make themselves available to students and are helpful. They make sure that students understand what's going on."

Study Assistance Programs are available in math, computer science and physics, writing lab, science, nursing and reading. For non-academic advice, minority students serve as peers and peer advisors for the Peer Counseling Group. One respondent says, "I truly appreciate the counseling advise that I received from my advisor. She gave me hope when I thought all was lost." Workshops are offered through the Counseling Center and include study skills, text anxiety and taking better notes.

Black student groups include two Greek organizations, the TWU Gospel Choir, the Southern Christian Leadership Conference, Alpha Omega Literary Social Club and the Society of Black Journalists. One student says the Gospel Choir is "the most visible black-oriented organization on campus other than the Greek organizations." Also quite active is a black Bible study group.

On the social side, participation by blacks at Greek parties is high, as one student reports. As far as university-sponsored activities, students report that many blacks do not generally attend these activities, unless it concerns blacks. One student says, "There are not many black speakers invited to TWU. This has been a concern of the politically oriented students."

Black participation in intramural and varsity sports receives mixed comments. One student maintains, "TWU has the best turnout for varsity sports," while another student says, "There's not much activity."

"The Fundango picnic," declares one senior, "gets quite a few black students out." And one student simply states, "Participation is high if there is food involved!"

Black History Month is celebrated on campus with many programs, activities and seminars.

Another student says, "It would be great to have more influential, successful black men and women come to talk with students." On racial tolerance, one student says there are a few seminars and workshops, but, "There needs to be more available, for all students."

Black students are involved actively in student government. One sister is a member of the Student Government Association Board and says, "We have a lot of other black students involved in the senate voting body. The university committees are voluntary for any student, and a number of blacks are on each committee."

Any off-campus community interaction seems centered on church activities. Reports one student, "The churches are really the only places in this town that truly accept us black students. We are welcomed and encouraged to participate in church activities."

Students note that interaction with white students is good, but some still notice some tensions and prejudice. A respondent's assessment: "Students are easier to get along with than some faculty members, but there are still some problems." Another notes, "There exists some prejudice, but it's not as prevalent here as in other places." One student finds some of the white faculty and administration to be both helpful and friendly, while others are not.

One student says, "I do not see TWU as a predominantly white school, but I do see it as an educational environment. I am having an excellent education and social experience."

TOUGALOO COLLEGE
Tougaloo, Mississippi 39174

Undergrads: 1,105
Black Undergrads: 1,105
Faculty: 91
Black Faculty: NA
Tuition: $5,940
Total Expenses: $8,484

Most respondents say they are satisfied with Tougaloo. Argues one brother, "There are no unattractive features of the school." Yet another student is quick to point out that city folks might find the atmosphere "too quiet." Most students cite the closeness between the staff and students as the major highlight of their school, and as one student put it, "You really feel like someone cares about you at Tougaloo."

Small, historically black and liberal arts-oriented, Tougaloo represents pride, tradition and a caring attitude. "Tougaloo doesn't turn down people who aren't extra smart," says one student, describing its less selective admission policy. But the private, coed institution has produced 40 percent of the black doctors and lawyers in Mississippi.

Geographically, the majority of the students come from a variety of states: the North is represented by New Yorkers, the Midwest by students from Illinois, and the Southern states can boast of people from Mississippi and Tennessee.

According to one informant, Tougaloo is noted for its education, social science and pre-med departments. Approximately 26 percent of the graduating class goes on to pursue full-time graduate or professional school.

The Recruiting Office not only uses its staff and faculty to attract students; it also has a definite plan of action for alumni to recruit students on the state and national level. Arrangements can be made for sub-freshmen to stay overnight as guests of the faculty and staff as well as guests of undergraduates.

Incoming students at Tougaloo are assigned a peer counselor, and chaplains and faculty are a part of an academic advising program. The Basic Studies Program provides tutorial services such as a study skills and test preparation class. Tutoring is done through a free, student-to-student service. Instructors also tutor. Academic subjects are divided into tutorial centers focusing on math, reading, writing and logic, all of which are "very helpful."

Special seminars led by guest alumni and specialists are offered for "motivational purposes." One respondent notes: "There is an assembly every Wednesday offering speakers and covering topics that aren't covered in the curriculum."

Tougaloo has good relations with Brown University's medical school, and Tougaloo and Brown have an exchange program for undergraduates. White and black students from both schools have learned a great deal from each other. One student comments: "It is a myth that academics in black colleges is inferior or easier than that of white schools. In fact, I had my hardest political science course at Tougaloo, not Brown."

There are 60 student organizations at Tougaloo, and many students are involved in as many as three clubs. One respondent claims that the pre-professional clubs are "very useful, and helpful in terms of guidance and direction."

Theater is represented by two groups at Tougaloo. The Pact performs plays on various subjects, and the Alkebulean Players perform "plays with meaning." Noonday prayer takes place at the College Chapel, which hosts Baptist services, Operation Somebody Cares and the Sunday School Club. The last two groups have made meaningful contributions to the town of Tougaloo.

The relationship between black and white students on campus is described by these two responses: "Every year there's about one white student on campus. Interaction is good"; "They get along very well; there is no partiality."

Interaction between students and black faculty and administration is "very close." And the faculty, says one sister, "Lets the students be a part of their social life; we always have dinners together." The same closeness seems to exist between black students and white faculty.

Tougaloo itself is a small town, but the adjacent city of Jackson has a strong African-American presence. Relations between the students and the local community is reportedly "very good."

Social life on campus seems spirited, with "parties every weekend, but never during the week." A student center boasts a pool and game room. Intramural sports is said to be "very popular," and there are "lots of picnics sponsored by Greek organizations and academic departments."

Cliques do exist at Tougaloo—the most common being fraternal and "the out-of-state students versus in-staters." Bonds between students at Tougaloo and Jackson State are well-developed, with Student Government Association sponsoring various activities.

Alumni seem to work conscientiously for the school. The national alumni fundraising effort is very effective, and alumns help with special projects such as "donating furniture, walkways, flowers and scholarships." Tougaloo grads do visit their alma mater, and the gathering at commencement is said to be "similar to a convention."

TOWSON STATE UNIVERSITY
Towson, Maryland 21204-7097

Undergrads: 13,089
Black Undergrads: 1,178
Faculty: 955
Black Faculty: NA
Tuition: $3,580; $6,104
Total Expenses: $8,090; $10,614

L ocated seven miles from downtown Baltimore and 47 miles from Washington D.C., Towson is a coed, liberal arts-based institution offering programs in the arts and sciences, professional and pre-professional areas of study. Under general studies, courses in African-American studies are available.

Towson recruits via black recruitment fairs throughout Maryland, New Jersey and Pennsylvania. Also, TSU provides a day on campus for two local middle schools with high minority student populations, and it sponsors a Minority Student Open House as well as other open house sessions in the fall.

The Office of Minority Affairs (OMA) sponsors programs to facilitate recruitment, retention and graduation of black students. It is here that the accomplishments, culture and character of people of African ancestry is reflected. In addition, the office helps black students negotiate the college environment, and it heightens awareness of racial diversity.

OMA sponsors *Mahogany Magazine* (a student-operated radio talk show), a reception for newly admitted black students and their parents, and the AIMS Program, which gives each black freshman a faculty mentor to ease the transition into Towson.

In addition, the center sponsors the Distinguished Black Scholars Series, the Distinguished Black Marylanders awards and *Ebony Notes*, a newsletter published by the African-American Cultural Center (AACC), which contains information of interest to blacks and is written by students, faculty and staff.

Support services include TSU's Tutorial Services Center and the Counseling Center's professional staff available for students with personal, social and career issues. The center offers workshops, discussion groups, referrals, outreach programs and a career guidance program. All services are free and confidential.

Towson also offers Career Counseling Services and Career Placement Services. The counseling services offer resources such as individual and group counseling workshops, and a course in Life and Career Planning. The Career Library and Cope-Line offer information on occupations and give assistance with career choice. The Career Placement Center offers seminars and workshops, career awareness programs, and job listings for full-, part-time and summer employment.

There are more than 70 student organizations on campus. Of particular interest to blacks are the Black Student Union, The Brotherhood/Sisterhood and NAACP College Chapter along with eight black Greek-letter organizations.

The Black Student Union sponsors several events: Kwanzaa, the Parent's Dinner, a speaker series and dances throughout the academic year.

The Brotherhood/Sisterhood groups provide social interaction and community involvement.

The NAACP College chapter fosters political awareness and allows for the exchange of ideas and minority concerns.

The African-American Cultural Center maintains books, records, tapes and periodicals about people of African heritage. The center also sponsors the TSU Gospel Choir.

Intramural sports is open to all students, with competition offered in 21 sports. Also available to all students is a recreation sports program with swimming, basketball, tennis, weight training, volleyball and badminton.

TRINITY COLLEGE
Hartford, Connecticut 06106

Undergrads: 1,944
Black Undergrads: 117
Faculty: 260
Black Faculty: 6
Tuition: $20,230
Total Expenses: $26,360

An undergrad says of this college, "I did know that I could get a good education that would help me in the future. Trinity is a good school, with a beautiful small campus."

Admission is highly selective at this liberal arts college nestled in a park-like haven in the midst of Hartford's urban environment. One undergrad says that the college's small size ensures smaller classes and more teacher-student interaction.

For courses in the black experience, students can sample from Black Americans (before and after 1865), Afro-American Experience and Music in Black America.

To enhance its recruitment efforts, Trinity holds a Minorities Admissions Weekend. "The school makes an effort during minority student orientation to inform students of support services," says one undergrad. The Writing and Math Centers provide English and math study skills workshops. Tutorial assistance is available through all of the departments. The Counseling Center lives up to its name, and the Dean of Student's Office provides both services. Students also seek informal counseling from faculty members or peers. In addition, the Office of Career Counseling helps students seeking both summer and post-graduation employment. Says one undergrad, "I have found both the writing center and the math center to be useful. Most professors set up help sessions that meet at least twice a week."

Counseling, however, receives criticism. One respondent says that since the administration, faculty and psychological center staff are predominantly white males, "black students are reluctant to seek counseling from these sources." However, some respondents report that the minority faculty and staff are very supportive and eager to assist black students.

Umoja House, the social and educational center for black students, has an African art museum and a library that contains African-American literature and periodicals. Activities held at Umoja House, including lectures and films, are sponsored by black organizations.

"The Trinity Coalition of Black Women strives for unity and cultural awareness," says one undergrad. Another adds that the Pan-African Alliance, a black political organization, makes sure that concerns of the black community are voiced and "provides an opportunity to develop leadership qualities."

Most respondents agree that black participation in student government is flourishing. "Blacks are beginning to realize the importance of these governing bodies," says one student. One undergrad says that there are also black dorm representatives and black members of the Budget Committee.

Trinity Gospel Choir members visit several black churches in the area to perform. "Some blacks go to weekly meetings at a Black Muslim Mosque in the Hartford area, so some ties have been established between blacks on campus and those in the community," says one undergrad.

According to one undergrad, several black DJs have had shows on WRTC-FM. One respondent says, "This programming is like a breath of fresh air on this white and conservative campus."

Black participation in intramural sports is active, according to several students. "When blacks participate in these sports, they do so together, forming their own teams," reports one undergrad.

One respondent says that as far as college-sponsored activities go, "The majority of blacks only go to activities in which there is a black interest." According to some students, black participation is high in activities such as music, dance and lectures (speakers have included Desmond Tutu and actress Margaret Avery), but "the majority of social events appeal mainly to white students, who set up these events."

Respondents say that black students go off campus to socialize, party together or meet at Umoja House. One respondent adds, "The Pan-African Alliance does a lot together."

Trinity has a formal policy against racial harassment. Workshops are held during freshmen orientation that discuss topics such as racism, cultural diversity and pluralism. In addition, Students Organized Against Racism (SOAR) sponsors programs that are designed to encourage racial tolerance.

One respondent says that these are good programs, but there are not enough of them. Another says that the few that are held "are usually attended only by black students and other students of color."

One undergrad has this to say about the relations between black and white students: "There is a little tension, but I do not think any more or less than at any other predominantly white institution." However, other respondents report that there is little interaction. "Most of the blacks stay together just because we have a lot in common, just like any other group," says one student. "However, whites take it as isolating ourselves, when they do the same thing. There are a few blacks who have more white friends than black friends."

One brother reports, "The white professors are always willing to help, and the white administrators always tell us to come by and talk if we need to." Another adds, "A few white faculty members have shown a special interest in black students."

"The interaction between the black students and the local community, which is predominantly black, is very good," says one respondent. "The Hartford community is very supportive of the black organizations on campus—they attend our lectures and other events."

"I feel that coming to a white school is a good experience, for it prepares me for the future," says one respondent. "It's a fact that black people must struggle in this society. Overall, I feel I made a good choice. The support groups created by black students have helped me greatly."

TRUMAN STATE UNIVERSITY
Kirksville, Missouri 63501

Undergrads: 6,043
Black Undergrads: 181
Faculty: 382
Black Faculty: NA
Tuition: $2,890; $5,152
Total Expenses: $6,514; $8,776

A school that lets students do the grading? Pack your bags and say hello to Truman State University.

The pride and glory of this highly selective public school is its nationally recognized assessment program, which gives students a chance to evaluate curricula and policies, measure their academic progress, and express their opinions about everything—including the food in the cafeteria.

Located in Kirksville, Missouri, 170 miles from Kansas City, Truman State, which recently changed its name from Northeast Missouri State University, is quietly becoming one of the best public colleges in the country. It offers majors in 60 areas including business, fine arts, liberal arts, education and computer science.

Students who minor in African/African-American Studies have a wide variety of courses from which to choose. Classes range from The History of Africa to Rhetoric of Race Relations to Jazz History and Appreciation.

Other programs of interest for black students are the Ronald McNair Program (named after the late astronaut) that prepares black students for graduate and professional entrance examinations and the Scholastic Enhancement Experience, a month-long summer residential program that helps underrepresented students adjust to college life.

Truman State sponsors tutors for several classes, and students can apply through the Office of Multicultural Affairs to receive individual tutoring for any subject. Professional and minority peer counseling are also available.

Students seem satisfied with the academic support services, especially professors' involvement. One student says, "Professors will call special class sections if students don't seem to understand the subject" and that professors will find tutors for students if they feel it is necessary. If he had to rate professors, one brother says they would be a nine on a scale of one to ten. According to another student, however, professors won't offer help unless students take the first step. "Students must make themselves visible and willing," she says. "Otherwise they may go unnoticed."

If you are interested in Greek life, Truman State has everything you could ever ask for. All eight black fraternities and sororities are active on campus. If the Greek experience doesn't appeal to you, non-Greek organizations include the Nia Dancers, the Black Association of Science Majors, the Black Pre-Law Students Association, the Unique Ensemble Gospel Choir and the Africa Society.

Understandably, fraternity and sorority parties are popular for black students. But one undergraduate complains, "Since there are so few of us and everyone does not attend parties, many of them are dead."

A unique activity at Truman State is the homecoming mixer that allows current black students and black alumns to meet. One student calls this event a "great success," adding, "the alumns were very impressive and excellent role models." Although a brother says alumns come back "with enthusiasm," another student senses that they are satisfied with the school academically but not socially.

To try to combat racial incidents, the Office of Multicultural Affairs sponsors seminars on racial tolerance throughout the year. It may be working. The majority of respondents do not report any major incidents of racism. Although one student mentions that tension exists between blacks and whites at times, she categorizes race relations overall as "fair." One brother says, "Everybody tries to be friends." And according to another sister, interaction is pervasive and extends to clubs, class, the cafeteria and even personal friendships.

Overall, black students have few regrets about their decision to attend Truman State, but for some acceptance comes with time. One intangible benefit, according to some respondents, is the supportive community. "This small black community is a strong community," a student says. "We help each other out when we can."

Some last minute advice from these undergrads— look before you leap. "I think blacks need to visit the campus and Kirksville. They need to know that Kirksville does not cater to the African-American student."

TUFTS UNIVERSITY
Medford, Massachusetts 02155

Undergrads: 4,531
Black Undergrads: 181
Faculty: 1,093
Black Faculty: NA
Tuition: $21,086
Total Expenses: $27,336

Some respondents feel that the environment here isn't secure enough. "I would recommend that black students support the black institutions of learning. You don't have to go to a predominantly white school to learn how to deal with white people," contends a sister.

Tufts seems to have integrated effectively the diversity and resources of the university with the intimacy of a liberal arts college. The 150-acre Medford campus caters to the undergraduate, while its campus in Boston concentrates on post-graduate professional education.

Students at highly selective Tufts come from all parts of the country. They find Tufts to have a tough, crisply honed curriculum that demands much. Classes are small by design. A writing seminar is mandatory for frosh, and there are distribution requirements. Although some black students find that the academic requirements are challenging, one student says, "It is frustrating to be enrolled in courses that weed you out eventually."

"Those from predominantly black settings find a major adjustment awaiting them, but there are resources at the African American Center in particular that make the adjustment as smooth as possible," says a respondent.

Tufts offers a wide range of services and organizations to help both in the transition from high school to college and in the solving of academic and social questions for the duration of the students' undergraduate education. Tufts students seeking academic or personal guidance may take Freshman Explorations, offered at the Experimental College, which offers an array of courses, programs and alternative teaching methods not found in the traditional university framework. The seminar explores such issues as academic adjustment and general college life. Freshmen are also assigned a faculty advisor.

The Academic Resource Center provides small workshops or individual sessions in study skills, such as managing time, taking notes, reading textbooks, organizing term papers and preparing for exams. One student says of the Academic Resource Center: "The tutors are students, and they are on salary so they are very accessible. I found that the professors themselves are very available at Tufts, and willing to provide any assistance they can."

Other resources are the Office of Career Guidance and Placement and the Counseling Center, which offers professional counseling. Yet even with all these services one student complains, "The school doesn't seem to have the financial resources available to really pull in strong academic support services. The programs here are just adequate."

The main social and intellectual gathering place for black students is the African American Center, which examines the intellectual and scholarly issues affecting blacks. Their ideology is based on sensitizing both blacks and whites so they will work for effective social change. Another goal of the center is to help black students adjust successfully to the university. Finally, the African American Center tries to create an atmosphere of community among blacks at Tufts in order to institute a greater system of support and participation within the entire Tufts community.

The center sponsors lectures by nationally prominent speakers, colloquia and a number of seminars. Seminars and workshops designed to improve the career decision-making skills of black undergraduates are offered. In addition, the center publishes a bi-weekly newsletter, the *Lighthouse*, which serves as a major communication device for the Tufts black community. Other activities include dance, monthly jazz forums, gospel choirs, theater parties and exhibitions of black art. A black cultural weekend occurs each April.

A key event of the Black Cultural Weekend is the Awards Banquet, where students are recognized for excellence in academic and community service.

Capen House, located in the upper two floors of the center, is a cultural residence for approximately 15 students who want an in-depth experience with black culture.

The African American Society, like the center, is designed to foster the interests of the African community at Tufts. The society sponsors the Student-Faculty Dinner, Kwanzaa Celebrations and the Campus Cabaret. Other campus organizations are the Academic and Career Enrichment Services (ACES) Program; the Committee for Black Involvement in Drama; the Office of Equal Opportunity, designed to oversee the Tufts Affirmative Action Plan; the National Association of Tufts Black Alumni; the Black Caucus, for black employees at Tufts; the Third World Admissions Task Force; and the bi-monthly *African American Newsletter*.

Students say that on-campus parties are usually lively but that they are rare and only go until 1:00 a.m. to 1:30 a.m. Support for parties is great at the beginning of the semester and tapers off toward the end. However, given all of the universities in the Boston area, one can find many parties and new faces away from Tufts.

The various interactions between black students, white students, administrators and faculty yield different responses. Personal and academic interaction seems to be frequent and cordial. But there are noticeable tensions in some situations. One student says: "There is a lot of interaction between white and black students. However, I do think blacks tend to keep to themselves as much as possible...I think the black faculty are very helpful and supportive to the black population."

Another respondent says, "Blacks and whites are not usually at the same parties. However, there are many black-white friendships. There is also an increase of whites attending black events." Of white faculty and administrators, one student says, "Some relationships are excellent. I know there are professors in the sciences that really 'push' black students. On the other hand, some black students have had difficulty with white faculty and administrators." But another respondent cautions: "There is an over-all distrust of white faculty members and particularly of administrators."

Although Tufts offers a wide range of counseling and recruiting programs and sponsors a number of black organizations and services, some black students feel that Tufts doesn't provide a secure environment for its students.

Says one student: "I would recommend this school for those who consider themselves active, both socially and politically. Tufts is not for those who demand a lot of privacy. The school is hungry for new ideas, so things can be accomplished."

TUSKEGEE INSTITUTE
Tuskegee, Alabama 36088

Undergrads: 2,726
Black Undergrads: 2,508
Faculty: 298
Black Faculty: NA
Tuition: $7,070
Total Expenses: $10,690

Socially and academically, Tuskegee is an attractive possibility for the prospective black student. Steeped in its historic tradition, Tuskegee is proof positive that predominantly black institutions are a viable alternative for today's black student.

For the past century, historically black Tuskegee Institute has been known as one of the "birthplaces" of higher education for African-Americans. This private, coed institution founded by Booker T. Washington offers undergraduate instruction in six areas including arts and sciences, nursing and education. Tuskegee prides itself on preparing its students for both graduate school and work in the "real world."

Most of the brothers and sisters come from Alabama, Georgia, Florida and New York.

While some brothers and sisters feel that the smoothness of the transition for Tuskegee freshmen depends mostly on student preparedness, others insist that the Freshmen Orientation Week is a significant help for incoming students.

For those students experiencing academic difficulties, the school offers both tutorial and counseling services. All respondents feel that the college's tutorial services are "pretty good." Yet some students express displeasure with Tuskegee's counseling services. Moreover, while most brothers and sisters feel the study skills workshops held at the school are adequate, some feel that the study skills workshops should offer information about a larger variety of courses.

Unfortunately the Tuskegee Institute has only two pre-professional organizations (the Pre-Veterinarian and the Pre-Nursing Societies). Yet students are quick to point to Tuskegee's black theater, which performs plays that emphasize black culture, music and heritage. There is a campus-based church, but most black students attend church in the community. The school's radio station seems to be very popular with most students.

Tuskegee's student center is called the College Union and is the focus of all campus-based club and organizational activity. Included in the center are a television room and rooms for informal lectures and discussions. Some students have a complaint—that there isn't enough university-sponsored entertainment. Yet this perceived lack is made up by black students' heavy participation in the school's intramural sports program.

In general, Tuskegee students are very proud of their student government. Many blacks participate each year in the maintenance of a strong yet flexible student government. Greek organizations are very popular on Tuskegee's campus. And while all black students feel that the parties are "on time," some feel that there is too much partying, deterring students from academics.

Interaction between black and white students is termed "adequate," and Tuskegee's black students communicate fairly well with the school's black and white faculty and administrative members. And while most students feel that Tuskegee students interact well with the general community, other blacks feel that communication is minimal at best between the two groups.

UNIVERSITY OF AKRON
Akron, Ohio 44325

Undergrads: 20,722
Black Undergrads: 2,279
Faculty: 1,737
Black Faculty: NA
Tuition: $3,384; $8,110
Total Expenses: $7,446; $12,172

Consider this senior's words before sending in your room deposit: "I do not feel that the University of Akron has helped to prepare me for my next step in life."

Big is a good word for Akron. It sits on a spacious, 170-acre campus 30 miles south of Cleveland. It is one of the 50 largest colleges in the country. Its big-time reputation attracts registrants from 34 states and 64 countries. And it gets big-time complaints from its black student body.

First, respondents feel that the school's academic resources need much improvement. The Academic Advisement Center is called "mediocre" by one. Another resents the university's practices: "Although tutorial assistance is available, it is not publicized. Athletes get first priority, and the average student gets shafted," she says. Still, another respondent feels that the tutorial services are fine because she never had a problem getting a tutor.

The one support service that black students regard highly is the minority peer counseling program. For some, this program is often the difference between sticking it out and dropping out. One brother puts it this way: "The students who participate in this program have gotten through college and graduated at a higher percentage that those who don't." Another undergrad adds, "Black students that are not involved in peer counseling haven't adjusted well at all. The University of Akron does not create an environment outside of peer counseling for their academic transition."

The school offers many majors for students in the areas of nursing, business, fine arts, engineering, and liberal arts, among others. African-American Studies is offered as a certificate, not a major, which upsets one sister. "My biggest problem with this is that the subject is treated like it's a fad," she says.

Campus organizations provide students with opportunities to develop themselves professionally, spiritually, and socially. National Association of Black Accountants (NABA), National Society of Black Engineers (NSBE), Black Law Students, and Black Education Students are a few organizations that allow students to network within their majors. A student notes that NSBE in particular helps students of all majors, not just future engineers. The active gospel choir "is uplifting and provides religious support for all students." Black Greek life is prominent on this campus too, with several black sororities and fraternities holding forth under a Black Greek Council.

Socially? The University of Akron is disappointing for black students. A respectable number turn out at parties sponsored by fraternities and sororities. The problem is that they are not held often enough. "There aren't many parties due to violence and the cost of renting the establishments," says one sister. A brother puts it matter-of-factly: "One or two parties in fifteen weeks is not good. Students are very unhappy."

Interaction with white students is usually limited to formal situations, according to respondents. Although some blacks are members of white fraternities, "most socialization occurs in class," one student reports. Others describe race relations as "poor" and "not well." Even more disturbing are the respondents' feelings about black faculty members. "Only a few seem to want to interact with us," complains one undergraduate. According to another, "A lot of our black faculty members become non-favorites among black students."

Unfortunately, some students feel that the university doesn't concern itself with the needs of its minority population. Some respondents were satisfied with their decision to attend the University of Akron, but several wish that they had mailed their acceptance letters elsewhere.

UNIVERSITY OF ARIZONA
Tucson, Arizona 85721

Undergrads: 26,153
Black Undergrads: 785
Faculty: 1,588
Black Faculty: NA
Tuition: $1,950; $7,912
Total Expenses: $6,140; $12,102

Arizona offers very little for the undergrad actively seeking to socialize and organize with fellow black students.

The large, coed university, founded in 1885 with a single building in the desert, now consists of 14 colleges with over 35,000 students. This selective school, even tougher for out-of-staters, prides itself on readying its students for careers in business and industry. The curriculum offers bachelor's degree programs in fields ranging from business, education, math and engineering to psychology, biology, philosophy and agriculture.

Arizona offers a number of counseling and tutorial services for its black students. The Student Encouragement Program and the Black Pre-Medical tutorial service are just two of the committees that try to help students who need special academic help. Yet despite these tutorial and counseling groups, black students still find it difficult to adjust to academics on the college level.

If students need academic counseling, they have to make an extremely strong effort to find the services that will fulfill their academic needs. And despite the wide variety of courses offered at the university, the school has only a few relating to the African-American experience.

The majority of parties and social events are given by the two Greek-letter organizations, but the number of parties is few. Rarely is there university-sponsored professional and semi-professional entertainment geared toward the black community at Arizona.

One encouraging note is that the university's Minority Medical Student Group remains very active despite its small membership. Students have also organized a Black Pre-Engineering society, an African American Leadership Alliance and an Association for African Women for Change. The Black

Law Student's Association program called "Ebony Incorporated," held each fall, brings together all of the black students on campus. It features music, food and much-needed social interaction.

UNIVERSITY OF ARKANSAS

Little Rock, Arkansas 72204

Undergrads: 8,754
Black Undergrads: 1,663
Faculty: 740
Black Faculty: NA
Tuition: $2,378; $5,664
Total Expenses: $4,788; $8,074

Since most black students at Arkansas are from the South (primarily Arkansas, Missouri, Tennessee and Louisiana), and a variety of black services and organizations are available, it is possible for a black student to feel "at home" here, if not literally, then at least spiritually. But feeling at home is still not that easy for the brothers and sisters.

The University of Arkansas at Little Rock presents some difficult obstacles for black students. Since its creation in 1969, the school has been state-supported and now offers a variety of graduate and undergraduate programs, including evening and off-campus classes. The curriculum, oriented toward the educational needs of urban Arkansas, is aimed primarily at preparing students for either a profession or a career.

More than 75 undergraduate degree programs as well as 24 graduate and/or professional programs are offered. Its admission policy is less selective than most. Under exceptional circumstances, admission can be obtained on the basis of an examination given by the university.

Freshmen and sophomores are required to fulfill distribution requirements in English, history, communication skills, mathematics and physical education. Academic support services include tutorials, faculty-to-student and peer counseling, and study skills workshops. These are reported to be quite helpful, although all students questioned claim that these services are not well-publicized or visible. The curriculum includes a few courses in black studies.

Students live at home; this is primarily a commuter school with no dormitory facilities. Also noteworthy is the fact that Arkansas has a large number of resumed education students, and the average age is 26. The non-residential quality and wide age range of students have a negative effect on social life, students report. Many organizations, including three black fraternities and two sororities, attempt to combat this problem.

Few other student programs are run especially for blacks. One of the most notable is the Gospel Chorus. Other student organizations include pre-professional societies, a student theatrical group and a radio station; reportedly blacks do not participate widely. In addition, there is virtually inadequate involvement, according to some respondents, by blacks in the governance of the university.

The intramural sports program is quite popular, and helps to compensate for the non-residential quality of the school by fostering interaction between black and white students. Black religious services are also offered and are seen as a positive aspect of campus life. One student calls the services "the foremost source of black unity" on campus.

Students are enthusiastic about community relations. But they still express a need for programs designed to help place blacks within community-based activities.

Black alumns play a vital role in implementing and organizing these events. Students report that black alumns are cooperative although contact has been limited primarily to recent graduates.

UNIVERSITY OF CALIFORNIA

Davis, California 95616

Undergrads: 18,001
Black Undergrads: 732
Faculty: 1,349
Black Faculty: 16
Tuition: $4,174; $11,873
Total Expenses: $9,694; $17,393

L ocated 15 sunny miles from Sacramento, the University of California
at Davis offers many programs for blacks and all students in general.
Recruitment is active and varied. One program involves black outreach
officers located in both Los Angeles and San Francisco who visit black high
schools, public and private. In addition, they attend black-student fairs and
work with alumns. UCal-Davis sponsors an early outreach program which
brings in black students from Los Angeles and Oakland to campus on a
regular basis. Further, the college hosts ethnic-specific scholar banquets,
including one for blacks. Twenty-five to thirty high-achieving black
students and their families (parents, brothers and sisters) are invited, and the
scholar is presented with a certificate.

UCal-Davis offers complete and comprehensive support services.
STEP is a Summer Transitional Education Program for new incoming black
students, and tutorial assistance is offered through the Learning Skills
Center. Minority peer counseling can be found at the counseling center,
while special forums and workshops are run throughout the year on career
planning, counseling and advising. Davis's Black Studies department has
an extensive list of courses with topics including culture and society,
politics, social organization and history. Noteworthy are Black Intellectuals, Introduction to Black Politics and West African Social Organization.

Social life for Blacks should be quite active. The African-American
Greek Letter Council represents eight national black Greek-letter organiza-
tions. Black students can gather at the Cross-Cultural Center and the EOP/
SAA Counseling Center.

UCal-Davis has sponsored forums for alumni to discuss outreach
priorities as well as the Black Eligibility Student Forum, which involves

Sacramento area business and professional leaders. The Career Planning and Placement Office provides assistance for seniors. The office is in touch with companies, school districts and graduate schools who are interested in black graduates. The office also has a summer employment board where black students can find summer jobs in both local businesses and in cooperative/intern education.

Five of the eight members of the Executive Council for the Associated Students (Student Government) are black. In addition, blacks hold many positions in the administration and academic offices, including Assistant Vice Chancellor (2 positions) and Director of Financial Aids. There are black faculty and administrators who advise the Executive Vice Chancellor and Chancellor on administrative matters and also in the Academic Senate who have a direct voice in academic matters.

Each May, students, faculty and staff sponsor a Black Family Week celebration of speakers, music, food and activities, which attracts more than 25,000 families and individuals to the campus.

UNIVERSITY OF CALIFORNIA
Los Angeles, California 90024

Undergrads: 23,769
Black Undergrads: 1,449
Faculty: 573
Black Faculty: NA
Tuition: $3,894; $11,593
Total Expenses: $9,649; $17,348

B efore you decide to venture to UCLA, take its academic and social life into account. These are issues that can "make you or break you," according to one brother who states nevertheless: "I am satisfied with my decision to attend this predominantly white school."

Large, coeducational and liberal arts UCLA has a selective admission policy and is one of nine different campuses of the University of California.

It's tough going academically, and the attrition rate for black students per year averages about 30 percent. To combat this, the university sponsors free tutoring for eligible students through the Academic Advancement Program (AAP), designed to help minority and low-income students survive the adjustment from high school to college through tutorial services in English and math as well as special counseling.

Many of the counselors at UCLA are minority students, and their efforts are combined with those of the pre-professional student organizations to reduce the attrition rate. "The Black Pre-Med society is very useful because it draws students together and also allows the graduate pre-med society to know and help undergraduate members," reports an undergrad. The Black Pre-Law Society provides another place to go for academic help, services or socialization.

The Center for Afro-American Studies (CAAS) also serves as an academic and social gathering place. Founded in 1959, CAAS has grown into one of the country's most prestigious institutions for teaching and research on Africa. In addition to its 50,000-volume research library, CAAS sponsors exhibits, cultural publications, concerts and other entertainment, cultural and educational events.

Black student interests are also served by *Nommo*, the black student newspaper, the Black Student Alliance (BSA), black Greek-letter organizations, black theater and a black gospel choir. The BSA's annual picnic at the end of the school year, to which all Third World students, black faculty and special interest groups are invited, is a major event.

Both intramural sports and student government have also been popular activities for black students at UCLA.

A Community Programs Unit, sponsored by UCLA, gives students an opportunity to develop meaningful relationships with blacks off-campus. Some black students tutor high school students in the inner city schools and at local camps. The UCLA Alumni Association's Advisory and Scholarship Program assists in recruiting and giving aid to high-achieving black high school students.

UNIVERSITY OF CALIFORNIA
Riverside, California 92521

Undergrads: 7,433
Black Undergrads: 279
Faculty: 672
Black Faculty: NA
Tuition: $4,093; $11,792
Total Expenses: $9,523; $17,222

Black respondents are satisfied with the greenery, landscape and quiet atmosphere of this small, coed school with a selective admission policy although the campus isn't huge like the University of California at Los Angeles and isn't as popular as the two "beach" campuses of San Diego and Santa Barbara.

Riverside provides its students with a wide range of courses and an extensive system of support services. Undergraduate courses are offered within the College of Humanities and Social Science, the College of Natural and Agricultural Sciences, and the School of Education.

Although the majority of black students at Riverside are from Southern California, the school recruits actively. For example, the Equal Opportunity Program and Student Affirmative Action Office identifies annually approximately 40 high schools throughout California that have a high enrollment of prospective black and minority student applicants.

The New Student Recruitment Office then sends to these schools recruiters who distribute information and discuss admission requirements and procedures. These recruiters also attend numerous college fairs. In general, say respondents, alumns who do not work at the university are not very helpful with recruiting.

Courses relating to the African-American and African experience include Introduction to Black Studies, History of Black Africans, Black Women in America and Surveys of Black Literature.

The university's academic support programs include tutorial assistance, counseling and study skills workshops. All undergrads are entitled to free tutoring in introductory and advanced courses.

The Black Retention Network matches students with professors and staff to facilitate better academic performance and increased self-esteem among black undergrads. Students can also obtain academic, peer and psychological counseling through various academic departments, student organizations and the Counseling Center.

The Career Planning and Placement Center at Riverside offers group counseling sessions that cover topics like career decision-making, resume preparation and job search. The Black Student Activities Office consults regularly with the Career Planning and Placement Center about black student placement. An internship program is considered especially helpful. Certain community agencies, like the Urban League, assist in providing summer employment for black undergrads.

Each quarter, the university gives a non-credit Study Skills class for eight weeks. Moreover, there are learning skills counselors and a Learning Laboratory to assist in developing effective study skills. Students can also view videotapes of study skills lectures at their convenience. The university encourages structured study groups so that students work together in learning course material. Overall, black undergrads say that the support system helps them adjust to Riverside's academic requirements.

Many brothers and sisters participate actively in Shades of Black, the black theater group, and consider their experience "very useful and entertaining." For those students interested in health careers, the Black Pre-Med Society is considered informative and helpful. Most black students participate in parties and other activities sponsored by the black Greek sororities and fraternities. And black students participate enthusiastically in intramural sports.

UNIVERSITY OF CENTRAL OKLAHOMA

Edmond, Oklahoma 73034

Undergrads: 12,048
Black Undergrads: 723
Faculty: 692
Black Faculty: NA
Tuition: $1,716; $3,630
Total Expenses: $4,107; $6,021

Students here appear to be pleased with their choice, with one stating that the "great nursing school is the reason I am here."

Twelve miles from Oklahoma City, large, non-selective, and coed Central Oklahoma offers a diverse undergraduate academic program and a definite sense of family among black students.

The majority of Central Oklahoma's black students hail from Oklahoma, Texas and yes, Nigeria. Recruitment efforts are led by two full-time recruiters aided by faculty and student groups who visit schools.

Courses in the black experience cover fiction and poetry, American history, African history and politics, among others.

A range of support systems for black students are in place. Tutorial assistance is offered through the Peer Counseling Center (PCC) in the University Counseling Center (UCC), and through Alpha Lambda Delta. The UCC, the PCC, and all black faculty members provide counseling. Study skills workshops exist too, and the remedial reading program is well-respected. Career guidance for black seniors is provided by the PCC within the University Placement Service.

A list of black student organizations includes the Afro-American Student Union, the NAACP, pre-professional clubs, and Ebony Gospel Choir. The Young Democrats and Young Republicans are popular groups. One student remarks that there is tremendous black participation in the Student Senate.

Fraternities and sororities are also popular, and the following chapters are represented: Alpha Kappa Alpha, Delta Sigma Theta, Kappa Alpha Psi,

Alpha Phi Alpha, and Phi Beta Sigma. The Baptist Student Union has a dedicated following as well. In all, "spirit" on the campus is reported to be high.

Greek organizations are responsible for most campus recreation; the university sponsors little except a Black Heritage Week. The Student Senate organizes picnics and get-togethers. In one student's opinion, "the overall turnout for intramural sports has been great."

The few black faculty foster what one student terms a "family-type relationship" with black students. Black students' relationships with white students and faculty are said to be without strain.

THE UNIVERSITY OF CHICAGO
Chicago, Illinois 60637

Undergrads: 3,453
Black Undergrads: 138
Faculty: 1,312
Black Faculty: NA
Tuition: $20,193
Total Expenses: $26,861

Reports from Chicago's black students reveal a relaxed racial climate, a school that has much to offer and the need to learn to cope with the predominantly white environment.

This is one of the country's wealthiest private institutions and features a small, coed and rigorous academic environment.

Located in the exclusive residential community of Hyde Park, the 165-acre campus is only seven miles from downtown Chicago. The college has a highly selective admissions policy which attracts students who have graduated in the top fifth of their high school classes and have scored over 1200 on the combined Scholastic Aptitude Test.

The late George Kent, an English professor in the college, once remarked, "One of the most impressive benefits of a Chicago education for black students is the opportunity to work effectively for self-education." Students are launched on the road to self-reliance by one of the most respected and traditional liberal arts programs in the country. The "common core," as it is called here, is designed to teach students the art of asking intelligent questions that have meaning for informed and responsible individuals.

During the first two years, students are required to complete four year-long course sequences. In their exploratory and analytical approach, in their emphasis on small discussion groups and work with primary materials, the courses are perhaps closer to work done in seminars or more advanced classes. Special opportunities in undergraduate research, tutorials, joint degree and professional option programs also exist.

University of Chicago offers a concentration in African and African-American Studies. Sample courses are Rethinking the Black Diaspora and

The Structure of African-American English. There is also an active Committee on African Studies, which has sponsored speaking engagements in past years.

The college does provide the following services free of charge: health care, psychological and career counseling, placement, and tutoring or remedial instruction. While the tutorial services get high marks from black students (particularly the freshman program on expository writing), study skill workshops are noticeably absent.

Each student is assigned an academic advisor from the staff of the Dean of Students; however, black students tend to rely much more on peer counseling. The Coordinating Council for Minority Issues (CCMI) sponsors an alumni mentor program that pairs students with minority alumni who have the same academic or career interests.

The principal organization for black students is the Organization of Black Students (OBS), a group that aims to not only serve as a cultural outlet for black students, but to share black culture with the school's entire community. The George E. Kent Memorial Lecture is an annual OBS event. Recent speakers include Imamu Baraka, Sonia Sanchez and Ivan Van Sertima. Other activities include a special Orientation Dinner for incoming students, a Spring Banquet to honor graduating seniors, dances, study breaks and jazz coffeehouses. There is also a cultural diversity workshop.

UNIVERSITY OF COLORADO
Boulder, Colorado 80309

Undergrads: 19,640
Black Undergrads: 393
Faculty: 1,350
Black Faculty: 23
Tuition: $2,769; $13,653
Total Expenses: $6,892; $17,776

All in all, a black student looking for a large predominantly white school in the West should definitely give UC-Boulder a shot. At the foothills of the Rocky Mountains, one of the nation's leading research universities presents an environment for blacks that features a healthy combination of courses, support services and racial sensitivity.

UC-Boulder sits on 600 acres of land 35 miles from Denver. Courses for black studies are plentiful, with more than two dozen. They cover dance, black women, film, literature, politics and the U.S. educational system.

Most black students come from Colorado, California, Texas and Missouri. To recruit them, the college works with the Colorado Springs Public Schools System, the Colorado Educational Services and Development Association and the Boulder/Denver Public Schools Partnership Program. Recruiters also visit parochial and private schools, attend minority student fairs and contact minority students in the state. The UC-Boulder Black Alumni Association helps attract black students in other states.

UC-Boulder holds a Black Student Weekend twice a year for high school juniors and seniors. Guest speakers provide information on admissions, financial aid and support services.

For admitted students and their parents there is the Black Orientation Program, which holds workshops on financing an education, social organizations and Greek life, and survival skills for black students. The program also gives participants an opportunity to meet faculty, staff, students, alumni and administrators.

Other recruitment efforts include a Pre-Collegiate Development Program for high school sophomores and juniors, Baxter Business Leaders of Tomorrow Minority Seminar for high school juniors interested in business careers, and the Engineering Honors Institute for talented minority students in math and science. The Office of Admissions offers special campus visits for middle school and high school groups.

The UC-Boulder Black Alumni Association encourages the recruitment, enrollment and graduation of black students. They are very involved in numerous programs including a scholarship fund and homecoming.

Tutorial services are free to all minority students. The Multicultural Counseling Center for Community Development (MCCCD) is the main support branch. Counselors assist students with career and academic planning/counseling, personal and social adjustment and cross-cultural awareness training. Peer counselors share their experience with students.

Additional counseling is available through the financial aid officer, and there are advisors in all colleges and schools of the university. Free workshops are offered on test- and note-taking, time management, writing skills, concentration and motivation.

The UCOP Fall Institute Program is designed to assure support and retention of higher-risk minority freshmen. These students must attend labs and see tutors in their more difficult subject areas. The courses offered through this program, General Expository Writing, College Algebra and Biology, have a reputation of academic teaching excellence.

The Minority Faculty-Student Mentorship Program helps students adjust to university life and establish a personal relationship with a faculty member.

There are plenty of black student organizations to keep one busy. Look for the Black Student Athletes Association, Black Student Alliance, Black Business Student's Coalition, Black Law Student's Association, Black Society of Engineers, UMOJA, UC Gospel Choir and six black Greek organizations. Some of the activities sponsored by these organizations are Black History Month, Black Student Welcome Week (first week of school), Harlem Cabaret Talent Show, Soul Food Night and Black Homecoming.

To encourage racial tolerance, UC-Boulder's College of Arts and Sciences has established a policy requiring all students to take at least one course in cultural and gender diversity. And the Multicultural Counseling Center for Community Development offers workshops in cross-cultural awareness training for faculty/staff and student groups.

THE UNIVERSITY OF CONNECTICUT
Storrs, Connecticut 06268

Undergrads: 11,333
Black Undergrads: 453
Faculty: 1,123
Black Faculty: 22
Tuition: $4,974; $12,306
Total Expenses: $10,276; $17,608

Y ou must be strong to survive here, is the general opinion. Here is the
University of Connecticut, offering a liberal education curriculum with
bachelor's, master's, doctoral and first professional degrees. UConn is
large, state-supported and filled with possibilities for the enterprising black
student.

The nearest city is Hartford, which is 30 miles away and has a black
population of 30 percent, contrasting sharply with UConn's black undergraduate population of only four percent.

Admission is selective, and recruitment efforts on the part of the school
are less than vigorous. Twice a year, a recruiter visits public and private
schools in the area to provide information on university programs. Few, if
any, admission officers attend black recruitment fairs, and except for the
school's Day of Pride, in which top Connecticut high school minority
students are honored by the university, seemingly little interest is shown in
the active recruitment of black high school students.

The solid educational curriculum of the University of Connecticut is one
of the few positive aspects students note. The school offers a wide variety
of concentration areas, especially in the fields of agriculture and pharmacol-
ogy. One student chose the school because of the "respect my school has in
the professional world."

For the black student who finds the adjustment to the competitive
academic demands of UConn difficult, the school provides a program called
Committee for the Education of Minority Students. CEMS provides free
academic and personal counseling as well as tutorial services for those
students who show high academic promise and demonstrate a need for
special services. Study skills workshops are also offered, including special

sessions to improve students' writing skills.

In addition, juniors, seniors and faculty members conduct counseling sessions. Respondents consider all of these programs helpful although not enough take advantage of these opportunities, one student reports. Special class sections are rare. One student says that because this is a large school, students rarely get attention on an individual level.

It is the consensus of black students that the rigorous academic life is the hardest obstacle to overcome, but some also feel that another lies in the overwhelming population of white students.

Black organizations on campus include West Indian Student Awareness, National Society of Black Engineers, Minority Students Business Association, Black Student Union, NAACP, and a full representation of Greek fraternities and sororities.

The Student Union is the center for all student activities. There is an Afro-American Cultural Center, established in 1968, but as its name implies, it is mostly geared toward providing cultural and entertainment programs rather than acting as a central gathering place for black students. In the past, the center has sponsored a jazz workshop and an annual cultural fair. It regularly offers dance concerts, plays, art exhibits, musical concerts, films and lectures.

Most blacks view interaction between black and white students negatively. Respondents list the lack of common interests and the giant disparity between the percentages of the two groups as barriers to better relations.

One highlight: UConn's black FM radio programming is easily one of the best in the country.

UNIVERSITY OF DAYTON
Dayton, Ohio 45469

Undergrads: 6,443
Black Undergrads: 193
Faculty: 781
Black Faculty: NA
Tuition: $13,640
Total Expenses: $18,070

University of Dayton students really appreciate the legacy of their school: "The campus has the look of tradition, which the university really promotes," one admirer says.

Located in a city which is 37 percent black, Dayton is a selective, Catholic institution whose campus sits on a hill overlooking the city where the great African-American poet Paul Lawrence Dunbar lived.

Dayton admissions officers make vigorous efforts to recruit black students. They visit predominantly black high schools, and a minority relations counselor conducts telephone conversations with students. Admission counselors attend NSSFMS fairs held in prime recruiting areas, and by invitation, any specifically designated black recruitment programs. Black alumns also assist in recruitment.

Students from Dayton's high schools have an opportunity to come to the campus for a day visit where they receive an admission and financial presentation, lunch, tour, departmental meetings, and sports interest meetings. The university also receives names through the SAT Search Program, and students earning certain PSAT scores are sent mass mailings in the spring. Current minority students visit their former high schools to talk with prospective students and to distribute literature. Two special visitation programs for accepted black students take place in the spring, offering an early university experience prior to attendance.

Course offerings appealing to the black experience have a historical bent, the more unusual being North Africa in Modern Times, South Africa in Modern Times, and West Africa in Modern Times. Mini-courses like The Black Family, Criminal Justice and Minorities, Black Women in America, and Contemporary Issues of the Black Experience may also interest students.

The school's support services are complete and plentiful. Examples include the Tutorial Program, the federally funded SURGE assisting 100 freshmen annually, and Peer Counseling.

One student comments on the "beneficial" Afro-American Center Study Skills Workshops. BATU (Black Action Through Unity) offers tutorial assistance for black students as well. The university holds several special seminars and forums that cover a wide variety of subject areas including career preparation, how to study, interviewing, college orientation, and a speaker series.

One black pre-professional organization, a Society for Black Engineers, is quite active. There are a Black Concert Choir and a black dance group on campus. Black students produce programs on a radio station and publish a black newspaper.

Many social activities are not geared to black students, but blacks do attend black sorority and fraternity parties and private parties. Blacks also go to clubs off campus. BATU sponsors parties, speakers, and intramural sports teams. The Afro-American Center sponsors a Labor Day picnic, and sororities and fraternities offer happy hours. Cliques do exist at Dayton, largely in accordance with sorority/fraternity affiliation and academic concentrations.

Black alumns are very active. Besides attending reunion activities held during Homecoming Weekend, black alumns participate in a Career Volunteer Program, with students spending time with alumns at their jobs. Career placement for black seniors and summer employment leads for black students are available through the Center for Afro-American Affairs. Alumns keep in touch through the Advisory Committee and an alumn newspaper; they also share their expertise through workshops, mini-courses, and internships.

A student says, "I am very satisfied with my decision to attend a predominantly white school. The school has more money than the average black school, so the facilities are better and there are more programs academically and socially going on...I wish there were more blacks here so I could interact with more people from my own race, but I have adjusted to there being only a few."

UNIVERSITY OF DELAWARE
Newark, Delaware 19716

Undergrads: 14,870
Black Undergrads: 677
Faculty: 1,013
Black Faculty: 31
Tuition: $3,690; $10,220
Total Expenses: $8,330; $14,860

"**A**ctually," says a student, "the whole university prepares blacks for the real world because the world is white. Therefore, going to this college is doing exactly what it's supposed to—prepare me (us) for life."

Located 12 miles from the small town of Wilmington, which has a six percent black population, Delaware is a major research institution with a selective admission policy.

Most of the brothers and sisters here are from Pennsylvania, Maryland, Delaware and New Jersey. To recruit them, Delaware employs a variety of strategies. They contact as many as 4,500 black students during its fall recruiting activities. Black alumns help out with telephone campaigns aimed at admitted black students, and a Youth Development Conference for Delaware junior and senior high school students dispenses valuable college advice for first-generation college-bound students.

Each summer, *Initiatives*, an exceptionally handsome four-page newsletter, covers activities of African-American and Latino students.

Delaware offers a minor in both African Studies and Black American Studies, and its courses deal with historic, cultural and social phenomena of people of African descent. Sample listings include Pan Africanism, History of the Caribbean, Images of Race and Ethnicity in American Culture, and Race, Class and Crime.

In addition, the library houses the Ishmael Reed Papers and the papers of Alice Dunbar Wilson.

When academically challenged, help is available from the Academic Services Center, the Writing Center and the Math Center. Plus, SkilMod, one-credit courses to assist in critical thinking, study skills, problem solving and academic self-management, can help keep you afloat. Need more personal contact? Then try Each One Reach One, a mentoring program matching upperclass minority students with frosh.

Ongoing cultural diversity workshops—for students and employees—are sponsored by the Multicultural Affairs Offices, and during New Student Orientation, all frosh attend a diversity workshop.

"Tutorial assistance is available to students in all areas of study," says a respondent, and he reports that the schedules are flexible.

At the same time, Delaware boasts an impressive set of support programs including mentoring, tutoring, study skills classes and career development based on majors: ASPIRE is in the College of Education, FORTUNE 2000 in the College of Business and Economics, HORIZONS in the College of Human Resources, NUCLEUS in the College of Arts and Science, and RISE in the College of Engineering.

The hub of activities is the Center for Black Culture, home of the historically black sororities and fraternities, the Black Student Union, the Cultural Programming and Advisory Board, the campus chapter of the NAACP, and a host of other activities.

At the center, you may find the Dance Theater of Harlem, a step show, a play, a lecture by Afrocentrist Dr. Asa Hilliard or the Gospelrama annual spring concert. "They do all they can," reports a brother, "but students still don't attend the functions."

Social life can be cliquish with the frats and sororities holding dominance, and one respondent insists that there is not enough programming relevant to black students.

Relations with white students are considered good for the most part. "At times," says a respondent, "it seems like as black students, we have to prove more to the faculty than non-blacks."

UNIVERSITY OF THE DISTRICT OF COLUMBIA
Washington, D.C. 20004

Undergrads: 9,179
Black Undergrads: 6,609
Faculty: 615
Black Faculty: NA
Tuition: $1,228; $4,142
Total Expenses: $1,228; $4,142

Blacks at UDC must be careful not to get caught up in the school's hectic and time-consuming social life, advise respondents. Self-discipline is a must, and the disciplined student will best be able to handle UDC's academic challenge.

Large and mostly black, the University of the District of Columbia is an urban commuter school offering the usual array of big city amenities and challenges. Publicly controlled, the university provides liberal arts, teacher education and technical programs.

Most of the black students at UDC come from Washington, D.C., Maryland, Virginia and West Virginia.

The UDC curriculum includes only a palmful of courses that relate to the African-American experience.

UDC has an open admission policy, and the transition from high school to college-level academics has not been that "rough" for most blacks here.

Brothers and sisters finding the academic environment too difficult can call on the university's tutorial and counseling services. Considered quite beneficial by students, these programs include peer and psychological counseling, honors class sections focusing on basics "for students who aren't ready," and special seminars on financial aid, testing and skills assessment. Yet some blacks wish that tutorial assistance could be enlarged to meet the needs of even more students, and one sister says that alumni counseling and support could stand improvement.

UDC has a University College which provides study skills workshops primarily for freshmen. The program has a good reputation, but a few students say that it should offer more workshops dealing with cultural and ethnic perspectives.

One respondent judges contact between UDC's black students and black alumns to be "adequate," thanks to the black alumn association.

When it comes to parties, there are very few complaints. Moreover, the black population supports university-sponsored entertainment.

UDC offers an abundance of service opportunities. The majority of the schools clubs and organizations are black. Most notable are campus-based radio programming and a National Association of Black Accountants. A drama/theater group and a student run newspaper are other popular organizations.

For the student seeking an inexpensive option in an urban setting, UDC is worth a shot.

UNIVERSITY OF FLORIDA

Gainesville, Florida 32611

Undergrads: 29,637
Black Undergrads: 1,778
Faculty: 2,225
Black Faculty: NA
Tuition: $1,705; $7,403
Total Expenses: $6,015; $11,713

G reatly outnumbered by the tens of thousands of white students, many
brothers and sisters here think that the school's concern for their
interests may be getting better—but is still not where it should be.

Florida's first university, coed with a selective admission policy, is also
among the nation's 25 largest with 18 colleges and schools. Its School of
Journalism is nationally ranked.

The majority of the university's black students come from Florida,
Georgia, Alabama and Mississippi.

Most black students feel that the collegiate transition is not intolerably
rough. And for those who do have academic or personal problems, the
university's tutorial and counseling services are more than adequate. For
example, the Reading and Writing Center is a free service offered to students
at all levels. The reading program offers individual and group courses
designed to improve one's vocabulary and study skills. The writing program
is offered to students on a voluntary basis, and help is provided in such areas
as writing thesis statements and developing essays from outlines.

The students also make use of the university's Division of Student
Support and Special Program (DSSSP). Services include academic and
career counseling, free tutoring, financial assistance, and reading and study
skills assistance. The Program for Academic Counseling and Tutoring
(PACT) offers tutoring and counseling especially for educationally disadvantaged students.

The curriculum does not include a degree in this area, but does offer nine
courses related to the African-American experience. The school also has an
Institute of Black Culture, which offers cultural programs, music, art and
literary works.

Many of the university's brothers and sisters "dig the social life." The University of Florida has more than its share of black fraternities and sororities, which students rate highly for throwing the best parties.

Pre-professional societies include the Association of Black Communicators, Black American Law Society, the Minority Business Society and the Society for Black Engineers.

The school has a black gospel choir that sings on campus and at black churches around the Gainesville area. Intramurals are not as popular as one would think at the university.

THE UNIVERSITY OF GEORGIA
Athens, Georgia 30602

Undergrads: 23,572
Black Undergrads: 1,650
Faculty: 2,179
Black Faculty: NA
Tuition: $2,508; $6,282
Total Expenses: $6,328; $10,102

"If you're not used to being around white people, you will definitely experience culture shock," declares one brother. "You'd better be sure you really want to be here," he adds.

Founded in 1785, the first state-chartered university in America remains a large, liberal arts and co-educational institution whose admission policy is selective and whose black students are under pressure.

Advises one undergrad, "It's a unique experience to have to live, work and compete with white students. Be serious! Be confident!" Some blacks say that the most attractive feature of the University of Georgia is its outstanding football team.

Because large classes can often be a drawback, the University of Georgia provides a counseling program and a testing center wherein "tutors are provided, up to five hours a week, for just about every class." Everyone has a concentration advisor, and "there's always someone to talk to," remarks one student. Topics for study skills workshops range from How to Test with Stress, to Personal Time Management, while special seminars and forums have included titles such as "Reaganomics and the KKK."

With five courses offered on African issues and a black director of Development Studies, black students are able to relate at least culturally to their curriculum. Yet, there is little interaction with black faculty and white professors.

Black pre-journalism, pre-med, business and computer societies often help to relieve some of the academic pressures at the University of Georgia. The Black Theatrical Ensemble (BTE) performs throughout the year; black radio airs three hours a day.

Blacks usually attend area churches, despite the fact that, from one

perspective, "the university doesn't really deal with the local community."
Because the Black Student Center and the Black Student Union are fairly inactive, social life for blacks is dependent upon the Greek-letter organizations, which give the majority of black parties on campus and which sometimes sponsor athletic events. There is also a Committee for Black Student Programs, which plans special events relating to the black experience.

Many blacks participate in dorm activities through intramural sports. Blacks in the same dorms, as well as sisters and brothers with similar tastes, form cliques. Unfortunately, many students do not know about the University of Georgia's Black Alumni Chapter, which actively recruits black students from local high schools.

UNIVERSITY OF IDAHO
Moscow, Idaho 83843

Undergrads: 8,103
Black Undergrads: 81
Faculty: 625
Black Faculty: NA
Tuition: $1,620; $5,380
Total Expenses: $5,220; $8,980

B lacks describe the surrounding community of northern Idaho as an area "not yet reached by the Civil Rights Movement" and a place where "whites view blacks as they saw them in the 1950s." Consequently, black students travel eight miles to Washington State University in Pullman for black religious services and to participate in Alpha Kappa Alpha Chapter activities. Even here, black athletes reportedly receive favorable treatment in terms of housing and employment.

Despite the problems, one student writes, "It would be an injustice to warn blacks not to come here because nothing will change unless more blacks choose to attend." Nevertheless, the respondents seem unanimous about the special problems awaiting the out-of-state black student who is not an athlete.

Surrounded by mountains, the campus is 90 miles southeast of Spokane, Washington. Idaho offers open admissions to state residents. Out-of-state applicants must have a "C" average and rank in the top half of their graduating class.

The University of Idaho is composed of eight colleges and a graduate school. Students can obtain bachelor's degrees in area studies (America, Latin America), business education, English, fine and performing arts, and pre-professional areas, among others.

Student responses reveal a sharp dichotomy between the experiences of black students and black athletes. Some respondents complain that black athletes receive special help in making the academic transition at the university.

The university provides free tutorial assistance and counseling through the Office of Special Services, the Learning Resource Center, and the

Minority Advisory Services.

Although they acknowledge the hardships facing black students, several students express satisfaction with their decision to attend the University of Idaho. They cite the small community which "enables a black student to concentrate on studies" and "the fairly based competition" which allows a student "who works hard enough to get ahead regardless of race."

UNIVERSITY OF IOWA
Iowa City, Iowa 52242

Undergrads: 18,740
Black Undergrads: 375
Faculty: 1,803
Black Faculty: NA
Tuition: $2,558; $8,636
Total Expenses: $6,108; $12,186

The lack of role models in this white environment demands strong, mature individuals. Says one brother, "It was quite a change, but one I considered necessary in order to make it and to be able to adjust in the predominantly white real world."

The black community is very small at large U. of I., and many brothers and sisters have difficulty adjusting to the overwhelmingly white atmosphere. But there is a great deal of academic support for them.

Says one undergrad: "If one wants to stay in the Midwest, not be in the big cities, then this is a good place to study." He adds, however, that Iowa winters can be "awfully cold."

Self-contained on a campus by the Iowa River, 25 miles from Cedar Rapids, the University of Iowa is a large, selective, coed school with five graduate and professional colleges.

Most of the U. of I.'s black students are from Iowa itself and the neighboring states of Illinois, Missouri, Michigan and Nebraska. One student describes Iowa as a "law and order" state, and many students consider Iowa City a safe place to live. The U. of I. is strong academically. It has a long history of academic innovation, having been the first state university in the nation to admit women and men on an equal basis, and the first to accept creative work for graduate degrees instead of the traditional academic thesis.

There is an abundance of academic support available to students, including a reading lab, a writing lab and a network of advising centers in the dorms. Minority students have access to special academic, financial and personal counseling, and the offerings include tutoring and study skills assistance in math and science. Among other campus support organizations, the black pre-med and pre-law societies are great according to respondents. The Greek system is a strong source of black community at the university, and social life here revolves primarily around the Greek party scene, considered the most important form of entertainment for blacks on campus.

A major reason for attending the University of Iowa, according to many of its black students, is the low tuition. However, most consider the school to be academically challenging, and only a few respondents have reconsidered their decision to attend.

Interaction between whites and blacks at U. of I. is comfortable but cool, say respondents. Most white students come from small towns where they have had little or no contact with black people.

Fighters and go-getters will do well here. Others...?

UNIVERSITY OF MARYLAND, BALTIMORE COUNTY

Catonsville, Maryland 21228

Undergrads: 8,899
Black Undergrads: 1,335
Faculty: 696
Black Faculty: NA
Tuition: $4,540; $7,992
Total Expenses: $9,074; $12,526

Among UMBC's special academic programs is one in African-American Studies, which some black students cite as the most attractive feature of the school.

UMBC, founded in 1966, sits on 476 acres eight miles from the Baltimore city line. Students say this modern, coed, suburban school with a selective admission policy is dominated by whites.

The majority of black students at UMBC come from Maryland, New York, Pennsylvania and New Jersey. Many are commuters, and many complain about white student insensitivity to them.

UMBC recruits at inner city high schools and offers a workshop to help the brothers and sisters prepare for college. A role model mentor program matches black frosh with faculty members for four years and has a tutoring component to boot. Respondents also rate counseling at the Learning Resources Center as adequate.

But the standout is the career counseling program; many students consider it to be excellent.

The Black Student Union, the most visible non-Greek organization for blacks on campus, is a source of cultural unity. Look for lectures and workshops to be sponsored by them. Moreover, black religious services also provide a source of strength and identity.

Blacks at UMBC depend upon the school's two black sororities and one black fraternity to fill their social needs.

Most black students don't attend the white-oriented parties that are the heart of organized social activity here. Participation in intramural sports, however, seems to cut the tension between black and white students.

Since most black students here give the local community poor grades and even term it racist, they take advantage of nearby Baltimore's features as often as possible.

For the serious student who is serious about a good future, the feeling that UMBC offers black students solid academics and outstanding career guidance may make UMBC a good no-frills option. In the words of one brother, "The most attractive thing about this school is the opportunity to meet intellectually bright blacks who are headed for a good future and who care not only about themselves, but also about their people."

UNIVERSITY OF MARYLAND, COLLEGE PARK

College Park, Maryland 20742

Undergrads: 22,922
Black Undergrads: 2,980
Faculty: 1,638
Black Faculty: NA
Tuition: $4,169; $9,553
Total Expenses: $9,420; $14,804

"It isn't always a good decision to attend a predominantly white school," advises a senior. "You receive added pressures, and you have to show yourself even more."

The flagship institution in the Maryland state system, UMCP with 2,500 faculty members and 35,000 students ranks ninth among the ten largest campuses in the country. It also ranks, if you listen to some brothers and sisters, at the top for the amount of pressure put on black students.

With a projected 15 percent rise in tuition, a curriculum that students say is racist and fuels the ideals of white supremacy, and a heated discussion about the funding of a black student center, one brother asks, "What next?"

Maryland's admission policy is selective, and its black students are predominantly from Maryland, D.C., New Jersey and Virginia.

Afro-American studies flourishes here, with a B.A., B.S. or certificate available. The department offers more than a dozen courses, including history and politics.

Since many black students are not prepared for the demanding college-level academics, they must rely upon the school's support services, including tutorial and counseling services, the writing center, minority peer advisors and the writing and study skills lab—most of which are part of the Office of Minority Student Education (OMSE).

The nexus for UMCP black student activities is the Nyumburu Cultural Center, providing programs relating to the black experience and located in Stamp Union. Respondents say that the offerings are culturally healthy and deserve greater participation by black matriculants.

The Black Student Union is the major political group for black students on campus, while the Black Student Summit Committee carries additional clout. Other activities are sponsored by pre-professional societies, black theater (mostly limited to one-act plays) and the campus radio's daily program geared to black students called "Yester Now." The NAACP meets at Nyumburu, the University gospel choir dishes out musical inspiration and a Black Ministry Society provides religious solace.

"The most attractive thing about this school is probably the number of things to do," claims one student. Other opportunities include the Black Student Athletic Council, created to support black athletes; the *Black Explosion* newspaper; an African-American Writers Workshop; and the Caribbean Student Association.

The social atmosphere is one of the more positive aspects of the University of Maryland although students warn that the initiative must be taken by the black students: "Any catering to black tastes must be done by blacks."

Black Greeks' parties, often held off campus, are the main source of entertainment. This and other social outlets include the Miss Black Unity Pageant; the yearly unity picnic for first-year African, Asian, Hispanic and Native Americans; happy hours; pool parties; and spades tournaments.

Students applaud happy hours soundly because "they give you a chance to meet a lot of people, have a good time, and provide social stability and an outlet from classes." These activities are necessary because the mixers and other university-sponsored social gatherings are "geared to and organized by the white student." Despite these drawbacks, black students find no shortage of social activity, citing in addition to the parties, "many up-to-date movies and good plays," as well as very good concerts.

Even those students who are happy about Maryland admit, "You need to have the idea that you are here to better yourself so that you can survive in the real world."

UNIVERSITY OF MASSACHUSETTS
Boston, Massachusetts 02125

Undergrads: 7,851
Black Undergrads: 1,178
Faculty: 835
Black Faculty: NA
Tuition: $4,405; $8,568
Total Expenses: $8,405; $12,568

One of the campus highlights here, according to one respondent, is the return of black alumns to speak on campus. "Those alumns on the faculty and administrative staff are very helpful and sensitive to the problems and challenges of student life," assesses one undergrad in describing the unique environment of black students at UMass.

UMass, with its affordable education, is a large, state-supported, coed institution with a selective admission policy. Approximately 95 percent of the students come from Massachusetts, and most commute from the Boston area.

The university has Colleges of Arts and Science, Management, and Public and Community Service. Each college provides its students with academic support in the form of free tutorial help, peer advising and study skills workshops. One contented respondent considers these to be "very good, informative and useful."

In addition, UMass/Boston offers fundamental skills courses in English and math, while the College of Arts and Science features an honors program in which high academic achievers enroll in small classes and have special opportunities for informal exchanges with faculty members. Additionally, the university sponsors a six-to-eight-week summer program emphasizing reading, writing, math and study skills. Participants who successfully complete this program enroll as full-time students in the fall.

Moreover, the university offers various pre-freshman programs to students from Boston public high schools who are highly motivated but economically and educationally disadvantaged. These students undertake two to three years of tutorial and remedial work in preparation for college-level study.

Finally, there is the Flexible Campus Program for high school students from the Greater Boston area who wish to enroll in UMass/Boston classes free of charge. These students learn first-hand about the university experience and can explore subjects not offered at their high schools.

Reports one black student: "Although this transition is difficult, the academic support services available have helped many students make the transition from college a smooth one."

The Career Services Office provides counseling about employment outlooks, job options and graduate schools.

Counseling Services offers personal counseling in both individual and group formats. Bilingual counseling is available for Hispanic students. The Campus Ministry, which includes representatives of all faiths, is also available for counseling and discussion.

For student-parents, the Day Care Center offers child care services on a sliding fee basis.

The Pan African Students Organization (PASO) brings black students and faculty together by organizing conferences, parties and other cultural activities. One student notes that a large number of black students participate in PASO-sponsored events. Black students also get together through the university's growing athletic programs. Black undergraduates participate actively in both intramural and varsity sports.

On campus, interaction between black and white students is generally friendly and constructive. However, one student says, "Interaction depends on individual students." Student respondents feel that white faculty and administrators are helpful and approachable, though sometimes condescending. Black undergraduates say that black faculty and administrators serve as role models and are very supportive and encouraging. Black student interaction with the local communities is generally good.

With access to strong academic and extracurricular support services, black students here seem generally satisfied with their decision to attend UMass/Boston. Concludes one student, "I am receiving a great deal for my money."

UNIVERSITY OF MICHIGAN
Ann Arbor, Michigan 48109

Undergrads: 23,575
Black Undergrads: 2,122
Faculty: 3,520
Black Faculty: NA
Tuition: $5,546; $18,025
Total Expenses: $10,443; $22,922

According to one respondent, "I am satisfied with my decision to attend this university for academic reasons—but socially and culturally, it leaves much to be desired."

Large, coed and very selective Michigan is revered for its excellent and respected academic programs, but black students should be prepared to combat possible culture shock and social alienation, say respondents.

The university attracts black students mostly from Michigan, Ohio, Illinois and New York.

Students describe the academics as rigorous and emphasize the necessity of a solid high school background and a lot of determination and perseverance. They can enjoy an extensive range of courses, including several dozen courses in African-American Studies as well as a flexible concentration program in this area.

Looking for academic and personal counseling? The Comprehensive Studies/Opportunity Program provides academic advising, tutorial assistance, personalized counseling and career-oriented work study to incoming freshmen. The Office of Academic Counseling assigns concentration and scheduling advisors to students, and a Minority Study and Survival Skills program offers additional assistance.

Writing workshops evaluate students' strengths and weaknesses. At the same time, acquiring tutorial assistance requires that students be assertive. Most comment on the value of the Minority Peer Advisors who serve as role models, programmers, resource people, personal and academic counselors and referral agents within the housing units.

The most extensive counseling network is within the residence halls themselves.

Black organizations on campus are not strong, with the exception of Greeks. The black pre-med society receives ratings of "moderately useful" to "useless," and other black pre-professional societies seem unused or unheard-of. The Minority Student Services program offers Trotter House as a facility for a variety of educational and multicultural activities. But one student mentions that "the house is not really theirs, and students don't use it that much." There is a black student union, but one brother discards it as a "lifeless organization."

The Special Programs Office, a part of the Housing Division, is the major source of cultural events and provides funding for Black History Month, The Minority Arts and Cultural Festival, Kwanzaa, Minority Freshmen Weekend, Martin Luther King Celebration and various lectures and workshops.

When it comes to partying, black students at the University of Michigan are "Greek happy." There are three black fraternities and three black sororities which provide the major social outlets for black students. Dorm parties and university-sponsored activities are not met with enthusiasm by blacks unless they are specifically geared to them. Intramural sports are "serious stuff" and draw a significant number of black athletes. A few mention that intramurals lessen racial tension and break down barriers, to some degree.

Subtle as well as blatant racism is a concern of black students on the Ann Arbor campus. Superficial relationships are easy to establish, but there is much underlying hostility. There seems to be little exchange of ideas, and both sides practice segregation. Black students coming from mostly black environments tend to cling to each other and blacks coming from predominantly white environments have a difficult time finding their niche. Says one sister, "The black student here must make a choice between being 'white' or 'black'; there is a kind of double anxiety within the mind of the upper middle-class black."

Black faculty are a source of support for students, and the relationships between the two are good. "The problem is that there are so few," according to one student.

Black alumns participate moderately in recruitment efforts. They organize and contribute to scholarships for black students and participate in the Student-Alumni Mentorship program.

Preparation for the working world is a high priority at this institution. A job placement manual is available which thoroughly outlines the requirements and opportunities for specific areas of employment and gives useful pointers for job seekers. The emphasis on post-graduate work is an attractive feature to students, yet some mention that Michigan's large size dehumanizes; students feel like numbers, and the faculty devotes more time to research than to teaching.

UNIVERSITY OF MISSISSIPPI
University, Mississippi 38677

Undergrads: 7,946
Black Undergrads: 715
Faculty: 526
Black Faculty: NA
Tuition: $2,546; $4,816
Total Expenses: $4,146; $6,416

Ole Miss has some very good things and some very bad things on its campus. Although it has a diverse curriculum, an active Black Student Union, frequent parties and good intramurals, students point to superficial race relations, an overemphasis on fraternity and sorority life, poor student-faculty and student-administrator relations and questionable relationships with the community as potential drawbacks.

Located on a 2,000-acre campus, Ole Miss is a selective, public institution offering bachelor's degree programs in liberal arts, education, and the sciences.

Seventy percent of the students attending Ole Miss are from within the state. Other states with high representation are Tennessee, Alabama, and Illinois.

Ole Miss has a diverse curriculum, so trying to decide what to take may be a problem. Courses offered in the African-American experience encompass the study of politics, literature, community research, and culture.

Students warn that the adjustment to college work requirements is a challenge; Ole Miss is definitely not to be played with—or partied with. In order to ease the transition from high school, the Learning Development Center offers tutorial assistance in English, math, and reading. Academic, personal, and career counseling is available through the Student Counseling Center. A campus-wide three-hour credit course is open to students who wish to improve their study habits, note-taking skills, and time management.

Resident Hall Advisors living in dormitories also provide personal and academic counseling on a one-to-one basis.

The Black Student Union sponsors several events and activities including the Miss Ebony Pageant, a homecoming dance, a speaker's forum, Black History Month, Afro-Ball, and a Gospel Extravaganza. The popular Gospel Choir travels nationwide with its harmonies.

The Office of Student Activities for Minority Affairs publishes a monthly newsletter to provide black students with a forum for relevant issues and events. The office further assists students in planning and coordinating social, cultural, and recreational events.

During the yearly National Achievement Conference, approximately 85 outstanding black high school seniors from Mississippi are invited to be guests of the university for three days during Black History week. The students attend class, talk to professors and staff, hear guest speakers, and attend social activities sponsored by the black campus organizations. Black students say the university sponsors entertainment geared to white students. Yet the brothers and sisters do find happy hours to be a popular and relaxing alternative to fraternity and sorority social events.

Intramurals at Ole Miss are highly competitive and are considered one of the university's most successful programs. Black students tend to participate in the heavily competitive intramural sports because they see it as a great way to relax and stay in shape.

Through both the campus radio station and televison studio, black students promote news and other programs of interest to African-American students.

Race relations? They're described as superficial, with much prejudice underneath, despite the outward appearance of friendliness. Relationships with members of the community are said to be strained.

Like most things in life, Ole Miss mixes both good and bad.

The good part is that Ole Miss is considered "one of the most partying schools in the South." The bad part is that you could party yourself right on out the door.

UNIVERSITY OF MISSOURI
Columbia, Missouri 65211

Undergrads: 16,784
Black Undergrads: 1,007
Faculty: 1,599
Black Faculty: NA
Tuition: $3,771; $9,954
Total Expenses: $7,370; $13,553

Consider: Mizzou-Columbia offers a significant variety of degree programs, and certainly the tuition cost has to be considered a bargain. With these two advantages weighed, Mizzou-Columbia may deserve a serious look-see.

Students say it is easy to feel lost on the 3,600-acre campus of the oldest and largest of the four colleges which make up the University of Missouri system. Coed Mizzou-Columbia, located 35 miles north of Jefferson City, employs a selective admission policy. Eighty-five percent of Mizzou-Columbia's student body are natives of Missouri, and 95 percent of them have attended public high schools.

The range of bachelor's degree programs includes almost everything from the fine arts to the natural sciences. But education, engineering, and business and public administration are the most popular concentrations.

The curriculum provides several courses in history and literature related to the African-American experience.

Because of the large size of most classes, faculty access, say students, is limited. Meanwhile, black students face long adjustment periods due to the rigor of college academics, and the attrition rate is high. Many come from inner-city high schools which have not adequately prepared them for college.

The university offers tutorial assistance to all students, but reportedly, few black students participate.

At the forefront of cultural life is the university's Black Culture Center, which sponsors events and speakers. Fraternities and sororities sponsor most of the campus parties, and as a result, cliques tend to emerge on the basis of Greek affiliation.

There seem to be very few connecting points between native black and white students, and similarly, relations between black students and the community seem extremely limited.

Students interested in the University of Missouri at Columbia have some serious considerations to make: attrition rates for blacks are high; counseling services need improvement; class size is large in most cases; cliques abound; fraternities and sororities dominate social life; and there is limited interaction between black students and the rest of the campus.

UNIVERSITY OF MISSOURI
St. Louis, Missouri 63121

Undergrads: 9,464
Black Undergrads: 1,325
Faculty: 970
Black Faculty: NA
Tuition: $3,383; $8,681
Total Expenses: $7,724; $13,022

If you want a commuter school that has one of the best business schools around, you'd better look at the University of Missouri at St. Louis.

Famous for its business school, the University of Missouri is ideal for the career-minded and commuter-minded. This liberal arts, coed institution is one of four campuses that make the University of Missouri the ninth largest in the country. Located five miles from downtown St. Louis, the school has a selective admission policy.

Still, because of its commuter status, UMSL draws most of its black students from Missouri and nearby Illinois.

Unlike many commuter schools, UMSL has a reputation for high-quality academics. Students are advised to come here to learn. Bachelor's and graduate degrees are offered in areas of liberal arts, business, education, optometry and nursing.

The library holds manuscripts related to St. Louis's black history.

For support services, you can find tutorials, peer counselors, faculty advisors and plenty of academic workshops ranging from from test-taking to math anxiety.

For African-American activities, students depend upon the Associated Black Collegians and the Black Culture Room, which serves as a meeting and party area.

Socially, black students complain. Parties are infrequent and off-campus; interaction between black and white students is minimal. White faculty are deemed insensitive. Thankfully, the few black faculty members help lift black students' spirits.

UNIVERSITY OF MONTANA
Missoula, Montana 59812

Undergrads: 9,675
Black Undergrads: 97
Faculty: 640
Black Faculty: NA
Tuition: $2,414; $6,562
Total Expenses: $6,200; $10,348

Well, it's in Montana, what were you expecting? Like to ski? Only 12 miles to excellent skiing, according to its brochure, state-supported and coed Montana offers the usual range of undergraduate degrees in liberal arts, science and other areas. Its admission policy is not very selective, and seven out of ten students come from Montana

Still, Montana seems to offer a challenging academic atmosphere and a willingness to accommodate the special needs of its black undergrads. Most come to the Big Sky State from Montana, California, Washington and Illinois.

Of the transition from high school to university life, one black student says, "some have, and some haven't" made the adjustment well. For those students with transitional or academic difficulties, tutorial assistance, offered by the Special Services Program and the Center for Student Development, is available.

"Counseling," one student says, "is a valuable service, once the student finds out where help is." Another says that counseling "was lacking when I first came here, but now we have a minority counselor, which should help." Academic departments pitch in too. Study Skills Workshops, including a "fairly effective" reading course, are offered by the Center for Student Development.

Special class sections, special seminars and forums complement the workshops.

UM also provides a Black Student Advisor to help with counseling and summer employment with the U.S. Forest Service and area agricultural resources.

Over a dozen courses, including Afro-Americans Since Emancipation, relate to the black experience. Archival material on the black military experience in Montana is available, and the African-American Studies Program has its own private library.

Relations between Montana's black students and the school's white students get mixed reactions. "Good," one student says. Another calls them "okay, at times—nothing great or extremely bad. Sports help to provide interaction." Reports another: "The black students here are from larger cities and have no real experience with an almost totally white environment. As a consequence, they have trouble relating to white students."

Relations with white faculty and administrators are said to be without stress. Relations with black faculty and administrators are "fair," one student says, and "could use some improving." Interaction with the local community is said to be comfortable. Says a sophomore: "The community is very liberal—unlike the state as a whole, which is conservative."

University-sponsored entertainment is considered to be adequate by the black students. A brother says that the school has brought "one black jazz band, which is all I am aware of." Social life seems to revolve around intramural sports, infrequent parties and mixers, all of which are moderately satisfying for Montana's black students.

The Black Student Union organizes various cultural and educational activities, including a Black History Month, picnics, happy hours and "other social functions."

According to one student, there is "zero" participation in university government other than the Black Student Union. Another student says that blacks "do not hold any [governmental] positions that I am aware of."

UM's alumns have contributed money to pay for a speaker during Black History Month. Given the potential for a satisfying black collegiate environment—beautiful locale, interesting curriculum and a range of support services—the alumn effort could be instrumental in aiding Montana's recruitment efforts.

UNIVERSITY OF NORTH CAROLINA
Greensboro, North Carolina 27412

Undergrads: 9,931
Black Undergrads: 1,490
Faculty: 700
Black Faculty: NA
Tuition: $1,868; $8,904
Total Expenses: $5,373; $12,409

Most students choose UNC, Greensboro for its high academic rating. One student proclaims, "Overall, UNC, Greensboro is what you make it. There are plenty of opportunities to get involved, and I'm really glad I chose this school. Why? Because it's a challenge."

State-supported, large and coed, the University of North Carolina, Greensboro is a selective, coeducational and liberal arts school that provides real challenges for black students. This large, public university attracts most of its students from North Carolina, New Jersey, Virginia or Florida.

Unfortunately, one quarter of the black students who enter UNC, Greensboro become discouraged by the class work and peer pressure, and drop out after one semester.

Many feel that a possible cause for the high attrition is the lack of university-sponsored support services. A federally supported Special Services Project, the counseling supplied by the Neo-Black Society (NBS) and occasional study skills workshops are the only sources of academic support to which a black student can turn.

Yet one student says, "The counseling has been extremely helpful to me in overcoming the fear of the university and the rapid pace of life here. It has provided me with encouragement to improve my grades and to work harder towards a goal."

In addition, the black church also helps to inspire black students. "Several of the community churches send buses over to pick students up on Sundays." Students do volunteer work in the community under church auspices, which helps students to develop meaningful relationships with blacks off campus.

On campus, because there is very little university-sponsored entertainment for blacks; students mostly interact through events sponsored by the NBS. "NBS sponsors a choir, a dance group, drama and other black arts," proclaims one student. Most parties are sponsored by the black fraternities and sororities.

Some students feel that UNC, Greensboro's greatest weakness is its lack of football and basketball teams although students are very active in intramural sports. Another weakness which students point out is the lack of interaction between black faculty and students. On the other hand, according to one student, relations between black students and white faculty are "surprisingly compatible." The interaction with alumns is also fairly good.

One student notes that "many people in the local community are alumns of this school or one of the 16 other UNC campuses. So they understand exactly where we are coming from and where we want to go in life."

UNIVERSITY OF NORTH TEXAS
Denton, Texas 76203

Undergrads: 18,654
Black Undergrads: 1,306
Faculty: 1,005
Black Faculty: NA
Tuition: $1,713; $7,472
Total Expenses: $5,372; $11,131

State-supported, coed, and selective, this large university 35 miles from Fort Worth and Dallas promises an atmosphere in which you "won't lose your identity." However, a common complaint is that both black and white students are "treated like numbers."

Academics at University of North Texas focus on practical education based on a liberal arts foundation. The university has programs in 87 undergraduate fields. An honors program offers an inter-disciplinary approach to learning for 50 academically superior beginning freshmen each year, and five national honor societies have chapters on campus.

The emphasis is on broad education with a career preparation bent. Juniors and seniors can participate in paid internships through the Cooperative Education Program. The UNT-Meadows Teaching Excellence Program is a collaborative effort offering practical experience to educators.

The university offers guidance to students through its Center for Career Choice, and the Career Planning and Placement Service helps them in the mechanics of starting a career.

Some black students have found the transition from high school to college-level academics at UNT to be difficult. Support services exist, but respondents seem to feel they are not well-utilized. However, each department has its own tutorial service, and tutorial efforts on campus are generally termed "good." Peer counseling is considered especially useful. One feature is the university-sponsored Campus Chat, "a peer-group talk about anything."

Organizational support at UNT can most easily be found in the Greek organizations. There are 15 national fraternities and nine national sororities on campus, and they sponsor sports, dances, and parties. Most blacks belong to a Greek organization. There is said to be some keen competition among them. The position of the Greek groups in the mainstream of campus life, as well as the inter-group competition, is seen by one sister as a source of division among blacks.

There is healthy interaction between whites and blacks at UNT. The two groups often attend the same parties, which are often sponsored by individual dorms. But the need to assimilate and become part of the general "school spirit," as well as the small numbers of blacks on campus and the absence of overt racism, tend, she says, to make blacks "forget where we come from."

The residence halls at University of North Texas have distinct flavors, from Bruce Hall, known for fine arts, to Clark Hall, which encourages participation in intramural sports, to Kerr Hall, "full of school spirit and an active social pace." All but two of the halls are coed. In the coed dorms, men and women share dining facilities and recreational space, but live in separate wings. The separate wings have their own upperclass resident counselors.

Black students have generally adjusted well to life at North Texas, but do not play a visible role in campus affairs. University committees are "mostly white," and black theater is active "mostly during Black History Month." Black faculty are few in number, and one student writes that he has "never had a black teacher."

However, campus radio is said to have "a lot of black influence," and the Voices of Praise, a gospel group, offers students a creative outlet. Church activities in the town of Denton are also important to black students, and buses are available for that purpose.

On the whole, University of North Texas offers a good academic education to the black student who is able to find his niche in a white environment.

UNIVERSITY OF NOTRE DAME
Notre Dame, Indiana 46556

Undergrads: 7,600
Black Undergrads: 228
Faculty: 924
Black Faculty: NA
Tuition: $17,971
Total Expenses: $22,471

A brother admits that the school has opened his eyes, like many other blacks, "to the harsh realities of our American system." Yet he concludes that although "the environment of the school is far from being perfect, there are dedicated individuals who are trying to change things for the betterment of all mankind." Essentially, as one brother puts it, "It takes a very special black student to 'survive' in a mystical environment like Notre Dame."

One of the premier Catholic universities in the country, with a highly selective admission process, Notre Dame is considered an athletically inclined university, but its academic reputation is just as impressive.

Although most black students at Notre Dame hail from Illinois, Indiana and Louisiana, Notre Dame's national recruitment program covers more than 29 cities with large black populations. As part of the recruitment effort, admission officers visit private and public secondary schools, college-bound programs and NSSFMS events. On campus, black students get involved in the undergraduate schools committee, which trains student volunteers in admission recruitment. They also help organize a spring visitation program.

Students can pursue a bachelor's degree in the social sciences, natural sciences, humanities or business-related fields. Notre Dame has a Minority Engineering Program for black students who are serious about pursuing an engineering degree. The Black Studies Department features courses in Afro-American literature and black American politics.

During the first year at Notre Dame, black students can call upon counselors in the Freshman Year of Studies Office, senior advisors and minority peer advisors for academic and personal advice. And if these support bases aren't enough, they can drop in the Minority Affairs Office for consultations, even though one black student claims that the office is "seldom utilized by students until problems get large."

To sharpen student's academic tools, the Freshman Learning Resource Center organizes study skills workshops, tutoring sessions and other support services.

After the first year, black students are assigned a faculty and a minority advisor in their major area of study. Several black students feel that support services, particularly tutoring, "tend to drop off slightly after freshman year." Nonetheless, many classes with an enrollment greater than 25 students have weekly tutorial sessions run by teacher assistants.

Academic adjustment is facilitated by these services, says one brother, but he thinks emotional stability deserves attention too.

Organizations like the Society of Black Engineers and the Black Business Students exist primarily to assist the black student's struggle on the psychological as well as academic level.

Although Notre Dame is a religious school, there is no worship service on campus frequented by black students. Instead, most black students attend church services in the black community in South Bend, especially since the churches provide transportation. A radio station catering to the cultural rhythms of black students is missing at Notre Dame, prompting one brother to speculate that a campus-based black radio station would "help students, if only to boost morale, since there is no black radio or T.V. programming in the vicinity."

Parties thrown by black students lack some spirit because brothers and sisters attend the functions "as though it were their duty" and not for the pleasure of it. Sometimes parties, as well as meetings, seminars and study sessions, take place in the Black Cultural Arts Center, a one-room center under the supervision of the Director of Minority Affairs.

Every year, a committee is formed to organize the big spring fling, the Black Cultural Arts Festival, which helps to forge ties between the black community at Notre Dame and the black community in South Bend as well as compensate for the paucity of university-sponsored entertainment.

Though black students' past involvement in university governance has been characterized as "non-existent" by one sister, "participation is now on the upswing." Nevertheless, there is some tradition for black students at Notre Dame, such as their annual effort to have a keynote speaker at commencement.

During freshman year, black students have more contact with white students because roommates are chosen by the university. The only other sphere where interaction occurs is in the classroom. Despite these structured situations, which don't lead to much voluntary interaction, relations between black and white students remain superficial. Then one brother complains: "Some black students try to assimilate instead of being themselves."

One sister notes: "The small number of black faculty enhances the relationship because we become like extended families." This family feeling seems to exist within the black student body also, except that some sense certain drawbacks.

"Students have a tendency to adopt one another as sisters and brothers, but the relationships and social gatherings are limited to platonic ones."

The few black graduates of Notre Dame manage to stay in touch with the present black undergraduates and pay their dues to prospective black undergraduates by plugging into the national alumn network, the alumni schools committee (recruitment program) and participating in on-campus workshops. Already, they have developed a black alumn directory, and according to one administrator, the "network is beginning to take shape."

UNIVERSITY OF PENNSYLVANIA
Philadelphia, Pennsylvania 19104

Undergrads: 11,504
Black Undergrads: 805
Faculty: 3,853
Black Faculty: NA
Tuition: $19,898
Total Expenses: $27,398

Warns one respondent: "It is important that a black student who applies to Penn have confidence in his/her abilities. A student with low self-esteem will not survive four years here."

Founded in 1740 by Ben Franklin and academically rigorous, the University of Pennsylvania is a large, coed Ivy League institution. Its admission policy is one of the most selective in the country. Here are Penn's undergraduate schools: the School of Nursing, the only one in the Ivy League; the School of Engineering and Applied Science; the College of Arts and Sciences; and the Wharton School of Business.

African-American Studies offers a wide range of courses covering anthropology, religion, politics, music, and history, including Black Psychology, African-American Literature, and Black Intellectuals.

The academic pressure that characterizes the University of Pennsylvania makes the transition from high school to college especially tough. One participant places the responsibility on the student: "If one has initiative and takes advantage of the support services on campus, one will find the transition to college life a little easier."

Tutorial assistance is available through the Tutoring Center. A study skills workshop focuses on time management and term-paper writing. The large number of black political, social, and pre-professional organizations on campus should help your academic survival. These groups include the Black Student League, Black Pre-Health Society, Black Pre-Law Society, Black Economic Society, Society of Black Engineers, Black Wharton Undergraduate Association, Minority Student News, Groove Phi Groove Social Fellowship, Alpha Kappa Alpha sorority, Alpha Phi Alpha fraternity, Kappa Alpha Psi fraternity, Delta Sigma Theta sorority, Eta Phi Beta sorority, and the Council of Black Organizations.

The W. E. B. Dubois College House (a dormitory) serves as a gathering place for black students. They sponsor study breaks and get-togethers and have recreational facilities. The Penn Black Drama Ensemble may interest actors, and for those with good voices there is a Gospel Choir.

The Black Alumni Association works directly with the admission officers in recruiting. Also on the recruiting agenda are introductory receptions in areas with traditionally high application rates. These receptions get alumni and current students involved in sending out letters inviting students to visit the campus. Admission officers visit public and private high schools, attend local college fairs, and receive names of prospective black students from the National Scholarship Service and Fund for Minority Students (NSSFMS).

Staying enrolled at the University of Pennsylvania may be as difficult, if not more so, than getting in, considering the pressure. One student's advice is to put academics first. "In the wake of ever-increasing racial problems, it is necessary for black students to continue to put their school work first, and then fight to eliminate such problems."

Another believes these issues to be of equal importance. "Each of us has something to contribute to the world; Penn is a good place to start. There are opportunities to do most anything. I feel that one cannot truly enjoy the Penn experience without experiencing involvement in those activities that facilitate interaction with many different types of people."

UNIVERSITY OF PITTSBURGH
Pittsburgh, Pennsylvania 15260

Undergrads: 16,447
Black Undergrads: 1,480
Faculty: 3,410
Black Faculty: NA
Tuition: $5,638; $13,854
Total Expenses: $10,472; $18,688

"At the University of Pittsburgh, black students are not held back," says a student. "Come with an open mind. Feel that you have as much a right to be here as anyone else."

Admission at this large, coed, public institution is selective. Located three miles from downtown Pittsburgh, the university attracts black students mainly from Pennsylvania, New York, New Jersey and Ohio.

Degrees are awarded in the liberal arts and sciences, business, education, health, engineering, pre-professional and professional fields. The African-American Studies department offers courses in Afro-American, African, and Caribbean affairs. States the university bulletin: "Contrary to popular myth, black studies occupies a central—not peripheral—role in understanding modern American life and global linkages tied to American life."

The university's size may interfere with a student's transition from high school to college. "I had a problem at first," states a student. "It seemed that I just became a number." Since the information about academic services is poor, many students may not know that tutorial assistance is rather helpful. Explains a dean, "The University-Community Educational Program (UCEP) exists for students whose educational opportunity and growth may have been hindered because of their academic, economic or cultural backgrounds and experiences."

Counseling services are offered by UCEP, Pitt Engineering Impact Program for minorities, The Counseling and Student Development Center, faculty advisors and peer hotlines.

Study skills workshops, basic skills and instruction classes, special class sections and special seminars and forums exist but may not compensate for over-crowding in certain classes. Program organizers experience difficulty in motivating students to attend lectures given by guest speakers or to take advantage of other resources. At this campus within a city, an undergrad remarks, "I could go to all my classes in one building and never find out what's going on in another area."

Palms, the pre-medical organization for minority students, fosters a sense of unity, and helps students involve themselves in learning experiences offered with the participation of three major hospitals and the university-affiliated medical school.

A black American law society, an engineering caucus and a graduate and pre-professional caucus have also been established. Minority students see these self-segregated societies as beneficial because many students have not had much experience interacting with whites. As a result, they tend to shy away from societies that do not address problems unique to them. "With shared backgrounds and similar goals, these societies help people to overcome isolation and to become involved," responds a participant.

The Kuntu Repertory Theater is an outlet for black student and community actors, actresses, writers and directors. Plays produced by the university at large do not always have what one student describes as "black parts."

There are no black churches in the immediate area. To compensate, an all-black student organization provides a bus service to local churches. A gospel group, Some of God's Children, also holds Bible studies.

Organizationally, the Black Action Society does attempt to change things. Another organization, The Black Active Student Inter-Collegiate Struggle, represents blacks at the University of Pittsburgh and surrounding schools in the greater Pittsburgh area. Emphasizing communication and unification among black student organizations, the society attacks discrimination, prejudice and other injustices at institutions of higher education.

Students have a good time at parties, many of which are sponsored by black sororities and fraternities. When it comes to off-campus night life, people from the cities of New York, Philadelphia and D.C. may be disappointed. Bars close at two. A young woman depicts Pittsburgh as a "slow town, twenty years behind the times. It is a good place for the career-minded and family-oriented."

Black students have no principal gathering place, but fraternities, sororities and the Black Action Society hold activities throughout the year. Black Week, lectures, workshops, conferences and entertainment are open to everyone, and people of different backgrounds attend.

Blacks participate in intramurals, which are racially integrated. Still, blacks and whites tend to be self-segregated. "Since there is little interaction between blacks and whites, feelings don't always surface. There is little racial conflict," says a respondent. Within black cliques, people from the same hometowns tend to stick together.

Although professors are extremely busy, interaction with them is good. Regardless of race, students are treated equally. Likewise, the students get along well with people in the community. Black students tutor and help register citizens to vote. A Prison Academic Program and Forum keeps inmate-citizens in touch with the black community. The Black Studies Research Unit studies the socioeconomic and political conditions of blacks in Pittsburgh. Black alumns, on the other hand, do not maintain much contact with the campus community.

The campus, which is in fact a part of the city, only appeals to some. The quiet social life appeals to those not seeking a party atmosphere. Academics at the University of Pittsburgh keep black students, for the most part, busy enough.

UNIVERSITY OF PORTLAND
Portland, Oregon 97203

Undergrads: 2,044
Black Undergrads: 41
Faculty: 205
Black Faculty: NA
Tuition: $13,250
Total Expenses: $17,400

"Good" seems to be the word most often used to describe the University of Portland. Not great, not terrible—just good. And your grades have to be good to get in because the admission policy is selective.

B.A.'s and advanced degrees are offered in the humanities and sciences.

Blacks are not left out totally when it comes to recruiting. In fact, the admission staff recruits black high school seniors aggressively. The staff visits approximately 400 to 500 private and public schools each year, and interviews college-bound black students. In addition, the university sponsors a High School Engineering Seminar for Minorities, as well as a High School Career Day and a High School Weekend Campus visitation.

Still, the aggressive recruiting efforts on paper have only yielded a few blacks on campus. The majority are from nearby California, Oregon and Washington.

Study skills workshops are available through the Office of Counseling and Consulting. A Big Brother/Sister Program is also active in counseling. Counseling is highly rated by one student, while another sees it as "limited." Special class sections are offered through the communications, languages, literature and mathematics departments only, and this handful of departments leaves a lot of students without supplementary sections.

Tutorial assistance is also organized on a departmental basis. So students go to other students for help. "Usually students tutor students for free or for a minimal fee," says one respondent. And the study skills workshops are few and far between: "The workshops provided are good but are only offered once a semester."

The closest thing to career preparation are the Resume Writing and Interviewing Skills workshops.

There is a radio station and a T.V. station, but neither has much black programming. And for black religious services, as one student writes, "you must leave campus." Blacks play "a very limited role" in the student government, reports a sophomore.

Black alumns show a lack of interest in their alma mater. According to one respondent, about the only thing alumns participate in, a few of them anyway, is a Family Away from Home support program.

Socially, blacks are left to fend for themselves. "There are no cultural events for blacks," one student says flatly. There is no black student center—and only one black student organization, the Third World Coalition, a much-needed outlet for student concerns.

Nevertheless, interaction between black and white students is described as "good." Another respondent calls it "fair—surface interaction. Basically friendly greetings—politeness." But another student describes it as "excellent."

Safeway Stores and local banks sponsor summer employment programs for black undergraduates. There is also no problem with cliques among blacks. Explains one student: "Most blacks stick together, since there are not many of us. The few that are here are adjusting well."

Seemingly, the University of Portland needs a great deal of help to increase not only the number of black student organizations, activities, faculty and administrators, but also the number of black students, period.

UNIVERSITY OF RHODE ISLAND
Kingston, Rhode Island 02881

Undergrads: 10,531
Black Undergrads: 316
Faculty: 665
Black Faculty: NA
Tuition: $4,404; $10,846
Total Expenses: $9,754; $16,196

URI can offer a black student a solid liberal arts education and a pleasant environment in which to study. Black culture is barely present, but students continue to make efforts to change things.

As one student puts it, "URI is in a phase of major transition towards improvement for blacks."

Sprawled across 1,200 acres and located 35 miles from Providence, The University of Rhode Island is a state-funded, coed school with selective admission policies. Seventy percent of URI's black students are from Rhode Island, but there are also large contingents from New York, Connecticut and Massachusetts. Ninety percent of URI students are products of public school systems.

URI offers undergraduate programs in the colleges of arts and sciences, business and administration, engineering, human sciences and services, nursing, pharmacy, and resource development. African and Afro-American Studies is offered as a minor, consisting of English, history, sociology, and Afro-American Studies courses; permission is given on an ad hoc basis to various students who wish to substitute other black studies courses.

Most blacks seem to have adjusted well to URI's academic demands, and the consensus is that the first two years are the most difficult. The university provides free tutorial services to guide students through the rough spots, and students who have used these services deem them "useful." However, one student complains that sources of aid are "not well advertised," and another claims that knowledge of academic support systems is disseminated mostly by "word of mouth."

Special sections or labs are often scheduled for individual classes, and academic and psychological counseling is readily available. The Special

Programs for Talent Development program offers tutoring and counseling specifically geared toward minorities.

The usual pre-professional organizations, like pre-med and pre-law societies, are absent, but there is a fine network of other organizations, such as nursing and pharmacy groups.

A little over half of URI's student body actually lives on campus in the university's residence halls. Housing is assigned on a first-come, first-served basis; freshmen are assured housing if their room deposits are made on time. The fact that many students who are Rhode Island residents go home for the weekend puts an understandable damper on social life, but the dorms are still a great source of activity. (There are also weekly happy hours, with disc-jockey hosts.)

Social activities revolve around the Greek system, which is largely white. Their parties are often well-attended by blacks, though, as relations between black and white students on campus are not strained. One student notes that there is "no overt racism" at URI, and another maintains that you can "make friends with the white students here."

Perhaps because of their small numbers and because of their absorption into the mainstream of university life, many black students at URI sense a fragmentation; says one sister, "black students don't live together in dorms and stick together."

There are, however, expressions of the black experience at URI. There are "a few black-focused radio shows" on the campus radio station, and a monthly black newsletter called the *Rapport*, which carries news of minority affairs, profiles of prominent campus and community figures and schedules of upcoming minority-sponsored activities. Black History Month is a university-wide event and is generally quite popular. The Uhuru Sasa House provides students with a black student center on campus.

Ties to the surrounding towns of Peace Dale and Kingston are not strong; but one sister notes that this is true for both blacks and whites. One student finds the "rural area of Kingston" much more friendly than the "urban area of Providence," where he grew up.

THE UNIVERSITY OF THE SOUTH
Sewanee, Tennessee 37375

Undergrads: 1,242
Black Undergrads: 25
Faculty: 146
Black Faculty: NA
Tuition: $16,315
Total Expenses: $20,595

"The University of the South is the perfect place for a student who is serious about learning more about the world and himself," says a student. "It is a demanding school academically."

Few black men and women have graduated from the University of the South—a historic American college that was destroyed during the Civil War and rebuilt with gifts from England. But those who have survived the rigors of this highly selective Episcopalian university can boast that they have received one of the country's best liberal arts educations.

Sewanee, as the college is more popularly known, is situated on a brow of the Cumberland Plateau between Nashville and Chattanooga. The 10,000-acre campus, which includes forests, lakes, gardens, bluffs and trails, has 36 academic buildings and dormitories.

Entering students, 51 percent of whom are Episcopalians, have a high school grade-point average of B. Men at Sewanee are expected to wear coats and ties; and women, dresses and skirts.

Most of the black students at Sewanee are from Georgia, Tennessee, Alabama and North Carolina. The Minority Affairs director recruits minority students at fairs in Atlanta, Miami, Memphis and Birmingham. The director also attends high schools with sizable minority enrollments in Tennessee, Georgia, Alabama, Florida and North Carolina.

Sewanee has two divisions. The College of Arts and Sciences offers 500 courses in 31 subjects in the humanities, social sciences and natural sciences. Cooperative programs with graduate universities in forestry and engineering, and a teacher certification program are also available.

The School of Theology is a three-year program that prepares men and women for service in the ordained ministry of the Episcopalian Church. The college also offers pre-professional programs in medicine, law, dentistry, veterinary medicine and business.

The strong academic program produces impressive results. Sewanee is distinguished as the number one college in the country in the production of Rhodes Scholars. Ninety percent of the college's pre-medicine students are accepted to medical schools, and 95 percent of pre-law students into law schools.

Despite the absence of a sizable black population, the college is not short on courses relating to the African-American experience. Indians and Blacks in America, African Art and Culture, and Economic Development in the Third World are typical offerings.

If a student is having trouble, academic or personal, "Minority, psychological, faculty and administrative counseling are all top quality at Sewanee," a student says. "Faculty counseling is superb. Professors keep long office hours for the student's convenience." The college's counseling office conducts workshops on leadership skills, assertiveness training, sexual attitudes and responsibilities, alcohol awareness, interpersonal communication and stress management. Also, remedial and developmental programs are available to meet emotional, behavioral and educational needs of students.

With such a small percentage of black students attending the university, racial tolerance programs would be expected to be nonexistent. However, the black students attending the university have recently formed an organization that enlightens the non-minority community about the problems black students and individuals experience at the university—as well as throughout the nation.

Blacks on campus recently revived the once defunct Black Student Union. It is the only black organization on campus. Cultural Awareness Symposiums are held periodically.

On the whole, students describe the black-white interaction in positive terms. The same applies to the faculty and administration. Students and faculty at Sewanee enjoy a particularly close relationship. The student-faculty ratio is 11:1 and all faculty members live on campus. Students are welcome in faculty homes and offices.

As for relations with the community, things are not perfect but are getting better. "In the past the interaction between local blacks and whites, and black students has been poor. This interaction, however, tends to be improving with the increasing enrollment rate," according to one student.

"There is not much of a social life for many of the black students that attend the university. Nonetheless, most black students that attend Sewanee are happy with their choice. The most attractive feature that Sewanee has to offer is its long-held reputation as one of the best schools in the nation," maintains one undergrad.

UNIVERSITY OF SOUTH FLORIDA
Tampa, Florida 33620

Undergrads: 23,994
Black Undergrads: 1,920
Faculty: 1,652
Black Faculty: NA
Tuition: $1,877; $6,764
Total Expenses: $6,297; $11,184

It's said that you may be floundering if you are too unprepared for the special environment of this large, white state university. Respondents agree that the University of South Florida provides its students with a good academic education. However, you must take the initiative for academic success and not rely on the university's support services.

You won't be bored—academically anyway. Opportunities range from degree programs in business administration, education, engineering, fine arts, medicine, language and literature, natural science, nursing, and the social sciences to dual degree programs, opportunities for independent study and study abroad, cooperative work-study programs, and a major in general studies.

The Bay Campus at St. Petersburg is the headquarters for the university's Marine Science Department. USF also offers its students on-the-job experience through employment options ranging from graphics to programming at the University Center.

Most black students agree, say respondents, that there is great potential for academic success at USF, but many say that success often eludes minorities. One brother cites the "high dropout and academic probation/dismissal rate" as evidence that the transition to college-level work is not an easy one for USF blacks. Says another: "Most black students are not very active. Too much time is spent trying to stay in this place."

Support services are available (workshops on time management, test anxiety and math anxiety, a for-credit reading and study skills class, and a few special sections in math and English). But respondents rate these as only "fair," and many students are unaware of their existence.

One brother claims that the use of supplementary academic services is essential to success at USF: "If you're having problems, you either get help or drop out." Another black student believes that the USF system is actually "made to weed out those students who aren't steadfast, zealous, and serious about continuing their education."

Although it appears to students that there is little institutional academic support for minorities, there are other sources of strength on campus. The black business and engineering groups are quite popular. The black pre-med society (known as the Bio-Med Society) is generally accepted as "grounds for exchange and support" although one student claims that many blacks opt for "regular" pre-med meetings, hoping to make better contacts there. Interaction between black faculty and administrators and black students is rated good, with "some room for improvement."

About four percent of all undergraduates at USF are black, and this fact is reflected in its campus activities. There is no black radio, no organized black theater group, and university-sponsored events are felt to be geared toward whites.

Black political organization is also weak, but present to some degree in the Black Student Union. Blacks are quite active in varsity and intramural sports. The USF Gospel Choir is almost unanimously praised as a "good opportunity for creative expression" on campus.

The black community at USF is small and, therefore, quite cohesive. Black social life revolves, to a great degree, around Greek parties. (There are six black fraternities and sororities on campus.) "Most blacks," explains one sister, "avoid dorm parties." Social interaction with white students is minimal but described as "more positive than negative." The races are not adversarial at USF, merely separate. Says one brother: "Simply put, blacks party with blacks, and whites party with whites."

"The most unattractive feature of USF for blacks," says one student, "is the alienation we face, culturally and institutionally."

For black students, the University of South Florida is no vacation. Ninety-eight percent of USF's blacks are from Florida anyway, and, according to many, life on the university's 17-acre campus is a "sink or swim" situation.

UNIVERSITY OF TENNESSEE
Chattanooga, Tennessee 37402

Undergrads: 7,015
Black Undergrads: 912
Faculty: 551
Black Faculty: NA
Tuition: $1,932; $6,062
Total Expenses: $3,362; $7,492

When will the school help improve the quality of life for them? That is the question on the mind of most respondents. At the top of their wish list is a reversal of their isolated social life.

There are, of course, good and bad facets to life at the University of Tennessee at Chattanooga. On the good side, students say that you can get to know your teachers well and that classes are small. Academic life here, one student says, is "stimulating."

Coed and part of the state college system, Tennessee is located in the center of Chattanooga on a 60-acre campus. Admission is less selective than most schools. Most matriculants come from the South, and most of the black students come from Tennessee, Georgia, Alabama and Florida.

Black students here offer a variety of responses about the transition from high school to college academics. "College isn't as structured as high school," and so difficulties arise, says one. "The main problem is dealing with independence," declares a brother. Another student believes that many of the black students have adjusted "very well, very quickly." Another says that Tennessee's black students "tend to help each other out," and so the transition is made easier.

For those students in need of academic help, tutorial services are offered by graduate students, undergraduates and faculty. One student calls the services "good" but adds that more tutors would be welcome in certain academic departments.

The school's Black Student Association also offers tutoring. Counseling services are provided through faculty advisors and through counselors at the school's Counseling Center; the community medical center also offers counseling services.

"The faculty-to-student counseling has been good for me," one student maintains. "The faculty member has always made me feel relaxed and has always been truthful." Study Skills Workshops are called "real useful." Special seminars and forums—some mandatory—are provided. Seminars, considered helpful by most, are also offered during the school's Black Awareness Week.

For cultural renewal, Black Awareness and Black History weeks are celebrated each year. There is not a black student center; black students, like white students, hang out in the University Center. The Black Student Association, in addition to providing tutoring, organizes rap sessions and parties.

Off-campus parties, one student reports, take place more often than on-campus parties. The off-campus parties are "popular" though another student adds that Black student activities in the dorms "are improving." Mixers at the school, one student reports, take place within academic departments. Mixers are also provided, another student says, by Greek societies and are "fun."

University-sponsored entertainment is called "average." There are good concerts and movies, one student says. Another student, however, says that more entertainment is needed "in terms of the black experience."

Intramural sports, primarily basketball and football, are "very popular" among black students. Picnics sponsored by the Black Student Association are "on time." There are also picnics sponsored by Greek organizations.

Interaction between white and black students? "I don't see very much interaction," reports one. Others use terms like positive and relaxed. But prejudice is said to exist. Black students and white faculty and administrators "get along well," one student says. Another says that relations are "good in some areas and bad in others," while one respondant asserts that some teachers have a reputation for being prejudiced.

Relations between black students and black faculty and administrators are considered positive and "no problem." Another student, however, is aware of only a few black faculty members on campus and knows very little about them.

Relations with other non-white faculty and administrators are called "good." "There are all kinds of ethnic professors here," one student reports.

Of interaction with the local community, a student says that it is just adequate. Another uses the term "fine." This student says that community members attend "many" university functions and that students, too, are involved with the community. Internships, for example, involve students in community political activities. The school's Black Student Association also provides tutoring opportunities.

Concerning black participation in university governance, one student declares the percentage to be "of a respectable size." Another says that blacks are "very active" in student government, dorm councils, student boards and orientation boards.

UNIVERSITY OF TEXAS
Austin, Texas 78712

Undergrads: 35,088
Black Undergrads: 1,404
Faculty: 2,367
Black Faculty: NA
Tuition: $2,208; $6,660
Total Expenses: $6,758; $11,210

To get through here, "Be sure you put your priorities straight: academics first," advises one sister.

There is no doubting the academic excellence of UT. The 11 undergraduate divisions use a selective admission policy, so get ready for some stiff competition from fellow classmates. It has one of the nation's top architectural schools and an internationally recognized College of Business Administration.

And if you want to study African and Afro-American issues, you won't have any trouble finding courses to take. UT's catalog lists more than 65 courses, including Geography of Africa, Racial and Ethnic Politics, The Black Family, and Swahili Language and Literature. Plus, UT's College of Liberal Arts offers two degree programs relating to Africa and Afro-American studies.

But whatever major you choose, "Be prepared to be challenged quite rigorously," advises one sister.

UT has the services and programs that will help you meet that challenge. The Welcome Program matches black freshmen with black upperclassmen to act as "buddies" and give academic pointers to the newcomers. The Minority Mentor Program pairs black students with faculty members for one-on-one academic counseling. For hard-core study skills training, head for the Reading and Study Skills Laboratory (RASSL). Tutoring, anxiety-reduction workshops, test-taking tips, and more are available at RASSL. One believer in RASSL sums the program up this way: "Lots of workshops and seminars on everything from leadership to relationships."

Even with all of these services available, the jump from high school to UT-level work can still be difficult. According to this brother, "There is an overall poor transition. The services are there, but most students are either unaware or afraid to use them." Another student cites this reason: "Black freshmen may have come from a predominantly black high school and therefore are going through psychological changes already, making their transition to academic requirements hard."

Unit, a program for entering black freshmen and overseen by a black counselor, is designed to make that transition easier. Unit supplements both the Welcome Program and the Minority Mentor Program.

Although blacks only make up about four percent of UT's student population, over 20 black student organizations exist. These include eight fraternities and sororities, and three pre-professional groups. Look out, too, for a black choir, a black dance ensemble, and a black student's association.

These groups are crucial to a black student's success at Texas, according to this respondent: "It is so easy to get lost in a school with forty-five-thousand-plus students, but if you find people that you can identify with, you will make it." You won't find a black student's center at UT, but blacks do have a setting of their own—the Afro-American Culture Room, where students study, hold activities, and display their artwork.

"The majority of blacks stick with black students; the majority of whites stick with white students." That is how one student sums up race relations at UT. Another describes interaction with white students as "fairly positive."

In fact, however, the campus has a long history of racial tension that is still prevalent. One brother has termed the environment "racially hostile" and insists he has been called "nigger" several times. Other brothers and sisters define their existence at UT in terms of isolation and intolerance.

White faculty and administrators are criticized by one respondent as being "too busy thinking about how to make minorities feel that this is not a racist institution to take time out to actually talk to blacks." Another sister gives white faculty members a more favorable review: "The faculty here are color-blind to those they pass and fail, meaning that as long as their curve comes out balanced, it makes no difference who is where."

What about black faculty and administrators? "Very helpful to blacks." Although blacks make up little over one percent of the faculty, "the interaction is very close and rewarding," says one respondent. "As students, we don't feel so alone."

You won't feel alone at the parties given by Alpha Phi Alpha or Delta

Sigma Theta. "The Greek parties are the most popular," reports one brother. UT's varsity sports are popular too, including its football team (the Texas Longhorns), basketball, baseball, swimming, and diving teams. Of the 65 blacks on varsity teams, most are active in football, basketball, and track. University-sponsored concerts and activities do not draw a large black audience.

However, UT's Afro-American Student Affairs Advisory Committee on Cultural Diversity is working to provide more programs relating to blacks. Religious groups are active both on and off campus. And black involvement in UT's Student Association is on the upswing. As one student explains: "We are finally realizing that the only way to get something done is to get through the red tape."

"You should be able to accept and function on a white campus with no discomfort. Expect some prejudice; it will happen," adds another student.

Being black on a white campus like UT's does not bother this sister, who concludes: "It doesn't take a black school to make a black man or woman. It takes a black mind, body, and soul with a dedication to the advancement of his or her people."

UNIVERSITY OF TULSA
Tulsa, Oklahoma 74104

Undergrads: 3,025
Black Undergrads: 212
Faculty: 405
Black Faculty: NA
Tuition: $12,300
Total Expenses: $16,660

Although it is the state's largest private university, Tulsa stresses individual attention, say respondents. Students are known by name, and professors are accessible. Faculty frequently serve as mentors for students, and academic advisors provide guidance in course selections.

The University of Tulsa (TU) is located on a beautifully landscaped campus near downtown Tulsa. It's noted for its excellent liberal arts-based curriculum and fine petroleum engineering program.

TU houses five colleges and one school: the College of Arts and Sciences, College of Business Administration, College of Engineering and Applied Sciences, College of Nursing and Applied Health Sciences, College of Law and School of Graduate Studies.

TU encourages prospective students to visit the campus so they can determine if TU is for them. Visits include meeting an admissions counselor, touring the campus and talking to professors about your particular field of interest. Tulsa also sponsors special campus visitation programs throughout the year for prospective students. These special programs address the issues and needs of students who are interested in multicultural programs.

Black students should take advantage of the Office of Minority Student Affairs, set up to help students develop leadership and social skills, to represent the interests of minority students, to inform minority students of special opportunities and to promote cultural awareness within the university community.

The Office helps organize various organizations and clubs, including the Association of Black Collegians. It also serves as a resource center with information on study skills, scholarship and grant opportunities, and each semseter it publishes a newsletter reflecting the interests of minority students.

Some of the programs include the Multicultural Student Council, Academic Study Group, Multicultural Orientation Program, University Big Brothers and Sisters, World of Work Seminars, Adjustment Seminars and Cross-Cultural Exchanges.

ABC, or the Association of Black Collegians, is a support group for black students. ABC helps new students get acquainted and sponsors social activities. In the past ABC has sponsored a homecoming dance, the Minority Orientation Program, Minority Campus Visitation Program, the Martin Luther King Celebration, Black Heritage Month, Gospel Extravaganza, Black Business Fair and Muilticultural Awards Banquet.

ABC has brought to campus speakers such as Jesse Jackson, Randall Robertson, Yolanda King, Dr. Asa Hilliard and Scott Momaday. ABC social events include bowling, ice skating and parties. During Black Heritage Month, an annual fashion show takes place. ABC meets weekly.

Other social events have included a Kwanzaa Holiday Celebration, a Multicultural Holiday Celebration and speakers for African-American Heritage Month (one year Dr. Na'im Akbar, the African-American psychologist, was the main speaker). Also for the African-American Heritage Month events such as films, music (soloists and choirs), dramas, a panel discussion and exhibits are part of the fare.

Other black student clubs and organizations include the Unlimited Praise Choir, which is a gospel choir, and three Greek organizations, Alpha Phi Alpha, Delta Sigma Theta and Alpha Kappa Alpha.

And if there is not enough on campus for students to do, there is always downtown Tulsa with its museums, dining, shopping and recreational activities.

If you're looking for small, Southwest and a healthy number of support services and black student organizations, you might want to stop by to see what's happening at Tulsa.

UNIVERSITY OF VIRGINIA
Charlottesville, Virginia 22903

Undergrads: 11,949
Black Undergrads: 1,314
Faculty: 2,022
Black Faculty: 35
Tuition: $4,614; $13,140
Total Expenses: $8,476; $17,002

As one sister points out, "If you're outgoing and vivacious, no problem. If you're not, it's difficult, especially because things at UVA are totally student run."

"If I had to do it all over again, I would still come to UVA," is one respondent's reflection.

In the spirit of Thomas Jefferson, the University of Virginia's founder, standards at this large, coed, public institution are high. The admissions policy here is extremely selective; only a handful of out-of-state applicants are accepted.

UVA has three merit-based financial awards for black students. The Jerome Holland Scholarship offers 10 annual awards of $10,000. During the fall of their junior year of high school, students may qualify for the National Achievement Program when they take the PSAT. The award ranges from $750-$2,000. There are also University Achievement Awards for UVA students.

At least once in two years, the school offers more than 70 courses relating to Afro-American and African Studies.

"Choose a goal and keep going for it," advises one brother. Academics are rigorous, and the heavy workload gives some students the feeling of being closed in. In general, black students adapt successfully to their environment; prep-school graduates seem to have an advantage over public school ones.

Accepted students who indicate potential academic difficulties attend a six-week summer preparatory program to enhance their academic skills. Athletes receive special tutoring if they need it, and there is a Writing Center for the general population.

UVA offers special programs for its black students as well. Assistance is available through the Office of Afro-American Affairs. And as one brother states, "It is comforting to know that blacks have a strong bond and help each other out. After the first year, school is okay." The people at the Luther P. Jackson House are "extremely tight," and offer tutoring, counseling, and activities dedicated to the preservation and dissemination of the black culture.

In the past year, UVA also established a new program for minority students who have potential but need extra help. "What it amounts to is individualized guidance," according to one respondent.

The black pre-med society offers special tutoring, review sessions, trips, and a scholarship for black high school students. Opportunities to meet with senators and congressmen in nearby Washington, D.C. are provided by the black pre-law society. A black pre-engineering society is not quite as active as these other two. UVA also sponsors a black nursing support group.

Although the theater and intramurals are racially intermingled, few blacks are involved in student government. Those who may be interested feel insecure about getting involved or experience difficulties in getting elected. One student comments: "White people don't want us, so we don't want to get involved." Blacks do participate actively in the Black Student Alliance and the university's chapter of the NAACP.

"You can segregate yourself, or you can integrate yourself," remarks a sister. Students' mixed responses about black and white student interaction support this view. One respondent is enthusiastic about the apparent integration; another is disillusioned by the extent of segregation. The general opinion is that students express a Southern hospitality and kindness for one another but remain racially segregated, especially in social circles.

STARS (Students Together Against Racial Separatism) was founded to address the problems of social integration and the common misconceptions blacks and whites hold about each other. But, claims a sister, the group disbanded because it had reached the conclusion that students at UVA really don't have the interest to integrate.

Social activities—parties, black student center activities, mixers, and university-sponsored events—are appreciated and well attended at the beginning of each semester, but their popularity tends to fade as the academic year progresses. Some blacks follow the common bonds of fraternities, sororities, hometown acquaintances, sports, and socio-economic status, but their numbers are limited; isolating oneself in small groups is seen by many as disadvantageous.

Since the University of Virginia was not integrated until 1971, black alumns are not that easy to find. Contacts outside the university may be made with the community of Charlottesville through programs which center around tutoring and counseling. Fraternities and sororities have Big Brother and Big Sister activities, and the university sponsors Upward Bound—aimed at helping community youngsters.

Church services provide another setting for student-community relations to develop.

Socially and academically, the student must take the initiative to get the most out of UVA. But black students respect their school and their choice. A degree from the elite University of Virginia is meaningful both for its prestige and for the effort that goes into it.

"UVA," concludes one respondent, "is a school that gives you a great deal of freedom. It gives you room to experience much and to test your maturity."

UNIVERSITY OF WISCONSIN

Madison, Wisconsin 53706

Undergrads: 26,361
Black Undergrads: 1,054
Faculty: 2,475
Black Faculty: NA
Tuition: $2,870; $9,580
Total Expenses: $7,390; $14,100

For one brother, "The University of Wisconsin-Madison is a challenge." This coed university is large and state-supported. As one of the schools in the University of Wisconsin system, Madison has more than 400 buildings on its 569-acre suburban campus and is located 70 miles from Milwaukee. The school's admission policy is selective.

Consistently ranked as one of the top universities in the country, Madison has 13 schools and colleges and 133 academic departments. Few universities can match the quantity and quality of the academic programs and research projects available at Madison.

A majority of the university's black students come from Wisconsin, Illinois, Ohio, Michigan, Indiana, and Iowa. Most black students seem to like the city of Madison, which is Wisconsin's capital and second largest city. One student describes the city as "clean, liberal, and free."

Despite few black professors, the university has excellent African and Afro-American programs. And the university's undergraduate and graduate libraries contain special collections in Africana and black studies materials.

Overall, black student respondents say that although the first year is often difficult, most black students adjust well to the university's academic requirements. The university's extensive academic support program helps students with any curricular or extracurricular problems. Students say that tutorial assistance is available and very helpful.

The most popular tutorial programs are the Greater University Tutoring Service/Help at Student Housing (GUTS/HASH), the chemistry tutorial, and the math tutorial. In addition to tutorials, the university has a Study Skills program and a Writing Lab. The university Counseling Service provides personal, vocational, and educational counseling on an individual or group basis. For interested minority students, the university offers the Faculty Mentor Program, which enables a student to work closely with a faculty member who has similar intellectual interests.

Madison also reaches out to adults interested in continuing their education, pre-college minority students, and academically disadvantaged students. Continuing Educational Services provides adults with counseling, testing, and referral services. Group workshops on subjects of interest to adult students are offered regularly. The Academic Advancement program provides access to higher education and support services to students from minority and academically disadvantaged backgrounds. And in addition to its regular summer session, the university offers several summer programs for students interested in particular fields of study.

The Multi-Cultural Program office works with other campus groups and departments to develop and sponsor a variety of cultural events, extracurricular programs, and student services that assist in meeting the needs of ethnic minority students.

Twenty predominantly black student organizations hold forth on campus. However, black respondents feel that black students should be more active in academic, cultural, and political events. One sister says that most activities revolve around the black Greek organizations. While some brothers play basketball, football, and baseball, most black students do not participate actively in intramural and varsity sports.

Notwithstanding some racial problems, the campus atmosphere is generally friendly. According to one student, "Black and white students interact everyday in classes, libraries, lunchrooms and dormitories. But, there is still a separation between races."

Another student agrees that black-white student relationships are usually casual. Black students seem to get along well with the university's white faculty and administrators. One sister suggests that black students should introduce themselves to professors and teaching assistants. A brother describes black faculty and administrators as "very helpful." Relations between black students and the local community are "generally good."

Black undergrads who have met black alumns say that the alumns are genuinely concerned about them and their university experience. The new Afro-American Alumni Association plans to raise funds for scholarships, assist in recruiting black students, and become a communication network for black graduates. Black alumns have already helped establish the Chancellor's Achievement Scholarship for minority students.

Black student respondents are thoroughly satisfied with their decision to attend the University of Wisconsin-Madison. At the same time, they advise prospective black students from predominantly black high schools to be prepared for a "big" cultural transition to the predominantly white campus. The university also has students from 108 foreign countries.

For some black students, the university's most unattractive features are the lack of black students and black-oriented activities. Moreover, the competition among students, including black students, is viewed as sometimes too intense. On the other hand, a sister says, "The courses are rigorous and hard, but they are also stimulating."

UNIVERSITY OF WISCONSIN
Milwaukee, Wisconsin 53201

Undergrads: 15,557
Black Undergrads: 1,400
Faculty: 1,354
Black Faculty: NA
Tuition: $2,947; $9,398
Total Expenses: $5,841; $12,292

"My decision to attend a predominantly white college has good and bad points," one brother says, summing up his stay at Wisconsin-Milwaukee. "Racism is apparent, but it exists within the society. Dealing with it makes one more tolerant, and one is able to handle problems that may arise."

The University of Wisconsin at Milwaukee, one of 13 schools in the University of Wisconsin system, is a state-run, coed school which offers a wide range of undergraduate major degrees—68 in all. The school is located on a 90-acre campus in urban Milwaukee, near Lake Michigan; downtown Milwaukee is 15 minutes away by bus. The university employs a selective admission policy.

For the university's black students, most of whom come from Wisconsin and Illinois, there are, one student says simply, those who have adjusted well to college life and those who have not. Says another student: "College-level work can be a shock, though, a shock which too many black students never overcome."

For those students in need of academic help at the school, tutorial assistance, offered by the school's Department of Learning Skills, is called "very available" by one student, who adds that services could be improved. Another student feels that the tutorial services are excellent but that the program isn't large enough for a school of Milwaukee's size.

Counseling services at Wisconsin are provided by academic advisors, by advisors in the school's Department of Educational Opportunity, and by peer counselors under the auspices of the Black Student Union; one student calls the counseling services "adequate." Study skills workshops are provided by the Department of Learning Skills "but could be better."

Special class sections are available through the Department of Educational Opportunity. Courses are offered in English, psychology, biology, Spanish, and other subjects.

The university offers many courses in black studies; 47 courses are taught at least once every two years. A hefty addition is the school's library, which includes over 5,600 volumes related to Afro-American studies.

Relations between black and white students at Wisconsin are "generally okay although black students and white students tend to have their closest alliances" with one another. Says another student: "Some whites will converse, and some will not. Many have not seen people of color before, so it is hard for them to speak with us." Relations between black students and white faculty and administrators vary: some "are open-minded and really care," while others are "biased."

Says another, "I feel there is a tremendous, perhaps insurmountable, rift. White faculty often seem to talk down to black students, and white administrators shift between not recognizing black students to wanting to 'showcase' a chosen few in an attempt to disprove prejudice." Relations between black students and black faculty and administrators are "pretty good" although "it seems the higher up a person is in the administration, the more inaccessible they become. Blacks, too, are a casualty of the 'superior aloofness' syndrome."

Another student disagrees, describing relations between black faculty and administrators as being "very close since we are in a predominantly white institution."

Cliques? "Sure," one student says. "Blacks from well-off families hang together; fraternity and sorority members associate with one another." Yet the student says this as well: "On the whole, black students on this campus are warm and friendly to everyone. If you pass a black student here, you always speak to each other."

The Black Student Union at the school organizes cultural, social, and educational programs; the Union also publishes a biweekly newspaper, *Invictus*. There are plenty of other organizations: The Black Achievement Organization, The Future Black Nurses Association, The Black Graduate Council, The Black Student Psychological Association, The National Society of Black Engineers, and The Minority Business Student Association.

Black students at the school are active, one student says, in university governance, and the numbers of those participating is increasing. Says another: "Black students have always been at the forefront of student government." Blacks have held prominent positions, including student body president, in recent years.

There are no black theater groups, no black religious services, no campus-based black radio or television, and minimal university-sponsored black entertainment at Milwaukee. One student says, "There are not enough parties, from what I've seen...but being in an urban area, with the black community readily accessible, this is not a priority." Twenty-three percent of Milwaukee's residents are black.

Students here, on the positve side, enjoy a rewarding academic life, and they speak highly of the different black organizations which support them.

UPSALA COLLEGE
East Orange, New Jersey 07019

Undergrads: 579
Black Undergrads: 214
Faculty: 110
Black Faculty: NA
Tuition: $12,400
Total Expenses: $17,532

R ace relations are frequently listed as the most negative feature of their school by Upsala's black student respondents, but most agree that the college's academic offerings compensate for social difficulties. Says one brother of his time at Upsala: "I've kept my black identity while learning about other people and cultures."

Small, coed, and selective, Upsala is located in a residential area of predominantly black East Orange, 16 miles from New York City. The college was founded in 1893 by Swedish Lutherans, and the school catalog calls this affiliation "a source of strength."

Upsala offers B.A., B.S., and master's programs, and seven honor societies maintain chapters here. Classes are generally small, and professors are viewed as accessible and willing to give extra help. According to one student, "You are not a number in a class; the professors get to know you. If you have any problems, they try to help you solve them." An honors program is available for superior students, and 30 percent of Upsala's graduates go on for advanced degrees. The college offers a Black Studies concentration, composed of five courses in history and politics. The concentration is designed to stress the historical, economic, political, social, and cultural achievements of blacks in Africa and America.

Black students at Upsala occasionally have some difficulty in adjusting to college-level academics, but there is a good support system on campus. Each student is assigned a faculty advisor, and the Office of Academic and Career Counseling offers advice on course selection, academic difficulties and study skills, personal and social problems, and careers and life decisions.

Personal counseling is also available from the dean of students and his staff, and resident students are eligible to participate in an informal peer counseling program. The Educational Opportunities Fund (EOF) also offers study skills, stress, and writing workshops. Says one student: "Tutoring at Upsala is very good for any subject." There are no black pre-med or pre-law societies on campus, but pre-professional groups do exist in other disciplines.

Sixty percent of Upsala's students live on campus, and housing possibilities range from the Townhouses, a relatively new complex of air-conditioned, carpeted four-to-eight person units, to Bremer, Froeberg, and Nelsenius Halls, more traditional coed dorms. (Froeberg Hall houses the campus radio station, WFMU.) All residents must be full-time students and must be on the meal plan.

For commuters, Kenbrook Hall offers lounges and a snack bar where hot meals can be purchased. The college publishes an annual commuter directory, and residents and commuters alike have mailboxes in the Agnes Wahlstrom College Center.

Blacks compose just over 20 percent of Upsala's student body, and several feel neglected by college programs and student activities. One brother remarks that activities seem to be "zeroed toward the white crowd."

There is a Black Women's Organization, but the Third World Student Organization is generally felt to be the "primary unifying force for African-American students." No black Greek organizations exist on campus, and blacks do not frequent parties given by white groups. Says one sister: "Blacks who interact with whites don't interact with many black students."

White fraternities and sororities are said to "basically have a monopoly" on university governance. For black undergraduates, most college-related activity comes in the form of varsity basketball and football.

Black-white relations at Upsala are separate at best. One brother calls his white acquaintances "phoney, two-faced, and prejudiced," and another says that "racism is the order of the day."

Another student feels that "whites and blacks are both prejudiced." Racial awareness workshops are conducted for freshmen during Orientation and included in training for resident counselors; however, one sister thinks the workshops "cause more damage than encouragement."

Ninety percent of Upsala's students are from New Jersey, and the surrounding black communities of East Orange and nearby Newark are very supportive. Whites tend to focus their day-to-day lives on campus, while blacks find their niches in town.

At Upsala, says one undergrad, students must be "open-minded and willing to give a little as well as take a little." Blacks will encounter obstacles on campus, but none is insurmountable.

U.S. AIR FORCE ACADEMY
USAF Academy, Colorado 80840

Undergrads: 4,117
Black Undergrads: 247
Faculty: 547
Black Faculty: NA
Tuition: $0
Total Expenses: $0

With all expenses being paid by the government, and employment guaranteed upon graduation, the academy does represent an attractive option for higher education. Blacks are "forced to do a lot of things here that would not apply to other schools," says one cadet. But he says that in the long run, it could be well worthwhile.

The U.S. Air Force Academy, sitting eight miles from Colorado Springs in the mountains, employs a most selective admission policy while offering its graduates a commission as second lieutenants in the Air Force. Graduates must serve a minimum of five years active duty.

The academy offers the bachelor of science degree in the social sciences, humanities, science and engineering fields, and offers an interdivisional degree in aviation sciences and operations research.

Air Force has an early decision plan, so students are encouraged to submit applications as early as possible. Prospective cadets receive a monthly stipend upon admission to USAFA. Although students are actively recruited, they are also encouraged to write their congressmen, senators or representatives from their congressional district for letters of nomination.

The majority of the black cadets come from California, New York, Texas and Maryland. Only four percent are from Colorado.

Most cadets are prepared to deal with the academic aspects of the academy. There are, however, adjustment problems for students who don't have the background for college-level academics. Says another, "Adjustment hasn't been detrimental. Special honor sections are available, and classes are generally sectioned according to ability." Other special class sections are designed for cadets for whom English is a second language.

For cadets who have adjustment or academic problems, various support services are available. The Extra Instruction Program, the How to Study program and the informal academic program of each squadron are all designed to promote academic success. In addition, the Minority Retention Office is set up to cut down on the attrition rate of minorities. The tutorial and counseling services are described as very good and highly encouraging by various respondents. The one pre-professional group on campus is the Mechanical Engineering Club.

Although there are few black faculty members, the black cadets seem to have a very positive relationship with them and respond favorably to the advice, counseling, extra instruction and encouragement they receive.

The USAF Academy has been described as "quite a cultural shock for most black cadets." Blacks, however, seem to be able to get along reasonably well with white cadets and white faculty members. Relationships with white faculty members are described as being more professional than relationships with black faculty members. Minimal interaction with the local community also results in better-than-average relationships with whites. According to one student, "The environment here forces interaction." Still, the black cadets "basically stick together."

"Because blacks are just now becoming active in student government," according to one respondent. "They don't play an important role." Heavy academic loads account for previous lack of interest in student government. Despite the fact that eight graduates from each class remain at the academy to help improve minority affairs, black cadets still have very little contact with black alumni.

The controlling force of black social activities is the Way of Life Committee. This organization of black cadets sponsors parties, mixers and picnics designed especially for blacks. Black Heritage Week is an annual event designed to inform the local community of black achievement and black culture. A black religious service is held during that week, and throughout the year the Gospel Choir is "very active," usually booked a year in advance.

Although there is little entertainment designed specifically for blacks during Black Heritage Week, the academy does sponsor black-oriented entertainment during the year.

Cadets are forced to comply with high academic standards, yet the parties, termed "frequent and well-attended" by several, as well as the intramural sports program, serve as important avenues for easing the pressure.

"To be successful at the academy the transition has to be a fast one," warns one black cadet. "And the transition from civilian to military life can be tough."

U.S. COAST GUARD ACADEMY
New London, Connecticut 06320

Undergrads: 862
Black Undergrads: 60
Faculty: 111
Black Faculty: NA
Tuition: $0
Total Expenses: $0

"**B**ecause the opportunities and education at the academy differ so greatly from those at civilian institutions," reports a black cadet, "the decision to apply must be weighed carefully."

Coast Guard Academy, overlooking the Thames River in New London, has one of the most selective admission policies in the country as it prepares its graduates to become ensigns for five years. It provides all cadets with fully funded scholarships and has put minority recruiting at the top of its priority list.

Coast Guard recruits black cadets by targeting schools producing both large numbers of black Merit Scholarship achievers and black students who do well on the PSAT. Academy reps also attend minority fairs and other conferences including the NAACP fairs.

They advertise in *Ebony* and *Essence*, and send direct mailings in the spring of the junior year and the fall of the senior year to black students whose PSAT scores are impressive. The academy hosts a minority-introduction-to-engineering program and funds visits to the academy for black students who are offered appointments.

On the positive side, argues one brother, is the wealth of opportunity in professional military service. On the other hand: "There is a small community of blacks here," advises a cadet, "and there can be culture shock from living with white people all the time."

But generally, black cadets here speak proudly of the need for integrity, will-power and an open outlook on one's future as the basis for surviving Coast Guard's rigorous academic and emotional demands.

The curriculum is by definition a technical one, and the needs of black students in particular are not met with special course offerings.

One student states that the transition from high school to college-level courses is difficult. There are no formal black student support systems, but cadets generally agree that the tutorial system (teacher-to-student and peer level) is very helpful. Special after-school sessions are available for those having difficulties. The Cadet Counseling Center assists in personal and career decisions, and peer facilitators are available at the barracks.

Study skills workshops are also offered. A student says special class sections known as "tree classes" are held once a week in all of the mandatory subjects. Attendance is required if a cadet is failing a basic course.

"The special seminar programs are informative," reports one midshipman. Very popular are the academy spotlight lectures given by prominent military officials.

Since one's vocation after graduation is pre-determined, the only preprofessional program at the academy is the Institute of Electrical and Electronic Engineers. The society offers insights into the job market. There is no black theater. "Our chaplain does try occasionally to bring in a black choir group," says one upperclassman. And about once a year, a black minister from a local church holds services at the academy chapel. Otherwise, church services are available in the community. Coast Guard does not have its own radio station, but a few of the black cadets have anchor time on nearby Connecticut College's station. One minority club, Genesis, fosters social interaction.

"Most of the black cadets attend off-campus parties," reports an upperclassman. Genesis sponsors campus parties occasionally and has sponsored dance troupes and lectures in the past. Mixers offered by the academy are not well-attended by the black cadets; they don't like the music. Now and then a band will play. "The United States Coast Guard Academy is not a place to come for the social life," states one respondent.

"All cadets participate in intramural or collegiate sports," says one brother. "Blacks are active in student government, but overall black participation is low," explains a cadet. Cadets also participate in Big Brother, which fosters friendships with children in single-parent families in the community.

A cadet states, "Overall, the relationship between black and white cadets is pretty good." Another believes that it is very good because it is "pretty much demanded that there be good, normal interaction."

But a third cadet warns, "There is a very small black community, and we seldom see each other. You have to fight to retain identity as a black." Black and white faculty and administration alike are reportedly very supportive and helpful. A cadet regards his contact with black alumns as "very encouraging. There aren't that many black officers in the Coast Guard, so each chance I get to meet one, it encourages me all the more to work hard and succeed."

Advice from a black cadet: "If you have doubts about your ability or your self-esteem, don't apply. The academy is for people who have heart."

U.S. MERCHANT MARINE ACADEMY
Kings Point, New York 11024

Undergrads: 950
Black Undergrads: 20
Faculty: 82
Black Faculty: NA
Tuition: $0
Total Expenses: $0

For a quality education without financial strain and almost guaranteed employment, Merchant Marine Academy presents quite an attractive option.

Located on 80 acres on the posh north shore of Long Island, 20 miles from Manhattan, U.S. Merchant Marine Academy is a federally funded, coed specialized college that prepares its grads to become mates and engineers on merchant vessels and ensigns in the Naval Reserve.

Cadets receive four-year scholarships and a monthly stipend while on summer training ships.

Admission is highly selective. Concentrations include marine engineering, marine sciences and maritime sciences.

Admission officers frequently visit inner city high schools with large black populations. Alumns assist by attending College Night/Days and fairs at high schools in large cities with heavy black populations. And the college sponsors trips to the campus from local high schools with large black populations.

Students come from various states, with the majority from Maryland, Rhode Island, Texas and New York.

Tutorial assistance is offered for any student having problems in mathematics, and is provided by upperclassmen and faculty. Academic counseling is provided by assigned faculty advisors, while personal counseling is available through the medical department, the Office of External Affairs, the Admissions Office, the chaplains and officers of the Commandants Department. Remedial studies and special tutoring are provided for students who need extra help.

The Black Culture Club is the only black-oriented organization. The club has sponsored Black History week and a visit to an ethnic restaurant in New York City.

Many sport activities are offered, including baseball/softball, basketball, football, cross-country running, golf, ice hockey, riflery, tennis, swimming and volleyball.

Black seniors can receive placement assistance through the USMMA Placement Office, which arranges company campus presentations. Unlike other colleges, summer employment is not an option: all undergraduates are at sea or attend classes during the summer.

U.S. NAVAL ACADEMY
Annapolis, Maryland 21402

Undergrads: 4,080
Black Undergrads: 286
Faculty: 650
Black Faculty: NA
Tuition: $0
Total Expenses: $0

Most respondents seem to agree with one black midshipman's comment: "The Naval Academy is the ultimate education."

There is, by definition, a pervasive military atmosphere at USNA, complete with many regulations and restrictions. You must be ready to deal with the pressure of the challenge to excel, both physically and academically.

Admission policy at the academy, as at all the nation's military service schools, is highly selective. Candidates must be able to prove good academic performance, produce high scores on the SAT or ACT exam and secure a Congressional nomination to be selected for appointment.

Naval Academy is a coed undergraduate school that places heavy emphasis on the fields of engineering, science and mathematics; at least 80 percent of the students in each class must be enrolled in one of these programs of study.

The remaining 20 percent are enrolled in a B.S. program with majors in English, history, political science and economics. Specific, or designated, bachelor of science degrees are offered in seven areas of the engineering field: aerospace, electrical, mechanical, marine, naval, ocean and systems engineering. In addition, programs leading to a B.S. degree are offered in more general areas of math and science, with majors in chemistry, mathematics, applied science, oceanography, physics, physical science and general engineering.

The first-year, or "plebe-year," program consists of a core of courses offered to all midshipmen at a level determined by an individual's ability and academic background. Although there are no formal tutoring programs available at the Academy, students agree that tutoring by both faculty and classmates is readily available "whenever needed."

In the academy library is an Educational Resource Center which contains a lending library of videotapes and films. Videocassette programs are utilized by midshipmen as remedial and tutorial tools. Students are also assigned faculty advisors in the spring of plebe year, after a major has been chosen.

Both academic and psychological counseling are available.

Computers play an integral part in academic life at the academy, and there are hundreds of remote terminals connected to an extensive time-shared multi-computer system. In addition, minicomputers and microcomputers are located throughout the academy.

As the sciences are the emphasis of academic study, so are athletics the focus of extracurricular activities at USNA. All students are expected to participate in at least one sport. There are intercollegiate teams in 21 sports for men and six for women, and there are 23 intramural sports. As one midshipman sums up the situation, "Everyone is engaged in sports."

Midshipmen are not involved in political activities since "you can't get into politics while in uniform." But they do participate in the governance of the academy. There are bands, a radio and a television station, and a theater group at the academy although none of these organizations are black-oriented. There are no fraternities or sororities.

The Black Studies Club is the only black-oriented organization on campus. The club sponsors several dances in the course of the school year, schedules speakers and plans special events for Black History Month.

Social life at the academy is not extensive. The major events are Homecoming and Commissioning Week.

Human relations seminars, including such topics as relations among the races and equal opportunity, are held periodically during all four years of a midshipman's attendance.

Relations between black midshipmen and white midshipmen, faculty, and members of the local community of Annapolis, which is 35 percent black, are reported to be cordial, on the whole.

Blacks stress that all at Naval Academy are "treated according to rank," that "with the Naval Academy being a military school... midshipmen are midshipmen...whether they are black, white, any other minority, male or female."

One student cautions: "The applicant ought to be able to work and live with white students and should expect a lack of black interest on campus."

Brothers and sisters inclined toward a career in the military, who seek a "rigorous and serious challenge," and who are not afraid to be "pushed to the limits, and then pushed some more" may well consider application to the United States Naval Academy.

VANDERBILT UNIVERSITY
Nashville, Tennessee 37212

Undergrads: 5,792
Black Undergrads: 232
Faculty: 1,968
Black Faculty: NA
Tuition: $19,422
Total Expenses: $26,078

One student says, "Vanderbilt has one of the best campuses that I have ever seen. Everything is taken care of, and there is constant renovation. Although it is located in a city atmosphere, Vanderbilt is its own little microcosm. It is separated from Nashville by greenery instead of gates."

Admission is selective at Vanderbilt—coed, private and moderately sized.

Vanderbilt offers several courses in the black experience, and the library has several collections, including the Lost Cause Press Collection.

Admits one undergrad, "First year at Vanderbilt is usually the worst as far as GPA goes. However, most of the upperclassmen seem to have adjusted."

To assist them, a bevy of support services are offered and include tutoring, counseling and study skills workshops. Sources of tutoring mentioned by respondents include the Tutorial Service for Minorities and Women, major departments, the Black Cultural Center, professors and teaching assistants, upperclass volunteers, paid peer tutors or organizations such as the Black Student Alliance (BSA) and the National Society of Black Engineers.

One undergrad says, "Our university provides excellent counseling resources for all types of situations, ranging from religious counseling to a crisis center."

In addition, one brother says that although there is a small number of black faculty members, many of them are very dedicated and willing to help their students.

Study skills workshops are available through the university and the Black Cultural Center. Respondents mention several special classes and other programs, including honors courses, workshops and seminars given by visiting professors and other guests.

Black student organizations include NAACP, the African Student Association, a fraternity (Alpha Phi Alpha) and two sororities (Delta Sigma Theta and Alpha Kappa Alpha). According to respondents, the Black Cultural Center, "a central hang-out for a majority of the black population," sponsors cultural programming, special seminars and workshops on various topics, parties, movie nights, picnics and "political activities."

Vanderbilt is within walking distance of many churches and synagogues. "There are black religious groups in the area," says one sister. However, another adds, "There is no black religious group supported by the university other than the Muslim Society." Most respondents report high black student involvement in intramural sports. In addition, one sister says that black participation on varsity sports is excellent. "Vanderbilt takes very good care of our black athletes," she says, adding that the university promotes academics by requiring a certain GPA for athletes to remain active. Vanderbilt has NCAA status. According to respondents, the percentage of black student athletes is the same as that of black students in the school as a whole, except in football, which fields a large number of African-American players.

Students have varying opinions about black student attendance at university-sponsored activities. Some say that participation is excellent, but others report that fewer blacks attend than would be expected and that many of these attend only events of an ethnic nature.

According to some, blacks participate heavily in Greek, off-campus and dormitory parties although some say that since Vanderbilt is located near black universities like Fisk and Tennessee State, an "excellent network of friends and social release" is provided.

Interaction between black and white students is "mostly superficial," according to most respondents. One brother says, "There are some sincere relationships, and some black students associate totally with whites." Another says, "Wherever you go, you will always find an ignorant person."

Responses are mixed concerning interaction between white faculty and black students. One undergrad feels that relations are "better than average." On the other hand, another student says, "Interaction is not encouraged unless absolutely necessary—for example, to check grades or talk about homework."

Relationships with other non-white faculty members are reportedly fair. One sister says, "As with whites, sometimes you may run into a rotten apple, but as a whole, they realize that the stereotype of blacks is a lie."

According to another sister, "The black faculty are very supportive. They are great at making time for black students." Although many respondents agree, others feel that there are too few black professors for all black students to have much contact with them.

Regarding the surrounding community, one undergrad says, "Interaction is good for me with both blacks and whites, yet I suspect that others would not feel the same." Another reports, "Whites refuse to believe you go to Vanderbilt until you prove it, and blacks assume that you're snobbish until you reach out and show you're not."

One sister advises that prospective students "must keep in mind that racism is still in existence. There will be some encounters of the worst kind when attending white institutions. That's a fact we have to live with."

However, she continues, "I am pleased with my decision to come to Vanderbilt. My two-year journey through this school has made me one strong black woman."

"The school that best serves your interests in the long run is the school to choose," says one undergrad. "You can find a rewarding academic challenge at Vanderbilt, and the faculty welcomes students seeking challenges. The school's environment is steadily improving, it has a very good reputation and the increasing black population keeps a black student from feeling alone."

VASSAR COLLEGE
Poughkeepsie, New York 12601

Undergrads: 2,344
Black Undergrads: 141
Faculty: 223
Black Faculty: 9
Tuition: $20,330
Total Expenses: $26,480

Most black student respondents are quite happy with their decision to attend Vassar. Although perhaps a bit overwhelmed at first by the school's white atmosphere, they have found that relationships with white students and faculty are quite beneficial, providing a good foundation for the future.

Says one brother: "Because Vassar is predominantly white, the school helps to program you for dealing with whites in the outside world."

Founded in 1861 to provide a quality education for young women, today's Vassar is a highly selective, private liberal arts college 75 miles north of New York City.

Although Vassar went coed in 1968, it is still widely known as a women's college, contributing to a somewhat lopsided gender ratio. Says one sister: "I wish more blacks realized that Vassar is coed. I believe that everything we have here would be enhanced by the presence of a larger number of blacks, especially males."

Academically, Vassar enjoys top-notch status. The college offers the B.A. degree and a four-year course of study leading to a combined B.A-M.A. in chemistry, French, Hispanic Studies, or physics. Independent study plans are encouraged, and internships are available through the Center for Career Development and Field Work. Eight national honorary societies, including Phi Beta Kappa, have chapters on campus, and 50 percent of Vassar grads pursue advanced degrees.

Black students at Vassar occasionally encounter academic difficulty. Says one brother, "We always complain and do fall behind at times, but it always gets done." However, another insists, "There is always assistance at hand for those who need it." Assures a fellow student: "Once you make it through your first semester of freshman year, you are bound to come through the entire four years."

Support services at Vassar are described by many respondents as "excellent." Freshmen are assigned pre-major advisors, and after majors are declared, departmental advisors. Further counseling is available from the dean of studies, the dean of freshmen and the sophomore and junior advisors.

Tutoring is offered by the Academic Resource Center in all academic subjects. The Listening Center is a forum for phone-in peer counseling. Day-to-day advice is available from Student Fellows—upperclassmen who live in the dorms. More informal settings are encouraged by House Fellows, faculty members who live with their families in special dormitory apartments. Says one student: "Help is available at all times to students who express a need."

Vassar's most prominent black organizations are the Black Student Union and Ebony Theater, which occasionally sponsors black theater productions and other cultural events, and has brought to campus such speakers as Imamu Baraka, Gil Noble, and Kwame Toure.

Vassar's gospel choir is predominantly black and "very active," and many black students participate in the Africana Studies program, through which students go to nearby Greenhaven Prison and conduct workshops. Occasional mobility problems crop up to mar the social scene; a brother notes, "Cars are necessary, and most black students don't own them."

Dorm life at Vassar revolves around 10 residence halls, including a cluster of townhouse apartments. Most of the student body comes from New York state, but students also come to Vassar from across the continent.

The hub of Vassar's social milieu is the College Center, which houses a post office, the campus radio station, a snack bar called the Retreat, and Matthew's Mug, a pub/dance floor. Says one brother, "You can usually count on a good night out at the Mug."

Black-white relations at Vassar are without serious strain. "Most people," claims one sister, "are associated with a mixed group of friends." Another agrees that there is "lots of interaction, and each respects the other's views and ideas." A brother remarks: "Of course we do have our black tables."

The Black Student Union sponsors programs on racial tolerance and supports a Black Alumni Forum.

"Vassar," says a satisfied sister, "is an excellent place to grow."

VIRGINIA STATE UNIVERSITY
Petersburg, Virginia 23803

Undergrads: 3,484
Black Undergrads: 3,484
Faculty: 265
Black Faculty: NA
Tuition: $3,256; $5,960
Total Expenses: $8,101; $10,805

A satisfied VSU student urges all blacks to consider the spiritual impact of attending a historically black school. There is more to college than classes and parties, he suggests about century-old, state-supported, and coed VSU, committed to educating blacks. Its admission policy is not selective.

The college offers a variety of degrees in liberal arts, education, and business to its largely Virginian (80 percent) student body. The most popular major is business administration. Cooperative education and work experience programs, and summer and mid-winter internship programs provide valuable job training.

An exchange with Old Dominion University in engineering and math has been established.

Most students find the school challenging. According to one respondent, "Only half are able to meet the academic requirements beyond freshman year." Some students have trouble adjusting to college-level academics.

Therefore, VSU offers various tutorial and counseling services designed to ease the transition. Among these are a summer skill-building session for credit, developmental courses, extra class sessions for review, tutoring, and faculty counseling. However, there are no pre-med, pre-law, or pre-professional clubs, and not enough special class sections, according to students. Career counseling also appears to be limited although students say faculty are accessible for discussion about professional options and graduate school.

Students find faculty to be congenial on the whole, but one brother notes that "the students and black faculty don't see eye-to-eye at times," and another suggests that non-white faculty and administrators are "more concerned" than their white colleagues.

Despite a student body somewhat older than the norm (one third of VSU students are over 21 years old), with a large percentage of part-time (16 percent) and off-campus (50 percent) students, and alcohol forbidden on campus, VSU offers a lively, entertaining, and not atypical social scene, according to respondents. Frats and sororities are very active in sponsoring mixers and other events. Intercollegiate and intramural sports are quite popular, despite the small number of teams. For the student who wants more excitement, Richmond, Virginia's capital city, is just 25 miles north of Virginia State.

The university choir performs at local churches, and students tutor and counsel college-oriented high schoolers through the Upward Bound Program. While there is little campus theater and no radio, and students are not certain they have any real power in helping decide matters relating to university governance, VSU's blacks are not dissatisfied. And they feel, as one respondent says, that there are "no racial problems that would cause great concern." Relations with the small number of whites on campus is said to be fairly smooth, if not entirely trouble-free.

"An education from a historically black school is one that will leave a lasting feeling in your heart," one respondent writes.

VIRGINIA UNION UNIVERSITY
Richmond, Virginia 23220

Undergrads: 1,057
Black Undergrads: 1,046
Faculty: 65
Black Faculty: NA
Tuition: $3,256; $5,960
Total Expenses: $8,101; $10,805

Small, coed, not very selective and liberal arts-oriented, the university is located in the urban environment of Richmond and is affiliated with the American Baptist Convention.

Virginia Union is among the first of the traditionally black institutions in America. Unlike many of them, it makes no bones about the foundation of its curriculum. It is decidedly a combination of Western civilization and black heritage.

Founded in 1865 on the site of a former slave jail, the goal of the university has been to provide quality education and leadership development opportunities, originally for newly emancipated blacks, and now for all students. It can now take pride in the fact that one of its alumns, Governor L. Douglas Wilder, was the nation's highest-ranking black elected official as Virginia's governor.

There are several academic divisions within the university: Education and Psychology; Humanities; Natural Science and Mathematics; Social Sciences; and the Sydney Lewis School of Business Administration.

The well-respected Graduate School of Theology rounds out the school's offerings. Its most popular concentrations are business, biology and education.

The university continually seeks ways in which to upgrade its undergraduate programs. For example, with the establishment of the City of Richmond Police Academy on campus, the criminal justice program has changed from a minor to a major course of study.

Music majors will study black music as part of the basic music theory and history courses. These students can take advantage of the University Choir, Chapel Choir, Concert Choir, University Band and Stage Band.

All students are required to take a least one course in religious studies, regardless of area of concentration. Chapel is mandatory.

In addition to the emphasis on liberal arts and the humanities, the university promotes a better understanding of the significance of African-American history, literature, arts and other contributions to society.

To get away from the academic pressures, four national fraternities, four national sororities and a full slate of organizations are available for artistic, physical, social, spiritual and community service activities. A drama/theater group and a student-run newspaper as well as a nationally recognized sports program will also keep you busy.

WASHINGTON UNIVERSITY
St. Louis, Missouri 63130

Undergrads: 4,993
Black Undergrads: 250
Faculty: 3,619
Black Faculty: NA
Tuition: $19,291
Total Expenses: $25,323

They love it here. And overall, blacks are at peace with their decision to attend Wash U. They emphasize that the university is academically challenging, and unless a student is prepared for this challenge, it can be a difficult adjustment. They also appreciate the school's ethnic diversity.

Coed, medium-sized, and independent, the undergraduate college has a highly selective admission policy. Located seven miles from downtown St. Louis, the university's 17-acre campus borders Forest Park, one of the largest municipal parks in America.

Washington University students represent all 50 states and more than 70 foreign countries and territories. Most black students at Washington University come from Missouri, Illinois, Tennessee, and New York.

Undergraduates here can take courses in the arts and sciences, business, education, health fields, and engineering.

The university, now with an African-American Studies major, also offers dozens of courses that relate directly to the black experience. A few examples are "The Black Woman in Contemporary Society," "Modern African Writers," and "Blacks in Science and Technology."

Overall, the black students interviewed feel that most blacks at Washington University adjust well to the academic requirements. However, students with weak high school backgrounds tend to have more difficulty with the adjustment process than do other students.

Students describe the university's academic support services as "very helpful." One brother says, "A student who wants help can always get it."

The university provides tutorial assistance and study skills workshops throughout the school year. During the summer, Washington University offers pre-freshmen a five week, all-expenses-paid summer program featuring workshops in calculus, English, and communication skills.

Washington University offers its freshmen an innovative one-year program (FOCUS) which brings them into close contact with professors and fellow students who have similar interests. Central to each program is a seminar examining the core issues of the general topic. Some FOCUS plans have included Law and Society, Text and Context, Humanities for the Science Student, and Technology and Society.

Besides academic offerings and support services, the university has a large network of counseling services. The professionally staffed Student Counseling Service works with students to resolve personal and interpersonal difficulties. Similarly, Uncle Joe's, a student-run peer counseling center, operates at night in the residential area and enables students to talk with their peers in a confidential and supportive atmosphere. Most black respondents say that counseling services are generally very good.

For the post-collegiate world, the Career Planning and Placement Office assists students in making career decisions, securing employment when they leave the university, and obtaining part-time and summer employment.

There are four active black student organizations on campus: Association of Black Students (ABS), St. Louis Black Pan-Hellenic Council, Black Pre-Med Association, and the Society of Black Engineers. Students say that the Black Pre-Med Association provides many helpful workshops and activities for its members. It also has strong ties with students in medical school.

ABS is actively trying to improve relations between black students and the local community—especially the local black community. It seems that black students from the St. Louis area have less difficulty establishing positive relations with the local community than do other students.

Student descriptions of the interaction between black and white students range from "superficial" to "very good." According to one student, "There is some racial tension between groups, but not as much between individuals."

Several university groups jointly sponsor programs to encourage racial tolerance. Among these programs are the Martin Luther King Symposium, a Black Arts and Sciences Festival, the W.E.B. DuBois lecture series, and the campus YMCA's Interracial Awareness Committee. In general, the Office of Student Activities is responsible for providing out-of-class activities and encouraging social interaction between students and other members of the university community.

Interaction between brothers and sisters and white faculty and administrators is said to be positive. However, a few students say that some white faculty and administrators are known for their insensitivity to black students.

Black students seem to relate well to the few black faculty and administrators on campus. A black undergrad says that the black faculty should become more involved in activities that would make them more visible to the university community at large.

The Residential Life Center coordinates and promotes social, cultural, educational, religious, and recreational activities for students. Nonetheless, "Black students refuse to participate in white Greek life," according to one black undergrad. Black students usually attend the few parties given by black organizations. If they have the transportation, they sometimes attend off-campus parties. The university's athletic teams are not usually conference champions, but brothers and sisters participate at both the varsity and intramural levels. The most popular sports are football, basketball, and baseball.

Blacks are also becoming more active in student government. One sister says, "Unfortunately, black students are either very active or not active at all."

"The diverse student body at Wash U forces you to learn a lot about people from other parts of the country and the world," says one undergraduate.

WEBER STATE COLLEGE
Ogden, Utah 84408

Undergrads: 13,840
Black Undergrads: 138
Faculty: 506
Black Faculty: NA
Tuition: $1,854; $5,148
Total Expenses: $4,644; $7,938

Students point to Utah itself as a challenge to any black student. One thinks, "Any black student coming from out of state probably wouldn't enjoy Weber State because of the Mormon culture and also because blacks in Utah are not as united as they should be."

Situated in Ogden, Utah, WSC draws most of its small black population from Utah, California and Arizona. The school, coed and less selective, offers degrees in the traditional arts and sciences as well as in business and education.

According to one respondent, the English, business and education programs here are attractive academic features.

While students find getting into Weber "no problem," adjustment once they are in is not always easy. To help students in difficulty, the school has a counseling center to assist with personal problems and offers a full-credit course in "Effective Study Skills." There is no tutoring center, but student tutors are assigned to those who ask for help. While tutors are "excellent and very willing to help," in one student's opinion, the lack of a more organized system is discouraging.

BSU, the Black Scholars United, is the one black support and cultural organization; it provides some tutoring assistance as well as serving as a forum for complaints and sponsoring a few activities for Weber's black undergrads.

WSC's environment is another reason that adjustment to college life is tough for some. Because they make up such a small percentage of its student population, blacks experience some awkwardness in their relations with white students and faculty. White and black students get along fairly well, although a sister also notes "apprehensiveness" and offers this analysis: "I think black and white students have a hard time dealing with each other because it takes intellect to be understanding."

As for relations with white faculty, respondents report "racial slurs" or "racial jokes." And one student says, "Black people here have to earn their attention." Still, some professors and administrators are rated "excellent" and although one brother notes a few barriers, black faculty are supportive, and interaction with them is generally good.

Given the lack of black organizations, most parties and other social events take place off campus. Says one student, "There is no place for on-campus blacks to go where they can really feel at home." There is, however, one chapter of black Greeks, and efforts are being made to establish several others.

Participation in other events varies from student to student, but it is especially heavy in intramural and varsity athletics. The latter, claims one student, "is why most of the black males are here." There is one radio spot on radio KJQ which, according to another, "gives students a chance to voice their opinions."

Life for black students is no crystal staircase at Weber State, say respondents. Another believes that increased understanding and interaction with the community would make life at this college better. But for now, a student must rely on a strong sense of self to make something of Weber. In the words of one undergrad, "He must realize his character is an asset," and work from there.

WELLESLEY COLLEGE
Wellesley, Massachusetts 02181

Undergrads: 2,299
Black Undergrads: 138
Faculty: 320
Black Faculty: 20
Tuition: $19,610
Total Expenses: $25,810

In brief, "Wellesley is reality," writes one sister. Despite the racial tension, most black women adjust well to the environment and appreciate the opportunity to learn how to cope with this societal problem before entering society. They want to reap the benefits of the Wellesley experience.

And prestigious Wellesley, 35 minutes from Boston and among the most selective schools in the country, strives to produce well-educated women that can hold their own in society.

Bachelor's degree programs are offered in the arts, social sciences, education, humanities, sciences and math. A concentration in engineering is established by combining physics courses at Wellesley with engineering courses at M.I.T.

For the Afrocentric, the curriculum includes Black Studies courses like African-American Music and Black Women Writers.

The Black Alumnae Network, whose 185 trained representatives avidly recruit qualified black students worldwide, has solid input in the admission process.

Most of the blacks at Wellesley come from Massachusetts, New York, New Jersey and the Maryland/Washington, D.C. area.

An attractive feature of Wellesley's special academic programs is the Spelman-Wellesley Exchange program whereby Wellesley students can spend one or two semesters of their junior year at this historic, black women's college in Atlanta. In turn, sisters from Spelman learn and share their interests and experiences with Wellesley women.

The shift from high school to college is not especially difficult for black students entering Wellesley. An individual's background is cited as the central factor which determines how well a student adjusts. "Those who have problems should take advantage of the support systems offered," advises one black student. The support systems at Wellesley are indeed extensive, with services provided by the dean's office and the black student organization, Ethos, among others. The dean's office provides free tutorial sessions with trained student tutors and holds study skills workshops on such topics as time management, note-taking and memorization. Both services are offered in the dormitories and are open to the entire student body.

The math department also holds study skills workshops for freshmen at the start of the school year. The workshops are described as "very helpful" but under-utilized. For counseling, students have the choice of talking to professional counselors of the college counseling service at the Stone Center for Mental Health, resident counselors within the dorms, faculty advisors and deans.

Of special interest to black students is the peer counseling group of Ethos, Sisters Helping Each Other (SHE). Members are black student volunteers trained in academic and social counseling techniques. The Director of the Black Cultural Center, Harambee House, also acts as a counselor. In addition, weekly discussion groups are led by a black member of the staff at Stone Center.

There are no black pre-professional societies at Wellesley, but the black pre-medical students work closely with each other and with the black pre-med advisor. A Premedical Advisory Committee informs students about med school requirements. Although one sister claims that Wellesley is not the place for pre-meds, 70 percent of its pre-meds are accepted to medical school each year.

The Black Theater, offering two productions yearly, is one of Wellesley's black cultural outlets. Some black students have daily slots on the campus radio station. Although there are no regular black religious services on campus, Wellesley's Black Christian Fellowship is active and sponsors buses to community churches on Sundays. The non-denominational campus church gives a black service once each year during Ethos' Black Quintessence Weekend.

Wellesley's black faculty and administrators are considered a source of pride and encouragement to the sisters, and they help with social planning.

Yet, the sisters definitely sense racism on campus and in the community. Black and white students interact mostly on an individual, academic basis. "In the classroom there are no problems," says one respondent. "But outside the classroom blacks tend to deal with blacks, and whites tend not to deal with blacks. Blacks sit with blacks because they are friends and share similar backgrounds, and whites, Iranians, etc...do the same."

The black students find their role models and strongest support in the black faculty and administrators. Members of the two groups interact as friends and tend to be close. Relationships between black students and white faculty and administrators are generally not close, "but there are exceptions." Interaction with the community is infrequent.

The participation of black students in university governance is not substantial. Many are on various committees as representatives of Ethos, but few are on the student governing board. Wellesley's black alumns remain in close contact with the undergraduates, and their network provides leads on job opportunities, speakers for special forums, and summer and winter internships. Area alumns also attend Ethos meetings occasionally and give an annual dinner for black students at the home of one of the alumns.

Most sisters seem to mind the absence of men, who are nevertheless frequent visitors at social functions. Integrated parties are popular. Harambee House is the social and cultural center for black students, has a black director, and features diverse program offerings, including class dinners for black students and faculty, dance performances, speakers, movies, pizza and ice cream parties, a record library, and a growing library on African and Afro-American history and culture. The house also has offices for staff members, Ethos and *Brown Sister*, a literary magazine. The college rarely brings black professional entertainment to the campus.

Word has it that black women usually fare well at prestigious Wellesley. They view the academic and social challenges at this small, private women's college as preparation for the real world.

Finally, explains one student, as a women's college, "Wellesley helps you to grow and develop your abilities as a woman."

WESLEYAN UNIVERSITY
Middletown, Connecticut 06457

Undergrads: 445
Black Undergrads: 76
Faculty: 356
Black Faculty: 13
Tuition: $20,820
Total Expenses: $26,630

B rothers and sisters will doubtless find an extensive support network and a solid family atmosphere among the black community here. The congenial relationship with the white community, as well as academics "as fine as one can find" make it a top choice. Wesleyan's black students, on the whole, speak of their school in superlatives.

Founded in 1831, this most selective, private, coed university offers first-rate undergraduate instruction in the liberal arts and sciences.

Most blacks are from Massachusetts and the tri-state area; there's also a large contingent from California. Academics are rigorous at Wesleyan, and survivors enjoy a high acceptance rate at graduate and professional schools. Two honorary societies have chapters on campus, and honors work with thesis is offered in all departments. Students can even design their own majors.

An African-American Studies program—the first of its kind on the East Coast—consists of 25 courses, in fields like anthropology, art, linguistics, or dance.

The Center for Afro-American Studies (CAAS) also offers an academic program designed to "define the black American cultural and intellectual perspective through the liberal arts curriculum." The Center's African Studies Program places students for a semester at the University of Ghana.

Black students sometimes encounter adjustment problems at Wesleyan. "But," assures one sister, "there are just too many programs offered that help ease that adjustment." Another student feels there is a wealth of social support for the insecure freshman: "Because of the close-knit community and support groups, the adjustment is easier."

The black community at Wesleyan is very cohesive, and many academic and social support services are sponsored by black organizations. Ujamaa (meaning "familyhood"), the college's black political organization, offers a tutorial service as well as various cultural events. The Center for Afro-American Studies is also very active, co-sponsoring with the dean's office a peer tutorial service called Prospect Wesleyan. The Center fosters faculty-student relations through a weekly community meal in the Malcolm X House under the auspices of its Fellows Program. The faculty-student bond is said to be "tight."

Other support services at Wesleyan include an extensive network of resident advisors (there are usually two per freshman hall), a Sexual Help and Information Service, and a non-academic counseling system called "Eight to Eight." Writing workshops and math clinics are also available. One sister calls the support services at Wesleyan "extremely convenient and accessible."

Wesleyan has several black pre-professional organizations, including a pre-med and a pre-law society.

Alumns are also a great source of guidance for undergrads. Several students refer to their alumn contacts as "friends" who have provided them with valuable career information. Wesleyan graduates keep in touch with campus life through the annual Black Alumni Weekend.

Social life at Wesleyan is more or less restricted to on-campus activity. Little Middletown is not a cultural mecca; however, Wesleyan is only 30 minutes from Yale, an hour from the five-college area in Massachusetts, and two hours from Rhode Island's Brown University. Students make an effort to establish ties with the surrounding community, even appointing a "student liaison" with the town and participating in community tutorial programs and other projects.

Yet, with all this, campus-community relations are called "absolutely horrible" by one student, and several others express regret over the lack of interaction.

Life on campus is not, however, so horrible. Ten frat houses and 24 dormitories will keep you busy.

Dorm parties are "frequently fun" and well-attended by blacks. Although one student cautions that he has witnessed "some serious racial altercations," another calls interracial interaction "above standard." Another assures that it is "steadily improving."

The race relations question is officially tackled by the Student Community on Racial Awareness (SCORA). Most students emphasize that the ideal situation does not exist, and that most black-white relations at Wesleyan are positive.

Wesleyan's black students seem to have thrown themselves wholeheartedly into the school's social and cultural whirl. Ujamaa sponsors an annual five-day festival of artists, speakers, and films called Jubilee Week. The CAAS also sponsors a lecture series for which June Jordan, Gloria Naylor, Jay Mandle, Robert Thompson, and Ntozake Shange have been speakers. The Black Artists Collective, a forum for black student artists and writers, meets weekly to discuss student work and publishes an annual collection called *Expression.*

Black radio is very strong at Wesleyan; the campus station, WESU, has a show called Music for the People, which plays rhythm and blues, soul, and funk. Black programming is on regularly on weekdays and Saturdays.

Blacks take an active role in university governance, serving on most university committees. The senior class president has been black during several previous academic years. The only Wesleyan activity that has not drawn overwhelming support from black students is, in fact, athletics. Several students attribute this low participation rate to the varsity system at Wesleyan. One brother claims, "If black athletes are not exceptional, they will not play."

A strong sense of identity is needed here, says one student. "It is a place geared for students with inner strength and persistence."

Finally, Wesleyan's black students exude enthusiasm when it comes to supporting their college's national reputation. "I love this school and what it has to offer me," raves one sister.

WEST VIRGINIA STATE COLLEGE
Institute, West Virginia 25112

Undergrads: 4,486
Black Undergrads: 538
Faculty: 242
Black Faculty: NA
Tuition: $2,050; $4,866
Total Expenses: $5,500; $8,316

"Our campus is full of the pride and rich heritage of a black college although the majority of our students are non-black," one student writes. "I am very satisfied that I chose a historically black school."

The mission of West Virginia State College—a multipurpose, undergraduate institution with a "hometown atmosphere"—is to educate the "whole person."

Located in the capital region of Charleston, West Virginia, the institution is dedicated to providing students with the academic, social, psychological, cultural and moral support they need to excel in the "real world."

Originally, the college was predominantly black—open to young men and women who were otherwise denied equal educational opportunity. However, the institution desegregated in 1954 and now has a racially mixed student body.

The campus is situated on a spacious 83-acre tract of land in the Appalachian foothills along the Kanawha River. Most of the students are residents of West Virginia, Ohio, Pennsylvania and New York.

Alumni chapters assist in recruitment efforts by referring students, covering college fairs, bringing students for overnight visits and hosting special events in their cities. In addition, admission counselors participate in several college fairs throughout the year.

West Virginia State maintains a strong general education program. It offers day as well as night academic programs.

A variety of courses, too many to list, are offered on the subject of African and American experiences. One course, African Textiles, may give some idea of the range of subjects covered.

The library has an extensive collection in African, Afro-American and other black history and literature. The school is in the process of developing an Archive Collection of materials that document the history of black West Virginians.

A wide spectrum of academic support programs such as workshops on memory testing, test-taking, relaxation, speed reading, assertiveness and study skills improvement are offered at the college.

The Collegiate Support Services and Counseling Center Staff screens students to determine areas of need, and match them with help services on and off campus. Also, personal counseling and referrals are available.

A West Virginia State College counselor assists full-time students who are handicapped, including those with non-visual handicaps such as asthma and heart conditions. Special counselors are on staff for the two-year degree student who needs educational counseling and for students who are eligible for Vocational Rehabilitation Services.

Peer tutoring in most subject areas is offered through various departments, as is extra counseling for students from other cultures. The college also boasts a comprehensive career planning and placement service that assists everyone from pre-college students to college alumni.

The list of student organizations at West Virginia State College is also long. Groups include Kappa Delta Pi, an honor society in Education; Alpha Kappa Mu, a national honor society; and Alpha Kappa Delta, the national sociology honor society.

In addition, West Virginia State has the Greek-letter organizations of Alpha Kappa Alpha sorority, Alpha Phi Alpha fraternity, Delta Sigma Theta sorority and Omega Psi Phi fraternity.

As for sports, the college sponsors men's varsity teams in football, basketball, track, baseball and tennis. Women's teams include tennis, basketball and track. Cross-country and golf are also sponsored, but considered coeducational.

In general, students say race relations are very good between black students on campus and white students, and white faculty and administrators; black faculty and administrators or other non-white faculty also get along well with WVSC's black undergrads. They say the occasional problems that do arise because of racial tensions are due to personality or individual conflicts.

This land grant college has prided itself since 1891 in, as one student put it, providing students with "encouragement and understanding and an increased awareness of what it means to be black in American society."

WHEATON COLLEGE
Norton, Massachusetts 02766

Undergrads: 1,319
Black Undergrads: 26
Faculty: 110
Black Faculty: NA
Tuition: $19,140
Total Expenses: $25,190

Despite the criticisms about the social life, black respondents say that they are satisfied with the educational options and instruction they receive. "Wheaton has helped me develop myself as a young black woman," says one woman. "Since I have been at Wheaton, I have learned that I must challenge myself, make difficult decisions and stand on my own two feet."

A willingness to "sacrifice your social life" is a key to getting through Wheaton College, the oldest women's institution in New England. The college is small, private and has a selective admission policy.

Most black students at Wheaton are residents of New York, Massachusetts, Pennsylvania and New Jersey. Admissions counselors visit schools with significant numbers of black students as part of an effort to recruit black students.

Wheaton is known for its quality academic programs. "Wheaton is very challenging academically," a student confirms. "Sometimes it's a lot easier to get accepted than it is to stay and maintain good grades." Another says, "I think a black student planning to attend Wheaton should be prepared to compete in rigorous academics."

Thirteen courses in African and Afro-American study are offered as part of the college curriculum including Black America, Systems of Social Inequality and Women of Sub-Saharan Africa.

The school participates in a 12-college exchange and has junior year abroad programs. Students interested in business, engineering, journalism or religion may enroll in the dual degree program, which Wheaton offers in cooperation with other institutions. Participants spend their first three years at Wheaton and transfer for the last two years. Upon completion, the student will receive both her Wheaton B.A. and the advanced degree from the cooperating university.

Wheaton's career planning program has earned national recognition. The Mentor program matches juniors with career professionals in their areas of interest. A-Plus (A Program for Learning and Utilizing Skills) provides workshops designed to meet social, emotional and career development needs of Wheaton students through topics like career life planning, decision making and assertiveness training. Students who need tutorial assistance in a particular subject area may make arrangements to find a tutor through the advising office. Most of the tutors are students. Special class sections are at the request of students, as are special workshops and seminars.

The college has declared its interest in increased programs on racial awareness and now holds a black alumn weekend. Also, a workshop on intercultural awareness during orientation is mandatory for freshmen. And special seminars and workshops such as a "Teach-In on Racism" are offered. Wheaton also sponsors other programs, such as the Intercultural Awareness Committee, Committee to Improve Diversity and the Society Organized Against Racism (SOAR), to encourage racial tolerance.

Students contend, however, that the programs haven't made a significant impression on the campus. "I feel that it is relevant for a black student to be prepared for racism in all its subtle forms," one complains.

Students rate the interaction between themselves and white students, white faculty and administrators, black faculty and administrators in the community as fair to bad. "Most blacks associate with the whites on campus, but they associate more with the other blacks." Many of the whites living in Norton are not civil to black students, one woman reports. Others add that students are often subjected to name-calling.

The college sponsors one black student organization, the Union of Black Students. A Black Cultural Center is located in the Student Activities building.

Some sisters report a feeling of isolation when they speak of this 151-year-old college in Norton, Massachusetts. Interaction between black women on campus and everyone else—white women, white and black faculty members and Norton residents—is "shaky" at best and "real bad" at worst, respondents say.

"I've made a lot of social sacrifices in exchange for a quality education," says one black woman.

Black women say they go to Boston for social activities because the social life on campus is often nothing more than "drinking coffee and chatting over dinner." A Wheaton bus, which runs several times daily to and from Boston, provides students with regular, moderately priced transportation to theaters, museums, whale watches and other events.

WILBERFORCE UNIVERSITY
Wilberforce, Ohio 45384

Undergrads: 848
Black Undergrads: 814
Faculty: 90
Black Faculty: NA
Tuition: $7,360
Total Expenses: $11,260

No matter what the pace of life, after 126 years of service to the African-American nation, Wilberforce will continue to be a "force" among the historically black colleges and college-bound black students, asserts one respondent.

From the time Wilberforce opened its doors in 1856, it has played a vital role in the education of black students. Under the direction of the African Methodist Episcopal Church, the first African-American church established in America, Wilberforce has attracted black students from the surrounding states of Pennsylvania, Michigan and Illinois as well as from the Caribbean and Africa.

With a relatively small student body that is equally divided between males and females, it has an atmosphere for the black student seeking an "intimate small college." Furthermore, Wilberforce's less selective admission process leaves the door wide open for many black students who might not attend college because of fierce competition.

Since Wilberforce is on a tri-semester system and happens to be one of about 200 U.S. colleges that operate a cooperative education program, all undergraduates must spend at least one semester per year, beginning in the sophomore year, in a work environment. Credit based on the co-op experience is applied toward the degree. For the student who wants to work very hard, Wilberforce has dual degree programs in engineering, mathematics and science.

Although the frosh dropout rate is about 20 percent, the same percentage manage to complete their studies at Wilberforce and go on to graduate school.

Recruitment efforts at private and public secondary schools are supplemented by visits to churches, career fairs, and recruitment functions sponsored by NSSFMS and the United Negro College Fund. Alumni play a vital role in recruiting by disseminating literature about Wilberforce and sometimes contacting "pre-frosh." Throughout the year, prospective students visit the campus for overnight visits.

Getting used to campus life is a real challenge here because the many fraternal and social organizations distract one from academic pursuits, say students. One sister claims that it "usually takes two tri-semesters, the junior counselors and some resident assistants to help freshmen adjust."

The General Studies Program ensures that free tutoring is provided to students, by students. And faculty make themselves accessible for additional academic assistance. Mandatory workshops on "college survival skills" are held for frosh.

Wilberforce students form study groups often. Academic support organizations, like the Pre-law Club or the National Student Business League, do their share in easing the academic tension.

Wilberforce has a theatrical organization that aims to dramatize the African experience. Also a campus-based radio station, WURS, entertains and educates the student body. Since the university has an affiliation with the AME church, religious services are made available—even for non-Episcopalians.

Despite their "minority" status, one black student claims, "The white students don't feel isolated." Interaction between black students and faculty is described as "good and positive" primarily because "the campus community is so small that professors often act as counselors."

Parties thrown on campus are well-attended because there are no discos in town. Yet when Wilberforce students get tired of campus parties, they may visit one of the surrounding colleges like Central State to socialize. Although the various black Greek fraternities and sororities sponsor parties throughout the year, the university sponsors only one jam—the annual "dawn dance" for seniors. When off the dance floor, many students find time to engage in sports activities.

Almost the same amount of energy that goes into socializing is expended in the politics of university life. Through the Student Government Association, students sit on various university committees. They feel they have some leverage in the decision-making process. Unlike most schools in the country, point out respondents, a student representative sits on the Board of Trustees at Wilberforce.

In Xenia, a town about six miles away from the university, with a 50 percent black population, students find the time to party, counsel in the community health center and tutor youth. However, the "desolate" immediate surroundings of Wilberforce impose restrictions on students' community involvement. Since most Wilberforce students come from large cities, life can be quite slow around school or, as one sister analyzes the situation: "This isolation creates a strong dependence on and interest in campus activities."

WILLIAMS COLLEGE
Williamstown, Massachusetts 01267

Undergrads: 2,053
Black Undergrads: 123
Faculty: 251
Black Faculty: 13
Tuition: $20,790
Total Expenses: $26,780

Assessing Williams College, respondents point out these advantages: a small school, a prestigious degree, individualized attention from professors, fairly easy access to college money to fund creative ideas, and the opportunity to establish close relationships with other blacks.

Tucked away on 450 acres in western Massachusetts, a few miles from both the Vermont and New York borders, coed Williams is as beautiful as it is pretigious.

Williams has always maintained a tradition of academic excellence, and its admission policy is one of the most selective in the country.

Support services include a special black pre-freshman weekend, peer and professional counseling, career counseling and placement, tutoring and remedial instruction, special class sections, and formal as well as informal faculty counseling.

The black faculty, while perhaps too small a percentage of the teaching staff (three percent), is very accessible, according to brothers and sisters. "A number of white faculty and administrators have been particularly concerned with or helpful to black students," a respondent notes.

Another student describes this relationship as "something extra which makes you that much more comfortable." Although there are no black pre-law or pre-professional groups, there is a "successful" black pre-med society and active, integrated pre-law and pre-professional clubs. A black alumn network has just been established, and the alumn association (the nation's oldest) does maintain a meticulously updated directory of all Williams' alumns.

In general, students at Williams adjust well to the college, as the low freshman attrition rate (two percent) and the number of students who remain to collect their degrees (90 percent) demonstrate. "The work at Williams is definitely challenging. However, in general the black students seem to make the adjustment," a sister states. Presumably, the various counseling services help ease the transition to college-level studies.

Still, academics at Williams is never easy. Williams students are achievers and the academic pressure can be intense at times.

All freshmen are required to participate in special Winter Study interdisciplinary seminars which are designed "to stimulate synthetic thinking and to improve writing ability." Over 60 percent of Williams grads go on to further study, with 11 percent attending medical school and 7 percent enrolling in law school. Graduate school admission officers respect the Williams degree. Businesses do too: Williams has been called "the West Point of Wall Street."

Although the academic and physical environments are invigorating and pleasing, the social environment is less so. Williams is hours away from any major city (three hours from both Boston and New York) and students must content themselves with whatever is at hand, which means whatever the college sponsors.

There are no fraternities or sororities on campus, so mixers and other social and cultural events are sponsored by the residential houses and various clubs and departments. "Black party life is limited because we're not close to other schools. Parties are usually small and informal. All-campus parties are not usually attended by blacks," a respondent says, and adds, "Black Student Union activities aren't very well attended by black students, except for a few core groups."

The college newspaper, the literary magazine, and the radio station attract a few blacks, and "the black singing and dance groups are popular throughout the college community." There is also a large number of integrated musical groups, both vocal and instrumental, with some black membership.

The Lehman Service Council sponsors Big Brother/Big Sister programs, as well as programs for the Williamstown Boys Club, the Berkshire Farm Center for delinquent youth, and the Williamstown Day Care Center. Also under its auspices are high school equivalency exam tutoring for adults, instruction to foreign nationals in English as a second language, and ABC, a high school tutoring program.

Sports, too, are important to black Williams students. Basketball is the most popular intramural activity for blacks.

Williams sponsors professional entertainment, some of it black-oriented, and "sometimes makes very impressive attempts to show their appreciation for black culture," a student suggests. However, commenting on the lack of a black theater, one student exclaims, "We definitely need this."

On the whole, most blacks are satisfied, if not entirely delighted, with Williams. They cite the social life as the major drawback. Relationships with whites, while for the most part "superficial," are not antagonistic. Interracial dating occurs. But the school's isolated location, lack of a local black community, and small black student body "can sometimes make for a stifled social life," one sister points out.

Says one black woman: "No matter how much complaining we do, we usually come back every September."

WRIGHT STATE UNIVERSITY
Dayton, Ohio 45435

Undergrads: 12,254
Black Undergrads: 858
Faculty: 950
Black Faculty: NA
Tuition: $3,429; $6,858
Total Expenses: $7,785; $11,214

B lack students here are having their share of problems adjusting to this predominantly white institution. But the Bolinga Center has helped with the transition, and after the first quarter, most of the brother and sisters are on firm footing.

Its 618-acre, wooded suburban campus is about nine miles from the center of Dayton. The curriculum offers bachelor's degree programs in over 12 fields, including accounting, education and liberal arts. Its admission policy is less selective.

The change from high school to college-level academics has not been an easy one for most black students at the university. This difficulty may result from school's change from a commuter to a residential school.

A freshmen-level assistance program is designed to tutor freshmen in specific courses, free of charge. Yet, a few students complain about the lack of such facilities for upperclassmen.

Wright State's primary tutorial arm seems to be the Developmental Education Special Services Program, tutoring students in fundamental English skills, study skills, reading skills and basic math skills.

In the summer there is subsidiary effort: Wright State's Special Services Program (SSP), for students having trouble in English, biology, chemistry and business courses. What's more, the university gives college credit to all of the students who can complete this program satisfactorily.

Each student in this summer program has a peer counselor who continues to advise the student for the first two years at Wright State University.

Although Wright State has a few black students who are from out of state, the university's recruiting efforts are restricted mainly to Ohio residents. Because of the seclusion of the campus, the majority of the university's black students interact mostly among themselves and only communicate and socialize with white students and faculty on rare occasions.

And while some students feel that interaction between black faculty and black students is "pretty good," others feel that the communication between the two groups leaves much to be desired. Several black students have participated in Dayton high school programs as tutors and counselors. The school's black community does not interact much with the community surrounding Wright State, however.

In general, black students play a very small role in university governance, with few participating on important committees or councils of the university. And although some students have had some contact with black alumns, for the most part, their interaction is non-existent.

Despite the rough transition that some black students face at the university, the Bolinga Black Cultural Resources Center tends to smooth things out for them through the Peer Supportive Service Program (PSSP). The services offered through this program are the MODELS (Mentors Offering Direction, Encouragement, and Leadership Strategies), Black Men on the Move, and tutoring.

MODELS promotes the adjustment of first-year minority students and helps assure retention and graduation of students. MODELS also sponsors activities including lectures, forums and artistic events. Black Men on the Move promotes academic achievement among the black undergraduate male population.

The center also houses a Paul Lawrence Dunbar Library, the Black Student Union, Association of Black Business Students, Student Chapter of NAACP, Society of Black Engineers and Scientists, the Ebony Majestic Singers, the Bolinga Dancers and The Wright State University Black Gospel Choir.

A joint program of the Dunbar Library and the Bolinga Center, the Paul Laurence Dunbar Writers Workshop identifies, promotes and develops writers.

The Bolinga Center has also brought many prominent black speakers and writers to campus. In addition to tutorial and counseling services, the Bolinga Center has a scholarship fund for black students. Furthermore, the university's radio station, it is said, has made a conscious effort to implement music and other programs pertaining to its black community.

Yet, it is with the Bolinga Center that support services begin and end for Wright State's brothers and sisters. The university has no black theater, no religious services, no black pre-professional societies.

Parties sponsored by black Greeks are popular. One student says, "Greek [black] parties are always fun because they attract other Greeks from other campuses." Students sometimes go off campus to other universities for parties. And "When the university sponsors black speakers, they get black participation," responds one student.

Blacks participate in both intramural and varsity sports. One student says, "Of course, the stars are black."

Students are content with their experiences—filled with obstacles and opportunities—at Wright State. One student states, "I am satisfied with my choice, and by going to Wright State I haven't lost sight of what black means to me."

YALE UNIVERSITY
New Haven, Connecticut 06520

Undergrads: 5,326
Black Undergrads: 479
Faculty: 2,802
Black Faculty: NA
Tuition: $21,000
Total Expenses: $27,630

R igorous and demanding, Yale reminds black students that they must be assertive and "not fear changes that might need to be worked on," according to one undergrad.

Academics are rated among the finest and admission is most selective at renowned Yale College, third oldest in the country. A private institution that has been coed since 1969, it offers endless resources and rigorous academics.

Three major divisions—humanities, social sciences and natural sciences—offer over 50 majors. The African-American Studies Department is among those dedicated to the study of particular ethnic groups and includes the James Weldon Johnson Collection, one of the most significant holdings in Afro-Americana in the country.

Admission officers from Yale attend black recruitment fairs such as the NSSFMS College Fair Program and the Martin Luther King Educational Service Fair. Alumns interview across the country, drawing black students mainly from New York, California, Pennsylvania and Washington, D.C.

At the heart of support services is the tutoring program. Regarding the helpfulness of tutoring, one student exclaims, "Oh God, yes." An effective introduction to college is Prop (Pre-Registration Orientation Program), an opportunity for minority students to preview college life at Yale during the month of August.

Every first-year student has a freshman counselor. For black students who desire a supportive link, a "floating counselor," a black upperclassman, is provided.

Pre-meds are assisted by the Pre-Med Advisory Committee for Minorities, established by the Afro-American Center. The Black Pre-law Society is considered effective in helping students learn what to expect in their prospective careers. The Minority Business Association, similarly, supports internships, different educational programs and personal contacts in their field.

The Afro-American Cultural Center also celebrates the heritage of the black community with the Nzinga Dancers, Heritage Theater Ensemble, Black Church at Yale and the Yale Gospel Choir. The Center coordinates such events as Black History Month and Third World Weekend (for accepted black high school applicants).

One of the advantages of attending school in New Haven is a campus radio station (WYBC) which caters not only to the black student population, but also to the city's black community. Athletes find support in BAY (Black Athletes at Yale).

Black students are active in politics. The BSAY (Black Student Alliance at Yale) reportedly has pull both on campus and in the local community.

Black students often find the Yale faculty somewhat detached. "There are times when I have a rough time with the white faculty," remarks a student. "They don't seem to believe that we can do well, even though we are at Yale and we qualify." Black faculty and administration do not give black students any special treatment, but black students feel a natural link. They can always be reached; they keep consistent office hours and lend an open ear. Students interact with them on a first-name basis.

The parties held by black students are enjoyable, but because blacks are spread out on campus (at about 12 per residential college), they may be hard to find. These parties seem to be less rowdy, less expensive and less focused on alcohol than racially mixed parties. The Cultural Center provides an outlet for black students: "It is more than adequate. Students that don't come out to the house may not think so, but there is always something going on."

Women, on the other hand, are distressed by the two-to-one ratio of black women to black men. Comments one sister, "Good parties are rare unless you're into drugs or liquor."

In general, students at Yale seem to segregate themselves. Existing cliques among blacks form along ties of socioeconomic status, personal magnetism, hometowns and native countries. There are also some blacks that "just wanna hang white," but they are in the minority. Black-white interaction is "pretty good" in the classroom, in sports and in the residences. Some white students at Yale have little experience with blacks, and interaction with them can be frustrating. Yet, little racial strife seems to exist.

Yale's interaction with New Haven seems productive when programs are sponsored by formal organizations. Students tutor and counsel city youngsters, and participate in political and religious affairs.

By contrast, interaction on a one-to-one, personal basis is poor. Yalies are apathetic about New Haveners; New Haveners do not relate well to the students. Black students have an easier time than whites in avoiding outside hostilities. "Since Yalies are usually white, black students can fit in well as long as Y.A.L.E. is not plastered all over us." In the areas of black social and cultural activities, students agree that the city of New Haven is inadequate.

"Yale is what you make it," says one brother, adding, "it is definitely for those who want to lead."

GEOGRAPHIC INDEX

GEORGIA
Agnes Scott College
Emory University
Fort Valley State College
Kennesaw State College
Morehouse College
Morris Brown College
Savannah State College
Spelman College
University of Georgia

IDAHO
University of Idaho

ILLINOIS
Illinois State University
Knox College
Lake Forest College
Saint Xavier College
University of Chicago

INDIANA
Earlham College
Indiana University
University of Notre Dame

IOWA
Coe College
Grinnell College
University of Iowa

KANSAS
Kansas State University

KENTUCKY
Kentucky State University
Murray State University

MAINE
Bates College
Bowdoin College
Colby College

MARYLAND
Coppin State College
Johns Hopkins University
Morgan State University
Towson State University
University of Maryland,
    Baltimore County
University of Maryland,
    College Park
U.S. Naval Academy

MASSACHUSETTS
Amherst College
Boston College
Boston University
Brandeis University
Harvard and Radcliffe Colleges
Mount Holyoke College
Smith College
Tufts University
University of Massachusetts
Wellesley College
Wheaton College
Williams College

OHIO
Case Western Reserve University
Denison University
Kent State University
Notre Dame College of Ohio
Oberlin College
Ohio State University
Ohio University
Ohio Wesleyan University
University of Akron
University of Dayton
Wilberforce University
Wright State University

OKLAHOMA
Langston University
University of Central Oklahoma
University of Tulsa

OREGON
Linfield College
Reed College
University of Portland

PENNSYLVANIA
Bryn Mawr College
Carnegie-Mellon University
Cheyney University of
    Pennsylvania
Dickinson College
Eastern College
Franklin and Marshall College
Gettysburg College
Haverford College
Lafayette College
La Salle University

PENNSYLVANIA (CONT.)
Lehigh University
Lincoln University
St. Joseph's University
University of Pennsylvania
University of Pittsburgh

RHODE ISLAND
Brown University
Bryant College
Rhode Island College
Rhode Island School of Design
Roger Williams College
University of Rhode Island

SOUTH CAROLINA
Furman University

TENNESSEE
Lane College
Memphis State University
University of the South
University of Tennessee
Vanderbilt University

TEXAS
Rice University
Sam Houston State University
Texas Women's University
University of North Texas
University of Texas

UTAH
Weber State College

ABOUT THE AUTHOR

B arry Beckham is a novelist, former English professor and president of Beckham House Publishers in Silver Spring, Maryland.